LIFE AND DEATH ON
MT. EVEREST

Life and Death on Mt. Everest

Sherpas and Himalayan Mountaineering

SHERRY B. ORTNER

OXFORD
UNIVERSITY PRESS

OXFORD
UNIVERSITY PRESS

YMCA Library Building, Jai Singh Road, New Delhi 110 001

Oxford University Press is a department of the University of Oxford. It furthers the
University's objective of excellence in research, scholarship, and education
by publishing worldwide in

Oxford   New York

Athens   Auckland   Bangkok   Bogota   Buenos Aires   Calcutta
Cape Town   Chennai   Dar es Salaam   Delhi   Florence   Hong Kong   Istanbul
Karachi   Kuala Lumpur   Madrid   Melbourne   Mexico City   Mumbai
Nairobi   Paris   Sao Paolo   Singapore   Taipei   Tokyo   Toronto   Warsaw

with associated companies in   Berlin   Ibadan

Published in India
By Oxford University Press, New Delhi

Published by Oxford University Press 2000
under license from the original Publisher
For sale in India, Pakistan, Bangladesh, Bhutan
Myanmar, Nepal and Sri Lanka only

ISBN 019 565211 8

Typeset in Janson
Printed at Pauls Press, Delhi 110020
and published by Manzar Khan, Oxford University Press
YMCA Library Building, Jai Singh Road, New Delhi 110 001

For my families

TIM AND GWEN

DADDY AND MEL

Kinship matters

CONTENTS

ILLUSTRATIONS

PHOTOGRAPHS

FIGURE

MAPS

ACKNOWLEDGMENTS

Like most books, and certainly most of mine, this one has a long history and has accumulated a long list of debts. I wish to thank most profoundly the following agencies and people for the many things they have done to make this project and book possible.

For money (*sine qua non*): The John D. and Catherine T. MacArthur Foundation, the National Endowment for the Humanities, the National Science Foundation (Grant No. BNS-8206304), and the University of Michigan (Faculty Assistance Fund and Faculty International Travel Fund).

For detailed comments, close readings, and other kinds of major critical help and advice in the creation of this book: Arjun Appadurai, James F. Fisher, Harka Gurung, Peter H. Hansen, David Holmberg, Mary Murrell, William H. Sewell Jr., Timothy D. Taylor, and one anonymous Press reader.

For interviews and other assistance in Nepal (1990): Mr. Banskota (Ministry of Tourism), Elizabeth Hawley, Ang Nyimi Lama, Lhakpa Ongju Lama, Pemba Lama, (Col.) James Roberts, Ang Kami Sherpa, Ang Karma Sherpa, (Takto) Ang Karma Sherpa, Ang Nyima Sherpa, Ang Nyima Sherpa (Nauje), Ang Pasang Sherpa, Ang (Tsak) Pasang Sherpa, Ang Purwa Sherpa, Ang Rita Sherpa (f.), Ang Rita Sherpa (m.), Ang Tshering Sherpa, Apa Sherpa, Au Norbu Sherpa, Lhakpa Gyelzen Sherpa, Lhakpa Norbu Sherpa, Lobsang Tsering Sherpa, Mingma Tenzing Sherpa, (Jiri) Norbu Sherpa, Nyima Tsering Sherpa, Pasang Sherpa, Pasang Nuru Sherpa, Pasang Temba Sherpa, Pema Sherpa, Pertemba Sherpa, Phu Dorje Sherpa, Sangye Sherpa, Sonam Gyalchhen Sherpa, Tsultim Sherpa, and Urkyen Sherpa.

For valuable readings of chapters and pieces of this book: Lila Abu-Lughod, Vincanne Adams, Laura Ahearn, anonymous reviewers for SINHAS (Studies in Nepali History and Society), Eberhard Berg, Emily Chao, Nancy Chodorow, Elaine Combs-Schilling, Coralynn Davis, Clifford Geertz, Stephen Greenblatt, Liisa Malkki, and Abigail Stewart.

For diverse smaller, but nonetheless indispensable, contributions: Arlene Blum, Pat Cahill, Brot Coburn, Tom Cuddy, Michael Fahy, Michael Falter, Linsay French, Barbara Kaplan, Gwendolyn Ida Ortner Kelly, Mountain Travel/Sobek Himalayan Library, Lars Rodseth, Jessica Sewell, Ruth Shamraj, Robert Yale Shapiro and Harrison White, Ang Rita Sherpa of the Himalayan Trust, Pemba Tsering Sherpa, Tara Susman, Timothy D. Taylor, and Joan and Will Weber.

For their years of friendship, and for their personal support in Nepal in 1990: Mingma Tenzing Sherpa, Pasang Lhamu Sherpani, (Tawa) Dorje Sherpa, and Ang Gyelzen (A. G.) Sherpa. (Ang Gyelzen Sherpa, whom I have known since he was ten years old, and whom I was fortunate to count as a good friend, died in a plane crash as this book was going into production. He was a young man of incredible character—smart, kind, hardworking, generous—and his death at the age of forty-two is a terrible tragedy.)

For domestic love, support, and distraction: Gwendolyn Ida Ortner Kelly, Timothy D. Taylor, and Paddy the Cat.

Deepest thanks to all.

NOTE TO THE READER

I have used real names throughout this text except when noted. I have only changed or omitted names when I was concerned that the party might be embarrassed by what I had written or quoted.

A different version of chapter 3 is forthcoming as "The Making and Self-Making of the Sherpas in Early Himalayan Mountaineering," in *Studies in Nepali History and Society*.

A different version of chapter 5 was published as "Thick Resistance: Death and the Cultural Construction of Agency in Himalayan Mountaineering," in *Representations* 59 (summer 1997): 135–62.

A different version of chapter 8 was published as "Borderlands Politics and Erotics: Gender and Sexuality in Himalayan Mountaineering," in S. B. Ortner, *Making Gender: The Politics and Erotics of Culture*, 181–212. Boston: Beacon Press, 1996.

LIFE AND DEATH ON
MT. EVEREST

1

BEGINNING

In May of 1996, eight people in three different parties died in a storm on Mount Everest. It was not the worst Himalayan mountaineering disaster in history, but it received enormous public attention, perhaps the most since the time in 1924 when George Leigh Mallory disappeared with another climber into the mists near the summit of Everest and never returned. It was Mallory who had said that he wanted to climb Everest "because it is there."

The public drama of the 1996 Everest fatalities was the result of several late-twentieth-century developments. There was first of all the growth in communications technology, such that several parties on the mountain had the capacity for live communication via computer or telephone to any part of the world directly from the mountain itself. One of the macabre effects of this was that one of the climbers, Rob Hall, who was stranded high on the mountain, spoke to his pregnant wife in New Zealand several times as he lay dying. A second factor bringing the events to world attention was the rise of so-called "adventure travel" in the last decade or so, wherein relatively inexperienced individuals pay large sums of money to participate in dangerous sports that were normally the preserve of highly dedicated aficionados in the past. In the 1996 case, two of the parties that suffered fatalities were such commercially organized groups, whose clients had paid about $65,000 each to be guided by a professional to the top of Mount Everest.

The 1996 disaster was also unusual in that no Sherpas lost their lives.[1] Sherpas are members of an ethnic group who live in the environs of Mount Everest and some of the other highest Himalayan peaks, and who have provided climbing support for Himalayan mountaineering expeditions since the first decade of the twentieth century. They are the usually silent partners to the international mountaineers, carrying supplies, establishing routes, fixing ropes, cooking, setting up camps, sometimes saving the climbers' lives, and sometimes themselves dying in the process.

Who were these climbers? Who were these Sherpas? What did they think they were they doing on the stunning and lethal walls of the tallest mountain on earth?

As an anthropologist I have been studying the Sherpas since the mid-sixties. I have felt a growing urgency to write about the Sherpas' role in mountaineering, to tell the story of Himalayan mountaineering from the Sherpa point of view. This enterprise is part of this book. The Sherpas have made major contributions to Himalayan mountaineering, have made money, become famous, and often died in the course of it. But Himalayan mountaineering was originally, and is still, for the most part, defined by the international mountaineers. It is their sport, their game, the enactment of their desires.

Thus to define the book as a history of the Sherpa role in mountaineering, or mountaineering from the Sherpa point of view, is to situate the Sherpas from the outset within the frame established by these men (and later women) and their ideas. There is an important story here, a history of ways in which, despite the mountaineers' control of the sport, the Sherpas managed to make extraordinary gains in their position over the course of the twentieth century. We will see a history of strikes on expeditions, from the earliest to the present, for better pay and equipment and—always at the same time—for more respect. In addition, Sherpas and international mountaineers have competed with and teased one another within a (would-be) shared masculinity, have entered into father-son-like relations, and have occasionally managed to become something like equals and friends. The story of Himalayan mountaineering "from the Sherpa point of view" is the story of these complex and changing relations.

But if one part of a Sherpa-centered history of Himalayan mountaineering is the Sherpas' changing role in and relationship to the enterprise, the other must be the role of the enterprise in relation to the Sherpas' own agendas. It has become increasingly common in recent years to note that the Sherpas are not given adequate recognition, but this usually means recognition for their support and successes in mountaineering itself. Yet if this book has one refrain, it is that the Sherpas have a life off the mountain, a life with its own forms of intention, desire, and achievement, and a life with its own forms of inequality and pain as well. The other story of this book situates itself off the mountain, as it were, in the Sherpa villages of their home region of Solu-Khumbu, in their Buddhist temples and monasteries, and in their urban neighborhoods in Kathmandu, the capital of Nepal. Here we will see the pressures of social and economic life that sent, and continue to send, many young Sherpas into mountaineering; we will see the religious beliefs and gender assumptions that they brought with them to mountaineering, but that they also changed, over the course of the twentieth century; and we will trace the changing shape of Sherpa "identity," as the mountaineering experience connected with their lives in the local, national, and even global contexts they have inhabited.

Sherpa life before mountaineering was different, but it was not idyllic. Solu-Khumbu was (and still is) very beautiful, but agricultural labor is hard, the terrain is rough, and there are no roads and no wheeled vehicles. There were relationships of inequality in Sherpa society; even within relatively equal relationships, there were patterns of competitiveness and conflict. For Sherpas situated in the contexts of village, and later urban, life, mountaineering provided ways of addressing these problems in their lives. One may think of mountaineering as having had an "impact" on the Sherpas, but one may also think of it, as I will do in this book, as providing ways for them to transform and remake their own society at least partly in terms of their own agendas.

A note on terminology. Until the 1970s, the Sherpas both addressed and referred to the international mountaineers as "sahib" (usually pronounced as one syllable, "sahb"), a Hindi term meaning "boss" or "master." The fact that they stopped using it in the 1970s was one piece of the campaign for respect and recognition alluded to above. I will, however, continue to use the term throughout this book in my voice as writer, for several reasons. For one thing, it (or "memsahib" for women) is a handy one-word tag for the international mountaineers in general, when there is no necessity for breaking them down by other specific characteristics. For another, it places the sahibs in the same frame as the Sherpas, a single category of people being subjected to ethnographic scrutiny. And finally, though I do not accept the implication of superiority embodied in the term (which is of course why the Sherpas stopped using it), I do not think it is possible to avoid the (ongoing) fact of sahibs' power over the Sherpas on expeditions; my continuing, somewhat ironic, use of the term signals this continuing fact.

RISK

High-altitude mountaineering is one of the most dangerous sports on earth. The most frequent kind of death is sudden and shocking, a slip or drop off a sheer face, a fall into a crevasse, or—the biggest killer in terms of numbers—burial in an avalanche. But there is also slow death from "altitude sickness," an innocuous sounding phrase that refers to the consequences of an inadequate supply of oxygen reaching the bloodstream, producing strokes, cerebral and pulmonary edema, and other bodily breakdowns.

It is difficult to get precise statistics on death rates in Himalayan mountaineering; a variety of numbers are bandied about.[2] "One out of ten Himalayan climbers does not return."[3] "The death rate on expeditions to the Everest area runs about one in eight."[4] "For every ten climbers who enter the ice fall [on Everest], one does not emerge."[5] "For every two climbers to reach the summit [of Everest], another has died in the attempt."[6] Elizabeth Hawley, an extremely knowledgeable journalist who has lived in Kathmandu for many years, told a reporter in 1996, "Some 4,000 people have tried to climb Everest, 660 have succeeded, and 142 have died."[7] This puts the ratio at about one death for every five successes. Concerning Sherpas alone, "from 1950 through the middle of 1989, 84 Sherpas died on mountaineering expeditions."[8] Specifically with reference to Everest, "of the 115 climbers who have died on Everest, 43 have been Sherpas."[9]

The imprecision and incomparability of these figures—not to mention the impersonal quality of statistics in general—should not lead one to glide over them too quickly. If one looks at the question from the points of view of those actually engaged in the sport, the sense of sudden, close, and relentless death becomes almost overpowering. There is probably not a single Himalayan climber who has not lost at least one close friend—and usually many more—to a mountaineering accident, and who has not been on at least one expedition that suffered a fatal accident or other death. The great British climber Chris Bonington totaled up what he called his "catalogue of deaths": Of eight people he climbed with on one expedition, four are now dead; of ten people he climbed with on another expedition, another four are dead; and so forth to a total of fifteen out of twenty-nine people.[10]

Much the same can be said for the Sherpas. Of the more than thirty climbing Sherpas I interviewed about their climbing experiences, there was not a single one who had not lost at least one (and usually more) close friend, covillager, or—something that is not true of most sahibs—kinsman in a mountaineering accident, and not a single one who had never been on an expedition with a fatal accident. Indeed for some climbing Sherpas, nearly every expedition they worked for had had a fatal accident. And it is probably fair to say that there is no Sherpa at all—man, woman, or child, climber or nonclimber—who does not personally know a fellow Sherpa who was killed in mountaineering.

In relation to this level of risk and sudden death, my own attitudes about mountaineering have changed over time. I think I began with relative neutrality on the subject, taking the idea of "adventure" and the exhilaration of success and triumph at face value. My neutrality was in part generated by the fact that my first fieldwork was located in a time and place that rendered Sherpa involvement in mountaineering almost invisible. I lived in a village in the Solu valley, and far fewer men of Solu had been involved in mountaineering work than had the men of Khumbu, which is at a higher altitude and closer to the peaks. In addition, that first fieldwork took place in 1966–68, when much of mountaineering was shut down in Nepal, because the "Great Cultural Revolution" was taking place in China, and the

Chinese were extremely sensitive about border violations. For these reasons, and also I think because I fancied myself as an anthropologist getting to the "real" Sherpas behind their popular image as mountaineers, the whole question of their involvement in mountaineering hardly impinged on my consciousness, and I had no particular judgments about the enterprise. Indeed I was concerned about the economic hardship caused for the Sherpas by the shutting down of climbing at that time.

In the interim between my first and second field trips, I saw the film *The Man Who Skied Down Everest*, an account of a Japanese expedition on which six Sherpas were killed. When I went back to the field in 1979, I lived in the Khumbu (higher valley) village of Khumjung, probably the single biggest source of mountaineering Sherpas. My landlord in Khumjung, as it turned out, was the *sardar* (foreman of the Sherpas) of the Japanese ski expedition, and I learned that he was devastated by the deaths. Most of the men who were killed were his relatives, and he never climbed again. In addition, there was a Yugoslavian Everest expedition in progress while I was there, and one of the leading high-altitude Sherpas was killed on the expedition. He was also from Khumjung, and I was able to see at first hand and with total immediacy the intensity, even the violence, of the grief that coursed through the village. I was stunned by the extravagant purposelessness of the deaths of these young men, and I became extremely hostile to mountaineering. Words like "lunacy" and "bizarre" were sprinkled through early drafts of some of the chapters that appear in this book.

It was not just my grief for the Sherpas that led me to be appalled by mountaineering. Reading the mountaineering literature over the course of this project, I was exposed to what felt at times like a relentless chronicle of death for sahibs and Sherpas alike.[11] I was mystified as to why anyone would voluntarily take these extraordinary risks. I came to know all the kinds of things sahibs say about this, but I could not say, for a very long time, that I felt I had come to understand them in any deep sense. The mountaineering sahibs seemed in many ways much more alien to me than the Sherpas.

In the end I think I "got it." I have not entirely lost my critical sense about the ~~senseless~~ risking of lives, and I could not imagine doing it myself. But I have come to see the ways in which climbing, for all its participation in certain problematic cultural scenarios (personal glory seeking, hypermasculinity, and so forth), nonetheless also stands at a somewhat critical angle to the dominant culture. That is one of the major themes of this book.

EXPEDITIONS

The Himalayan range contains the highest mountains in the world. There are only fourteen mountains on the earth over 8,000 meters high, all of them in the Himalayas, with eight of them in Nepal alone. (A meter is a little over 3 feet; 8,000 meters is over 26,000 feet.) Of these, the tallest is Mount Everest, at 29,028 feet. It is worth noting at the outset how extraordinarily difficult a task it is to climb an 8,000-plus-meter peak. At high altitudes there is very little oxygen in the air, and the difficulty of completing even the smallest tasks becomes enormously magnified. As Eric Shipton wrote in his diary in 1938, "a climber on the upper part of Everest is like a sick man climbing in a dream."[12] Thus, although the efforts to climb peaks over 8,000 meters began in earnest in the early 1920s, the first success—on Annapurna, in Nepal—was not achieved until 1950 (by the French climber Maurice Herzog). To this day, only about one-third of the expeditions that attempt peaks over 8,000 meters succeed.[13]

An expedition is a self-created group of people who decide to climb a mountain and then try to do it. Expeditions were once all-male, but that has changed significantly. Sahibs also used to be predominantly white and Western, but that too changed significantly starting in the sixties and seventies. But there is one respect in which mountaineering has remained relatively constant, socially speaking: by and large it has been, and continues to be, a sport of the middle class, generally but not entirely of the well-educated upper-middle class. Although there were a few highly visible upper-class individuals involved in the early years, and although there has been an increasing number of working-class (especially British) climbers since about the 1970s, nonetheless the majority of climbers have been middle to upper-middle class, and the culture of the sport has (as I will discuss) reflected that class composition.

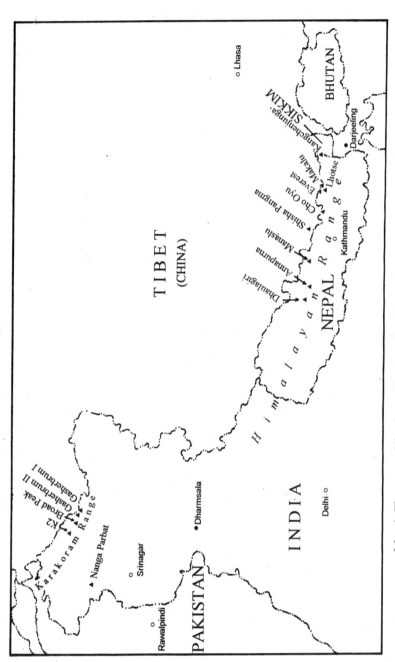

Map 1. The greater Himalayan-Karakoram region, showing all 14 over-8,000 meter peaks in the world.

Launching an expedition is a major undertaking. Funds must be raised, although the modes of fund-raising have been enormously variable across different expeditions, different nationalities, and over time, and that itself is part of the story. There is usually a core group, who then consider how many more people to bring in. Individuals are invited to join or not, with all the pleasures of inclusion and the pain of exclusion. Expeditions may be enormous high-tech affairs with many members, many tons of equipment and supplies, a large number of Sherpas, and literally hundreds of porters. At the other extreme they may (increasingly) be relatively small and low-tech. All of these choices are consequential.

And then there are questions of the social and psychological dynamics among the members of the group. Once the group gets to the mountain, differences of personality, nationality, climbing values, and many other things are enormously magnified by the close quarters, the stressful physical conditions, and the difficulty of the task. Although physical abilities, technical skills, and equipment are fundamental to success, the job of climbing the mountain involves as well an enormous component of interpersonal relations.

Finally, from the point of view of climbers from Western and/ or "first world" nations, highest-altitude mountaineering generally takes place in distant locales (basically the Himalayas and the Andes) populated by people who are seen as importantly different in terms of any or all of the following: "race," culture, religion, degree of "modernness," and personal characteristics thought to be related to the above. Expeditions depend on these people for permits, supplies, and especially labor, and thus relations with them are as much a part of the dynamics of high-altitude mountaineering as relations within the sahib group, and the technicalities of the climb. Which brings us to the Sherpas.

SHERPAS

Most Himalayan expeditions throughout the twentieth century have relied on people called Sherpas for general portering, skilled high-altitude portering, and all-around expedition support. Casual observers are often confused as to whether "Sherpas" are an ethnic

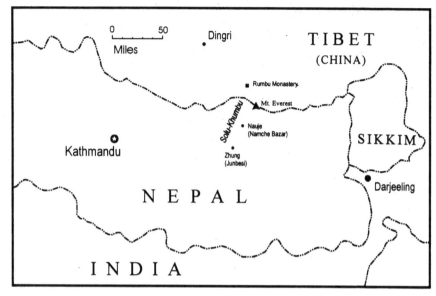

Map 2. Eastern Nepal, showing the Sherpas' home region of Solu-Khumbu in relation to key points of regional travel.

group, a role category, or both, and their confusion is not unjustified.[14] I will clarify this briefly here, but the question of what a Sherpa is will, like most of the other things mentioned briefly in this introduction, arise in different ways throughout the book.

The Sherpas are indeed, first of all, an ethnic group who live in northeast Nepal, in the mountains and valleys surrounding the Everest massif. Their ancestors migrated from eastern Tibet in the sixteenth century, and they remain closely related ethnically to Tibetans. In the second half of the nineteenth century some Sherpa men began migrating (for the most part seasonally) to the Darjeeling region of India in search of economic opportunity with the British, in the form of both petty and grand enterprise, and of wage labor.[15] Along with members of other ethnic groups, the Sherpas presented themselves for "coolie" work on road-building projects in the Darjeeling area, for exploration and surveying projects in the surrounding mountains, and for climbing expeditions as these became a distinct form of activity. The Sherpas quickly distinguished themselves: as early as 1907 climbers were marking the Sherpas as particularly well suited for the support work involved in mountain exploring and climbing.

Exactly what such work involves has gradually changed over time. Minimally, it has always involved portering as well as what might be called domestic support—setting up the camps, fetching wood and water, cooking, serving, cleaning up, and so forth. There was always less of a notion of "guiding" than was apparently true of European Alpine guides.[16] But as we shall see, the definition of "Sherpa work" has expanded over time, to the point where most present-day expeditions make at least some Sherpas members of the actual climbing party.

The category of "Sherpa" too kept undergoing changes. Originally referring to members of an ethnic group who happened to be good at high-altitude portering and generalized expedition support, it eventually became both a role and a status term, meaning essentially a specialized high-altitude porter with at least some (and sometimes a lot of) climbing expertise. As a status term, it was distinguished, on the one hand, from "local porters" (i.e., low-altitude porters who might or might not be ethnic Sherpas; nowadays they are mostly Tamang people), and, on the other hand, from "members" (the climbing party itself, normally composed exclusively of sahibs). If an ethnic Sherpa, who had been functioning as a climbing "Sherpa" (i.e., a high-altitude porter), was picked to join an assault team for the summit, then in theory he became a "member" and not a "Sherpa" for these purposes.

Although the early sahibs tried to pick their own Sherpas individually, it quickly became the practice to simply hire a good sardar and allow him to choose his own team. A Sherpa seeking expedition work, then, had to connect with a sardar, whether through kinship or other forms of personal acquaintanceship, or through bringing him gifts in the normal Sherpa mode of requesting a favor. There are several different career patterns for a mountaineering Sherpa. A young man might start as a kitchen boy or even a local porter, and hope to be hired up, after working at this level on one or two expeditions, to the "rank" of climbing Sherpa. Some young men, however, might be lucky enough to break into Sherpa work directly. After a few years as a climbing Sherpa, in turn, an ambitious young man might hope to become a sardar. But not all Sherpas become sardars, and some men simply climb as "Sherpas" for their entire careers. Indeed, some of these men say that they do not want to be sardars, that the job is too stressful. But sardars may make very good money, and many of them are able to retire relatively early.

Some Sherpas have become mountaineering legends and heroes. Some have sacrificed their lives; others have climbed Mount Everest multiple times (at last count Ang Rita Sherpa was up to ten successes, and Apa Sherpa was up to eight);[17] many—also very much deserving of note—have led or supported large numbers of expeditions up the mountain and down again without a fatal accident. While some of these individuals will be noted in the course of this study, this is not primarily a chronicle of individual achievements. Rather—in time-honored anthropological fashion—I try to understand what drives both sahibs and Sherpas, what they have done to and for one another, what they have brought to and taken from their encounters, and—for the Sherpas especially—what effect all this has had on their world as they define it.

THE RESEARCH

Mountain climbing has recently been called "the most literary of all sports."[18] Mountaineers tend to be relatively highly educated and articulate, and they write large numbers of articles and books, including accounts of particular expeditions (sometimes several people on the same expedition write about it) and personal memoirs. I have read literally hundreds of their works, which I have consumed with a certain amount of guilty pleasure insofar as they were rather more gripping than some of the usual research reading. I have mined this literature in depth for the sahib side of this book: for their detailed accounts of events and interpersonal dynamics on expeditions, for insights into "sahib culture," for sahib views of the Sherpas, and for a historical sense of how all of this has changed over the course of the twentieth century.

Second, I have drawn on the by-now voluminous ethnographic literature on the Sherpas, including my own past ethnographies. I draw on these for "data" about the Sherpas; I also view them as part of the general pool of "sahib representations" about the Sherpas that need to be critically examined in much the same way as the mountaineers' writings.

Third, for some of the earlier parts of the book, I draw heavily on two Sherpa autobiographies, by Ang Tharkay Sherpa and Tenzing Norgay Sherpa.[19] These works have their own complexities (they were told to Western authors, sometimes through interpreters, and thus cannot be taken as unmediated self-representations of Sherpa individuals). While one could certainly take these texts apart in terms of the ways in which (for example) Sherpa "voices" have been distorted, overwritten, and so forth, I have for the most part by-passed that question in favor of a fairly straightforward use of the autobiographies to learn about these men and their times.

And finally, of course, I draw on my own fieldwork. A few brief notes on my fieldwork practices that will be relevant for this book. I was committed from the outset of my research to learning Sherpa (a dialect of Tibetan), and my Sherpa language skills got fairly good. But I always worked with an assistant who wanted to practice his English as much as I wanted to practice my Sherpa; the outcome was some sort of working hybrid of Sherpa and English. My primary area of research for earlier projects was Sherpa religion, and most of my interviewing on religion was conducted in Sherpa, with backup from my assistants. But a good bit of the interviewing for the present project on mountaineering was done in English, as the English of many mountaineering Sherpas was at least as good as my Sherpa.[20]

I rarely used tape recorders as I found them to be intrusive. During formal interviews I took copious notes; on informal conversations I jotted down key items immediately afterward; in both cases I went home and wrote things up as soon as possible, in as much detail as I could remember, often questioning my assistant and whoever else had been around about their own memories of what was said or what it meant (their input in turn being, of course, more data). One effect of this practice, which the reader might find somewhat jarring, is that accounts of interviews are quoted from my field notes in the third person ("he told me he was very pleased

. . ."), which is how I wrote them up. I thought about converting things people said into the first person for greater immediacy, but my general approach to my field notes is that they constitute a set of fixed texts, like published works and historical documents, and I do not like to tamper with them except occasionally to clean up some grammar.

Returning then to the construction of the present book, the field notes constitute my final main source of information. Some of them go back to my first research trip, in the Sherpas' home region of Solu-Khumbu, Nepal, in 1966–68; there were later trips to Solu-Khumbu in 1976 and 1979, and finally the interviews for this book were done in Kathmandu, the capital of Nepal, in 1990. Although I have already published a number of books and articles on the Sherpas based on the earlier fieldwork, I nonetheless view all of the field notes from all of the trips as having a certain independent and ongoing existence. I thus return to old field notes not only for material bearing on questions that I have not addressed before, but also as part of attempts to rethink issues that I *have* addressed before.

One body of ethnographic material presented here has been almost entirely unpublished previously; namely, the material on the religious aftermath of the foundings of the monasteries. In the book *High Religion* I presented a cultural history of the foundings of the Sherpa Buddhist monasteries in the early twentieth century. Once the monasteries were founded, the monks embarked on a low-key but extensive campaign to upgrade Sherpa popular religion, and to bring it more into line with monastic ideals. I had originally planned to make this clean-up campaign part of the discussion in *High Religion* itself, but that book got too long, and in any event the post-founding events made a very different story from the story of the events that went into the foundings in the first place. Instead they form a major strand of the present work, one of the "serious games" (I will return to this phrase in a moment) that were in play for the Sherpas throughout the twentieth century, intertwining with mountaineering and with other dynamics of social transformation within the Sherpas' home community.

As noted, my last stint of fieldwork was in 1990, when I spent a month in Kathmandu interviewing mountaineering Sherpas specifically for the purposes of this project. Although I had always spent some time on past trips visiting Sherpa friends who lived in the capital, I had never really done urban fieldwork before, and in any event Kathmandu had changed a lot since my previous trip in 1979. (I couldn't get over the ease of urban fieldwork—electricity! photocopying machines! twenty-four-hour photoprocessing!) In addition to the interviews with thirty or so climbing Sherpas and sardars, I was able to acquire a somewhat fuller sense of the urban Sherpa community, and got caught up as well on the gossip from Solu-Khumbu, much of which will appear in the later chapters of this book.

This Book and Anthropological Debates

This is a history of a long-term encounter between two groups, two sets of people—one with more money and power than the other—coming together from different histories and for different reasons to accomplish a single task. The choice of focus on an encounter, rather than on a single group, immediately contextualizes this study within a certain trend in contemporary scholarship, a trend that emphasizes the intertwining and mutual production of the histories of the West and the Rest. Such work includes the study of encounters between "explorers" and native peoples in the course of early capitalist expansion;[21] of colonial and postcolonial regimes of power and knowledge;[22] and of global flows of people (everything from labor migration, to refugee flight, to tourism) in late modernity.[23] Within all of these contexts, what is at issue are the ways in which power and meaning are deployed and negotiated, expressed and transformed, as people confront one another within the frameworks of differing agendas. These are not necessarily agendas of power and domination as such; often they are not. But the de facto differentials of power and resources shape even the most well-meaning encounters, and produce the ongoing friction—sometimes pleasurable, often tragic, always generative—of history.

Studies of encounters between cultures, almost always involving asymmetries of power, share a common methodological problem: it is usually the dominant party that writes the (hi)stories of the encounter, and indeed it often continues to be (other) dominant parties who interpret those dominant texts. Faced with these materials, one appears to have only two choices: to focus on and "deconstruct" the texts for the kinds of power and social difference they embody and express, or to attempt to read through the texts for the "voices" of the weaker party, the "subaltern." Either way, in the haunting phrase of Gayatri Chakravorty Spivak, "the subaltern cannot speak":[24] either the less powerful parties are not heard at all, as the writer focuses largely on the dominant representations, or the less powerful appear only as the Other, defined wholly by their oppression, their only agency being expressed through "resistance."[25] Within this framework, then, the idea that the less powerful might have other agendas—lives that have meaning and purpose other than those defined by the relationship with the dominant party—tends to get lost.

In the past, anthropology was the field that offered a way to hear the voices and desires of others "in their own terms." Yet the anthropological project itself has become enormously problematized. What does it mean to understand others "in their own terms"? Who is the "they" whose terms are being heard? Is not the anthropologist simply another "dominant party"? And so forth.

These and related questions have been brought together under the notion of the "crisis of representation" in anthropology.[26] This idea actually contained several different, though interrelated, points. At the simplest level there was a sense that the traditional genre through which anthropologists represented other cultures, the ethnography, was stylistically exhausted. At the very least, conventional ethnographies were often boring, numbing, cutting up other cultures into dry bits labeled "kinship," "economy," and "ritual," for example, and putting the bits into boxes in the name of "objective" description and "analysis." Further, being for the most part based on fieldwork at a single point in time, often with people who did not have their own written history, ethnographies were also usually ahistorical, frozen; they had no story, no narrative, no past and future.

These points about the ethnographic genre had a darker side as well, and were subjected to a more pointed political and ethical critique. It was emphasized that the ethnographic project—originally

defined as the recording and detailed study of non-Western and
nonmodern cultures—was born in the age of empire in the nineteenth century, and could be seen as part of colonial projects in that
era. The objectification of other cultures in the name of science was
thus not merely an innocent (if dull) exercise in classification and
description; it embodied the same kinds of "orientalism" (the specific form of racism embodied in Western scholarship about non-
Western cultures)[27] that generated and were further elaborated
through regimes of colonization and exploitation. Moreover, the
representations themselves—catalogues of groups, tribes, castes; descriptions of habits, customs, practices—were seen as having an
enormous controlling power, defining and regulating populations in
the name of health, order, and civilization itself.

Many of the newer trends of contemporary anthropology have
taken shape at least in part in response to these critiques. There is
first of all a range of "experimental" ethnographic work that explores
various modes of writing in an effort to get around numbing positiv-
ist representations and to capture more vividly the voices and the
experience of those being portrayed. Much of this work is highly
"literary"—ethnography as poetry, fiction, surrealist text. Responding in part to these questions, my own work has changed stylistically as well, although the shift has been in rather the opposite
direction, toward realist history, true stories, exciting (hopefully)
narratives. If there is a literary model behind it at all, it is probably
the detective story.

A second kind of contemporary work responding to questions of
representation tends to focus on deconstructing dominant representations, considering the ways in which the categories and images of
colonial authorities, state apparatuses, mass media, anthropologists,
and so on, have "constructed" other peoples, cultures, and places.
This "constructing" may be examined either in the relatively weak
sense of exposing the orientalism and/or racism of the representations, or in the stronger sense of arguing that the dominant representations (and practices) have literally remade others in keeping
with dominant projects.

Such work is important, but it raises new problems. Too much of
a focus on dominant representations often comes to operate as an

evasion of actual ethnographic writing.[28] Because of the various critiques of ethnography—positivism, objectivism, colonial complicity—there may be an abandonment of ethnography as such, the abandonment of the attempt to understand the point of view of those not usually heard from, especially the distant and the weak, but also occasionally the very powerful as well (who are "not heard from" for other kinds of reasons). Yet it is this profound attentiveness to other perspectives that has always redeemed the classic ethnographic project, whatever its other faults; it is this that continues to make ethnography as an enterprise desirable to other disciplines, even as anthropologists engage in important critiques of the concept.

The challenge for the present project is to embrace both kinds of work within a single text, to recognize the power of the sahibs' representations in defining the practices of mountaineering, including the role of the Sherpas, but at the same time to see the Sherpas' role in mountaineering in a relatively classic ethnographic way—as emerging at least in part from their own perspectives, their own community of social relations, their own contexts of life. To define the project in this way is to explore, rather than to presume, the many forms of relationship that have obtained over time between sahibs, Sherpas, and their respective understandings of the enterprise. In some cases it is clear that sahib representations and practices over the course of nearly a century have had a large impact on the Sherpas. In other cases it is clear that Sherpas have both evaded and "resisted" sahib constructions of them and of the enterprise, and have reshaped both mountaineering and their own identity in ways that grew more from their own concerns than from the sahibs'. Most of the time all of these things are going on simultaneously.

It is important to insist on keeping the two kinds of work together, and in tension with one another. Too much emphasis on the defining and constructing power of dominant representations—anything from state propaganda, to advertising, to mass media, to informal discourses (like that of mountaineering sahibs)—creates a picture of a world in which dominant parties' views have the capacity to reshape the world entirely in their image. On the other hand, too much insistence on the power of the weaker party to evade, resist, or otherwise stand apart from dominant discourses and practices produces an equally unreal pricture of the workings of social life, given ongoing asymmetries of power and resources.

The opposition between these two perspectives has been variously labeled: "cultural studies" versus "ethnography"; "constructionism" versus "resistance" and "agency"; "postmodernism" versus a committment to the "real"; and there are no doubt others. My interest, however, is not in the dichotomy as such but in forging a practice of writing and a kind of text (like this book) in which these two processes are recognizably at work at the same time, but in ways that are not entirely predictable in advance. With these points in mind, then, let us return to the history of encounters between Sherpas and sahibs in Himalayan mountaineering. How shall we understand these encounters? What can they tell us about sahibs, about Sherpas, and about the particular history that unfolded for them jointly? Let me here make a preliminary sorting of what is involved in the enterprise.

SERIOUS GAMES

There is first of all the question of "representations," the fact that much of what we know about specific expeditions, and about the history of mountaineering, comes from the sahibs' writings. In response to this, I play the double game already alluded to: on the one hand I deconstruct sahib representations for their orientalism, and for what they can tell us about the sahibs' perspectives; at the same time I seek to establish Sherpa perspectives ethnographically, in part through my own fieldwork, but also from anything that yields access to (diverse) Sherpa perspectives—other ethnographies, Sherpa autobiographies, and—reading through and around their Orientalist biases—the mountaineering sahibs' texts themselves.

There is second of all the question of who all these people, both sahib and Sherpa, are. While older ethnographies often had problems of homogenizing the groups under study ("the culture of the

Soandso" was presented as if there were no differences of perspective within the group itself, or no changes in cultural beliefs and values over time), newer ethnographies often have their own problems of homogenization. There are several different traps: an emphasis on power may homogenize the dominant group (e.g., "colonial authorities") or the dominated group (who may appear to have nothing on their minds but "resistance"); an emphasis on transnationalism or globalization may homogenize "the West" or "modernity" as a monolithic force that transforms everything in its path in relatively predictable ways; and so forth. In contrast I have found it essential to situate both sahibs and Sherpas within the specific contexts from which they came. Thus, it is relevant that the sahibs are largely from the educated upper-middle classes, and that they have been, until recently, mostly men; and it is relevant that the climbing Sherpas come mostly from less privileged positions within their own society, and also that they too have been, until recently, mostly men. The sahib-Sherpa encounter, in other words, is not simply an encounter between two culturally different groups; each group in turn is the embodiment of other forms of difference, differences that they bring with them and that shape the enactment of difference between them.

Next, and very important, are questions of purpose or intention. The place of intention or purpose in the social process and in cultural thought is much contested in the worlds of theory and philosophy. I am aware of these debates but will spare the reader any extended discussion. Here, I will simply say that I follow Clifford Geertz's views, which underlie much of his work and are articulated particularly in "Thick Description,"[29] to the effect that cultural forms are not merely sets of terms and codes and categories, but emerge from structures of purpose and desire, and only make sense in relation to those underlying purposes and desires. Thus, in the case at hand, "mountaineering" for the sahibs can only be understood in terms of the intentions and desires that it is fulfilling, including desires grounded in sahib notions of modernity, class, and manhood. "Mountaineering" for the Sherpas is grounded in different desires and intentions, desires for (among other things) "money" and "modernity," which themselves carry different meanings for the Sherpas than they do for the sahibs. Understanding mountaineering at this level, then, is a matter of understanding the different sets of intentions in play, intentions in turn deriving their meanings from the social contexts, cultural categories, and historical moments in which they have taken shape for both parties.

Finally, there is the encounter itself, the actual experience of expeditions in which these people of different backgrounds and different purposes come together, in a context that is organized by both the specific nature of the task, and by one more form of difference— that of power between the parties. The encounter—in this case involving a group of men (later also women) pushing their bodies and each other up some of the highest mountains on earth—has its own dynamics, what Marshall Sahlins has called "the structure of the conjuncture."[30] The encounter is precisely the orchestration of the many forms of difference in play; the history of the encounter is the history of the changes not only of expeditions, but of all the other forms of difference as well. Himalayan mountaineering will change as we move through the twentieth century, but so will the social backgrounds, gender assumptions, and structures of desire that both sahibs and Sherpas bring to the enterprise.

I have recently conceptualized some of these issues in terms of the idea of "serious games."[31] By the term "games" I mean to capture in one image, perhaps impossibly, most of the points just made: that people do not just enact either material necessity or cultural scripts but live life with (often intense) purpose and intention; that people are defined and redefined by their social and cultural contexts, which frame not only the resources they start with but the intentions and purposes they bring to the games of life; that social life is precisely social, a matter of relationships—of cooperation and competition, of solidarity and exploitation, of allying and betraying. By the adjective "serious" I mean further to emphasize the constant play of power in the games of life, and the fact that, for most people most of the time, a great deal is at stake. And by the whole phrase, "serious games," I mean as well to sustain a sense that human experience is never just "discourse," and never just "acts," but is some inextricably interwoven fabric of images and practices, conceptions and actions in which history constructs both people and the games that they play, and in which people make history by enacting, reproducing, and transforming those games. Thus, for Himalayan mountaineering, both a dream and a practice, both a form of solidarity and a form of power, I will argue that the engagement between Sherpas and sahibs can only be understood in terms of the different ways in which each entered into the reality and the imagination of the other, in relation to the games they brought with them and the games that evolved in place.

Finally, I should address at this point my own games as writer of this book. One of the things I realize I have been doing throughout my writings on the Sherpas, and that I continue to do here, is to position myself at least partially in opposition to whatever the dominant image of the Sherpas has been at any given moment. In contrast to what I saw as the romanticism of the first ethnographer, Christoph von Fürer-Haimendorf, and of the early mountaineers, I emphasized in my first book some of the darker sides of Sherpa life—inequality, competition, selfishness. Today, however, it has become somewhat fashionable among both mountaineers and anthropologists to denigrate the Sherpas, to see them—as I will discuss later—as "spoiled," as having fallen victim to the lure of money and fame. In this context I feel called upon, once again, to take the other side, and I tend to emphasize the kinds of qualities—friendliness, warmth, dignity—that have been celebrated (however romantically) by both mountaineer and anthropology sahibs in the first place. Yet my purpose through all this is not to evaluate the Sherpas one way or another, but rather to try to counter *any* one-sided representation, and to try to render the Sherpas simply as real people, with complex lives and intentions of their own.

Throughout this book, the "I" of the author will appear in different guises, some of which I have chosen, and some of which were chosen for me: ethnographer of Sherpas and (more recently) of the Western middle class; memsahib with certain privileges (even if I did not want them); academic anthropologist staking out and defending positions against colleagues; a personal self who was shaped by many of the histories (the fifties, the feminist movement, the counterculture) that have shaped the people I talk about; and there are no doubt others. Each of those guises claims certain kinds of authority and disclaims others, but I will leave it to the reader, who comes to this book both positioned within, and actively playing, his or her own serious games, to sort out the details.

And now let us plunge into the ~~strange~~ world of early Himalayan mountaineering.

2

SAHIBS

The British in the Himalayas

In 1852, the Great Trigonometrical Survey of India triangulated a seemingly unprepossessing peak in the Himalayas and found it to be the highest mountain in the world. They named it Mount Everest, for Sir George Everest, the head of the Survey from the 1820s to the 1840s, and the man responsible for measuring the great meridional arc of India, on which all later measurements within the subcontinent and beyond were based. (The mountain is called Chomolungma in Sherpa and Tibetan, and Sagarmatha in Nepali, and these names will increasingly be used in public discourse as the century progresses. But as I will mostly be discussing Western accounts of expeditions, in which the mountain, until recently, has always been called Mount Everest, I will use the English name most of the time.)

The Great Trigonometrical Survey contained both the best and the worst of the British Raj. On the one hand, it was a stunning achievement of science, not only mapping virtually all the peaks of the Indian subcontinent, but providing "the basis for mapping the whole continent of Asia. . . . [It] has been described with justification as 'perhaps the greatest geographical achievement on any continent in any age.' "[1]

On the other hand, the whole project was predicated on the labor power of the native populations. Native surveyors set up instruments and took measurements at the tops of peaks that "were more difficult and a full 10,000 feet . . . higher than the European summits which were defeating contemporary alpinists in Europe."[2] Moreover, they undertook their charge with a kind of seriousness and devotion that the British (or anyone else) had no right to expect. Kenneth Mason, a superintendent with the Survey of India and a professor of geography at Oxford, revisited one of the Survey's observation posts in the Karakoram (western Himalaya) Range in 1911 and "found the original raised platform, 14 feet square, still intact, with [the surveyor's] finely chiselled marking-stone firmly in position; nearby was a ruined stone shelter, in the corner of which was a human skeleton."[3] Another author, summarizing Mason's history, goes on to say,

> It will never be known how many dedicated surveyors—*khalasis* [porters, "coolies"][4] employed by the survey on a salary of no more than six rupees (about 60 British pence) a month—died of cold, starvation or exposure on some isolated peak. It is not known how many peaks they climbed, nor which of these peaks was the highest—although Mason suggests that the khalasi who in 1860 struggled with a 14-inch theodolite to the summit of Shilla (23,050 ft.) may hold the record.[5]

Throughout the late nineteenth century, British army officers, naturalists, and travelers explored the peaks and valleys of the Himalayan range,[6] and by the end of the century were making serious attempts to climb the mountains.[7] Always they took "coolies," porters to carry their gear and to provide various support services. In general they took men from whatever ethnic group was available locally in the region of the peak, although the military officers also tended to bring along a few choice men from the Gurkha regiments (made up of soldiers from various ethnic groups and castes in Nepal) that they commanded.[8]

The 1895 British expedition to Nanga Parbat in Kashmir, for example, included the then-young Major Charles Granville Bruce, later to play a key role in the early Everest attempts. Bruce brought with him two Gurkha soldiers who "proved to be excellent porters and loyal servants."[9] In addition, a "huntsman" named Lor Khan from a region the author earlier described as populated by "savage tribes . . . against whom military operations were still being conducted" also joined the group.[10]

The responses of the British climbers to both the Gurkhas and Lor Khan give some sense of the kinds of qualities they sought and appreciated in mountain porters, and also previews a language of praise—for cheerfulness, loyalty, and bravery—that will later be reserved almost exclusively for the Sherpas:

> Lor Khan, who came behind me on the rope, seemed to be enjoying himself immensely; of course he had never been in such a position before, but these Chilas tribesmen are famous fellows. What Swiss peasant, whilst making his first trial of the big snow peaks and the ice, would have dared to follow in such a place, and that, too, with only skins soaked through by the melting snow wrapped round his feet? Lor Khan never hesitated for a moment; when I turned and pointed downwards he only grinned, and looked as if he were in the habit of walking on ice slopes every day of his life.[11]

Later, on the descent, one of the Gurkhas was put in the lead:

> He led us down the most precipitous places with tremendous rapidity and immense enjoyment. It was all "good" according to him, and his cheery face down below made me feel that there could be no difficulty.[12]

The expedition would also end, as so many Himalayan expeditions do, in violent death. The leader and both of the Gurkhas were killed.

British activity in the Himalayas always consisted of that peculiar combination of economic, political, scientific, Orientalist,[13] and "sporting" interests that was characteristic (in different mixes, in different times and places) of the Raj as a whole. While geographers in the Himalayas were peacefully measuring elevations,[14] naturalists studying plants,[15] and assorted observers making ethnographic observations,[16] all in the name of "science"; while Orientalists were studying Eastern religions, and particularly Buddhism, in the name of the spiritual improvement of the West;[17] and while mountaineers were exploring and climbing mountains in the name of both science and sport,[18] the economic/political aspect of the British interest in the region came to the fore with a vengeance in the disastrous 1904 Younghusband "diplomatic mission" to Tibet, which is now widely recognized as an invasion.

The British were hoping to strike up diplomatic agreements with the Tibetans, in order to ward off encroaching Russian influence in the region. Sending a large number of Indian troops with British officers, they entered the closed country and, in several engagements, massacred over seven hundred Tibetans. The casualties to the "British" (that is to say, Indian) troops were much smaller, although they experienced great misery at the 15,000 foot altitude and sub-zero temperatures of the Tibetan plateau.[19]

The "mission" accomplished very little in terms of diplomatic outcomes. An agreement was reached but had little legitimacy, because the Dalai Lama was not a party to it. He had fled to China at the start of the invasion, and had sought Chinese support against the British. The effects of this were played out in the mid-twentieth century, as the Chinese themselves invaded Tibet in 1959 on the pretext of an ancient suzerainty that had essentially lapsed until the Dalai Lama had been forced by the British invasion to seek their support. The Chinese occupy Tibet to this day.

The only concrete benefit for the British at the time was the one that has direct implications for this story: some shaky concessions of the right to send missions of exploration and to climb some unspecified peaks. Thus, three years later (1907), Charlie Bruce, who had fatally brought the two Gurkhas to Nanga Parbat, tried to organize the very first Everest expedition. Bruce sought to activate the Younghusband concessions and to get permission for the expedition to go in through Tibet (the southern approach to the mountain, through Nepal, was closed until the 1950s). But the bad taste of the invasion still lingered. The Tibetans were extremely resistant to a new expedition, and those British officials who had disapproved of the invasion in the first place also refused to support the request.[20] The first expedition did not take place until 1921.

The "Discovery" of the Sherpas

Because Nepal was closed to foreigners in the first half of the twentieth century, climbing in the central Himalaya was organized out of
Darjeeling, a town in north India about ten days' walk east of the
Sherpa region in northeast Nepal (see Map 2). The Sherpas had
been coming to Darjeeling for work since the mid-nineteenth century. Many had engaged in some kind of petty, and even grand, enterprise,[21] but others simply had taken construction work as "coolies," manual laborers. From the beginning, many of the Sherpas
migrated seasonally, but enough stayed so that by the time of the
first Darjeeling district census in 1901, 3,450 Sherpas were
counted.[22] Portering for survey work, for exploration and naturalist
expeditions, and for the early mountaineering expeditions was all of
a piece with construction labor—it was all "coolie" work, and the
Sherpas along with people from the many other ethnic groups in
the region signed up for this labor when it was available. Although
Darjeeling is in geopolitical India, it is located within the Himalayan
range: Kangchenjunga (8,598 meters, or 28,028 feet) gloriously rises
up to the north of the town, and is only a few days' trek away. Darjeeling is a trading town, bringing together people from many different
mountain groups: Tibetans, Sikkimese, Bhutanese, Rai and Limbu
from the middle hills of eastern Nepal, and Sherpas.

   In 1907, the same year that Bruce failed to get permission for the
first Everest attempt, two little-known Norwegians, C. W. Rubenson and Monrad-Aas (his first name is never given), came to Darjeeling to attempt to climb Kabru, a peak of 24,015 feet in the Darjeeling district. They took with them an ethnic assortment of porters,
and though they failed to reach the summit of the peak, they came
back singing the praises of the Sherpas. Rubenson wrote,

   The chief thing is to have as good and willing coolies as we
   had; properly fitted out and with kind treatment they will sur-
   mount what would seem impossible. . . . Our experience is that
   the coolies, especially the Nepaulese [sic] Sherpa, are excellent
   men when treated properly, and our success is only due to the
   willingness and brave qualities of these people.[23]

Bruce supported Rubenson's appraisal of the Sherpas, although not to the exclusion of other "Bhotia" or "Bhutia" (ethnically Tibetan) groups, and not so much on the grounds of their willingness and bravery as on the grounds of their being better adapted to cold and altitude:

[A] good many of the porters employed by Messrs. Rubenson and Monrad Aas [sic, no hyphen] were Sherpas from the actual Dudh Kosi, a branch of the great Kosi river, which rises in the lower slopes of Everest itself. All the higher valleys have excellent porter material, but the clothing of the different districts varies considerably. . . . The Bhutias (Thibetans) [Sherpas are included as Sherpa-Bhutias] are generally much better fitted out in this respect, and have a great power of resistance to cold.[24]

Reports similar to these came in a year or two later from an English research chemist by the name of Dr. A. M. Kellas, who began coming to the Darjeeling district in 1909 to study the effects of high altitude on the human system. Kellas traveled without other Westerners, and formed close relationships with his porters. Again the Sherpas stood out. At the end of his first expedition he wrote:

Their behaviour was excellent. By the end of the trip we were all working together most harmoniously. Really they are the most splendid fellows. . . . Of the different types of coolie, the writer has found the Nepalese Sherpas superior to all others. They are strong, good natured if fairly treated, and since they are Buddhists there is no difficulty about special food for them—a point strongly in their favour at high altitudes."[25]

Kellas returned nearly every summer until the outbreak of the First World War, and apparently took only Sherpa porters, who returned to work for him again and again. He pioneered many of the features that would become standard in later mountaineering. As a result of his research he came to promote the value of supplementary oxygen for high-altitude work. Through his appreciation of the Sherpas, he came to promote them as the best of the high-altitude porters. And through his continuing work with the Sherpas, he came to persuade them of the value of roping together, thus beginning to socialize them into some of the technical assumptions of Western mountaineering.[26]

Kellas joined Bruce on the Everest reconnaissance in 1921, though he died en route to the mountain. It is clear, however, that he passed on his strongly positive views of the Sherpas to the 1921 party, and the Sherpa reputation as outstanding high-altitude porters was launched.[27]

WHO WERE THE SAHIBS?

In order to get any depth of insight into the dynamics of the relationship between Sherpas and sahibs, we must situate both groups very carefully in their own contexts, both within a given historical period and across time. Although it would be tempting to treat the sahibs within the mountaineering arena as some undifferentiated mass of people from powerful nations who in turn exercise power over some undifferentiated mass of Sherpas, in fact this gives us little purchase on what is going on. Power, as Foucault has taught us, is in the details—in the very specific identities and very specific practices through which people engage with one another as they try to accomplish something in the world. Throughout this book, then, I will put great emphasis on distinctions among both the sahibs and the Sherpas. Here I focus on the sahibs.

A word first on "race." Virtually all the early sahibs were white, and thus of a different "race" from the Sherpas, but race does not so much describe physical differences as it describes differences of power based on alleged physical differences. Thus, later sahibs came from other "races," but a Japanese or Korean sahib (for example) is still a sahib in relation to the Sherpas, and "race" will not be a significant category in this study.

Next, nation. National differences are quite salient in Himalayan mountaineering in a number of ways. Expeditions have tended to be labeled nationally: the British Mount Everest expedition, the German Kangchenjunga expedition, the Japanese Dhaulagiri expedition, and so on. For specific historical reasons, some expeditions have became highly politicized in their own nations. Climbing in general has been of variable interest in different nations and at different points in time, and the level of national interest (and of politicization) has had effects, for example, on the funding available for expeditions. And individual climbers have varied significantly in their own personal nationalist sentiments. These various ways in which issues of "nation" impinge on Himalayan mountaineering can be quite interesting, but as they tend to be somewhat remote from the on-the-ground operation of expeditions, and of the sahib-Sherpa relationship, I do not for the most part pursue them in this book.

The one area in which national differences might be thought to be relevant to actual expedition practice and to sahib-Sherpa relations would be in what used to be called "national character." Do the British, or the Americans, or the Germans, or the Koreans organize expeditions differently, and/or treat the Sherpas differently because of their own cultural styles? It is certainly the case that both sahibs and Sherpas *think* these are relevant factors; almost everyone has his or her own stock of ethnic and national stereotypes about everything from expedition food to gender to authority relations. But these are precisely stereotypes, and as such I have not found them very useful for gaining insight into what is going on. For the most part I avoid them.

Gender, on the other hand, is highly relevant to this study—virtually all the early international mountaineers were men (and "sahib" is a male term); virtually all of the Sherpas were men. Sahib and Sherpa women came into mountaineering in large numbers starting in the seventies, and this had quite a dramatic impact. I will save questions of gender for later in the book.

Finally, and most relevant for immediate purposes, is the class positioning of the sahibs. From the earliest expeditions on, a very large proportion of international mountaineers were drawn from the relatively well educated, relatively well-to-do, upper-middle classes. Looking just at the British for the moment, the mountaineering historian Unsworth says of the 1933 Everest expedition, "The climbers came from the same class that had traditionally provided the membership of the Alpine club for three quarters of a century: the well-to-do middle classes, with a background of Oxbridge and a decent sprinkling of Army officers and Government officials."[28] From the beginning there were very few upper-class climbers, and they were generally held in deep suspicion unless they could prove themselves to be unsnobbish and socially egalitarian. For example, concerning the 1921 Everest reconnaissance, we are told that the "neosocialist" George Mallory could not stand the elite leader, C. K. Howard-Bury, who was "an old Etonian, descended from the illustrious Howard family, Earls of Suffolk, . . . [and] also High Tory."[29] At the same time, there have been relatively few working-class climbers (although middle-class climbers sometimes affect a working-class style). Unsworth has a good sense of the class factor in British mountaineering. Writing of the 1933 Everest expedition again, he says:

> Ruttledge recalled that applications to join the [1933 and earlier] expeditions were received for "pugilists, a barber, and a steeplejack"—thereby implicitly inviting his readers to scoff at such notions as preposterous. . . . In any case, no working class climber could afford to take the time off to go to the Himalaya. So the gulfs were practical as much as social."[30]

It was not only a question of time off. Expeditions could also often be costly to the members. Even when funding was raised from outside sponsors, as has normally been true for European and (later) American expeditions for most of the century, climbers had to pay some of the costs themselves, and for expeditions in the Himalayas—far away and of long duration—these costs could be quite substantial. Looking at other nationalities, the point about class positioning holds with minor variations. The membership of the 1929 German expedition to Kangchenjunga included a physician, an "agriculturalist," a chemist (pharmacist), a veterinary surgeon, two "political economists," a medical student, an engineer, and a notary.[31] As with the British case, the membership was not only middle class, but professional middle class, highly educated, and no doubt with some financial resources.

The high education level of mountaineers showed up in their leisure activities during expeditions. Bill Tilman gave a sketch of such activities on the 1938 Everest attempt, which included playing chess and reading *Gone with the Wind*, *Seventeenth Century Verse*, Montaigne's *Essays, Don Quixote, Adam Bede,* and *Martin Chuzzlewit.*[32] Not every mountaineer in the twentieth century sat around reading seventeenth-century verse in his or her tent. There were in fact some upper-class climbers, some working-class climbers, and some educational dropouts, among others, and the representation of the working class, and the less highly educated lower-middle class, grew somewhat over time. Nonetheless, it was and remains true that the educated upper-middle class has been the dominant social group in Himalayan mountaineering.[33]

Yet at the same time these people are not, when they are climbing mountains, sitting in clean and comfortable middle-class drawing rooms. They are living in cold, dirty, and uncomfortable conditions, eating bad food, and forcing their bodies to do extremely difficult things. And this is precisely the point: mountaineering as a sport both emanates from and addresses itself back to (and back against) the normal patterns of middle-class life. One of the dominant discourses of mountaineering, as we shall see, positions it critically against "bourgeois" existence, even as the sport demands the resources made possible by such an existence. This then brings us to the ways in which sahibs thought and talked about what they were doing.

SAHIB GAMES

The idea of "games" as a metaphor for how social life is lived is peculiarly relevant to this study. For one thing, mountaineering itself is a "sport," something close to a "game" in ordinary language. For another, the British in the Himalayas in the early decades of the twentieth century were engaged in quite serious political and military maneuverings with the Russians for influence in the region, and these maneuverings—memorialized in, among other works, Kipling's *Kim*—were called "The Great Game." And finally, I (along with many other interpreters of social and cultural life) have used the idea of the game as a way of thinking about the way in which people are defined and constrained by the intersections of culture, power, and history in which they find themselves, and yet at the same time are active players in making (and sometimes remaking) those worlds that have made them.

Games are not so much objects in the world as ways of interpreting objects in the world. One can think of "mountaineering" as a game, with its own rules and definitions and relations of power and solidarity, and I will think of it that way at some points in this book. By and large, however, I try to make sense of mountaineering by figuring out how it fits into other, or larger, games. One is a game of masculinity, of defining and enacting the masculine self. Another is a game. of "adventure," in which the point of mountaineering is that it entails, as Georg Simmel put it, "dropping out of the continuity of life."[34] Although there is a sense in which probably all human beings and all cultures have some sort of notion of "adventure," that this is part of simply being human, the kind of adventure involved in mountaineering—a basically twentieth-century phenomenon—is very specifically constructed in relation to issues of "modernity"; one drops out of the continuity of (modern) life because one finds it lacking—lacking in "adventure," among other things. A discourse in which the adventure-ness of mountaineering is linked with a critique of modernity is perhaps the dominant (though not the only) discourse of the sport, and a brief survey of the counter-modern discourse of mountaineering across the whole of the twentieth century will lay the groundwork for more historically specific variations.

THE CRITIQUE OF MODERNITY

For many, perhaps most, climbers, the point of climbing is to find something that one cannot find in modern life, that indeed has been lost in modern life. What exactly it is about modern life that is most problematic changes over time, and also varies from climber to climber, but a few broad clusters may be sketched.

The earliest climbers seemed to view climbing as embodying a spirituality that was lacking in modern life. Trying to raise money in 1920 for the very first Everest expedition, Sir Francis Younghusband, then the president of the Royal Geographical Society, argued that while "climbing Everest was not pragmatically useful . . . 'it would elevate the human spirit.' "[35] The much interpreted remark by George Leigh Mallory, that one tries to climb Everest "because it is there," seems to have referred to an ineffable spiritual quality embodied in this kind of enterprise; elsewhere he calls it "sheer joy."[36] We see another kind of spirituality in the comment by the Swiss climber René Dittert in the fifties who wrote that the top of Everest "touches the forbidden doors and limits of life."[37]

The spirituality and transcendence of mountaineering contrasts with the crass materialism and pragmatism of modern life. Bill Tilman argued in the thirties against bringing wireless radios on expeditions for purposes of receiving weather forecasts, as this would be both a sign and a manifestation of having made "an idol of 'success.' "[38] And the Canadian Earl Denman wrote in the forties, "I thought I saw in the vision of success [on the mountain] a wonderful meaning to life—my triumph over the gross materialism in which our civilisation as I knew it had been plunged."[39]

The crassness of modernity manifests itself among other things in its noisiness and busyness, which prevents reflection and the ability to commune with the self, nature, or God. Tilman's arguments against bringing wireless radios included the idea that in taking them climbers "lose one outstanding advantage of being in Tibet . . . [not having] their thoughts and feelings harrowed by listening daily to the news."[40] Another climber wrote in the fifties,

> [W]hen I return to what is called civilization and find myself once again in crowded, bustling cities, jostled by men and women whose minds are warped by fatuous illusions, I experience a sense of dismay, a sense of uneasiness; I feel I should like to escape, to run away at once to some distant land, to return into the midst of simple, humble, primitive people—best of all, to return to one of those barren wastes where a man can be alone with himself and his God.[41]

If modernity is vulgar and materialistic, crass and noisy, it is also soft, routinized, and boring. In this dull, modern world, the self loses its definition, its edge, its purpose, its honesty. Mountaineering on the other hand is difficult, dangerous, challenging; it makes the self sharper, tougher, more honest, more real. One Indian climber in the sixties emphasized the way in which modernity allows one to hide one's faults, but mountaineering forces one to own up to them:

The mountains are ruthless teachers! A man can hide his inner-self by putting on a cloak provided by so-called modern educa-tion—soft talk, polish, outward good-manners and an artificial smile. Thus, he can often fool even the cleverest people. But, in the mountains this camouflage mysteriously drops off and he stands naked in front of everyone. He cannot hide the awkward bulges and deformities in his mental make-up and character. What is more, he finds himself in front of a life-size mirror, as it were, and he can himself see what he really is."[42]

Norman Dyhrenfurth was unaware of his discontent with the insipidness of modern life until he went climbing in the fifties. He had what would appear to many of the people reading this book a choice job: He was founder and head of the Motion Picture Division of the Department of Theater Arts at UCLA. But after participating in the failed Swiss Everest expedition of 1952, he walked out of that job:

To help create a new department within a large university, de-voted to the development of a new and better generation of film makers, had once offered a great challenge. But now, sud-denly, it seemed terribly stale and uninspiring. The initial im-petus was gone; someone else could take over, someone content to spend the rest of his days in the academic world.[43]

Finally, in a language reminiscent of Mallory's emphasis on "sheer joy," an American in the seventies phrased the pull of mountaineering in terms of "real adventure" as against the "boredom" of modern life:

[O]ne of the principal reasons people today engage in danger-ous, risk-taking sports like mountain climbing is to fight bore-dom. Overcoming boredom is one of the main challenges to many people who find themselves in a world where it is nearly impossible to find real adventure.[44]

For these men, modernity is the problem, and mountaineering is the solution. Where the modern is vulgar and materialistic, moun-taineering is sublime and transcendental. Where the modern is noisy and distracting, mountaineering is peaceful and conducive to reflection. Where the modern is soft and boring, mountaineering is difficult, challenging, thrilling. The "there" of Everest contrasts with the "here" of the modern.

ROMANTICISM

Although the countermodern discourse of mountaineering runs across the entire twentieth century, it undergoes important variations in different eras. In the early period, which is to say essentially between the twenties and the forties, it bore a significant resemblance to late-nineteenth- and early-twentieth-century "romanticism," that is, to an ethos that is organized around the desire to transcend the limits of the self. It was a discourse and a set of practices directed toward disciplining the self to accomplish some very difficult task (such as climbing Mount Everest) so that one could rise above, transcend, previously assumed barriers and limitations. It could take various forms: moral, mystical, ascetic. It was often, though not always, highly serious. Its distinctiveness is clearer in contrast to later discourses, which reveal more sharply what this one was not: romanticism lacked the devil-may-care style of later climbing, which has a kind of heartiness and a cheerful refusal to appear to take oneself too seriously; it also lacked the machismo and joky sexualism of later climbing.

The other side of this romantic ethos involved a glorification of nature, a picture of nature as providing the extreme conditions under which the self could come to know and transcend its limits. Thus, when Younghusband argued in favor of the Royal Geographical Society sponsoring the first Mount Everest expedition, he talked of "this epic of man's struggle against the mountain—of his proving his own powers against the powers of the mountain, testing them to the utmost and unknown stretch of their capacity against the likewise unknown powers of the mountain."[45]

A German version of the discourse came from Paul Bauer, who attempted to climb Kangchenjunga in 1929 and 1931, and who closely echoed Younghusband:

It was not blind zeal or irrepressible pride that urged us on to the attempt; rather it was an opportunity for us to test those qualities which had become superfluous in everyday life, but which to us were still the highest qualities in the world: unshakeable courage, comradeship, and self-sacrifice.[46]

Two individuals who made solo attempts on Everest in this era participated in this discourse as well: an Englishman, Maurice Wilson, made the attempt in 1934,[47] and a Canadian, Earl Denman, tried in 1947.[48] In both cases we see, though in different mixes, the elements of asceticism, mysticism, and/or moralism that these early climbers brought to the Himalayas. Denman, as we have seen, thought the conquest of Everest would allow him to transcend Western materialistic values. But probably the most extreme mystic of the early period of expeditions was the Englishman Maurice Wilson, who in 1934 went secretly to Everest with two Sherpas and, leaving them at base camp, attempted to climb the mountain alone. Wilson "believed that if a man fasted almost to the point of death then all his physical and mental ills would drain out of him; and if he also had faith in the powers of God, then God would renew him in body and spirit, and he would emerge a stronger, better person."[49] Wilson thought that if he could successfully climb Mount Everest alone, while following this bodily regime, this would prove and publicize the truth of his views. He died trying.

Finally, although Bill Tilman may not seem at all "mystical" or "romantic" in any ordinary sense, his attack on the use of oxygen and other modern technology in mountaineering emerges as profoundly romantic, that is to say, not only antimodern but founded in the idea that mountaineering is about testing and refining the inner self. First he pointed out the contradictions of oxygen use for mountaineers:

The various other reasons which have been adduced [for climbing Mount Everest] in the past, such as demonstrating man's "unconquerable spirit," or increasing our knowledge of man's capacity, should not persuade us to alter our methods. . . . I take it that when a man has to start inhaling oxygen his spirit has already been conquered by the mountain and the limit of his capacity has been very clearly defined.[50]

He then takes on, with particular venom, the idea that the climbing
of Everest, even with oxygen, would have scientific value in increasing our knowledge of men's [*sic*] ability to climb at extreme high
altitudes. He talks of the scientists being interested in such things
"in their cold-blooded way"[51] and concludes:

> No, I merely ask that mountaineering and science should be
> kept distinct, in particular that the problem of climbing Mount
> Everest, like any other mountain, should be left to mountain-
> eers to solve, and that those actively engaged in solving it
> should not be expected to enter what Goethe calls the charnel-
> house of science.[52]

More articulate in ironic critique than in praise, Tilman rarely described the positive, unmodern, virtues of mountaineering in so
many words. Yet his conclusions to this whole discussion embody
the romantic sense of mountaineering as a matter of personal, inner,
value:

> Meantime let us count our blessings—I mean those thousands
> of peaks, climbed and unclimbed, of every size, shape and order
> of difficulty, where each of us may find our own unattainable
> Mount Everest.[53]

To understand sahibs' games—in this case games of countermodern "escape," and of testing and developing the self (which is, of
course, quite modernist)—is to begin to understand what the sahibs
thought they were doing, and why. It also helps us understand the
ways in which they constructed the various relationships involved
in playing the game, and in particular the ways in which they constructed their relationships with the Sherpas.

THE SHERPAS AS PART OF THE SOLUTION

Climbers in the Himalayas encountered two "others"—the mountains and the Sherpas. In the early period, the two were hardly
separate: both stood in contrast to a negatively figured modernity.
Like the physical mountains and the practice of mountain-

eering, the Sherpas stood for all that had not been corrupted by the modern world.

One set of representations of unmodernness—the most blatantly racist—placed the Sherpas virtually in the realm of nature. For example, the 1924 Everest expedition picked the Sherpas in part by facial and bodily types.[54] Other images in this era emphasized the Sherpas' physical strength and natural acclimatization to high altitude as a result of growing up carrying loads at high elevations. Although the point of the Sherpas' physical strength continued throughout the century, in this early era it was juxtaposed with the point that the Sherpas lacked the requisite "spirit" for mountaineering, thereby emphasizing their natural physicality. With respect to the 1924 expedition, for example, one of the members of the expedition wrote:

> It has been said that these men could easily reach the top if they themselves really wished to do so. I do not believe it for one moment. I think we are no less necessary to them than they are to us—they have acclimatized bodies, but lack the right mentality; we have the will power, the necessary spirit, but are woefully deficient in acclimatization.[55]

Younghusband said almost the same thing:

> So there, right on the spot, must be dozens of [Sherpa] men who could, as far as bodily fitness goes, reach the summit of Everest any year they liked. Yet the fact remains that they don't. They have not even the desire to. They have not the spirit.[56]

Perhaps the dominant strand within this discourse of the natural and the uncorrupt was the idea that the Sherpas were like children. This analogy went through some changes over time. At first the Sherpas were child*ish*, undisciplined. About the porters on the 1922 Everest expedition, Bruce wrote that "these hill people, whether Nepalese [i.e., Sherpa] or Tibetan, are very light-hearted, very irresponsible, very high-spirited," and very much given to drinking at any opportunity.[57] With respect to the 1924 expedition, Norton described the Sherpas as "singularly like a childish edition of the British soldier"; in both cases their natural "roughness" and lack of civilizational polish was considered both a strength and a weakness:

They have the same high spirit for a tough or dangerous job; the same ready response to quip and jest. As with the British soldier, the rough character, who is perpetually a nuisance when drink and the attractions of civilization tempt him astray, often comes out strongest when "up against it" in circumstances where the milder man fails.[58]

This whole discourse of childishness then got taken up in a more "scholarly" text of the day, Northey and Morris's *The Gurkhas: Their Manners, Customs, and Country.*[59] In his chapter "A Journey on the North East Frontier of Nepal," Morris—who does not appear to have actually visited Solu-Khumbu—first described the Sherpas as little more than bodies that carry: "It was from this race that the Mount Everest porter corps was recruited who performed such prodigious feats of endurance." He went on to say,

Left to themselves they are extremely lazy, and will spend the whole day in gambling for drink, of which they are inordinately fond. With a firm hand over them they will, and do, work extremely hard, but they lack that standby in times of distress—an innate sense of discipline.[60]

On the other hand, the idea that the Sherpas were like children could be taken in a different direction, seeing Sherpas as child*like* (rather than child*ish*), innocent and unspoiled. Of the 1922 expedition, George Finch wrote, "I felt responsible for these cheerful, smiling, willing men, who looked up to their leader and placed in him the complete trust of little children."[61] Like children, the Sherpas were frequently described as if they had no cares. Geoffrey Bruce described them as "light-hearted [and] care-free," [62] and we heard about their "smiling, happy faces" on the 1934 expedition to Nanga Parbat.[63] This discourse of innocence and/or happiness actually became the dominant version of the Sherpas-as-children in the 1930s (though the other line—lack of discipline—did not completely disappear) and continued on and off up to about the 1970s. Looking beyond the early period for a moment, James Morris wrote in the fifties about his "band of Sherpas, untouched by any tarnish of civilization, honest and faithful always." [64] John Dias, in the sixties, combined the Sherpas and their home region of Solu-Khumbu in one happy, untouched, unmodern package:

> Solo [*sic*] Khumbu and its Sherpa people retain an air of arcadian simplicity and happiness. Shangrila is an outworn idea, but it does spring to mind because these mountains and valleys do correspond to the secret retreat for which the questing mind of discontented Man has always craved. [65]

Kohli in the sixties, too, used a language of children, calling Sherpas "these cherubic men of the mountains, stocky and sturdy, happy and gay," [66] and Miura in 1978 pushed the cherubic image even further:

> I was very impressed by the loyalty and devotion they show each other, qualities that seem to be disappearing in the "civilized" world of today, but which still exist among these barefooted angels living in a forgotten corner of the Far East. [67]

The discourse of Sherpa innocence is closely related to another major theme about the Sherpas' unmodernity: it was consistently stressed in the early years that the Sherpas did not climb for money, and certainly not solely for money. Paul Bauer in the 1930s linked the themes of naturalness, innocence, and lack of interest in material reward:

> With such splendid fellows as these Bhutias [Tibetans] and Sherpas, our consideration was not wasted; they followed us to the last man in desperate places, with a trust and enthusiasm beyond rewarding, which had no thought of payment, but sprang purely from ethical motives, from noble natural instincts. [68]

Also in the thirties, Frank Smythe wrote that the Sherpas did not climb for money, that they made a "comfortable living" driving rickshaws, and that they climbed for essentially the same reasons as the sahibs: "adventure," "prestige," and "love of the mountains." [69] Hugh

Ruttledge wrote about the Sherpas on the 1933 Everest expedition: "The Sherpa does not come to Everest merely for what he can get out of it. He could earn as much money elsewhere."[70]

The discourse of the unmaterialistic motives of the Sherpas continued through the sixties. In 1961 Max Eiselin wrote about the 1960 Dhaulagiri expedition, "Most of our Sherpas were fine fellows who like climbing and did not join an expedition solely for what they could get out of it."[71] At about the same time, Ullman wrote about the 1963 American Everest Expedition:

> They were being paid, as all men are paid, for services rendered, but it was not primarily for pay that they were on that march. No less than the Western mountaineers who employed them, they were doing what they wanted to do, what they were born to do. They were not hired help but companions in adventure.[72]

The Ullman passage captures several dimensions of the Sherpa as unmodern or antimodern: naturalness (they were "born" to climb); the idea that they sought the same kind of "adventure" that the antimodern sahibs did; and the point that they were not in it for the money.

The discourse of the unmodern Sherpa is clearly "Orientalist" in Edward Said's (1978) by-now classic sense—born of the imperial project of the British in the late nineteenth century, sometimes racist, always "othering." Specific characteristics of the discourse can be tied to specific dimensions of the relationship between mountaineering sahibs and Sherpas: the sahibs' power and need for effective authority on the expeditions links up with ideas that the Sherpas lacked/needed "discipline"; the sahibs' intense romanticism, their desires to experience mountaineering as an escape from modernity, link up with the view of the Sherpas (like the mountains) as untouched, innocent, unspoiled. The idea, even the insistence, that the Sherpas were not in it for the money tied the two dimensions together in complex ways: on the one hand it was meant to stand for the point that the Sherpas were not part of the modern ("commercial," "materialist") world; on the other hand it was for the sahibs a peculiar denial of the knowledge of their own economic power over the Sherpas; they wanted—and it was clearly a very genuine, even urgent, desire in some cases—the Sherpas to share their reasons for and pleasures in this enterprise.

I leave aside here one of the key questions that has bedeviled the idea of orientalism almost from the outset: the question of the "real." Were the early climbing Sherpas really relatively undisciplined, relatively innocent and carefree, and not in this work primarily for the money? I will take these questions up in the next chapter, but we must consider now how sahib representations of the Sherpas as childish or childlike played themselves out in practice. This brings us to the other major sahib discourse of mountaineering, one that emerges from seeing mountaineering as part of a game of masculinity. The masculinity game, like the countermodern "adventure" game, runs through and informs mountaineering throughout the twentieth century. And like the countermodern game, it takes different forms at different times. For the early period in question in this chapter, and in fact up until the 1970s, it was largely framed in terms of military imagery. And in this context the view of the Sherpa takes on a slightly different cast.

The Military Model and Sahib Paternalism

If at one level it is relevant to see the sahibs as educated members of the upper-middle classes positioning themselves against a soul-destroying modernity, at another level it is relevant to recall that until the 1970s, sahibs were mostly male persons, highly responsive to certain values and ideals of Western masculinity, including physical strength, bravery and courage, authority and leadership, aggressiveness (within limits), and "paternalistic" responsibility for the socially subordinate and the weak. This is the side of the sahibs that has consistently endorsed certain dimensions of modernity even while questioning others. And although there are certain cross-cultural and cross-national variations in this picture, in general it holds up well enough to continue using the generic category of the sahib as the subject and object of this discussion.

A good part of the male-gendered dimension of sahib culture was embodied in the framing of mountaineering expeditions as military expeditions, a way of thinking that lasted from the earliest expedi-

1. Sahibs of the 1922 Everest expedition. *Back row, left to right:* Major Morshead, Captain Geoffrey Bruce, Captain Noel, Dr. Wakefield, Mr. Somervell, Captain Morris, Major Norton; *front row, left to right:* Mr. Mallory, Captain Finch, Dr. Longstaff, General Bruce, Colonel Strutt, Mr. Crawford.

tions to the mid-seventies. It was decided early on that the Himalayas could only be "conquered" through a military-style campaign, in which camps were set up and stocked with supplies at successively higher altitudes, thus forming a supply chain that would support the climbers making the final "assault" on the summit. This, of course, was where the Sherpas came into the picture, since their primary function was to carry all those supplies up the mountain.

Many of the leaders of the early expeditions were in fact army officers, but even if they were not, the military framework was used to define virtually every aspect of the endeavor, including the technical organization of the climbing, the language of the enterprise (siege, assault, conquest, etc.), and the forms of leadership, authority, and command.

The military model operated in a definite tension with the romantic and other countermodern yearnings that were central to much of early mountaineering. There were debates from early on about the size and organizational complexity of expeditions, and about the amounts and kinds of appropriate technology. One of the most serious debates concerned the use of supplementary oxygen. It was discovered early on—Dr. A. M. Kellas was a key player in this— that supplementary oxygen at high altitude made climbing much easier, and much safer as well insofar as the oxygen-deprived brain tends to lose focus and make mistakes. For many climbers, however, this kind of technological support precisely reduced the challenge that brought climbers to extreme high-altitude mountaineering in the first place. The arguments of the 1930s for and against supplementary oxygen continued to be heard for much of the twentieth century.

Nonetheless, the military model remained the dominant model well into the 1970s. Extreme romantics like Maurice Wilson and Earl Denman (discussed earlier), who tried to climb solo and without supplementary oxygen, either died trying (Wilson) or were extremely disillusioned when they failed (Denman). Despite the contradiction, however, there was one arena in which the military model and the romantic model dovetailed unfortunately too well: in the view of the Sherpas as childlike. In the romantic context Sherpa childishness was viewed as simple and winning. In the military context, however, it was seen as "unruly" and "undisciplined," requiring a firm paternalistic hand and a set of disciplinary measures.

One arena of unruliness involved Sherpa drinking and fighting on expeditions. This mostly took place along the approach march; alcohol was often barred on the expeditions (though some sahibs allowed it in base camp), but the Sherpas would stop and buy the local beer (*chang*) or spirits (*arak, rakshi*) in towns along the way to the mountain. The sahibs found it amusing or annoying but did not come down too hard unless the drinking interfered with the Sherpas' work. In fact it rarely did, but it was often a point of friction, and it clearly fed into the view of the Sherpas as self-indulgent and prone to letting themselves go without the firm hand of the sahib.

But the most serious arena of potential indiscipline concerned Sherpa willingness to proceed up the mountain under dangerous conditions. The sahibs required the Sherpas to carry loads to high camps; that, more than anything, was what they were there for. But the high slopes of the Himalaya can be quite terrifying—steep faces, slippery ice, deep crevasses, avalanches; there are numerous ways in which to get killed. At the very least the work can be utterly exhausting, with freezing temperatures, high winds, blinding snow, and air thinned of oxygen. There were in fact occasions when the Sherpas balked. Yet they usually had to be made to go on, and more generally they had to learn to be willing to go on (even, to desire to go on) without anyone making them do it; that is, to acquire self-discipline under the constant shadow of death.

DEATH AND DISCIPLINE

DEATH ON THE EARLY EXPEDITIONS

Nearly every one of the early expeditions in the Himalayas had a fatal accident, and in virtually every case one or more Sherpas were killed. It must be realized, too, that each and all of these deaths reverberated throughout the climbing communities, both Sherpa and sahib. Every expedition took place with an awareness of the deaths that had gone before. I give here a brief summary of the deaths in the pre-World War II period, essentially in the twenties and thirties.[73]

- On the British reconnaissance of Mount Everest, in 1921, Dr. Kellas died of a heart attack on the march, and one porter (no name or ethnic category given) also died on the march.[74]
- On the first full Everest attempt, in 1922, seven Sherpas—Lhakpa, Nurbu, Pasang, Pema, Sange, Dorje, and Remba—died in an avalanche.[75]
- On the third attempt, in 1924, two sahibs—Mallory and Irvine—died; two non-Sherpa porters died ("Lance-Naik Shamsherpun, a Gurkha, died of a brain haemorrhage, and Man Bahadur, Assistant Bootmaker, died of pneumonia following severe frostbite");[76] and four Sherpas were rescued in a state of extreme shock after being trapped for three days in a blizzard.[77]

- In 1930, the Germans attempted Kangchenjunga. Chettan, a Sherpa who had distinguished himself on earlier expeditions, was killed in an ice avalanche.[78]
- In 1931, the Germans tried again on Kangchenjunga. Pasang Sherpa was knocked off balance by a snow slide, fell off a cliff, and pulled a sahib, Hermann Schaller, with him.[79]
- The 1934 German-American expedition to Nanga Parbat had one of the great disasters of the period. One sahib (A. Drexel) died of illness. Three sahibs (W. Merkl, U. Wieland, W. Welzenbach) and six Sherpas (Gaylay, Dakshi, Nima Dorje II, Nima Tashi, Nima Norbu, Pinju Norbu) were killed in storms. Gaylay refused to leave one of the dying sahibs, Willy Merkl, and died with him in one of the legendary heroic Sherpa deaths of early mountaineering.[80]
- Also in 1934, Maurice Wilson died of exhaustion and exposure in his solo attempt on Everest.[81]
- In 1936, on the way back from yet another British Everest attempt, the expedition translator, a "Darjeeling businessman" named Karma Paul, ordered a Tibetan (or Sherpa; accounts vary) porter to cross a flimsy rope bridge over a high gorge. The porter "didn't dare refuse" and fell to his death.[82]
- Also in 1936, on the successful British-American attempt to climb Nanda Devi, one Sherpa, Kitar Dorje, died of dysentery in base camp.[83]
- The 1937 German attempt on Nanga Parbat was even more disastrous than the previous one. Seven sahibs (Karl Wien, Hans Hartmann, G. Hepp, A. Göttner, P. Fankhauser, M. Pfeffer, and P. Müllritter) and nine Sherpas (Pasang Norbu, Mingma Tsering, Nima Tsering I, Nima Tsering II, Tigmay, Chong Karma, Ang Tsering, Gyaljen Monjo, and Karmi) died in one avalanche, still a record for the number of deaths on a single expedition.[84]
- On the 1938 German attempt on Nanga Parbat, the climbers came upon the frozen bodies of Gaylay and Willy Merkl from the 1934 expedition.[85]

- In 1938 the British were once again on Everest. Pasang Sherpa had a stroke and was rescued in a controversial incident (see chapter 5).[86]
- In 1939 the Americans attempted K2 in the Karakoram, the second-highest mountain in the world and considered by many much more difficult than Everest. One sahib (Dudley Wolfe) died of illness high on the mountain. In the other major prewar story of Sherpa heroism, three Sherpas (Pasang Kikuli, Ang Kitar, and Pintso Sherpa) died trying to rescue him.[87]
- In the 1939 Swiss attempt on Garhwal Himal, two Sherpas (Ajitia and Gombu) were killed in an avalanche.[88]
- In 1939 Bill Tilman took three Sherpas on a trek to Assam. Nukku Sherpa died of malaria.[89]

SHERPA BREAKDOWN AND SAHIB CONTEMPT

In sum, Sherpas have died on expeditions, witnessed others (Sherpa and sahib) die, and have had terrifying close calls. Little wonder, then, that they have occasionally broken down and refused to go on in a situation of potential or actual fatality. The sahibs themselves have been upset by Sherpa, as well as sahib, deaths, sometimes extremely so.[90] Yet they have often had little sympathy for the surviving Sherpas' reactions, responding to Sherpa shows of fear or demoralization with contempt or worse. Their contempt, not surprisingly, has consistently been framed in terms of the Sherpas' childishness or primitiveness—their lack of bravery and self-control, their excessive vulnerability to fear. On the 1922 Everest expedition, for example, when seven Sherpas were killed in an avalanche, John Noel wrote that the surviving Sherpas "had completely lost their nerve and were crying and shaking like babies."[91] On the 1931 German expedition to Kangchenjunga, when one of the top Sherpas was killed, the other porters became extremely upset and only three would climb above the place where he fell. [92] Later, two of those who continued "broke down and cried," largely it seems because, after so many others had left, they were seriously overworked. Yet the leader, Paul Bauer, wrote: "They needed some connection with the world they left behind to strengthen their hold on reality and prevent superstitious feelings arising."[93]

On the 1938 German expedition to Nanga Parbat, when the expedition came across the dead bodies of Gaylay and Merkl from the 1934 climb, the sahibs tried to prevent the Sherpas from seeing the bodies, but Bauer wrote that "instinct is too powerful with these children of nature," and after that only one porter would work above Camp IV.[94] And in a later example, Klaus Becker Larsen, who tried to solo Everest in 1951, wrote: "When confronted by real hardships and dangers [the Sherpas] have their tails down like the majority of primitive people with whom the conception of honour has not yet arisen."[95]

When Sherpas refused to climb out of fear and demoralization, and yet, for whatever reasons, the sahibs absolutely required that they continue, the sahibs were known to resort to force to keep them moving. Thus, in the case of the 1931 German Kangchenjunga expedition, the Germans felt they had no choice but to force two of the Sherpas to continue. The leader's own contempt was both manifest in his actions, and projected onto his "loyal servant":

> [After the fatal accident] Dorji became hysterical, put down his load and undid the rope to go back. We took him firmly by the collar and forced both him and Pasang to go on with us up to the terrace. My loyal servant Kami curled his lips contemptuously when he saw them being dragged up by the rope.[96]

If the Sherpas were prey to what the sahibs saw as childish terrors and lack of self-control that threatened the success of the expedition, then from the sahibs' point of view the issue was one of disciplining them so that they would at least keep hold of themselves and at most internalize the proper "spirit" so that external discipline would no longer be necessary.

DISCIPLINING THE SHERPAS

The British in particular had a whole series of strategies for shaping up the Sherpas, most of them derived in one way or another from the model of military discipline and its underlying assumptions about how authority works.[97] For one thing, paternalism itself was put into service as a disciplinary technique. Geoffrey Bruce (Charlie Bruce's nephew, who was on the 1922 and 1924 attempts) wrote that it was important to look after the Sherpas daily, and to inquire personally about their welfare, as a way of insuring that they would not lose morale and refuse to go on.[98] Similarly, Norton wrote:

There is only one way of overcoming the difficulty I have mentioned—that of inducing porters to go to somewhere near their physical limit on the highest day—and this is for a large proportion of the climbers to acquire such influence over the porters that the latter will follow them.[99]

In other words, it was thought that the Sherpas as childlike people could be trained to do a good job not by appealing to their intelligence and rationality (which was in effect denied them) but by appealing to their very childishness, encouraging a childlike personal dependence on the sahibs who, with their superior rationality and intelligence, would guide and protect them. Thus, when Sherpas on expeditions did behave well, this was attributed to the sahibs having correctly elicited this dependence and loyalty. In a quote offered earlier, for example, Bauer wrote of the Sherpas "following us . . . with a trust and enthusiasm beyond rewarding" as a result of the sahibs having treated them with "consideration." [100]

Beyond a kind of strategic paternalism in the personal treatment of the Sherpas, the military model also suggested certain strategies for instilling the right "spirit" in them. Geoffrey Bruce tried to generate competition in the ranks of the Sherpas by promoting some individuals to leadership positions,[101] and Norton told the Sherpas that they would become very famous ("your names shall appear in letters of gold") if they surpassed previous altitude records.[102]

There was also the idea of awarding the Sherpas medals and badges. Sahib members of the 1922 expedition were given Olympic medals; additional medals were later given to "two porters."[103] But the most famous medal was of course the so-called Tiger medal, which the Himalayan Club in Darjeeling began awarding officially in 1939. The use of the term "Tiger" for Sherpas who put in outstanding performances began after the 1924 expedition. The award included not only the badge but "eight annas a day more than other porters for work above the snow line."[104] The first group of Tigers comprised twelve Sherpas, including Ang Tharkay, Tenzing Norgay, and "Wangdi" (possibly Wangdi Norbu, sardar of the 1933 expedition). Tenzing Norgay described himself as "proud and happy" about the award.[105]

Between the expeditions of the twenties and those of the thirties, at least on Everest, there was a definite break. The Sherpas on the 1933 (and subsequent) expeditions appear much more professionalized. We hear no more complaining from the sahibs about the Sherpas' lack of discipline—laziness, drunkenness, irresponsibility, lack of motivation, and lack of spirit. On the contrary they seem to have been more or less perfect, doing everything well, coming through in a pinch, ready and willing for anything:

> May 29th dawned very cold, though with a promise of fine weather. Now came the real test of the porters. On a similar occasion in 1924 Norton found himself in a four hours' argument, persuading the men to start. Nothing of the sort occurred this time. The climbers were up at 5 a.m., and found the eight [Sherpas] ready and willing. There can be no doubt that these Sherpas . . . have now developed an improved tradition, pride of achievement, standard of possibility.[106]

The discourse of childlike innocence persisted (at another point in his book Ruttledge described the Sherpas as "develop[ing] a pathetic reliance on the sahib,"[107] but the Sherpas' actual performance on the job was the subject of great praise.

Not surprisingly, the British took credit for whipping the Sherpas into shape. Ruttledge called it a "process of psychological evolution for which the credit must be shared by the men themselves and by the climbers who led them." [108] And Tilman wrote, "Amongst other factors which have brought about this change, and to which we are chiefly indebted, are the care, sympathy, and mountaineering skill, with which the porters of earlier Everest expeditions have been handled."[109]

Yet it is the nature of cultural encounters like those of Himalayan mountaineering that what goes on during expeditions is at least as much a function of what goes on at "home" as of the encounter itself. Home for the Sherpas was the Solu-Khumbu valley of Nepal, where extraordinary changes were going on, and the Darjeeling-Kalimpong region of India, where the Sherpas had been engaged in wage labor, a money economy, and dealing with a variety of sahibs for a good fifty years at the point at which mountaineering began.[110] Although there is no doubt that the rather creative array of British and other European disciplinary strategies had some effect on the Sherpas, their impact—not to mention the impact of that which the sahibs kept denying, the money—can only be understood in relation to the ways in which these things articulated with the Sherpas' own desires, intentions, and needs—their own "serious games"—to which we now turn.

3

SHERPAS

The Sahibs, from early on, had various ideas about the Sherpas. In the last chapter, I discussed the ways in which those ideas largely embodied the sahibs' own projected fantasies and prejudices. Yet the sahibs' assertions about the Sherpas make claims of describing something real, and this chapter turns to those "real" Sherpas. At the same time questions of representation cannot simply be dismissed.

There are at least two issues. The first concerns something like truth. If we recognize, as I do, that sahib representations of Sherpas embody various biases—not only the personal prejudices of individuals but the larger ideological ones of their times and places (colonialism, capitalism, masculinity, modernity, or, usually, several of these at once)—can we at the same time accept the sahibs as saying something true or real about the Sherpas? The problem applies not only to mountaineers' accounts but to anthropologists' descriptions as well. What can we know? The second question concerns the power of representations. If sahibs represent Sherpas in certain ways more consistent with their own fantasies and needs than with Sherpa "reality" (though of course there is never a single "Sherpa reality"), and if at the same time the sahibs have power over the Sherpas, then to what extent might sahib representations come to impose themselves on Sherpa reality?

Both sets of issues are questions of cultural or ideological construction. In the first case, the Sherpas are "constructed" in the sense that they are imagined or made up; they are constructed in sahib images that may have little to do with reality. In the second case, the Sherpas are "constructed" in the sense that they are "made," shaped by the images, and the power behind those images, to actually conform with the sahibs' desires. I need to say a few words here about both views, although the entire book is in some sense a response to them.

On the question of what we can know from sahib texts, I take inspiration from the work of Ranajit Guha and the members of the so-called Subaltern Studies school of Indian historiography,[1] who have devoted much attention to the problem of recuperating not only accounts of events and ethnographic descriptions but questions of agency and subjectivity from dominant (in that case, colonial) texts. I take inspiration as well from Louis Althusser's point that dominant representations ("ideology") always contains both "illusion" and "allusion," both distortions and truths.[2] In practice this means a kind of constant reversing of texts between an ethnographic reading and an ideological reading. Mountaineers' representations are mined for Sherpa ethnography, even as they are taken apart for their biases and fantasies. At the same time anthropological accounts of the Sherpas are criticized for their own theoretical and representational biases, even as a cumulative record of high-quality ethnographic work forms the touchstone against which mountaineers' views are interpreted. In Althusser's terms one might say that if one seeks the illusions within the allusions (the ideological biases within the seemingly realist claims), at the same time one seeks the allusions within the illusions, fragments (or more) of ethnographic truth in even the most eccentric sahib representations.

I have already indicated my position on the second question about "representation," the question of how much influence the sahibs' (including mountaineers, anthropologists, and—later—tourists) images of the Sherpas have had on the Sherpas themselves. In a recent book (1996) on late-twentieth-century Sherpa identity, Vincanne Adams argues that the Sherpas have been heavily reshaped by the sahibs' desires and fantasies. In her view, much of what we think of as Sherpa culture today has emerged through a process of mimesis, in which Sherpas—in large part but not entirely because of their dependence on the income from mountaineering and tourism—have sought to be the kinds of people and to have the kind of culture the sahibs have wanted. Sherpas today, she argues, have become "virtual Sherpas." James Fisher has made similar points in less extreme form,[3] and I would agree that some of this has occurred. But I would argue that Adams vastly overprivileges the effect of sahib perspectives and vastly underestimates the reality of a Sherpa world that bends sahib influence to Sherpa purposes. This entire book is meant to flesh out a position in which sahib construction of the Sherpas, and something like Sherpa self-fashioning, take place simultaneously, in a complex and unpredictable dialectic.

Returning, finally, to the early Sherpas, I begin again with sahib representations, in this case representations of Sherpa "excellence." I then move beyond them, into the Sherpa world of social relations and cultural understandings in Solu-Khumbu in the early part of the twentieth century.

VARIETIES OF SHERPA EXCELLENCE

The Sherpas began to be singled out by Western (mostly British) climbers as "excellent men," "excellent porter material," and "splendid fellows" in the first decade of the twentieth century. This excellence has been central to the conditions of Sherpa employment, and to sahib-Sherpa relations throughout the whole twentieth century, and I begin with an overview of the various dimensions of good Sherpa character that the sahibs have consistently remarked on and appreciated across time.

Originally, the sahibs valued the Sherpas primarily for their physical strength and stamina. Sherpas could often carry heavier loads for longer periods of time and to greater heights than most sahibs. An additional material factor, as General (then Major) Bruce noted in 1910, was that the Sherpas wore warm clothing and footwear (both indigenous woolen clothing and, as time went on, old expedition gear as well), and were better prepared to deal with extreme cold than the Indians and lowland Nepalis of the plains.[4]

The sahibs also commented, from early on, on a certain good-humored or good-natured style of Sherpa "character" or "temperament," including a tendency to smile or laugh easily, a willingness to enter into joking and teasing, and a generally affable manner that often made interacting with Sherpas pleasant and enjoyable. The climber who wrote the introduction to Tenzing Norgay's autobiography commented on

> the tolerance and good humor, spontaneity and lack of prudery . . . for which they are renowned. They are indeed a happy people, as anyone who has travelled with them will know, tolerant and good-humored to a high degree, finding enjoyment in almost anything they do, interested in everything and with a strong sense of fun.[5]

The notion that the Sherpas were cheerful, good-natured, and good-humored took various forms. Sometimes, as we saw in the last chapter, it entered into a near racist discourse that viewed their good humor as childlike.[6] Mostly, however, there was a straightforward appreciation of people who could keep up their good humor and good spirits under extremely adverse conditions. For example, after a hard day's climb at high altitude, or after a late night with little sleep, when the sahibs themselves were exhausted, they were astonished to find the Sherpas in good moods, laughing, joking, and singing. As Sir Edmund Hillary wrote: "I admired the Sherpas. Singing as they worked, and cheerful when most of the foreigners could barely raise an excruciating grin, they were slow to complain about their lot."[7]

Or from a Canadian: "[The Sherpas] seemingly weren't affected by the heat or the sun [which the Canadians found very debilitating] and were sunbathing, drying out their double-bootliners, drinking tea, laughing and joking."[8]

The appreciation for the Sherpas' good humor related to their value as support structure for the expeditions. For the most part they tended to be agreeable about, and willing to do, whatever they were asked to do; they cooperated with a smile and had a general "can do" attitude. The Swiss explorer Toni Hagen wrote of his "Sherpa, Aila, who normally in the most critical situations invariably said with a cheerful grin, 'all right sir.' "[9] And Ed Hillary wrote of Tenzing Norgay: "I was impressed with his strength, his sound technique, and particularly his willingness to rush off on any variation I might suggest."[10]

Then there is generosity. Sherpas have given up their oxygen if a sahib needed it;[11] given up their blankets or sleeping bags or waterproof gear when there was not enough;[12] slept outside of the tent when the sahibs had taken up all the room inside;[13] spent hours rubbing a sahib's hands or feet to prevent frostbite;[14] stayed behind to help a slower climber when all the other sahibs had rushed off;[15] carried sick and wounded sahibs twice their size down the mountain;[16] voluntarily made extra trips for supplies;[17] climbed part way back up a mountain with hot tea to meet a successful summit party coming down and to relieve them of their packs;[18] and more. In almost every case the Sherpas *offered* to do these extra things without being asked. While at some level they may have felt they had little choice, the offers still seemed genuinely ungrudging and communicated striking generosity. Hillary wrote about one Ang Nyima who was supposed to descend to a lower and more comfortable camp after portering goods for the first Everest summit party to the highest camp:

> He asked if he could be allowed to stay up [throughout] the night with us in order to help us down the next day. This demonstration of loyalty and unselfishness from a man who was obviously going to have great difficulty in getting down at all affected me deeply and seemed to epitomize all that is best in the Sherpas.[19]

These acts of generosity in turn shaded into acts of outright heroism in an accident or a crisis. Sherpas on expeditions have made extraordinary efforts, going out under terrible conditions, when everyone else was exhausted, to try to rescue stranded climbers.[20] In some cases they died trying. These stories are told and retold in the mountaineering literature, including that of Pasang Kikuli on K2 in 1939 trying to rescue a sick sahib,[21] and Chhowang on Cho Oyu in 1959 trying to render assistance to the summit party in a storm.[22] Both men passed up several opportunities to give up the rescue attempt and save their own lives. A major variant of this sort of story is the refusal by a Sherpa to leave a sick or injured sahib, even if staying with him or her would probably be fatal. The earliest of

2. Ajeeba Sherpa carrying the frostbitten Maurice
Herzog. French Annapurna Expedition, 1950.

these stories concerns "Gaylay" (Gyali) on Nanga Parbat in 1934, who would not leave the exhausted Willy Merkl and died with him on the mountain.[23] More recent examples include that of Sungdare in 1978, who bivouacked overnight just below the summit of Everest with the exhausted Hannelore Schmatz, and went down to a lower camp the next day for oxygen for her. When he came back up, he found her too weak to move and stayed with her until she died. He lost four toes to frostbite.[24] More recently, during the 1996 Everest disaster, Lobsang Jhangbu Sherpa insisted on staying with Scott Fischer, who was too ill to move, even when Fischer insisted that Lobsang Jhangbu go down. Lobsang Jhangbu left only when Fischer threatened to throw himself off the mountain.[25]

Underlying these and other acts of self-sacrifice and heroism is a more general pattern of Sherpa loyalty. Climbers have consistently remarked on the Sherpas' tendency to quickly develop loyalty to the expedition as a whole, and to individual sahibs. The modes of loyalty have been variable, from a filial devotion that fit in with sahibs' paternalism, more common on the earlier expeditions, to the loyalty of true and equal friendship, more common in recent times. In whatever form, the loyalty and solidarity that the Sherpas have consistently been willing to generate have clearly been major sources of the sahibs' positive views of them.

Probably the best overall summary of a sahib's appreciation for all the best in the Sherpas came from the great Bill Tilman, writing in 1935:

> For nearly five months we had lived and climbed together, and the more we saw of [the Sherpas], the more we liked and respected them. That they can climb and carry loads is now taken for granted; but even more valuable assets to our small self-contained party were their cheerful grins, their willing work in camp and on the march, their complete lack of selfishness, their devotion to our service. To be their companion was a delight; to lead them, an honour.[26]

Tilman's encomium summarized all the key characteristics that the sahibs felt they found in the Sherpas: their physical abilities, their cheerfulness, their lack of selfishness, and their loyalty.

But were the Sherpas really strong, cheerful, selfless, and loyal? The answer, of course, must be yes and no. We are sensitive to questions of essentialism and racism in these characterizations. Yet to recognize that representations are problematic in many ways—often Orientalist and racist, sometimes wholly phantasmic, and always, always, partial—is not to give up on the enterprise of understanding their relationship to some actual life-and-death world. It is the "yes and no" of the relationship between sahib representations and Sherpa "reality" that I pursue here and throughout this book. Let us begin with the question of physical strength.

STRONG SHERPAS: BUT WHO CARRIES?

Sherpas have been thought to possess tremendous strength and endurance. This, in turn, has been linked to a supposed physiological adaptation to high altitude, along with a cultural practice of carrying loads from early childhood on.

The Sherpas occupy two linked regions in eastern Nepal called Solu (the lower valley) and Khumbu (the higher). Solu villages are located between about 8,000 feet and 10,000 feet, with higher pastures above, while Khumbu villages—from which most of the early climbing Sherpas came—are located between about 12,000 feet and 14,000 feet, with higher pastures above. The two are linked by the Dudh Khosi, or Milk River, which flows down from Mount Everest; villages along the river between Khumbu and Solu occupy the Pharak region, which simply means the middle or in-between region. (See map 3.)

The basic economic activities are agriculture (mostly the growing of potatoes, wheat, and barley); the maintenance of herds of yak and cow for their dairy products and for sale (and more recently for rental to expeditions); and (until the Chinese invasion of Tibet in 1959) trading both north into Tibet and south and east into other regions of Nepal. Since Khumbu is located at a higher altitude than Solu, and since crops grow more slowly in Khumbu, there is greater emphasis on herds and on trade there than in the lower region.

There are no paved roads in Khumbu, and the trails are very steep. There are thus no wheeled vehicles in the region (not even wheelbarrows, although they would work). Virtually all transportation is on foot, and virtually all loads are carried on people's backs.[27] Sherpas start carrying loads up steep trails for long periods of time from an early age.

All of this would seem to adapt the Sherpas physically for mountaineering work, and no doubt it plays some role. From early on sahibs have assumed that the Sherpas have a genetic or an acquired physiological adaptation to high altitude, but in fact this has not been established with any certainty. Physician Charles Houston, re-

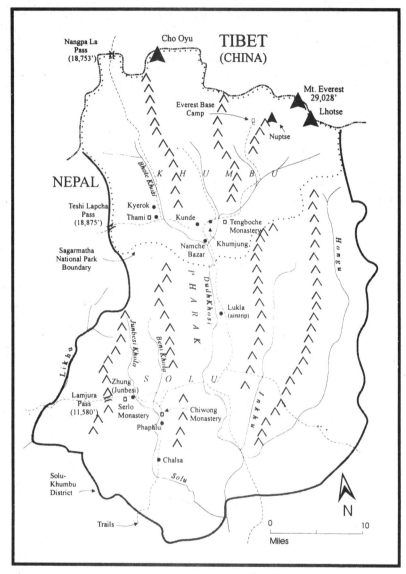

Map 3. Solu-Khumbu.

viewing the medical studies on the question, has argued that Sherpa success in mountaineering is more probably a matter of drive and motivation:

> Sherpas don't have more hemoglobin than their sea level co-horts. . . . Sherpas seem able to do more work at extreme altitude than can even well-acclimatized sea level natives, but there are few well-controlled studies to support this, and when the chips are down, willpower, motivation, spirit [N.B.] are probably more powerful spurs to summit Everest than is a slightly better level of acclimatization.[28]

Although bodies are not irrelevant, then, the more critical issue is the construction of certain Sherpas as being particularly strong or particularly willing to carry heavy loads, a question that brings us very quickly to social differentiation in Sherpa society. Differentiation is, again, absolutely critical to understanding people's intentions, that is, the serious games in which they are engaged, the resources they bring to playing those games, and the intensity with which they play them. In the case of the early Sherpas, as I will argue here, the game was a game of "liberation," of escape, often from poverty and dependence, but at the very least from certain tensions and constraints of traditional Sherpa society, even if one were not actually poor. We need to look briefly at the pressures that created these needs and desires.

In Sherpa society there were (and still are, but my discussion here is mainly about the early-twentieth century) categories of "big people," "small people," and everyone else in-between—"not rich, not poor," as they say. The big people were the wealthier people of the society; they owned more land and herds of animals; they lived better than others, with tenants and laborers to work their land and servants to help at home. The ordinary middle-level Sherpas made up the largest sector of the population. They were for the most part also independent property holders but they had less wealth and were less comfortable and less secure. A few people—the truly "small"— were landless and very poor and, if they did not migrate elsewhere, became tenants and servants for the big people.[29]

Being big meant many things, but one thing it meant, which is central to this story, was not having to carry loads. As noted, load carrying was a fact of life in Solu-Khumbu, including not only portering goods during travel but doing such mundane chores as collecting firewood, fetching water, carrying fertilizer to the fields, and carrying hay and crops from the fields. Some of this was burdensome and unpleasant in the extreme. Water sources might be far away; the water was ice-cold in the winter, and water for the household had to be fetched in either a heavy wooden container or a frigid brass urn several times a day. Although these chores were accepted as necessary, nonetheless people were delighted not to have to do them, and the good life was always partly defined as not having to carry loads.

And indeed, not everyone carried. Big people never carried. Middling people, ordinary Sherpas, carried their own loads, but it was something of a point of pride not to carry for others except as a favor, or in a reciprocal arrangement. On the other hand, the small people—the tenants, the servants, the hired laborers—carried not only for themselves but for the big people.

This in turn tells us something else: the physically "strong Sherpas" who could and would walk or climb for hours with sixty to eighty pounds on their backs were almost certainly from the non-big (though not necessarily "small") levels of Sherpa society. This meant one of two things: that they were very strong, because they were used to doing a lot of carrying and also needed the money, or that they were not necessarily very strong, but had to break their backs doing this work anyway because they needed the money. In either case, money or material well-being was central to the issue.

A note on money. Money is an extremely complex symbol that must always be interpreted. To say that most Sherpas climbed (and still climb) primarily for money is the beginning, not the end, of understanding why they climb. For money as a sign points to the Sherpas' own desires, their own notions of the good life, their own senses of what they would do and how they would live if they had the means. It may mean simply making a financial profit; it may also mean supporting kin or sending kids to private schools in Darjeeling, or traveling or sponsoring religious rituals, or contributing to the financing of a monastery. The point is that, for all its negative positioning within a certain Western countermodern imaginary, money points precisely toward (as much as it might seem to point away from) something we may think of as an "authentic" Sherpa cultural universe, a framework within which they articulate their own desires in something like their own terms.

This is not to say that the Sherpas do not have their own complicated feelings about money; they do. There are cultural notions that people can be powerfully seduced by the sight of money into doing things they do not want to do, or into becoming slaves of others' wishes on the analogy with (Nepali) love magic. People are certainly critical of individuals who seem driven solely by material greed and self-interest, by the desire for money for its own sake. Yet the Sherpas have no moral problem with the simple fact that they climb primarily for pay; whatever other motives may enter in, that is the bottom line. Moreover, their financial success on early expeditions was a major factor in their cheerfulness.

CHEERFULNESS AS A PREVAILING CULTURAL STYLE

I use the word "cheerfulness" to cover a range of characteristics noted appreciatively by the sahibs: that the Sherpas were "friendly," "good natured," "fun loving," or of a generally positive temperament, and that they were able to maintain this good humor even under fairly stressful conditions, especially after carrying heavy loads all day. Did this describe some piece of Sherpa reality? Again the answer must be yes and no, although the question is complex and the answer comes in several parts.

Let us start with "no." I have elsewhere presented a picture of Sherpa social life very different from the cheerful images we get from the sahibs.[30] In my first book, based on fieldwork in Solu (1978), I stressed a tendency toward "selfishness" in village life, grounded in the private-property system, and regularly generating disputes that escalated into violence.[31] (By violence I mean mostly fist- and wrestling-type fights, occasionally with rocks or chunks of wood. The use of actual weapons was extremely rare, but parties to fights might nonetheless get quite severely beaten up.) When I later did fieldwork in Khumbu, it seemed to me that people were individually somewhat more cooperative with one another, and that there was a fuller development of local institutions that worked for the collective good.[32] Nonetheless, there was a good deal of fighting and violence in Khumbu as well.

In this book I focus on the cheerfulness and good humor that have been so striking to the sahibs. But Sherpa fighting and violence are equally "real," and I am not denying them here. My point, however, is first, that virtually all of the violence (and 'selfishness') one sees in Sherpa village life is related to the structures of inequality in the society, and second, that a whole array of cultural values, beliefs, ideals, and notions of the good neither supports nor idealizes selfishness, fighting, and violence. This is what I mean by calling cheerfulness a prevailing cultural style. Specifically, from a Buddhist point of view, harming another person, even only with violent words, is sinful. Other beliefs stress not so much sin as the idea that fighting is disgusting and upsetting. To participate or even witness a fight generates *thip* ("pollution"), which is a state of being emotionally sickened in an extremely unpleasant way that may be a prelude to getting ill.[33] Fighting, beating up others, being able to "take it" oneself, are not significant components of Sherpa masculinity. Boys are not encouraged to be physically aggressive.

The Sherpas of course recognize that fights and violence occur, but they also make some key distinctions about them. At the simplest level they dismiss them as the effect of drink, something that happens when self-control breaks down, but that has no long-term causes or consequences and is easily repaired. Many fights are explained by the one-word answer: *chang* (beer). More serious conflict is viewed in two ways: as part of the rivalries for status, reputation, and influence ("name") among "big" people (including both wealthy lay people and lamas), and as part of the struggle for survival among non-big (both middling and small) people, especially focusing on property disputes. Big-man violence is disapproved of as fundamentally selfish and egotistical; the violence among non-big people over property and inheritance is viewed as unfortunate but understandable.

It seems reasonable to say that, despite a fair amount of social conflict in the community, cheerful friendliness is a style of social interaction that is culturally encouraged, valued, and—when possible—practiced. It is thus reasonable to ask, further, what it is in the Sherpa lifestyle that has produced and reproduced this cultural value. This question has been a major focus of prior anthropological research among the Sherpas, and there have been several answers.

The first ethnographer of the Sherpas, Christoph von Fürer-Haimendorf, took the question of Sherpa goodness of character as the central question of his monograph, and answered essentially that it was their Buddhism that made them so open and friendly, so generous and cooperative. It is true of course that Buddhism enjoins its adherents to be good people in these and other ways, and indeed Sherpa religion is central to many of the discussions in this book. Yet the connection as Haimendorf drew it is too broad to be of much use. All religions urge their adherents to be good, but few people, individually or collectively, follow the precepts of their religion in some clear-cut and direct way.

The other major explanation for the construction of Sherpa cheerfulness as a dominant cultural style has been put forward by anthropologist and mountaineer Mike Thompson, who has suggested that the good-natured Sherpa temperament derives from what is essentially a culture of trade and mercantilism.[34] At least since the Sherpas came into Nepal in the sixteenth century, they have been centrally engaged in trans-Himalayan trade, bringing salt down from Tibet and bringing rice up from the lower-altitude regions of Nepal. Almost every Sherpa man did a certain amount of small-scale trading, though only certain individuals were able to succeed in this enterprise on a large scale.[35] These successful men became the politically dominant actors of Sherpa society, and their interactional style, it is suggested, became the culturally dominant style. As Thompson put it, "Man, they have always felt, does not live by [potatoes] alone, and their individualistic, exuberant, risk-taking, reward-enjoying trade has formed the basis for a cheerful, convivial, easy-going, open and hospitable life-style that has endeared them to generations of Western mountaineers."[36]

Both of these interpretations—in terms of religion and of trade—are plausible, up to a point. Neither, however, takes into account the political and economic differences in Sherpa society. The prevalence of fighting and conflict in village life points to the ways in which friendliness and good cheer were always potentially subverted, on the Sherpas' home turf, by political and economic inequalities and rivalries. Pushing the argument further, then, I want to argue here that for the non-big people, cheerfulness had to be more actively and practically constructed, and that this, as much as any generic cultural style, was what the sahibs were seeing in the "cheerfulness" of expedition Sherpas.

Making Cheerfulness I: Money and the Escape from Smallness

The differences between "big people" and others (non-big, and "small") in Sherpa society were both a source and an outcome of other tensions in the society, tensions that propelled increasing numbers of young Sherpa men into mountaineering throughout much of the twentieth century. The continuities and changes in these patterns will be taken up in later chapters, but here I continue to focus largely on the early decades of mountaineering, the 1920s and 1930s.

PROPERTY AND INHERITANCE

The productive property of Sherpa society, including agricultural land and herds of dairy animals, was privately owned by families. The nuclear family was the property-owning unit of the society, and the ideal was for each nuclear family to have its own house and enough productive property to support its members. Inheritance was normally transmitted to young people at marriage, and that is where problems immediately arose for many families. The Sherpa inheritance rules are intrinsically problematic for all Sherpas, "big" or non-big. According to the rules, a father should divide his real property equally among all his sons. Within a generation or two, however, this would become impossible, as the subdivisions of property yielded parcels too small to support a family.

"Small people" with significant property problems in the past would, when all other options failed, have had to borrow money, work as laborers for other families, tie themselves to big people as tenant farmers and sharecroppers, or all of these. It is not clear how widespread indebtedness, tenantry, and debt bondage were in the past, and my sense is that real poverty among the Sherpas was not widespread, nor were the rich extravagantly richer than everyone else. But the differences were real enough, and the problem of the excessive subdividing and parcellization (reducing to tiny and scattered units) of property was pervasive. There was thus a sense in which some young men always had to go out and seek their fortunes elsewhere, that the Sherpa economic organization always produced "excess" sons and fraternal competition, and that there was always a need to find outside resources.[37]

Additional pressures were put on this system in the mid-nineteenth century. In 1846 a family called Rana, which had traditionally and hereditarily supplied the prime ministers to the king of Nepal, took power from the king and reduced him to a figurehead. The Rana accession had multiple effects. For the big people, in at least some cases, it allowed them to become bigger than ever, as tax collectors, traders, and through various business deals they were able to strike as a result of contacts with the Rana state in Kathmandu.[38] On the other hand, the Ranas also significantly raised the demands for taxes—in kind, in labor, and in cash—and expanded the means of collecting them more effectively.[39] For the small people, then, the need for additional sources of money was greatly intensified.

Thus, it is virtually certain that most of the Sherpas who showed up for mountaineering labor in Darjeeling in the late nineteenth century, and for a long time thereafter, were there because they needed the money. Some of them were very poor, with little or no land and a constant threat (or reality) of indebtedness. The story of Ang Tharkay, who became one of the greatest of the early Sherpa sardars, was a case in point. I take the following discussion from Ang Tharkay's autobiography; although it was composed with the help of Western scribes and translators, Ang Tharkay's voice, at least in the section to be discussed here, comes through very clearly.

Ang Tharkay was born into a very poor family in Kunde in 1907. Although his grandfather evidently had some land, his father's younger brother, Ang Tharkay's uncle, inherited the bulk of the grandfather's estate:

> My father had a younger brother and as such could not expect to come into the patrimony of the family, because it is frequent among the Sherpas that the youngest son inherits the paternal wealth. Thus it was that the younger brother of my father received the familial estate, leaving my father to get along however he could. At the death of my grandfather, my uncle then took possession of the fields and the house of my grandparents, which he still occupies to this very moment.[40]

When a neighbor with no family decided to enter a monastery, however, he gave Ang Tharkay's father, at no cost, a house and fields, thus saving the family from total impoverishment. Nonetheless, by the time Ang Tharkay was thirteen years old, the family had become heavily indebted and he was forced to go to work for other families:

> We contracted heavy debts which aggravated our already hardly brilliant situation. I was obliged to go to work for others, as a watcher of cows, a cutter of wood, and a [general] day laborer, in order to bring a meager supplement to the resources of the family. . . . I thus rented my services throughout the area and it was not until two years later that I was able to return home and take up my former occupations.[41]

Other early Sherpas were not necessarily poor, but they were sons of non-big families who were doing what, in effect, the system made them do: leaving the paternal property intact, at least for the time being, and bringing in additional resources from the outside rather than subdividing the limited internal pie. To see an example from a relatively middling family, we may look at the most well known Sherpa of all, Tenzing Norgay. Tenzing Norgay was born in 1914, the eleventh of thirteen children, seven of whom were sons. Although the family was reasonably comfortable, they were not enormously wealthy, and clearly the subdivision of the property among the sons would have significantly lowered the material conditions of life for all of them. Tenzing was sent off to the newly founded Tengboche monastery, but he did not like it and came home. Later he ran away to Kathmandu to see the big city, and finally he left for expedition work in Darjeeling.

Tenzing did not see himself as driven to leave by inheritance and property considerations. He simply viewed himself as having strong desires to see the outside world and to accomplish bigger things: "Always as a child, a boy, a man, I have wanted to travel, to move, to go and see, to go and find," he wrote.[42] The point is not that there is a direct line between material need or inheritance rules, on the one hand, and individual desires and plans, on the other. Rather, the property and inheritance organization of Sherpa society enduringly produced young men for whom going away was always an option if not a need. In addition, the centrality of long-distance trade (and pilgrimage) regularly produced individuals who had a sense of a larger world.

Indeed, even Ang Tharkay did not believe he was leaving simply to make money. In his case, his extreme poverty, his resentment of his uncle, his humiliation at having to work for other people, all condensed into a sense of the smallness, the backwardness, the almost suffocating closure of village life in Solu-Khumbu. At one point he called it "our lost country";[43] at another he described himself as "closed up [enfermé] within my natal village";[44] and finally, in the context of arriving in Paris and feeling particularly small, he piled up image upon image of backwardness and enclosure. He called himself "a poor little Sherpa from a miserable land lost in the shadow of the barrier of the Himalaya."[45]

As against all this, mountaineering labor quickly became invested with a particular glamour. Much of this glamour first took material form in the exotic clothing and equipment the earliest expedition Sherpas brought back from their climbs. Tenzing Norgay described himself as fascinated by the clothing of the men returning from the expeditions in the 1920s; he actually paid someone money in order to try on his expedition boots.[46] Ang Tharkay, too, invested mountaineering with an intense seductive power:

3. An early photo of Ang Tharkay (*left*) with Sen Tenzing
and Pasang Bhutia (no date).

I was a little more than 20 years old when I met one of my village friends, Nim Tharkay, who returned from the expedition of General Bruce and came to see me at our home in Kunde, carrying all his mountaineering equipment. He paraded from house to house as if he had accomplished some astounding feat. Being younger, my imagination became inflamed by the poetic descriptions that he gave of his adventures, so much so that it did not take long for me to feel a mad desire to follow his example and to seek to become a part of an expedition myself.[47]

There was also the possibility of a kind of personal advancement that was not available within the local village context, especially for someone like Ang Tharkay who started out quite poor and "small." From early on, the sahibs appointed one individual Sherpa, whom they deemed to be responsible and to have leadership qualities, to be the "sardar," the head Sherpa or foreman on an expedition. A bright young man would have ambitions beyond simply being a high-altitude "Sherpa" (skilled climbing porter); he would hope to become a sardar. Sardars were able to make significantly more money than the other Sherpas, both because they were better paid, and because they (or many of them) took "commissions" from the Sherpas and local porters, or at least, such was always the rumor. Sardars were often ambiguous figures in their communities of origin, as they did not fit neatly into the local status hierarchies. But all became famous and some became highly respected, and the possibilities of gaining recognition and perhaps respect, as well as money, added another layer of potential value to expedition work. Both Ang Tharkay and Tenzing Norgay became famous (and fairly wealthy) as sardars; Ang Tharkay was more famous as a sardar than as a climber.

For early Sherpas, then, mountaineering labor provided an almost perfect solution to the problems of property and inheritance in Sherpa society. For all but the biggest people it provided a way of making a living, and indeed a good living, for "excess" sons who in the worst case might have had to become servants or who, even in the best case, would have caused problems within the family by dividing the estate and pulling down everyone's standard of living. The glamour of mountaineering (as opposed to other kinds of "coolie work") allowed it to take on an additional positive charge, with exotic sahib clothing and foods, and other glimpses of the distant and the "modern." This sense of liberation from family and larger economic tensions was the first dimension of "making cheerfulness" for Sherpa men who went into this labor.

INDEPENDENT LABOR AND GOOD CHEER

There was one other factor that added to the liberating nature of mountaineering work, which is related to the free-enterprise (private property- and trade-based) nature of the Sherpa economy: the fact that the Sherpas came to the Darjeeling labor market, and to mountaineering, as independent labor. They were true capitalist workers, selling their own labor power on their own behalf, and

4. "Porters who went highest" on the 1924 British Everest expedition. *Left to right:* 'Bom, Narbu Yishé, Semchumbi, Lobsang, Llakpa Chedi, Angtenjin.

(apart from family claims) keeping their own wages..Odd as it may sound, the historical record suggests that the fact that the Sherpas were operating as independent labor was actually quite closely linked to the positive and energetic—"cheerful"—way in which they seem to have embarked on mountaineering work.

In order to see this, we need to compare the early sahibs' accounts of their dealings with the hill tribes in the western Himalayas and the Karakoram—Balti, Hunza, and others—with their accounts of their dealings with the Sherpas. The comparison is apt, since the ethnic groups in question are physically comparable to the Sherpas—mountain dwellers used to cold, to carrying loads, and to tough trekking. With a few exceptions (notably the cheerful Lor Khan seen in chapter 2), the western Himalayan groups were described in many expedition accounts as sullen, ill-tempered, and largely unreliable.

They complained, they stole, they went on strike at every opportunity, and often they simply walked out en masse on expeditions, stranding the expeditions in extremely isolated places (the Karakoram peaks, such as Nanga Parbat and K2, are much further away from inhabited villages than the ones further east (see Map 1), with no porter support and inadequate supplies.[48]

Although as a generalization it may be that the Hunzas (and other groups of those regions) are relatively less culturally inclined toward a "cheerful" and outgoing style than the Sherpas, it is also clear that these styles are situational. Thus, in one of the accounts in which the Hunzas are portrayed as having behaved very badly, we also read that "at home they ... display a fine cooperative spirit ... [and] among their neighbors they have a reputation for unruffled cheerfulness and friendly self-confidence."[49] We may say, in keeping with the language of the present discussion, that the Hunzas and similar groups, unlike the Sherpas, were unwilling or unable to "make cheerfulness" in the expedition context.

The relevant factors behind this difference appear to be the different political and economic circumstances in which the two groups came to mountaineering labor. The Hunzas seem to have come as *corvée* labor; that is, labor that is owed (like taxes) to a ruler, and for which they received little or no pay:

The Mir of Hunza, the autocratic ruler of the sturdy and independent mountain tribe, sent volunteers [*sic*] to undertake transport to the higher camps.[50]

There were three hundred porters at Talichi, hill peasants assembled there on the orders of the government.[51]

[They were under] the obligation not to abandon their post unless released by the expedition leader; otherwise they could expect to incur the contempt of their community and be sentenced to forced labor by their ruler, the Mir of Hunza.[52]

Given the conditions under which they were there, then, it is not surprising that the Hunzas were sullen and uncooperative, and also that the promise of better wages and equipment did not necessarily get them moving (as it would, in most cases, for the Sherpas). The

Hunzas simply did not want to be there; the expedition was taking them away from their own work and lives, and the Mir presumably took a big cut of their "wages."

The Sherpas on the other hand came—as much as one can say this about wage labor—of their own free will; their wages were theirs to keep, and they experienced these wages as liberating them from the various binds in the traditional economy. Moreover, they could perceive a close relationship between their own hard work, the success of an expedition, and their own money-making possibilities on a given expedition (as bonuses or baksheesh) and in the future. The difference between the Sherpas' relationship to their wages and that of the Hunzas seems almost directly related to the level of "cheerfulness" mustered for the labor.[53]

MAKING CHEERFULNESS II:
STRIKES AND IDENTITY

Mountaineering came to pay extremely well, but this was not always the case. The wages on the early expeditions were in fact poor, quite literally "coolie wages." Ang Tharkay describes the Sherpas as nearly starving on the return leg of the 1933 Everest expedition, and as not being able to buy enough food without pooling their meager travel allowances.[54] If the Sherpas were happy to be there, and it seems that they were, this did not mean that they found all the conditions of the work satisfactory. Almost from the beginning, they set themselves on a course of gaining improvements in those conditions, and in fact escaping the classification of "coolie" itself. They were, for the most part, enormously successful in all this, another major dimension of "making cheerfulness."

Ever since political scientist James Scott articulated the notion of "everyday forms of resistance," the boundary between "resistance" and many other kinds of behavior has become extremely blurred.[55] The question has been complicated because it seems to depend on the actor's intentions: Is a sick porter who refuses to continue "resisting," or is he merely sick and unable to go on? Obviously there is a large gray area between people who resist by going on strike with conscious intentions of making demands and unconscious persons who do not continue working because they cannot. But the point here is that labor relations are precisely relational; "illness" becomes "resistance" from the sahib's point of view regardless of the porter's intentions, simply because it does not carry out the sahibs' requirements. In fact, most of the cases to be discussed here are quite intentional instances of resistance; I simply leave room for the grey-area cases that occasionally arise.

Sherpas have enacted some form of resistance on probably the majority of Himalayan expeditions. The reasons have been various. At one end are the kinds of instances just mentioned: refusing to go on because they simply felt unable to go on. They might have been exhausted or sick; on the 1924 Everest expedition, although they performed extremely well overall and received high praise from the sahibs, there were several points high on the mountain where one or another small group of Sherpas simply could not or would not get out of the tent and get going, provoking hours of harangues and persuasions from the sahibs.[56] They might have been upset over a death: on the 1931 German Kangchenjunga expedition, after an accident in which a sahib and a Sherpa were killed, the Sherpas staged what appeared to the sahibs to be an irrelevant resistance about moving the camp.[57] Later, there was the incident of the porter Dorji, who became terrified and demoralized and tried to go down, but was dragged up the mountain by the leader, Paul Bauer.[58] The Dorji incident is a good example of the point that it is not particularly useful to try to draw the line between actual resistance and "accidental" forms of noncompliance, since Dorji's refusal to climb, which appears to be (in standard Western categories) for psychological rather than political reasons, nonetheless *functioned* as a political act, going up against the sahibs' desires and requirements and thus responded to with force.

A second cluster of reasons for resistance have related to the material conditions of the Sherpas' involvement in mountaineering—money, food, equipment.[59] On the very first Everest expedition, the 1921 reconnaissance, the "coolies" (which included a mixture of Sherpas and Tibetans; on the earliest expeditions the sahibs did not fully distinguish between them) staged "an attempted mutiny" over rations.[60] The sahibs ultimately blamed most of the trouble on the sardar. It is possible that the sardar was, as Mallory described him, "a whey-faced treacherous knave whose sly and calculated villainy . . . deprived our coolies of their food" (Howard-Bury et al. 1922, 216); the Sherpas themselves have on other occasions complained about unfair or dishonest treatment by their own sardars. It is equally possible, however, that the sahibs provided inadequate rations and that the Sherpas' strike was in fact just what it purported to be: a strike against the sahibs and the inadequate conditions on the expedition.[61]

The Sherpas made demands over money on the 1929 German Kangchenjunga expedition;[62] they actually brought a legal case over money against the sahib pay-officer of the 1930 International Kangchenjunga expedition.[63] On the 1933 Everest expedition, the Sherpas almost struck in base camp over the inadequate food and toilet facilities, but the crisis was averted by the order to start moving up the mountain.[64]

Although all of these strikes were directed against some aspect or other of the material conditions of expeditions, most of them had other dimensions as well. The question of the toilet facilities, for example, was clearly a matter of dignity for the Sherpas and not just physical discomfort or offense; Ang Tharkay described the sahibs as treating the Sherpas "in a manner barely human."[65] As for strikes over money (and later, even more centrally, over equipment) at one level these were just what they appeared to be; after all, money was the primary reason that the Sherpas were there at all. But the issue of wages and equipment for Sherpas has always at the same time been an issue of "distinction," in the double sense of prestige and distinctiveness; the Sherpas wanted recognition that the work they did was more skilled and dangerous, and hence more valuable, than the work of ordinary porters.

The question of Sherpa distinctiveness from other groups emerged very early as a critical question. After some initial sorting out of other groups (Indians and Nepalis from the plains who could not take the cold, or Hindus and Moslems who had too many eating taboos), the Sherpas' chief competitors emerged as their close ethnic cousins, the Tibetans and the "Bhotias" (other ethnically Tibetan peoples from the region). On the 1921 reconnaissance, the sahibs did not clearly distinguish between the Tibetan and Sherpa porters, but on the second Everest expedition, in 1922, the Sherpas made a point of competing with the Tibetans, volunteering for all the difficult high-altitude jobs, and bringing themselves to the sahibs' attention as less "superstitious," more willing, and more disciplined than the Tibetans.[66] This paid off on the 1924 expedition, as the sahibs created a sorting of low-altitude or "local" porters, who in practice were mostly Tibetans, and high-altitude porters, who in practice were mostly Sherpas. Presumably, although I have not been able to find any figures, there was higher pay for high-altitude work. On the series of Kangchenjunga expeditions (1929 German, 1930 International, 1931 German), the questions of money were also tied up with the Sherpas' competition with the Tibetans: in 1929 the Sherpas demanded more money "than ordinary coolies" who in practice were mostly Tibetans;[67] in 1930 they brought the legal case because they felt the Tibetans had come out unfairly better than they had; and in 1931, as a result of the 1930 events, they tried to get Bauer not to hire Tibetans at all—"otherwise they would not come."[68]

Finally, the issue of material conditions and the distinction that they signified took another turn with respect to carrying loads. When the high-altitude porters were sorted from the local or low-altitude porters in 1924, those designated for high-altitude work were given reduced load-carrying chores at low altitudes, to keep them "fresh for higher altitude."[69] It is not clear what happened on the next (1933) Everest expedition, but by 1935 the Sherpas took the distinction between local porters who carried loads at low altitudes, and high-altitude "Sherpas" who did not, as a given: they refused to carry loads on the inbound trek, and staged a strike when the sahibs tried to get them to do so.[70] The same thing happened in 1938, and Tilman was philosophical about it:

> The tradition has now spread beyond the confines of an Everest expedition, and it is wise to discount the Sherpas as a carrying force so long as any other transport is available. They either put their loads on the already sufficiently laden animals or hire animals on their own account and present you with the bill.[71]

5. Photo captioned "The 'Tigers' (except Kipa) who established Camp VI";
unidentified Sherpas of the 1933 British Everest expedition.

The relief from at least some carrying is another major dimension
of "making cheerfulness," and I will return later to the radical implications of the successful campaign to rise above local portering and
load carrying. More broadly, however, the whole sequence of sahib
demands, Sherpa resistance, and the establishment of progressively
more favorable working conditions over the course of the 1920s and
1930s constituted a moving front of tangible successes that must
have continued to add to the pleasure—the cheerfulness—of Sherpa
involvement in early mountaineering.

It is also important to note that the Sherpas were able to continu-
ously press for their interests while successfully retaining the sahibs'
affection and admiration. The same year, 1935, that they struck and
refused to carry loads on the walk-in, Bill Tilman wrote the greatly
admiring passage quoted earlier: "To be their companion was a de-

light; to lead them, an honour."[72] Part of this feat was related to yet another supposed character trait of the Sherpas that the sahibs consistently remarked on: loyalty, or what Tilman had called "devotion to our service."[73] Along with physical strength and cheerfulness, this too must be both provisionally accepted as "real" and deconstructed: de-invested of sahib orientalism, and re-invested with Sherpa meanings.

LOYALTY: THE IDEA OF
THE ZHINDAK

The Sherpas had the notion of a *zhindak*, a patron or protector, who would help a lesser person to succeed. People were often involved in competitive struggles with others—brothers for inheritance, others for political positions. But if one could find the right zhindak, and he took you under his wing, you might be able to defeat your rival. It is important to note that zhindaks do not directly bestow success—wealth, position and so on—but only facilitate achieving it, helping the hero to help himself.[74]

On the early expeditions, the British in particular played a highly paternalistic role in relation to the Sherpas. They also took it that the increasing "spirit" and skill of the Sherpas was the result of the ways in which they had, in effect, brought them up. It is not entirely improbable that the Sherpas did respond positively to the kindnesses of the sahibs, even if they were paternalistically bestowed. Many of the Sherpas were very young and sometimes very poor men. In addition, however, the Sherpas did have a strongly established notion, which ran through many aspects of their culture—folklore, religious ritual, social relations—of the value of a benevolent protector, a zhindak. Yet these cultural ideas have been consistently misunderstood. In particular, there has been a tendency to view the relationship precisely through the lenses of classic Western paternalism, in which the junior party to the relationship is viewed as childlike and dependent. Within the Sherpa frame, on the other hand, although one may occasionally hear some parent-child language, the relationship is actually embedded in a variety of profoundly egalitarian assumptions.[75]

In the first place, the idea of the zhindak operates within a culturally egalitarian world. This is to say that although there are significant differences of wealth and power in a Sherpa community, these differences are not given by birth but are achieved (both honestly and dishonestly) in a theoretically equal-opportunity system. Thus, all unrelated Sherpa men are considered equal in principle if not in practice, and everyone in theory has the possibility of advancing himself or herself as much as possible. Zhindaks are not part of a larger cultural system of hierarchical relations; they are hierarchical devices that are structurally harnessed to a world in which equality of opportunity is the basic assumption.

Second, the relationship between a person and his (or, less often, her) zhindak is a completely reciprocal one. The zhindak is more powerful than oneself, but this power must be augmented by the protectee caring for, feeding, and helping the zhindak. The zhindaks' strength comes precisely from those who are dependent upon them. The same mechanism works with the gods; they are able to help humanity because they are sustained by people's offerings; without those offerings they would be weak. As the Tengboche lama put it in an interview:

> The gods' power comes from the [spiritual energy] of men and is weak or strong according to our devotion to them. The fortunes of the gods rise and fall just like a family's might do, over time. When the gods are weak (when men's devotions lag or for other reasons) then floods and other things bad for man can easily happen.[76]

This, then, is the spirit in which Sherpas serve sahibs: if you take good care of them, they will take good care of you.[77]

Finally, there is a notion in the culture that hierarchical relations like the zhindak relationship may be transformed in a more egalitarian direction over time. If and when the junior party achieves some success, and if there is not a major age difference or formal status difference between the two parties, eventually things should even out. This is part of a larger cultural and religious pattern of both accepting and overcoming hieararchy. Thus, the same dynamic is embodied in certain religious ideas about the relationship with a tutelary deity, or *yidam*. Like the zhindak in the human realm, the yidam is a personal protector in the supernatural realm who must be given the utmost care. But at the same time the idea of Tantric practice is that the asymmetry of the relationship with the yidam is transcended over time:

> A well-known tradition states that on the lowest level (Kriya) [of Tantric practice] the practitioner's relationship with the Tantric god or *yidam* is as a servant to a lord, on the next level (Carya) the relationship is that of friend to friend, while on the higher levels the relationship is no longer dualistic, and the practitioner becomes identical with the Tantric deity.[78]

These various points are meant to indicate, in different ways, that there is a sort of egalitarian underpinning to the zhindak relationship. The junior party is not positioned as a child or a social inferior, but rather something more like a talented but disadvantaged protégé. In folktales, for example, the junior party is usually a bright young man who is down through no fault of his own, but who needs some extra help and power to come back strongly and defeat those who are illegitimately besting him.

To understand this is to understand one of the puzzles that runs through many sahib accounts of Sherpa "character": that the Sherpas seem to have an uncanny knack for being highly obliging, and for willingly doing what they are asked to do and even going beyond that, yet without seeming servile or subordinate. The Swiss climber René Dittert remarked of the Sherpas (including Tenzing Norgay) on a 1952 expedition, "I would not have thought it possible to be more obliging (*serviable*) and less servile (*servile*.)"[79] And Eric Shipton said in a 1969 interview that the Sherpas were "tremendously loyal and yet they never kowtow to people."[80] But the answer to this seeming contradiction is that, when the Sherpas are operating in a zhindak-type mode, these acts are not servile acts and to perform them is not to subordinate oneself.

We can watch this complex structure played out in the autobiographies of both Ang Tharkay and Tenzing Norgay. Both show a willingness to construct the sahibs as zhindaks and themselves seemingly as loyal servants, yet both show a sensitivity to being treated as not-equals, and a strong appreciation when relations with sahibs were egalitarian. Ang Tharkay, first, at one point described the 1950 Annapurna expedition as "like a big family of which the sahibs would have been the parents."[81] He also represented both himself and the other Sherpas as forming a deep, subordinately tinged admiration for the leader, Herzog:

> As primitive as we are, we other Sherpas, we are rarely mistaken in our appreciation for beauty and strength and, above all, in our intuition about qualities of the heart. Our admiration and our loyalty were immediately and spontaneously given to our leader.[82]

Ang Tharkay's autobiography has of course been filtered through several translators, each of whom no doubt added his own particular inflection to the text.[83] Nonetheless, let us assume a surplus of truth rather than an absence of truth: that if Ang Tharkay had constructed himself as excessively subordinate vis-à-vis Herzog, who had clearly been cast in a protector/zhindak role, Ang Tharkay had also refused to see any implication of inferiority in this construction. Thus Basil Norton wrote in the introduction to the autobiography that Ang Tharkay's one flaw was a hypersensitivity to perceived slight, and that "he reacted very sharply if he had the impression that someone was taking him for an inferior." [84] Moreover, the most important thing for Ang Tharkay about the 1950 Annapurna expedition was precisely its egalitarian style:

> The sahibs like us put their shoulders to the wheel and made no distinctions between themselves and us concerning the work. It was a new and very agreeable experience; this mode of acting filled us with enthusiasm. Never, in any expedition we had been on, had we had such an impression of freedom and intimacy with the sahibs. We felt that a tight link of comradeship united us to them.[85]

Looking next at Tenzing's autobiographies, we see the same combination of expressions and acts of seemingly subordinate devotion, on the one hand, and an appreciation—even a demand—for being

treated as an equal. Tenzing repeatedly cast in the zhindak role various higher figures who helped him. As a boy he dreamed of being
taken away by a zhindak figure:

> I remember I was very shy and stayed much by myself, and
> while the other boys chased one another and played games with
> mud and stones I would sit alone and dream of far places and
> great journeys. I would pretend I was writing a letter to an im-
> portant man in Lhasa who would come and get me.[86]

With the Swiss in 1952 there was a tinge of the Sherpas' using the
zhindak frame to get something from the leader. This was not necessarily cynical; it was what zhindaks were for. As Dittert wrote:

> And then [Sherpas] often find words which go directly to one's
> heart; the other day, Tensing, the sirdar, the head of the Sher-
> pas, having asked me for something, said to me: "I ask this of
> you because you are the father of the Sherpas." Try to refuse
> after that![87]

After the success of the British expedition in 1953, Prime Minister
Nehru of India took Tenzing (who lived in Darjeeling) under his wing.

> From the very first, Panditji [Nehru] was like a father to me.
> He was warm and kind, and, unlike so many others, was not
> thinking of what use he could make of me, but only of how he
> could help me and make me happy.[88]

Yet Tenzing, like Ang Tharkay, was extremely sensitive to slight.
After the success on Everest, he refused to attend a reception at the
British Embassy because he had been turned away from there once
before.[89] And he had no qualms about saying that he had "a difficulty
and a problem" with the British, compared to some other nationalities, because they drew an essentially racist line between themselves
and "Easterners."[90] Moreover, like Ang Tharkay, he was deeply ap-
preciative of egalitarian treatment. He wrote of a 1947 Swiss expedition in north India, "I had enjoyed this expedition with the Swiss.
For the first time on an expedition I felt on equal terms with my
employers; indeed I felt towards them not as Sherpa to Sahibs, but
rather as friends"; [91] and of a 1950 expedition with English climbers

(who here evidently transcended their alleged national character), he wrote that "this was one great thing about the expedition. There was no distinction at all between climbers and porters. We did the same work, shared the same burdens, everyone helping everyone else when help was needed. We were not like employers and employees, but like brothers."[92]

Tenzing tried to explain to his readers that even behavior that seemed subordinate or servantlike was not like that, but was actually done in a spirit of equality:

> We consider it our duty to take care of our sahibs. We cook for them, bring them their tea, look after their equipment, and see that they are comfortable in their tents. And we do these things not because we have to, but because we want to; *not in the spirit of servants but of good companions.*[93]

In sum, the Sherpas may, and frequently have, cast the sahibs as zhindaks, benevolent protectors who would help them in life. In turn they have often been willing to serve the sahibs with loyalty and devotion. This pattern has clearly played a major role in the sahibs' enormously positive reactions to the Sherpas in the early period, and well up into the present. But my point throughout this discussion has been that, however paradoxical it may seem, this apparently subordinate loyalty is built on a kind of egalitarian base; that the Sherpas actually dislike hierarchy and are sensitive to being taken as subordinates; and that the zhindak-Sherpa relationship is actually meant to be one of mutual and shared devotion, in which it happens to be the case that one party is temporarily in an advantaged position vis-à-vis the other, but that this inequality will level off or even be reversed over time.

THE MAKING OF THE SHERPAS / THE SHERPAS MAKE THEMSELVES

We may think of the outcome of the early decades of the twentieth century as the production and self-production of mountaineering Sherpas in a fused bundle of role, status, and identity that then remained relatively stable until the 1970s. We saw, first, that expedition Sherpas pressed successfully to be recognized as better than, and thus worth more in terms of pay and other privileges than, the other ethnic groups (mostly Tibetans) who also worked as expedition porters in the early years. This gradually produced the distinction between "local porters" and "high-altitude porters," with the high-altitude work reserved almost exclusively for ethnic Sherpas. It produced, in other words, the category of "Sherpa," as later mountaineers and even the "outside world," came to know it—a category that conflated the job and the ethnicity into a single identity.

To be a "Sherpa" in this sense carried multiple benefits. First of all, one was better paid. Second, high-altitude Sherpas won the extraordinary benefit of partial relief from the very thing that they were brought in to do in the first place: carry loads. Given what I said earlier about Sherpa attitudes toward carrying loads, and given the elite associations of not carrying (we shall see in the next chapter that not carrying loads is important to the identity and image of the monk as well), the idea that an elite Sherpa did not have to do mundane load carrying was clearly a major triumph, symbolically and practically. And, finally, there were issues of respect. Not only were the Sherpas distinguished from Tibetans, with attendant material benefits and symbolic pleasures, but the Tiger medals and other awards do seem to have meant something positive to the Sherpas. Again, these meant more money and more chances for future jobs. But beyond that the medals seem to have achieved, at least for a time, what the British intended: "Tigers" were proud of their awards, and they felt recognized in ways that counterbalanced and transformed the "coolie" nature of the work.[94] All of this is to say that the Sherpas continually shaped and furthered the conditions that made the work rewarding—more money, more recognition, and less domination—and that contributed to their own continuing empowerment—and cheerfulness.

4

MONKS

To the early twentieth century Western mountaineers, explorers, and researchers, the Sherpas were only what they appeared to be—men who showed up for a certain kind of work and turned out to be very good at it. But behind the scenes of mountaineering, there was a drama of major proportions—indeed of proportions larger than that on the Darjeeling scene—taking place in Solu-Khumbu. In precisely the same period in which the Sherpas got involved in making money, big and small, in Darjeeling, they also began a process of transforming their own religious system. In 1916 and 1924 they founded the first two monasteries in Solu-Khumbu.

The founding of the monasteries emerged from essentially the same trends that produced the move to mountaineering, although in this case from the effects of those trends on the big people rather than the non-big. That is, the rise of the Ranas in Nepal, which drove the smaller Sherpas to Darjeeling to make money (and the presence of the British in Darjeeling that allowed them to do so), also affected the Sherpa big people, who became the founders of the monasteries. Several of the wealthy founders got rich through dealings with the Ranas, and one of them also got rich through smart enterprise in Darjeeling. And the same inheritance structures that pushed less well off families to maintain undivided holdings and thus produced excess sons, had precisely the same effect on big people, who had economic and status interests in avoiding subdivisions and maintaining their properties intact. In this sense, the same forces wound up producing both monasteries and mountaineering in precisely the same period.[1]

We may think of the monastic movement as the other new "game," along with mountaineering, that came onto the Sherpa scene in the early twentieth century. It was a new game in the sense that the monks—like the mountaineers—had a new agenda that they were both offering to and pressing upon the Sherpas. The monks' game was spiritual improvement, both for themselves and for the Sherpas in general. There were even certain parallels between early monasticism and mountaineering as both sahibs and monks saw the ordinary Sherpas being in need of certain kinds of discipline, certain kinds of improvement. In this chapter, I consider the new dimensions and reconfigurations that the monastic movement began to bring to Sherpa popular religion, and also the ways in which some of the early mountaineering Sherpas responded to this other major new presence in their midst.

THE FOUNDING OF THE MONASTERIES

Although the Sherpas had always practiced a popular form of Tibetan Buddhism, before the twentieth century there were no monastic institutions in Solu-Khumbu; that is to say, no communities of monks who were celibate, who did not raise their own food, and who devoted themselves full-time to religious practice. The earlier Sherpa temples were presided over by married lamas (*banzin* or *ngawa* or *choa*), local ritual specialists who were part of the social life of the community. Much of the early history of Sherpa religion (indeed of Sherpa society) focuses on the foundings of these local temples at different times over the course of the Sherpas' residence in Solu-Khumbu, starting in the sixteenth century.[2] These foundings were deeply enmeshed in Sherpa politics, in rivalries between competing big people, and in the non-big people's roles in those rivalries.

The temples presided over by the married lamas served the religious needs of the lay population, with the lamas performing rituals for ensuring the well-being of people, crops, and animals. Within the framework of full-scale Buddhist ideology, these sorts of reli-

6. Tengboche monastery, with Everest appearing behind the Nuptse ridge, 1968.

gious institutions were "small," both because their lamas were married, and because their religious work, with minor exceptions, was directed largely toward worldly and practical concerns. Although higher Buddhism everywhere in the Buddhist world tolerates this lower level of religion, the absence of monasticism with its commitment to both maintaining and displaying the higher, other-worldly ideals of the religion threatens to leave lay people behind, to slide deeper into the sin and suffering from which Buddhism seeks to rescue them. Everywhere, then, the founding and sustaining of Buddhist monasteries is the sine qua non of a solidly Buddhist society. The position is that if a group that defines itself as Buddhist *can* found and support monasteries, it should do so.

In the second half of the nineteenth century, then, the Sherpas began a campaign of upgrading their religion. Starting in the 1860s, there were renovations of old temples, the founding of new local temples, and finally the innovative foundings of the first monasteries, Tengboche and Chiwong, for celibate monks. The building of Tengboche between 1916 and 1919, involving the volunteer labor of virtually every man, woman, and child in Khumbu, captivated the imagination of Sherpas to a degree that is hard to exaggerate. Two more foundings, closely related to the first, followed in this early period. Founded by a younger brother of one of the founders of Tengboche, Chiwong monastery in Solu was begun in 1924 and completed in 1929. The founder, Sangye Lama, provided full endowment for the support of fifty monks, creating the only monastery in Solu-Khumbu that would have such support. Finally, the first Sherpa nunnery, Devuche, was begun in 1925 and completed in 1928. Defined as a branch of Tengboche monastery, its major contributors included the wives of some of the same families involved in Tengboche and Chiwong.

THE MONASTERIES AND SHERPA IDENTITY

The question of ethnic identity within the larger region was an issue for climbing Sherpas in this period. Within the mountaineering labor market, Sherpas were competing with many groups, but especially with the Tibetans, from whom they sought (successfully, for the most part) to differentiate themselves. For "big" Sherpas, however, the configuration of identity issues was somewhat different. Most of these men made their money trading in Tibet. They had trading partners there, and in some cases they even had second homes in D'ingri, the Tibetan town in which they normally traded. They also developed religious ties with Rumbu ("Rongbuk") monastery after it was founded in 1902. The big traders were thus at the most Tibetan end of the spectrum of Sherpa identity possibilities.

The big men were also developing important political and economic connections with the Rana (Hindu) state in Kathmandu. These ties were of growing importance in the late nineteenth century, in terms of generating both political positions and economic opportunities for big Sherpas. But here the big men were at a cultural disadvantage. From the point of view of the Hindu rulers, the Sherpas (along with all the other Tibetan-related groups of the northern border areas of Nepal) were collectively situated fairly low in the caste hierarchy. Despite the wealth and status of Sherpa big men, and despite in some cases the development of warm personal relations between some of them and some Rana officials, there was an enduring asymmetry that they would almost certainly have found irksome.

Buddhism, of course, does not operate on a caste model. Without suggesting that the Sherpa big men sponsored the monastery foundings purely for reasons of regional identity politics, nonetheless an intensification of their Tibetan Buddhist identity though large-scale religious support would have flowed almost naturally from a situation like this. Founding the monasteries had the effect of solidifying ties in Tibet, and at the same time making a statement of caste-free Buddhist identity as against Hindu hierarchy. There are a number of indications that the monastery founders made a point of stressing their Tibetan-related ethnicity in their self-presentations to the Nepalis. For example, it was noted by one of his descendants that Karma Lama, the senior founder of Tengboche, always wore Sherpa clothing when he brought the taxes to Kathmandu (even though such clothing was far too warm for the capital), and that he always stayed at the Buddhist shrine of Bodnath when he was there. And in a studio photograph of Chiwong founder Sangye Lama, presumably taken in Kathmandu, he posed wearing Chinese-style clothing, which was the clothing affected by the Tibetan nobility in that era.[3]

Once the monasteries were founded, further identity issues came into play. In particular, the monks raised questions not so much about caste as about certain Nepali/Hindu religious practices that were creeping into the region. The monks thus added another line to the boundary between Sherpas and Nepalis that was taking shape in this era. One effect, then, of the conjunction of Sherpa involvement in mountaineering, on the one hand, and the founding of the monasteries, on the other, was the construction of the particular configuration of Sherpa ethnonational identity that persists to this day: firmly rooted in Tibetan culture yet historically distinct from ethnic Tibetans; firmly rooted in the Nepal nation-state, yet culturally distinct from caste Nepalis.

POPULAR RELIGION BEFORE
THE MONASTERIES

The founding of the monasteries represented an upgrade, and in
many ways a far-reaching transformation, of Sherpa Buddhism. In
order to understand this, and to understand the relationship between these religious transformations and the changes wrought by
the emerging involvement in mountaineering, we need to do a quick
sketch first of Sherpa popular religion at the time of the founding
of the monasteries.[4]

Sherpa religion—Nyingmapa sect Tibetan Buddhism—is prem-
ised on the idea that people need the protection of the gods if things
are to go well for humanity. Gods come in all shapes and sizes, and
at all levels of particularity and generality. Individuals, households,
and clans propitiate, in rites called *hla chetup* ("god-offering"), relatively local and specific spirits and gods to whom they are tied; the
community as a whole makes offerings (*hla-tso*, "god gathering,"
usually just called *tso*) to the higher Buddhist gods who protect "all
sentient beings."

Gods protect people from bad forces, which again come in many
shapes and sizes. There are local witches and ghosts, sorcerers and
poisoners, derived from living and deceased members of the local
community; there are "demons" of many kinds who are not tied to
any particular place, but who prowl the world causing injury, illness,
and death. In simplest terms, then, popular Sherpa religion is a matter of enacting rituals in which offerings are made to the gods so
that they will sustain their protection and ward off the forces of
evil. Beyond this, rituals called *kurim* (roughly "exorcism"), include
another stage, in which the forces of evil are, with the help of the
gods, conjured into receptacles of some kind and then ritually destroyed or cast out.

The gods do not normally bestow benefits. One seeks their protection against harmful forces that might subvert one's own efforts
to get those benefits. Moreover, if the god is touchy and irritable,
as many of the local gods and spirits tend to be, one seeks to keep

it happy so that it will not itself subvert one's efforts. In general, then, gods help those who both care for them and help themselves.

Some of the less elaborate offering rites may be done at home by a member (usually, but not necessarily, the male head) of the household without benefit of religious specialists. For the most part, however, rituals must be conducted by *lamas*, trained and authorized religious specialists who are able and empowered to read the relevant texts, make the appropriate offerings, and otherwise conduct the ritual with maximum effectiveness.

Before the foundings of the monasteries, the lamas were for the most part members of the village communities.[5] They were married, had families, and participated in the social life of the villages. (In addition to the terms noted earlier, these married lamas could also be called, descriptively, *gyudpi lama*, or "lineage lamas," emphasizing their descent from lamas in previous generations, and the transmission of ritual power through biological descent. Both their married states and the emphasis on at least partial acquisition of their powers through biological descent distinguished them from monks, as I will discuss in a moment.) As part of their training, they would have had to participate in retreats involving ascetic practices of fasting, silence, sexual abstinence, and continuous prostrations. These ascetic practices are not dissimilar from those of monks. But where a monk's asceticism is oriented toward moral purification and ultimate salvation, the married lama's asceticism was largely geared to the heightening of his ritual power. The important issue for married lamas was the effectiveness of their rituals in controlling the gods, sustaining the gods' protection for the community, and casting out evil.

The other major ritual specialists on the Sherpa scene were shamans, *hlawa*.[6] Where lamas did their work for the protection of families and community so that trouble would not happen, shamans were called in when it did, mostly in the case of illness. Shamans went into trance and contacted their tutelary deities whom they entertained with offerings, and who helped them diagnose the causes of illness—usually a specific local witch, ghost, or locality spirit who had been neglected or offended. The shaman then advised the patient's family as to what had to be done to pacify the illness-causing agent so that the patient would get better.

Sherpa popular religion was not utterly discontinuous with high monastic Buddhism.[7] Both monks and married lamas performed many of the same rituals. The premises of the religion, concerning the need for the protection of the gods against the forces of evil, were the same. Village Buddhism before the monasteries included many "higher" practices; village lamas observed certain ascetic retreats; a few hermits enacted the larger ascetic regime of monastic Buddhism; lay people observed partial fasts and temporary ascetic practices on certain days of the month (*sozhung*); funerals tended to be very "orthodox," with the deceased being read *The Tibetan Book of the Dead* and led through the orthodox Buddhist post-death sequence; and more.

Yet ultimately, once the monasteries were founded, village Buddhism in the hands of the married lamas was seen as "small," and the monks embarked on a campaign to improve it. What was wrong with popular religion?

The Monks' Campaign I: The Critique of Popular Religion as Undisciplined

The monks never articulated a general and systematic critique of popular religion, so one must piece together their objections from a variety of often oblique comments. As a summary statement it may be said that the monks viewed popular Sherpa religion as "small" or low in large part because it was "undisciplined," which in turn was a function of the undisciplined lives of its practitioners, the married lamas and the shamans.[8] Lack of discipline could take many forms— too sexual, too emotional, too materially self-indulgent, too violent. Here I will focus mainly on the question of violence; I will come back to sex later.

Killing is of course the supreme sinful act in Buddhism. But even fighting and other forms of violence are deeply abhorred. Fighting or physical abuse of another not only harms bodies; it emotionally agitates those involved and even those who witness or hear of it, destroying calmness and equanimity. Both shamans and married lamas were seen as participating in supernatural violence.

Shamans, first, were accused of (among other things) trafficking with demons, who are more or less nothing but bundles of viciousness and violence; they were accused of performing black magic and sorcery for clients in the community, involving harm and possibly death to others for reasons of personal gain; they were accused of causing conflict and discord, as they indicated possible witches (*pem*) in the community in the diagnosis of cases of illness.[9] The fact that shamans cured people of illness and thus could be seen as compassionate and helping receded into the background against this picture of shamans as troublemakers who both practiced and caused violence.

The monks raised an even greater range of criticism against the married lamas. Their general position was that the lamas were not very *khamu*, well-trained or skilled in ritual work, and not very *tsachermu*, ritually powerful. This was traceable to several "undisciplined" (from the monks' point of view) aspects of the lifestye of married lamas.

In the first place, of course, the lamas were married. It is worth noting at the outset that the religious critique of marriage is not primarily a critique of sex as such, but of what sex leads to: children, family. (Unlike the Christian position, this is not an issue of condemning "the pleasures of the flesh" but of condemning essentially socially generated demands, distractions, and moral faults.) The problems of marriage radiate out in many directions. Marriage means having a family, and a family must be supported by hard (agricultural) work. Work, in turn, is sinful in that it involves killing the myriad worms and insects that live in the soil. Marriage makes a man the head of household, which means always worrying about whether there will be enough food and other necessities for everyone. Morever, as a householder in a village, one is part of a larger network of social relations and social obligations. One must take part in the rituals and parties of others, and one must host one's own rituals and parties for neighbors and relatives. All of this takes time away from religious study and training; it also generates worry and stress that distracts the mind and disperses concentration. From the

7. Zhung married lamas leading a wedding procession, 1967.
Left: Lama Tenzing; *right*: Lama Kinziu.

monastic point of view, it is simply impossible to do a very good job of building up religious learning, power, and merit when one is embedded in normal social life. That is why one becomes a monk.[10]

The second "undisciplined" aspect of the married lamas' lifestyle was that the married lamas drank *chang* (beer) and *rakshi* (distilled spirits); the lamas' drinking was in effect the shorthand for all their other failings. Drinking is part of the normal social life of village relations; it is central to virtually all hospitality, festivity, and social interaction. But it is also the cause of all loss of self control, as illustrated by this often-told folktale:

Once there was a very high and holy lama who was approached by a *dirnmu*, a demoness. The dirnmu appeared in the guise of a beautiful woman, carrying a container of chang and leading a goat. She forced the lama to choose—kill the goat, drink the chang, or have intercourse with her. The lama chose the chang as seemingly the least of the evils, but then he got drunk and in his drunken state he killed the goat and had intercourse with the woman.[11]

Getting drunk, in other words, leads to all the other major forms of loss of control: it opens one to sexual temptation, which in turn connects back to marriage and children and all the problems thereof; it also leads to violence (killing the goat), which brings us to the final major aspect of the married lamas' lack of discipline.

Like the shamans, the lamas were seen as being deeply involved with sorcery and black magic, and some were considered to be exceedingly powerful and effective at this. Moreover, like the shamans, the lamas did not exactly disclaim this involvement. Again, their main function was to "help" people, to use their power to control the gods on behalf of the community. Nonetheless, the same powers that enabled them to do these things also enabled them to do harm. For example, the tales of the foundings of the ancient temples virtually dripped with the blood of the married lamas' political disputes.[12] And rumors of violent sorcery by contemporary lamas continued to circulate in village communities. In Khumbu there was one lama who was thought to be especially powerful for these things. He was said to kill people and to use their fat for burning his incense, and their thighbones and blood for ritual purposes. There was a death in the course of my fieldwork that was thought to be his doing:

Somebody had an argument with Lama X in Khumbu. The argument was some sort of land dispute. This man had been very sick in the past, but he had gotten better. After the argument with the lama, however, the man suddenly died. And to the [young man and middle-aged woman telling me the story] it was self-evident that this was the lama's work: The lama, they said, has a bad god.[13]

Another case, involving other lamas, concerned a *pem*, or witch. The lamas did a fire exorcism (*zingchang*), which was explained by an informant as follows:

> They cut some shoulder flesh from a corpse and saved it. They fry the meat in a large quantity of butter, and the frying attracts all the pem by the smell of the meat. Then they throw in rakshi and the brew catches fire and burns all the pem. In [another village] they did one of these rites. One known pem, who was peacefully sleeping in her own home, showed up next morning with half of her face burnt.[14]

Supernatural violence was invisible; perhaps it was not even "real." But the discourse was real, and it circulated in ways that had real effects in the community. Of course it coexisted with discourses and practices in which lamas helped and served the community in major ways. But as the monastic movement gained in charisma and influence, it was the undisciplined—"small"—aspects of village religion that came to the fore.

THE IDEAL OF THE MONK: INNER DISCIPLINE

In contast to the "undisciplined" lifestyles and ritual practices of the married lamas and the shamans, the monk was set up as the ideal embodiment of religious goals and religious practices. A monk (*tawa*) is an individual who takes a vow of celibacy and enters a monastery, theoretically for life. There, ideally, he[15] engages in sustained study and religious practice in order to achieve, at the very least, a better rebirth, and at most, transcendental salvation, defined as getting off the round of death and rebirth entirely.[16] Although there is a certain amount of collective ritual and community life, Tibetan Buddhist monasteries do not model themselves as alternative social forms—as brotherhoods, communes, or collectives. Rather, they are collections of monks whose primary tie to the community is through their individual ties to the head lama. The organization of the monastery thus both expresses and facilitates the focus on the monk's individual quest for salvation. Each monk lives in his own small private house, eats his meals alone, and studies and performs his devotions on his own.[17]

Central to the ideals of monasticism is the self-discipline of the monk, both in terms of his material life—the vow of celibacy, the withdrawal from normal social relations, the simple lifestyle—but also in terms of his emotional life. Ideally, one of the most important things the monk will learn, practice, and model for others is the ability to control and manage strong negative feelings, such as anger, fear, and grief, as well as strong positive feelings, such as love. Mostly it is the higher lamas—the reincarnates, the hermits, the older monks—who are believed to have genuinely acquired this ability. But it is understood that this is a major goal of monastic practice, that leaving society and taking a vow of celibacy is the first step toward this goal, and that this is one of the most important things monks will learn to accomplish. Monasticism is understood and appreciated as, among other things, a technology of emotional self-management.

It should be noted first that, although the ideas to be discussed here are general to Buddhism as a whole, and can be found in any set of relevant texts or secondary sources, I will draw all the examples for this discussion from local monks, lamas, and laypeople in the Sherpa area. Important as the knowledge of classical texts is for certain scholarly purposes, in the present instance—the study of popular knowledge and popular practices—it is much more important to show how these fundamental Buddhist ideas are refracted through the local Sherpa community.

In line with basic Buddhist ideas, then, strong feelings—cravings, desires, attachments, anger, pride—are understood to be the root of all evil. Strong feelings cause us to commit sins; anger leads to violence and killing, greed leads to stealing, sexual desire leads to adultery, and so forth. Strong feelings also lead to pain and suffering; attachments to others lead to grief when they die, attachment to things leads to pain at their loss. Controlling—calming, stilling, dissipating—all these feelings is the first step toward liberation. As one Sherpa monk said about the importance of managing his turbulent inner states, "If I don't think well, then I can't do any kind of good work."[18] Or as the great reincarnate lama, the Tushi Rim-

poche, wrote in a poem on the occasion of fleeing the Chinese invasion of Tibet, "When you tame the enemy within your own mind
. . . the demonic armies of the ten directions will just fall in defeat
by themselves."[19]

Emotional upheaval in general is disliked by Sherpas. This view
is embodied in, among other things, the idea of *thip*, or pollution,
which is imaged as a churned-up inner state, in which one feels
ill, and which is often the prelude to real bodily illness of various
kinds. Sherpas believe that pollution can cause states of permanent
mental disorder; polluting contacts are thought to be the cause of
cretinism, in which the mind is permanently rendered dull and stu-
pid and cannot think clearly. Many things cause thip, including
coming in contact with death, participating in or even witnessing a
fight, and being in a crowd, all of which trigger strong or disordering
feelings and a sense of being in the grip of potentially overpowering
emotional forces. Images of thip are images of darkness, muddi-
ness, and churning motions; images of purity are of clarity, lightness,
and calm.[20]

The religion specifically offers techniques for calming intense
and turbulent feelings. Such calming is the basis for virtually all
religious practice; it is the first step to all further ritual and meditational work. Explaining the basic morning devotions to me, the
Serlo lama said:

> When you do *kyamdu* in the morning, you first purge yourself
> by blowing your nose three times—this sends out the white
> cock of pride, the red snake of anger, and the black pig of greed.
> Then you imagine yourself like a full glass of milk, all white
> and pure inside, and then begin your prayers.[21]

Similarly, a former monk, now serving as a village lama, explained
the importance of the part of the offering ritual in which a dough
figure called a *gyek* is thrown out of the temple:

> [What we are doing is] calling all the beings from hell and send-
> ing them to heaven. . . . Actually, they are all inside us—when
> we get happy or angry or things like that. Thus we throw them
> out with the gyek and then we do cho [religion] with a pure

being. This is especially for the choa [trained religious prac-
titioner], but also for all of us. If the gyek is not thrown out,
then afterwards we (choa) feel angry, have ill feelings.[22]

For yet another example, a senior monk was explaining to me the
annual Dorsem ritual at Thami monastery, which is for the purification of the monks.[23] In the course of this ritual the head lama
includes among his ritual paraphernalia a large crystal. The monk
said that the crystal had heart-healing powers (he called it *nying chelap*, ritual medicine for the heart), that it "cleans out all the sin,
makes one clear as glass." As a result of the effectiveness of this ritual
in purifying the monks, they in turn are empowered to perform the
tse-wong, or life-power, ritual for the long life of the lay people.

The religious emphasis on inner discipline is profoundly linked
to issues of ritual power. It is through the ability to discipline themselves through meditation and other practices that all lamas (and not
just monks) gain the powers that allow them to control the gods. As
the Tengboche lama put it:

> In the practice of Buddha-dharma, by meditation training, our
> spirit becomes clear, and clean, and at this point great energy
> becomes possible for us. It was with this power the first lamas
> controlled the gods.[24]

The achievement of inner calm and control is thus central to monastic practice. Monks make an effort, in their public demeanor,
to present themselves as having achieved at least some degree of
emotional detachment, particularly in relation to lay people. I give
a few small examples from recent times; there is no reason to think
the pattern was any different in the early decades of monasticism.
During the observance of the annual Dumji festival in 1979, the
married lama who was to dance the role of a very important god got
very drunk, and could barely hold himself up, no less dance. The
monks who were chanting the texts put on a show of laughing about
this, and not appearing to be annoyed. Similarly, an informant said
that, as a child, he used to participate in lewd *tek-tek* dancing (to be
discussed later) during Dumji, and the monks just laughed about
that too. It was clear from other contexts that the monks disap-

proved quite strongly of both the married lamas' drinking, and of the tek-tek dancing, yet it was apparently important for them to act unperturbed in a public context. Indeed it is important for them to *be* unperturbed, particularly during the performance of a ritual, since strong feelings interfere with the capacity to *miwa* (visualize/identify with) the gods and may thus render the ritual ineffective.

Kinship and marriage are thought to create some of the strongest possible attachments, and it is thus particularly important for monks to be, or at least to appear to be, emotionally detached in relation to kinship upheavals or tragedies. In one case a monk's sister had been a nun, but then had broken her celibacy vow and "fallen." When I asked the monk if he had been upset about that he said, rather truculently, "No, why should I have been?" Later, however, a lay kinsman of the monk said that the monk had "cried and cried" at the time. In another case, a monk's brother, who was also a monk, had also fallen, and I asked this first monk, too, if he had suffered (had *dukpa*) over that. He cracked that he had not had *dukpa*, but his brother had—now the brother had to support a wife and children.[25]

The celibacy of the monk is both a sign of and a force for achieving this inner discipline. Tibetan Buddhism assumes that bodily disciplines—everything from celibacy to keeping a straight face in public—constitute the first step toward a larger spiritual and emotional discipline.[26] And beyond these simple, but often effective, practices, the monk learns a variety of more specialized techniques—meditational practices, mantra recitations, visualization techniques, and so forth, that aid in emotional management and the achievement of calmness and imperturbability.

ANG THARKAY'S LETTER

We get a rare glimpse, from Ang Tharkay's memoirs, into one lay Sherpa's engagement with monastic emotional discipline in the early decades after the foundings of the monasteries. Ang Tharkay was born in 1907 in the Khumbu village of Kunde. He remembered Tengboche monastery being built when he was about nine years old; he spent more than a day there watching the villagers bring blocks of stone to the site for the Tibetan masons to cut.[27] In about 1927

Ang Tharkay ran away from home and went to Darjeeling for work. He got his first break into the ranks of "Sherpa" on the 1933 Everest expedition. The expedition, like all the previous ones, stopped at Rumbu monastery and the "lamas" (presumably the monks) "gave [the expedition] their benediction. They told us," wrote Ang Tharkay, "that if we do our work honestly, faithfully, and with joy, nothing bad could happen to us." [28]

A bit later on the expedition, Ang Tharkay received an anonymous letter (he called it a filthy letter, *une lettre ordurière*) telling him that his wife had been unfaithful. He became extremely upset, and the leader, Hugh Ruttledge, suggested that he go back down to base camp "to rest and compose his thoughts."[29] But he decided instead to go back down to the monastery "to consult the lamas . . . who would deliver me from the bad fortune that had been sent my way, who would divert the wicked intentions of my enemies, and who would extract me from these encumbrances."[30] He described his experience with the monks as follows: "The lamas, after having blessed me, comforted me and told me to have faith in God and to continue my work with calm and confidence." [31] He stayed about two weeks at Rumbu, and then returned to the expedition, "relieved, and once again master of myself."[32]

Even allowing for muddled translations, the text nicely encapsulates the several logics operating in this early encounter between a lay Sherpa and some monks. Ang Tharkay was clearly operating in the folk/village religious mode: enemies had used sorcery against him and sent harm his way, the lamas were being asked to protect him from this harm, to divert it elsewhere (perhaps back to the enemies, though that is not stated), and to "extract" him from these "encumbrances." There is nothing here about inner discipline. The monks, however, offered the counsel of "higher" Buddhist theory for his troubles: quell strong feelings, regain inner composure, continue his work "with calm and confidence." Ang Tharkay's stay at the monastery and the experience there clearly had a positive effect. He returned to the expedition—it seems reasonable to accept the language here—"relieved" and "master of himself."

Unfortunately Ang Tharkay's father turned up and reinflamed his anxieties. He thus returned to Darjeeling after the expedition "with murder in his soul."[33] Everything in fact turned out to be all right with his wife and family, but if it had not, we are given the impression that more direct and rather less emotionally disciplined measures would have been taken against the enemies. Nonetheless, at the time of the incident, the monks clearly were effective in transmitting both the spiritual comfort and the practical value of inner discipline.

Following the foundings of the monasteries, and in line with their views about the "smallness" of much of village religious practice, the monks actively sought to bring about changes in Sherpa popular religion. Probably their earliest campaign, and also in some ways the most dramatically successful, was the campaign against the worship of a Nepali god that had been creeping into Sherpa religion.

THE MONKS' CAMPAIGN II: THE PROBLEM OF NUPKI GYELWU WORSHIP

At the time of the founding of Tengboche monastery, most Sherpa families had reportedly taken up the practice of worshiping a god called *Nupki Gyelwu* (literally, "Western King"). The performance of the Nupki Gyelwu rituals was thought to make the practitioners rich, and for this reason alone the rites were very popular. Apparently they were borrowed from the Hindu Nepalis, and they were performed in the Nepali language. (Interestingly enough, the god was given a Tibetan pedigree; see the text of the myth in Appendix A). They were apparently performed by individual families at their high grazing pastures and were conducted by heads of households without benefit of the assistance of Sherpa (or any) religious specialists.

The popularity of a new, and Nepali-derived, ritual for magically gaining wealth in this era may perhaps be linked—though not too literally—to the increased Rana tax demands noted earlier. The idea of a vicious Nepali god who eats Sherpa children may be taken as a representation of the Rana regime's exploitative practices, while the use of a Nepali-derived ritual to gain benefits from the god fits with Sherpa notions that one must fit the ritual practice (and ritual specialists, if needed) to the character of the god; that is, if Nupki Gyelwu is a Nepali god you need Nepali rituals to deal with him.

The god, like many Hindu gods (although unlike any of the twentieth-century Sherpa/Tibetan Buddhist gods), required blood sacrifice. According to informants in both Solu and Khumbu, Solu Sherpas were actually killing the sacrificial animals, while Khumbu Sherpas merely "showed" them to the god for the sacrifice. Even in the nonbloody Khumbu version, however, it was understood that the animal was being provided for the god's bloody appetite, and there would have been no question that this ritual was sinful in intention, which is almost as bad as in practice.

According to informants, the worship of Nupki Gyelwu was virtually universal at the time of the founding of Tengboche. But when the Zatul Rimpoche, the great Tibetan reincarnate lama who had been the spiritual force behind the founding, came to Khumbu to do the Tengboche consecration, he announced that people should stop sacrificing to Nupki Gyelwu. He said that Nupki Gyelwu was a bad god, a demon (du) god, and that the worshipers would accrue sin in performing his rituals.[34] They might get rich, but they would have short lives and go to hell afterward. One informant explaining all this to me made the distinction between the "white offerings" (karche) of "our inside [Sherpa/Tibetan] religion"—the food offerings given in periodic worship of the gods—and the "red offerings" (marche) of Hinduism, involving "cutting [animals'] necks and giving blood." Nupki Gyelwu is considered to be reincarnated in the god to whom the Nepali festival of Dasain is dedicated, at which thousands of goats and water buffalo are slaughtered in sacrifice, and the streets of Kathmandu run red with blood.

A pronouncement like this from the Zatul Rimpoche was very strong stuff indeed. Most Sherpas gave up Nupki Gyelwu worship almost immediately. The effective campaign against Nupki Gyelwu worship in turn seems to have had the effect of firming up a broader adherence to the Buddhist injunction against killing anything. It would appear that cultural and religious constraints against killing in general were weakening in that era. The willingness to commit live animal sacrifice in Nupki Gyelwu worship was the most obvious indicator of this point. But there was also a murder case in about

1915, when one of the major sponsors of Tengboche monastery, a wealthy trader and head tax collector (*gembu*) for the region, was alleged to have killed a political rival. Or in another register, Ang Tharkay in his memoirs described participating in hunting with guns on expeditions with some enthusiasm.[35] By the time of the 1938 Everest expedition, however, the climber Bill Tilman wrote:

> The Sherpas have a curious dislike of slaughtering a sheep. They love meat ... but they jeb at the actual killing of the animal. If no one else will oblige they cast lots amongst themselves, while the loser is usually so upset that he bungles the job and makes two or three half-hearted blows with the kukri instead of one, before severing the beast's head.[36]

This pattern remained consistent thereafter. An account very similar to Tilman's appeared in the fifties:

> The killing [of a sheep] was no casual affair, and in the darkness we found the Sherpas had erected a small altar and were gathered round it chanting prayers before a butter lamp illuminating it. . . . The conscience of Sherpas is very delicate in such matters, and it genuinely upset them to kill even a hen, or watch anything be killed.[37]

During my fieldwork in the mid-sixties, it was clear that people got quite upset if they even witnessed an animal being killed. They were disgusted by the sight of blood. Once some young boys found a snake on the path just outside the village, and stoned it to death. Adults gathered around, covering their mouths and spitting on the ground in a cultural gesture of disgust. I never saw a Sherpa adult willingly kill anything, and when my colleague Robert Paul and I asked our cook to find a Nepali to kill a chicken for our household for Christmas, he disappeared for six hours of anxious and ambivalent dawdling before getting the deed done. (As we ate an undercooked chicken in a very cold house late at night, we vowed never to do that again, and never did.)[38]

Connecting back to the Nupki Gyelwu issue, the Sherpas seemed so fundamentally upset by any kind of animal slaughter that I assumed they had always observed the Buddhist injunction against

killing. When I read Kathryn March's 1976 article saying that
the Sherpas used to practice live-animal sacrifice, I was utterly
startled. Later, in Khumbu, I asked people whether this was true,
and out came the stories and information presented above. It did
emerge that a few families in Khumbu (but not in Solu) had continued worshiping Nupki Gyelwu in private. Other people's attitudes
about this may be judged by the fact that the father of one of these
families was said to have gone mad as a result of continuing the
practice. The god was still felt to be powerful: The night after I
recorded the myth, there was a bad frost that killed much of the
budding potato crop in Khumjung village, and there was some sug-
gestion that this might have been the result of too much discussion
of Nupki Gyelwu.

In Khumbu, families have retained the practice of having a
butcher slaughter one yak or cow at the beginning of winter and
drying the meat to last throughout the year, but there was an awareness that even this act was sinful and required meritorious deeds
afterward to counterbalance the sin. In Solu, where fresh meat came
to be regularly available from Nepali butchers at the bazaar, not
even this annual killing of one animal was countenanced. As for the
killing of human beings, it was virtually unheard of. There was
never, as far as I know, another murder in Khumbu again.[39]

The Eliteness of Monaticism

Although virtually all Sherpas (big and small, as they say) seem to
have been caught up in the excitement of the early foundings, the
monasteries had certain elite associations that never entirely disappeared. For one thing, all the founders were wealthy traders and
businessmen, and three of the four also had close ties with the Rana
regime. I have discussed elsewhere in some detail the ways in which
the monastery foundings were enmeshed in status rivalries among
these big men, and in issues of political legitimacy of the big men
in relation to the ordinary people.

The monasteries also tended to draw their monks primarily from
the wealthier families, in part for practical reasons. With the exception of Chiwong, the monasteries did not support the monks except

for daily tea and during the performance of all-monastery rituals. Other than that, the monks' and nuns' families had to provide them with houses and with all of their food and other material needs, while at the same time losing their labor. Although not all monks and nuns came from elite backgrounds, the majority of them came from families that were at least comfortable, and this seems to have been true even at Chiwong.[40]

Next, monks lived lives that were seen, by themselves and by others, as soft and comfortable, similar to the lives of the rich. Although they renounced certain pleasures of worldly life, and although they had to study and apply themselves to their religious work, nonetheless one of the most prominent features of the monks from virtually all points of view was the fact that they did not do heavy labor. Because not working is not a formal vow, people do not mention it when asked specifically to explain the distinctive qualities of monks. The point emerged again and again, however, when one asked why monks were superior to married lamas, the answer being that monks did not have to work and so could devote full time to religion. The point also emerged again and again when monks were asked[41] why they chose to become monks or why they liked being monks: the life of the monk is *kirmu* (pleasant, happy), because monks do not have to work.[42] As one monk, Dorje, put it:

When I was studying religion, my father didn't make me do any work. If I weren't doing religion, it would be "go cut wood, go up, go down, go do coolie work, go do business." So many orders. If one does religion, then nobody gives you any orders. It's very high, it's very great.[43]

Finally, one occasionally heard comments to the effect that the monastic career represented a selfish choice. The monk retired to the monastery to pursue his own salvation; he became unavailable to others, both for practical assistance as a member of the social community, and even—in contrast to married lamas, who often stressed this point—for ritual assistance.[44] Although in later years this changed, in the early years in particular monks were only available for "high" ritual events, and did not dirty their hands with local needs for protection and purification.

I do not want to overstate the level of resistance to or skepticism about the monasteries among the Sherpas, but neither do I want to overly homogenize Sherpa views and feelings in the matter. A sense of the "selfishness" of monks, and skepticism about the value of monks to the community, were definite strands of thought among some Sherpas. An example from the early years was the famous Tenzing Norgay.

TENZING NORGAY'S RESERVATIONS

Tenzing Norgay was born in 1914 at a holy place where his mother had gone on pilgrimage, but he grew up in Thami village on the west side of Khumbu. His mother was very devout, and Tenzing notes that her brother "was once head lama" of Rumbu monastery. Tenzing's family was significantly better off than Ang Tharkay's, but they had a large number of children, and Tenzing was thus one of several "excess sons." Not surprisingly, he was sent off to the newly founded Tengboche monastery to be a monk. But that did not work out:

> I was sent to a monastery, my head was shaved, and I put on the robe of a novice. But after I had been there only a little time one of the lamas (who are not necessarily saints) got angry with me and hit me on the bare head with a wooden board, and I ran home and said I would not go back. My parents, who were always kind and loving to me, did not make me go back.[45]

His sister, however, did become a nun at Devuche, where she stayed for seven years before breaking her vow of celibacy with a Tengboche monk. Since, after being hit by a monk, Tenzing was basically uninterested in monasticism, he did not lament his sister's fall, and claimed, not quite in agreement with general views, that "in our religion there is no disgrace if a monk or a nun gets married." [46]

Driven, as he described it, by a burning desire to see the outside world, in 1927 at the age of thirteen Tenzing ran away to Kathmandu for several weeks, and in 1932, having heard about mountaineering expeditions from returning Sherpas, he ran away again to Darjeeling. He was eighteen. He specifically saw his decision as taken in opposition to the views of the lamas:

> The lamas told many stories of the terror of the snows—of gods and demons and creatures far worse than yetis ["abominable snowmen"], who guarded the heights and would bring doom to any man who ventured there. But I knew that men, and among them my own people, had climbed high on the other side of Chomolungma [Everest], and though some had been killed, more had returned alive. What I wanted was to see for myself; find out for myself.[47]

He tried to get hired on the 1933 Everest expedition but was not chosen, but he was hired for the 1935 and 1936 expeditions. In both cases we know that the expeditions stopped at Rumbu monastery; for the 1936 expedition Ang Tharkay said that the group took up a collection for an offering to the head lama, and that the lama in turn gave each one of them a charm for protection. Tenzing never mentioned the visits at all; it is possible that he did not join the group, but that in itself would have been extraordinary, especially if the head lama was indeed his mother's brother.[48] Given the earlier comment about how the lamas tried to hold people back from climbing, it seems that Tenzing—who was in other ways quite devout— basically had little use for the monastic establishment.

The most telling episode came after the conquest of Everest in 1953. Tenzing was overwhelmed by a whole range of changes in his life.[49] Among all these, however, he noted the following:

> After the climbing of Everest, I was asked to give money to a certain monastery near Darjeeling, but after thinking it over I decided against it. I preferred to donate it toward the building of a hostel or guest house which could be used by all poor people visiting the town, *rather than to a group of monks who would use it only for themselves.*[50]

But if monks were sometimes seen as selfish, this was counter-balanced to a great extent by another major figure in Tibetan Buddhism, the reincarnate lama, or *tulku*. There is almost a sense in

which the value of monasticism, for the Sherpas, was less that it
produced monks, who were largely pursuing their own salvation,
but that it produced powerful *tulku* who were much more oriented
toward the well-being of ordinary people in the world.

THE IDEAL OF THE *TULKU*: COMPASSION

The religion of the Sherpas, Tibetan Buddhism, falls within the Mahayana school of Buddhism as a whole. The Mahayana school arose
in the first century A.D. as a critique of the original form of Buddhism, called Theravada. Mahayanists criticized the Theravada
school for "selfishness," since the spiritual seeker was only concerned with his or her own salvation and not with the problems of
the world, which he or she in effect abandoned to its fate. Thus, the
Mahayanists emphasized the importance of "compassion" for other
beings as part of the quest for salvation, and argued that seekers
must engage in the quest (which is not itself radically altered from
the Buddha's original conception) not just for their own enlightenment, but as a model to help others achieve enlightenment as well.
In place of the Theravada ideal of the *arhat*, the "worthy one" or
saint, who seeks only his own enlightenment, the Mahayanists sub-
stituted the ideal of the *bodhisattva*, the individual who has achieved
enlightenment, but who remains involved in the world in order to
help others achieve enlightenment too.

The monks in the newly founded monasteries sought to enhance
the place of the religious ideal of compassion within the overall
shape of Sherpa popular religion. On the one hand they sought
to get rid of "low" and sinful practices like Nupki Gyelwu worship,
or like the "lower" work of the married lamas and shamans; we
may think of this as the negative campaign. On the other hand
they sought to institute newer and "higher" practices, oriented toward positive religious ideals like compassion. One of the first
moves in what we might think of as the positive campaign was the
establishment of a ritual for lay people called Nyungne, designed to
bring a greater degree of compassion into lay life. Nyungne was
originally performed inside the new monasteries, where lay people

would come for the observances; later it was moved out to the local village temples.

Nyungne is an observance in which individuals who so desire gather in the temple and observe fasting and silence over a two-day period, under the leadership of lamas or monks. During this period they repeatedly prostrate themselves, meditating upon and praying to the god Chenrezi, seeking identification with him. Chenrezi's chief characteristic is that he is all-compassionate; he feels tremendous pity and caring for all suffering creatures. In achieving identification with him and his great compassion, worshipers accrue enormous amounts of merit toward a better rebirth—perhaps more merit than can be achieved in any other context of popular religious practice.

Nyungne was somewhat unevenly observed among lay Sherpas throughout the twentieth century[51] (see also chapter 9). But it was only one of several contexts in which the idea of compassion was pressed to the fore of Sherpa religion. A much more salient and compelling one was the figure of the tulku, or reincarnate lama.

THE ASCENDANCE OF THE REINCARNATE LAMA

Reincarnate lamas were central to the development of Sherpa high religion, as they were throughout the Tibetan Buddhist world. The Zatul Rimpoche, at Rumbu monastery in the adjacent region of Tibet, was the spiritual instigator of the founding of the first Sherpa monasteries, and a continuing source of inspiration and blessing to Sherpas at all levels—big people, monks and lamas, expedition Sherpas—until his death about 1940.[52] The first head of Tengboche monastery, Lama Gulu, was retrospectively defined as an important reincarnation, and after his death in 1934 his reincarnation in turn was sought and found—the first home-grown Sherpa reincarnate lama. I will tell the story of his discovery in 1935 to conclude this chapter, but in order to understand where it fits in, I must give some brief background on reincarnate lamas, or *tulku*, in general.

Consistent with the elaboration of reincarnation ideology within Tibetan Buddhism was the elaboration of the Mahayana notion of the bodhisattva, the idea that certain individuals (including the Buddha) attain enlightenment, but refuse to enter Nirvana, choosing instead to remain within the world to help others attain enlightenment too. In Chinese and Japanese Buddhism (also within the Mahayana tradition), boddhisattvas remain in contact with the world only in spiritual form, as gods. In Tibetan Buddhism, however, the notion developed that bodhisattvas might reincarnate in human bodies, and operate within the actual physical world. Such beings are called *tulku* (Tib., *sprul sku*), "emanation bodies."[53]

Tulku are the highest—most sacred, most ritually potent, most merit-generating—figures in Sherpa/Tibetan religion. As gods, bodhisattvas, or simply highly spiritually advanced beings walking around on earth, they operate as what might be called religious force fields, attracting intense interest, affection, devotion, and respect. Monastic leadership is almost always in the hands of tulku. If the founding head lama of a monastery is not known to be a tulku, a reincarnation lineage for him may be discovered after the fact, as it was for the first head lama of Tengboche, Lama Gulu. But in any event, after he dies, the monks will certainly seek his reincarnation, or if for some reason that does not work out, they will seek some other tulku to head the monastery.

Tulku are great because they are at the pinnacle of power and virtue as defined by Tibetan Buddhism. Because they are tremendously spiritually powerful, their rituals and blessings are more effective, and donations given to them produce greater amounts of merit than donations given to lesser religious figures. One of the signs and manifestations of their great spiritual power is that they are said to "know everything"—to learn religious work easily because they knew it all in past lives, to read the minds of people who come to see them, to know intuitively whether another tulku claimant is authentic or not, and so forth. They have other great magico/religious/psychic powers as well; they are thought to be able to do almost anything if they want to.[54]

A tulku's magical and ritual powers, however, are functions of his spiritual perfection or near-perfection, and this relates to the issue of compassion. Tulku are by definition quite literally embodiments of the ideal of compassion in Tibetan Buddhism. They are here among us on a mission of purest virtue: although they could have left this world of suffering and pain, they have stayed behind to show the way to enlightenment to the ignorant and suffering beings who remain in this world. And their compassion is, again by definition, universal: they are here to help "all sentient beings." Sherpas I knew clearly felt this was really enacted in practice; it was often remarked of tulku that they were kind to everyone, "high and low," and that they would—unlike "smaller" lamas—do rituals for anyone, "high and low." On a related point, tulku seemed to be less rigid than monks about maintaining the boundaries between high and low religion, and more tolerant of various levels and forms of religiosity. Both the Zatul Rimpoche and later the Tushi Rimpoche were less critical of shamans than the monks; the Zatul Rimpoche also gave some contributions to Thami temple to improve its ritual life when it was still a community of married lamas.

In my own experience, actual living tulku have varied greatly in their personal styles, and not all of them would strike an outsider as being people of great warmth and compassion. Yet several things counterbalance this point. First, there are norms that produce practices of generosity and compassion on the part of tulku, regardless of personal style. Thus, when somebody dies in a Sherpa community, the family is supposed to bring the clothes of the deceased to the local *rimpoche* ("precious master," the normal term of address and reference for a tulku), who in turn will redistribute them to the needy. More generally, tulku who are loved and/or respected will attract a high level of donations, but in turn they will redistribute some of these resources for worthy causes. Thus, the founding of the first Sherpa monastery, Tengboche, was initiated by a large donation from the Zatul Rimpoche. Tulku then do visibly practice material generosity, and sometimes on a large scale.

It also seems to be the case that many tulku are in fact strikingly warm, generous, and kindly people, who go out of their way to perform acts of personal kindness, who take a personal interest in others' problems and needs, and who are maternal and caring about their monks. From everything one reads and hears, the Dalai Lama is such a personality; for believers it is no doubt particularly relevant that he is a reincarnation of Chenrezi, the all-compassionate god.

8. The great reincarnate lama, the Tushi Rimpoche, 1967.

Closer to my own experience was the Tushi Rimpoche, a Tibetan tulku who fled from the Chinese with his monks and settled in the Sherpa area. The Tushi Rimpoche positively radiated goodness and caring, and was adored by all who knew him, monk and lay person alike, not excluding this ethnographer. Among other things, the Rimpoche was said to read the minds of people who gave him offerings, and if he came to realize that a person could not actually afford to give what he or she was giving, then the Rimpoche would return the gift, sometimes with a supplement.

Tulku thus are meant to be—and one way or another generally are—living examples of *nyingje*, compassion. The presence and importance of tulku on the Sherpa religious landscape, starting with the Zatul Rimpoche over the border at the turn of the century, foregrounded a critical third dimension to Sherpa Buddhist religiosity over the course of the twentieth century. The tulku contains in his person the idea of "power" (which was and continued to be central to popular religiosity) and the focus on "discipline" (which was added by the monks), but leavens both with an emphasis on "compassion" for one's suffering fellow creatures.

THE DEATH AND REBIRTH OF LAMA GULU

Lama Gulu had created Tengboche monastery and led it for many years. He had been involved with it since it was no more than a idea in the Zatul Rimpoche's mind. He had raised the financial backing, overseen the construction, and provided the leadership once the monastery was built. He came to be held in great affection among both the monks and the lay people.

In 1933 there was a serious earthquake in Nepal. Along with many other things, much of the main temple at Tengboche was destroyed. Lama Gulu, then around eighty-five years old, was not injured, but he nonetheless died a few days later.

There was a presumption, especially among the monks, that Lama Gulu would reincarnate, and that his reincarnation would be the next head of Tengboche. This meant that the next head of the monastery would be a child born shortly after Lama Gulu's death, who would reveal himself as the tulku or reincarnation around the time he started talking, at the age of about two. The fullest version of the discovery of Lama Gulu's reincarnation was told to me by one of the oldest and most respected Tengboche monks, Au Chokdu, who was involved in the events when he was a young novice at the monastery.

The child in question was born in 1935 (the *chak pak*, or Iron Pig, year of the Tibetan calendar) to a trader of Nauje (the main Sherpa trading town) and his wife. The father had gone to Lhasa on business, and was later joined by his wife, who bore their son there. As the boy began to talk, he insisted that he was the Teng-

9. Au Chokdu, Tengboche monk and excellent
teller of histories and tales, 1979.

boche lama, and a Sherpa trader living in Lhasa sent messages to
both Rumbu and Tengboche monasteries that Lama Gulu's reincarnation had appeared.[55]

While the parents and the child were on their way back to Nauje,
the senior Tengboche monks were staying in Rumbu, and a number
of junior monks (including our informant) were at Tengboche. The
junior monks looked forward with great excitement to seeing the
child, whom they were already calling "our Rimpoche," even while
trying to contain their elation by saying that "nobody knows
whether he is the real reincarnation or not." Meanwhile, they also
received a letter from the Zatul Rimpoche and one of the senior
Tengboche monks (Gelung Umze, Lama Gulu's brother's son) at
Rumbu asking them to bring the child back from Nauje to Rumbu,
so that his authenticity could be established. When the parents and
the child arrived in Nauje, Au Chokdu and two other monks turned
the party around and escorted the boy and his mother back to

Rumbu. They carried the boy much of the way themselves, as well as carrying many of Lama Gulu's former possessions from his past life, which would be necessary for the authentication test. (The distances involved—about six days' trek—and the arduousness of the route over the 19,000-foot Nangpa pass between Rumbu and Khumbu, make all this running back and forth transporting a two-year-old child all the more impressive.)

When the traveling party was on its last night en route, the Zatul Rimpoche waiting at Rumbu had a dream in which he saw Lama Gulu very vividly. The next morning he told Gelung Umze that "Lama Gulu is coming today, you must go down to meet him with tea and refreshments," and this was done. The Zatul Rimpoche's prescience in foretelling the exact day of the child's arrival foreshadowed his later ability to know that the child was in fact the reincarnation without any formal tests. Indeed the lama indicated this knowledge here, as he was already calling the child Lama Gulu before the tests had been administered.

When the party finally arrived at the top of the steps of Rumbu monastery, the Zatul Rimpoche greeted them (for anyone lesser, of course, he would not have come out to the steps), saying "Lama Gulu has arrived." Our informant, the young novice, presented the Zatul Rimpoche with a kata, the traditional scarf of respectful greeting. Then the child reincarnate himself gave a kata to the Zatul Rimpoche. He also grabbed the kata his mother was holding and gave it to the great lama, and tried to take another woman's kata as well. At first the woman tried to hold on to it, but the Zatul Rimpoche said, "Give it to him, give him anything he wants." And so the woman released the kata and the child took it and gave it to the Zatul Rimpoche. The three-time repetition was seen as very auspicious.

Then the Zatul Rimpoche asked the child, "Do you know me?" And "our lama" (as Au Chokdu put it) answered, "Yes, I know you. You're my *tsawi* lama, my 'heart lama,' you're the Zatul Rimpoche." The Zatul Rimpoche said, "Don't make a mistake," and the boy said, "I'm not mistaken, you are really my tsawi lama."

The formal test for a reincarnation was then administered. All of Lama Gulu's possessions that had been brought from Tengboche

10. The Tengboche Rimpoche at Tengboche, 1979.

were laid out, and similar objects were mixed in with them. The child had to pick "his own" things from among the objects, and he did. The Zatul Rimpoche had been convinced without the tests, but he told the monks that it was important to repeat the tests in Khumbu, or people would not believe that this child was the real reincarnation. So, after some months, during which the Tengboche monks performed numerous rituals with the Rumbu monks, and also built a lavish reliquary for (the deceased) Lama Gulu's remains, they returned with the child to Nauje.

In Nauje the boy once again demonstrated his authenticity. He was shown a certain item that had belonged to Lama Gulu, a *dablam*, or small window box with a miniature statue of a god inside. The boy exclaimed, "Oh, that statue once spoke to me." When the group proceeded from Nauje to Khumjung village, the monks (including Au Chokdu, still present) pointed to Khumjung village temple from a distance and told the child it was Tengboche monastery. But the boy, demonstrating once again his inherited knowledge, said, "No, it's not Tengboche, it's not my monastery," and hit the monks for trying to mislead him. When they entered Khumjung temple, they encountered one of the local married lamas, who had once borrowed a book from Lama Gulu and not returned it. The boy spotted the book and said, "This is mine. Where did you get it?" And the lama apologized and prostrated himself before the boy.

This little boy, now a man, is still the head lama of Tengboche monastery. He has become a major figure in Sherpa religion, in mountaineering culture (as all the Nepal-side expeditions to Everest have stopped at his monastery and been blessed by him, as they were by the Zatul Rimpoche in Rumbu in the early years), and in late-twentieth-century transnational Buddhist politics. (We will hear about him again in future chapters). For purposes of this chapter, he represents the final piece of the religious mosaic put in place for the Sherpas by the foundings of the monasteries in the early twentieth century: the local emergence and development of the tulku on the Sherpa religious scene, a figure of power and discipline harnessed to the service of compassion.

5

DEATH

The thirties had been a heady time for the Sherpas. In mountaineering the number of expeditions had continued to increase every year, and the Sherpas were getting increasingly skilled and professionalized. With a few exceptions, they performed brilliantly on expeditions, in some cases sacrificing their lives. The sahibs could not stop raving over their performance and their general character. After the 1924 Everest expedition, the British began informally calling the Sherpas who had done well "tigers," and in 1938 they officially created the "Tiger" medal, and bestowed the first round of awards.

There were also changes in Nepal that were favorable to the Sherpas. The British Raj on the edges of the Nepal state was creating a labor drain, existing as an attractive alternative to exploitative, feudal-style political-economic structures in many parts of Nepal. The Nepal state attempted to counter this situation in a number of ways, including undermining the power and authority of traditional elites and landlords where it could,[1] and by creating better economic conditions for ordinary people. Debt slavery was officially outlawed in 1926. In 1931 there was an effort to recall people who had left Nepal for wage work, or who had left to avoid taxes, by setting aside land for resettlement.[2] Similarly, banks were set up to compete with the moneylenders, with low rates of interest, in the name of protecting the people against exploitation.[3] And in 1941 the tax laws were changed, linking taxes to land rather than to persons, further loosening feudal-style relationships.[4] Somewhere around this time, in the late thirties or early forties, the Sherpas succeeded in undermining the office of *gembu* (head tax collector), which stood above the traditional *pembu*s, and which was seen as particularly open to abuse. After that the state dealt directly with the pembu, but the pembus' authority, too, was weakened in various ways.[5]

Things crashed rather dramatically for the mountaineering Sherpas with the onset of World War II, and the war, followed by the Indian Independence movement, created a long hiatus in Himalayan mountaineering. Between about 1939 and 1947 there were virtually no expeditions in the Himalayas, and the Sherpas in Darjeeling, who by then numbered over six thousand people[6] had a difficult time.[7] Things were even worse between 1947 and 1950, with the British pulling out of India, and the postindependence turmoil continuing to cause even the tourist trade to dry up. There was only a small amount of expedition-type work during this period. In 1947 a Canadian named Earl Denman tried to climb Everest "alone," which is to say, only by himself with two Sherpas, including Tenzing Norgay, but he failed.[8] Also in 1947, there was a Swiss expedition in north India.[9] And in 1948–49 the Tibetologist Giuseppe Tucci traveled for a year in Tibet, hiring Tenzing Norgay in Darjeeling to accompany him.[10] But by and large, the Sherpas in Darjeeling had to find other kinds of work. Tenzing, for example, worked as an orderly for a British officer in the Indian army, and later in the officers' mess (where he was eventually made headman), for most of this period.[11] His wife worked as a maid.

Back in Solu-Khumbu, on the other hand, the impact of the war and subsequent events in India seems to have been relatively muted. Monasteries and nunneries continued to be built or developed. In about 1934, a nunnery was founded at Bigu, west of Solu, by the headman of Bigu village.[12] In the late 1930s the Zatul Rimpoche died, which was an unhappy event, but which set in motion the search for his reincarnation, a matter of enormous general interest. (Several claimants were found; see Appendix B, section on "Chiwong.") In the early 1940s Thami temple staged its first Mani Rimdu festival, the first move in its conversion to a celibate monastery.[13] In about 1946 a Tengboche monk inaugurated the founding of a new monastery at Takshindo, in his home region of Solu,[14] and at about the same time a monastery was founded in Thodung, on the western edge of Solu.[15] In about 1949, a Sherpa monk spent time at the great Nyingmapa monastery of Tashilhunpo in central Tibet and reported that there were about fifty Sherpa monks there.[16] The number may be inflated, but we may take it that there were a significant number of Sherpa monks in Tashilhunpo.

When expeditions resumed after the war, Sherpa religion continued to play an active role in the Sherpas' participation in mountaineering work, or rather a number of different roles. In the first part of this chapter, I will look at the ways the Sherpas deployed their religious practices for their most basic purposes: to get some protection from the gods for this dangerous endeavor. Yet given the omnipresence of the sahibs, the rites came to serve another purpose, drawing in the sahibs and thus exerting a certain amount of moral influence over them as well. This part of the discussion thus places the Sherpas' religious practices on expeditions in part within questions of "resistance"; that is, efforts to achieve some sort of control over the conditions of work within a framework defined and controlled by the sahibs.

In the second part of the chapter, however, I consider some of the ways in which Sherpa religion comes into play on expeditions once protections fail and a death has occurred. Here a number of issues related to the patterns of higher monastic Buddhism become relevant. Some Sherpas mobilize the kinds of emotional discipline emphasized by monks as a way of hiding and thus in some sense mastering the strong emotional reactions evoked by death, but other Sherpas refuse that particular emotional strategy. The issues here then are less defined by sahib power and Sherpa resistance, and more by the variable impact the monastic movement was having within the Sherpa community itself.

While the chapters of this book succeed one another in a rough historical trajectory across the twentieth century, there are certain subjects that seem better treated by looking at the whole century, including both stabilities and changes, within a single chapter. Risk, death, and the religious responses to both, is one of those subjects.

GODS AND MOUNTAINS

Mountaineering has always been very questionable from the point of view of Sherpa religious beliefs. The mountains are the abode of the gods, and the gods must be kept happy if things are to go well for humanity. One of the things that does not make the gods happy, and that indeed angers them, is polluting or profaning the mountains. Such pollutions might include going high on the mountain or stepping on the summit; killing animals or otherwise shedding blood on the mountain; dropping human excretions on the mountain; burning garbage on the mountain or otherwise creating bad smells; and finally, having women on the mountain at all, having women menstruating on the mountain, or having people engage in sexual relations on the mountain.

When the gods are unhappy, all sorts of bad things may ensue— illness, bad crops, bad luck—but for purposes of mountaineering expeditions the main threats are accidents and deaths. From the earliest times, the lamas warned against climbing the mountains. After seven Sherpas were killed in an avalanche on the 1922 Everest expedition, the monks at the nearby Rumbu monastery said funeral prayers for them. When the next Everest expedition came through in 1924, John Noel was shown a fresco that had been painted by the monks:

> This extraordinary picture shows the angered Deity of the mountain surrounded by weird, wildly dancing demons, white lions, barking dogs and hairy men, and at the foot, speared through and through, lies the naked body of the white man who dared to violate [Everest].[17]

Other lamas voiced similar kinds of concern or disapproval. Tenzing Norgay wrote about the lamas' warnings in the 1930s.[18] When Ang Tharkay was invited to Paris in the fifties, after the Annapurna success, some of his friends advised him not to "risk again the anger of the gods, after having profaned their abode at the summit of Annapurna, by going to the land of the 'white man.'"[19] Thomas Laird quotes a lama in the 1980s who was still saying that when the mountains are violated the gods will flee, and then all human endeavors will go badly.[20]

Not every Sherpa was impressed by the lamas' warnings. Tenzing Norgay, as we have seen, virtually scoffed at them. At the other extreme some Sherpas, and not just in the early years, refused to step on summits or tried to get sahibs not to step up on the very top for these reasons.[21] In general, however, all Sherpas, whatever their feelings, have had to overcome most of their concerns about making the gods unhappy in order to do this job. But their continuing anxieties about every kind of disrespect for the mountains, along with the completely objective danger of mountaineering, have led them to be very scrupulous about keeping up religious practices on the mountains.

There are actually several different issues here. At one level, Sherpas saying mantras or making offerings in a somewhat private way during expeditions was clearly a matter of their simply doing what they felt they needed to do, to get some supernatural protection in this dangerous activity. But at another level, Sherpa religion has never been a passive affair, wherein one says one's prayers and hopes for the best. The gods, as noted earlier, help those who *both* make the appropriate offerings *and* help themselves in a practical way in the real world. Thus, the Sherpas from early on have sought to gain some real-world control over the cause of their dangers in the first place, the sahibs. There have been efforts to get the sahibs to limit the extent of the offenses visited upon the gods, and there have been efforts to engage the sahibs in actively pleasing the gods.

SPIRITUALLY CLEAN MOUNTAINS

The mountain gods are offended by, among other things, killing animals and shedding blood on the mountains. The issue of killing in general had been made a focus of the monastic reforms, and the Sherpas' feelings about killing had grown stronger in the decades following the foundings of the first monasteries. Although not in fact vegetarians, the Sherpas never ate a great deal of meat (unlike most sahibs, who were seen as very heavy meat eaters), and when the need arose they availed themselves of butcher-caste Tibetans or Nepalis to do the killing. On the expeditions, however, the Sherpas were not free agents. They were at the bottom of the hierarchy, the climbing sahibs often wanted fresh meat, and unless the Sherpas could impose their anxieties on the sahibs in this matter, they would have to do the killing. Even if they did not, even if the sahibs did it or commissioned non-Sherpas to do it, the offensiveness of the act to the gods put everyone on the expedition in danger. Thus, getting the sahibs not to kill animals on the mountains has been an issue for Sherpas for most of the twentieth century.

The first example of trying to get the sahibs not to kill on the mountain came on the 1922 Everest expedition. The Zatul Rimpoche, who was none too happy about the sahibs being there at all,[22] asked the members of the expedition not to kill within twenty miles of the monastery, or on the mountain itself. General Bruce, the leader of the expedition, complied.[23] His compliance is famous, because it is taken to be one of the reasons the next (1924) expedition received permission to climb.[24]

But the early expedition Sherpas hardly had the power and authority of the Zatul Rimpoche, and in many other instances expedition sahibs continued to kill animals or require Sherpas to kill them, thereby producing some unhappy episodes, with miserable Sherpas doing a very poor job of the killing, and making rather fervent offerings to the gods afterward. Not until the 1970s did they begin to get up the courage to attempt to control the sahibs directly in this matter:

> Sonam Girmi arrived at French Pass to direct the movement of supplies just in time to save the hen from becoming a dinner. Without emotion, but with obvious concern, Sonam told us it would be inappropriate to kill anything on a mountain one is about to climb. His voice was patient; the proper action was clear to him, but long experience had taught him that the sahibs are often unaware of such simple precautions. The chicken went to Tukche with the mailrunner, and rice and cabbage was served for dinner.[25]

In another example, which I collected in an interview, the Sherpas were partly successful in controlling the sahibs on this issue, but then things broke down producing the feared results:

Mingma Tenzing told a story of leading a Dutch expedition on Makalu. The Sherpas made the Dutch promise to keep a very clean expedition—no killing animals, no burning garbage [bad smells offend the gods]. And the expedition was totally success- ful—no avalanches, no accidents, success. So when they all got back to base camp the sahibs decided to have a celebration, and they sent down to a nearby village to kill a buffalo. And that night there was a terrible rock and boulder avalanche which would have killed them all—it came all the way down to base camp, only splitting at the last minute and missing them on both sides.[26]

Controlling the sahibs in such situations could never be guaran- teed, especially, as Sherpa religion would predict, without the back- ing and authority of a figure like the Zatul Rimpoche. The sahibs' uncontrollability, while maintaining control over the Sherpas, is precisely part of what is meant by saying that they "have power." But if the question of killing on the mountain was never fully re- solved, there is another practice in which the Sherpas had more visible success.

THE EVOLUTION OF THE BIG BASE CAMP *PUJA*

If one side of gaining and maintaining religious protection is a mat- ter of avoiding offense to the gods, the other side is a matter of actively petitioning their support and pleasing them with offerings. Thus Sherpas on expeditions have been observed performing one or another of their religious practices from the very beginning of Himalayan mountaineering up into the present. Minimally, they chant mantras at almost any time—in the camp, on the climb, in situations of both great danger and routine activity. The sound of Sherpas humming their mantras has been remarked upon by nu- merous sahibs; it is virtually the background music of Himalayan expeditions.

Similarly, virtually all climbing Sherpas carry with them rice blessed by lamas (or, in a pinch, rice over which they themselves recite a blessing) to sprinkle to the gods in times of serious danger:

The next day we moved up to Camp 2. Nima Tenzing had with him a polythene bag full of holy rice which, whilst chanting prayers, he scattered over potentially dangerous-looking crevasses, slopes and seracs.... When Nima arrived at Camp 2, he took one look at the tier upon tier of seracs and threw the remainder of the rice in a sweeping gesture at the entire North West face of Kangchenjunga.[27]

In another example, a climber was knocked down and partly pinned down by a falling block of ice, and was dug out. "As he left he passed one of the Sherpas, a young kid who looked under twenty, standing over the hole created by the shifting block, chanting a mantra and tossing sacred rice blessed by a lama."[28]

In addition, the sahibs frequently recorded seeing or hearing the Sherpas conducting offering rituals and rites of protection in their tents or in a small and somewhat private way at base camp. Ang Tharkay mentioned that the Sherpas celebrated pujas in their tents on the 1950 Annapurna expedition.[29] Some Sherpas made some small offerings in the evening fire on the 1952 Everest reconnaissance.[30] On the 1973 American expedition to Dhaulagiri, on the night before first entering the icefall, the Sherpas did puja privately in their tent.[31]

But there is also a more public face to some of these practices. It seems clear that Sherpas have also used religious rites on expeditions as a way of involving the sahibs in some of their spiritual concerns, and of getting some sort of moral control over the sahibs. Thus, alongside the smaller or more private practices, there has been a pattern of performing more visible pujas[32] in base camp or at some other point on the expedition. For example, on the 1934 German expedition to Nanga Parbat, "the Sherpas spread out their prayer-flags . . . and with smiling, happy faces offered sacrifices to the gods of Nanga Parbat."[33] On the 1956 women's expedition to some peaks in central Nepal, when the party reached a high pass, the Sherpas asked the memsahibs to join them while they built a stone "cairn," because "nobody has ever been here before."[34]

These base camp pujas seem to have grown larger and more elaborate over time, and it has become more and more common to invite the sahibs to participate. On the 1975 Southwest Face Everest expedition, for example, the Sherpas organized a large puja in base camp and invited Chris Bonington to participate in it, which he did.[35] On the 1978 Annapurna women's expedition, the sardar Lopsang asked for quite a bit of cooperation from the memsahibs in order to stage a large opening puja, and they did in fact go along with his request:

> [Lopsang, the sardar] explained that before we could climb the mountain safely, we had to have a ceremony in which we would raise flags and make offerings of food and drink in honor of the mountain gods. Because this was an inauspicious time in the Tibetan calendar for the making of prayer flags, we would have to wait until September for the flags to be made at the Kathmandu prayer flag factory. Then it would be at least twelve days before the mail runner could return with them. . . . Fortunately, the timing of the ceremony fitted in reasonably well with the timetable I had planned for the climb.[36]

And while sometimes the sahibs were humoring the Sherpas, at other times there was even a sense of their sharing in the benefits of the rituals, if only at the Durkheimian level of promoting social solidarity among all the members of the expedition:

> A few of the Sherpas spent an afternoon building a six-foot stone altar on the edge of our camp, standing a pole in the center to serve as a central stringing point for our lines of prayer flags.
>
> A few mornings before we planned to take our first steps on the mountain, we climbed out of bed early and gathered at the altar for the Pujah, a Buddhist blessing ceremony. . . . We didn't comprehend the religious significance the Sherpas did from the ceremony, but it gave us all a chance to feel joined in a team effort.[37]

The expansion of base camp pujas over time, and the increasing participation of the sahibs, can be read in a number of ways. On the one hand we may see this as another way in which the Sherpas systematically succeeded in gaining respect from the sahibs, and perhaps even some measure of moral influence and practical control over them; that is how I have been looking at the phenomenon here.

11. Raising prayer flags for the Base Camp *puja*, American Women's
Annapurna Expedition, 1978.

On the other hand, one could argue that there is a kind of "staged"
quality to these more public pujas, that they should be seen less as
unself-conscious religious practices and more as performances for
sahibs who seek a certain kind of exoticism as part of the adventure
of the whole enterprise. There is no doubt an element of this in play
as well, and I will return to it later in the chapter.

But there are other aspects of the relationship between Sherpa
religious practices and expedition risk that we must explore first. In
the offering rites I have been discussing, the Sherpas mobilize
their religion in its most basic aspect: as a system of protection and
help, amplifying human efforts with the power of the gods. Yet
protections, both practical and supernatural, fail with great regular-
ity in mountaineering, and despite everyone's best efforts there are
terrible, and usually fatal, accidents. This brings other dimensions
of Sherpa religion into play, connecting back with the questions
of "high religion," the discipline of feelings, and the modes of
"compassion."

12. Unidentified Sherpas (Tenzing Norgay, *second from right*) at Mingma Dorjee's grave, Swiss Everest Expedition, 1952.

DEATH HAPPENS

On the earlier expeditions it was more common (though by no means completely standard) for some Sherpas to break down under the shock of a death on an expedition. It was often occasions of this sort that produced Orientalist readings of the Sherpas as undisciplined and childish. But there was another pattern of reaction, wherein the Sherpas would show little or no apparent reaction to a near miss or a death. This produced a different Orientalist reading, though one that was perhaps meant to be sympathetic, or at least enlightened and culturally relativistic: the idea that the Sherpas were less affected by death because of their Buddhist religion and a kind of fatalism that this produced.

I must say immediately that this is simply wrong. I have never heard a Sherpa shrug off an accidental or violent or sudden death with the notion that the person's time had come, or that it was ordained on high, or that it did not matter because the person would be reincarnated. From my own experience with Sherpas, they are very shaken up by such events, whether because of the personal loss involved, or because such accidents are always signs that something is seriously amiss. Nonetheless this view has been quite widespread in the mountaineering literature.

SHERPA IMPASSIVITY AND "ORIENTAL FATALISM"

We can find traces of this idea on the 1922 Everest expedition, when there was an avalanche and seven porters were killed. Although John Noel had observed the Sherpas to be "crying like babies" right after the accident, General Bruce also noted that they "dismissed their troubles very rapidly and very lightly, holding simply that the men's time had come, and so there was no more to be said about it."[38]

The Oriental fatalism view became much stronger after World War II. One of the most famous examples came from the 1963 American Everest expedition. After Jake Breitenbach's death, the Sherpas seemed to show little reaction:

"They seemed unable to understand," said Norman [Dyhrenfurth, the leader], "why we were so upset and disorganized. They couldn't see why we take life so seriously, and there was grumbling among them, particularly the older ones, who said in effect, 'Why are the sahibs making such a fuss?'" Most were ready to go ahead with a normal day's work.[39]

The Sherpas even raised what the sahibs felt were some trivial complaints at this time, triggering the Oriental fatalism interpretation:

One group even picked this particular time to complain about shortages in their own food and clothing . . . and Norman, with Gombu acting as interpreter, eventually had to give them a dressing down. At the same time he tried to explain to them the present feelings of the team members—"to make them understand," he said, "that we who are of a different background and religion do not for the most part believe in reincarnation, and therefore life and death for us are more important."[40]

There was a good bit more in this vein in the seventies. For example, on the 1975 British Southwest Face Everest expedition, a young deaf-and-mute porter fell into a stream and drowned. Doug Scott and Chris Bonington were extremely upset about the accident (Bonington's own son had drowned some years before), but "On our return to camp, the ever pragmatic Mick Burke pointed out that the Sherpas were not unduly troubled because they could shrug it off with a thought that his time had come and he had gone to a better life."[41]

Similarly, during Reinhold Messner's 1978 ascent of Everest, there was an avalanche in the icefall. No one was hurt, and the Sherpas were seemingly unfazed by it. The Austrians attributed their lack of reaction to their Buddhist beliefs, and then segued into the Oriental fatalism line: "It's easy for the Sherpas. They simply believe everything is ordained from above," someone said. "If one of them dies, then it must be meant to happen."[42]

Again, many Sherpas have been deeply upset by deaths on expeditions. Many stop climbing for several years, or permanently. Domai Tsering was the sardar on the 1970 Japanese ski expedition on which six Sherpas were killed, many of them his own kin. He finished the expedition, but he never climbed again. Tawa Gyeldzen had been a Tengboche monk who had broken his vows and taken a wife. He took up expedition work in the seventies, but gave it up after a few years because virtually every expedition he climbed with (including the Japanese ski expedition) had multiple deaths. On the 1974 French Everest expedition, there was an avalanche that killed the French leader and five Sherpas. Pasang Nuru's older brother was among the Sherpas who died, and Pasang Nuru stopped climbing for three years. Pertemba Sherpa stopped climbing for three years after the death of a sahib on the 1975 British Southwest Face Everest expedition. He started again because old climbing friends urged him to do so, but in 1979 he was on Gaurishankar (another mountain) when he learned of the death of his best friend, Ang Phu, on Everest. He finished the expedition and the season, but he never climbed again.

Yet to show any reaction was to risk the other Orientalist response, that the Sherpas were in some way childlike, and one reason for their not showing reaction may have been precisely to avoid this response from the sahibs. But there were others, which we must now consider. It will be useful first to distinguish near misses, and the question of showing fear, from deaths and the question of showing grief.

NEAR MISSES AND SHERPA MASCULINE CULTURE

As in the example of the avalanche on Messner's expedition, when no one was hurt, the Sherpas were more likely to laugh off the incident and show no reaction. Although it was usually the case that nothing serious had occurred, nonetheless in such situations the sahibs themselves were more likely to show, and to expect to see, at least a momentary registering of being shaken up by the close call. Here is an example from Hillary's account of the 1951 Everest reconnaissance, which obviously took him somewhat aback:

> Even as I watched, [Angputer] slipped and fell and shot past at great speed. I clung to the belay with all my strength. It seemed a lifetime before the rope came tight with a twang; the belay held, and Angputer was spreadeagled on the slope. For a moment there was no sound only our deep panting and then I heard the noise of laughing. I looked up and saw the other two Sherpas hanging on to the slope and almost bursting with good humor at Angputer's predicament.[43]

Here is another example, from the 1960 Indian Everest expedition, in which part of the Icefall on which the climbers were sitting collapsed. Collapsing blocks of ice in the Icefall is one of the most common causes of death in Everest climbing.

> All this lasted only a few seconds and then everything was still again. We were both very frightened but our friend Lakpa did not lose his smile. He felt intrigued and amused at our discomfiture and kept sitting on the ridge completely unconcerned![44]

What seems to be in play in these situations is a dimension of Sherpa masculine culture. Sherpa men tease each other about showing fear; it is part of cultural patterns of competitiveness, which will be discussed more fully in the next chapter. Thus Ang Tharkay wrote about some difficult climbing with another Sherpa on Nanda Devi in 1936:

> Ang Dawa found this too hard for him and abandoned the effort. He left us and went down by the quickest possible routes. When I found him again at our camp, I teased him about his lack of courage, which annoyed him intensely.[45]

Fifty years later, Sarkey Tshering Sherpa wrote about the first all-Sherpa climbing expedition, "We overcame our nervousness by teasing each other."[46]

SHERPA IMPASSIVITY: A MORE CAREFUL CONSIDERATION

In situations where the worst has happened, and a death has actually occurred, Sherpas have never been reported to have laughed about it, but they sometimes have seemed to react more casually, or less emotionally, than the sahibs would have expected or would think appropriate. The reasons for Sherpa nonreaction are highly variable; individuals differ, occasions differ, and any one person's reaction at any given moment is usually a mixture of several different feelings. Beyond this kind of individual variability, however, there are several general patterns.

One motive for a Sherpa, usually a sardar, to cover or clamp down on his own reaction to death(s) on expeditions is simply professionalism. He had said he would do the job, and he feels an obligation to complete it, no matter what he may be experiencing emotionally. Domai Tsering was the sardar of the 1970 Japanese ski expedition on which six Sherpas were killed, including his own younger brother. Domai Tsering never climbed again after this expedition, but he felt obligated to complete the expedition because he had made a commitment to the Japanese climbers, and he persuaded most of the other Sherpas (many of whom wanted to quit) to finish as well. Similarly, Pertemba was devastated by the loss of his best friend in 1979 and stopped climbing after that season, but he did complete the season because he had committed himself to do so:

In '79 he was on an expedition to Gaurishankar. They were having lunch in Chaurikot, when he heard on the radio about Ang Phu dying on Everest. Ang Phu was one of his closest friends. They had spent lots of time together since childhood. They had gone to school together, they had worked for the same trekking company, they had started climbing at the same time. Pertemba continued climbing in '79 because he had already agreed to do so.[47]

At one level the Sherpa idea of professional behavior is no different from the sahibs': fulfilling obligations, carrying a job through to completion, and so forth. At another level, however, Sherpas may mobilize different kinds of cultural resources in order to manage their feelings and perform as professionals. Two important religious dynamics may come into play, though neither of them has anything to do with "fatalism." The first is a cultural/religious injunction against exhibiting strong emotions around death, which itself has several rationales. One is that the deceased has not fully departed yet (and this is especially true in the case of violent accidents), and hearing the crying of the living will make it difficult for the deceased to sever attachments and move on. It is also sometimes said that too much crying at funerals will cause blood to rain from the sky, or cause a veil of blood to cover the eyes of the deceased so that he or she cannot find "the road," the way to a good rebirth. The issues here are, as with showing fear, somewhat gendered; in ordinary life women often display intense grieving at funerals, while (generally) men do not; women at funerals are often reminded by the lamas to stop crying, as hearing such crying keeps the deceased attached to his or her previous life and may cause blood to rain down. Thus whatever men are feeling about a death, they have learned long before coming to expeditions that they are supposed to keep it inside. Women should, too, but it is assumed that women are weaker than men about this kind of control.

There is a fine line between simply hiding or masking one's feelings and actually dispelling or at least distancing them so that they will not take over the self. For monks, as discussed in chapter 4, the first is a prelude to the second; monks are taught not only to hide

13. Lobsang Tsering Sherpa, sardar of the
American Women's Annapurna Expedition
and other climbs, 1990.

but to learn to "let go" of "attachments," for it is these attachments
that cause the strong feelings that threaten to overwhelm the person.
The monastic ideal of disciplining oneself to "let go" of strong feelings entirely has also come into play, in some cases, in relation to
expedition deaths.

One example of this comes from the Annapurna women's expedition of 1978. Two of the women had a fatal accident, and everyone
was extremely upset. In describing the aftermath the leader, Arlene
Blum, first successfully avoided the orientalism trap: "The Sherpas
believe in reincarnation and have had much experience with death
in the mountains, but they too were severely shaken by the tragedy."[48] This allowed her, I think, to hear more accurately the kind
of comfort the sardar, Lopsang, was offering her, which carries echoes of the monastic emphasis on letting go of attachments: "Lopsang
sat near me, looking at the serac with binoculars and shaking his
head. Then he came over, patted me on the shoulder, and said, 'Let
them go. You have to let them go.' "[49]

Another example of monastic emotional discipline being brought
to bear in the face of a mountaineering death may be seen in the
following incident. I was staying in Khumjung village in 1979 when
word came back that Ang Phu, of that village, had just been killed
on Everest. Ang Phu, whom I did not know personally, had by all
accounts been an enormously well liked young man, and the news

sent shock waves through the village. There was much weeping and anger; there was much speculation about what happened, seizing upon every scrap of information (and misinformation). People could talk and think about nothing else for days.

The day after we heard the news, I went up to Tengboche monastery, a few hours' walk from Khumjung, for a previously scheduled lunch date with the Rimpoche, the head lama. Several Sherpas and I were having lunch in the lamas' chambers when one of the Rimpoche's servants came in to say that Ang Phu's family had arrived and needed to see the Rimpoche immediately. The group was shown in, consisting of the father, who was a village lama (married, as opposed to a monk), a male cousin (who counts as a virtual brother), and two sisters. My fieldnotes give a sense of the intensity of the event, and also of my own confusion about it:

Ang Phu's father, cousin, and two sisters came in, the father quite hysterical. He did his prostrations to the lama crying and choking and saying they tell him his son isn't coming back, begging the Rimpoche for a blessing (*molom*). The Rimpoche, however, was quite cool. He told the man to collect himself saying, "You're a *choa* (religious practitioner), you should know better, instead of crying you should read *cho* (sacred text, "prayers") and calm your family." He then closed his eyes and chanted quietly to himself for two or three minutes (which *was* soothing) and then called for his divination book (*tsi*) and worked out some texts for the father to read.

[People did indeed begin to calm down and pull themselves together. But] I was quite shocked by the lack of *nyingje*—compassion, sympathy, pity—manifested by the lama. At one point he even seemed to crack a joke and laugh. But later another man who had been present said approvingly, this is how high lamas are. *If their own mother and father die they simply meditate for five minutes and that's the end of their grief.* Too much crying will cause it to rain blood. . . . In response to my saying that the lama showed no *nyingje*, he said that that *was* nyingje.[50]

There are many things going on in this incident, and I have discussed it in slightly different terms elsewhere.[51] For present purposes, however, there are several notable points. First, the incident is in some ways reminiscent of Ang Tharkay's visit to Rumbu monastery in great emotional distress: in both cases the parties arrived seeking more conventional forms of comfort but were offered an injunction to be calm and regain composure. In Ang Tharkay's case the monks were gentle, while in the case of Ang Phu's family the Tengboche lama was stern. But what I took to be the lama's coldness must also be understood as an act of modeling for the family the appropriate composure and management of feelings, thus indicating for them a way out of their grief and horror. That is certainly how the other man—my friend Nyima Chotar—saw it. Nyima Chotar approved of the lama's behavior, seeing it as a manifestation of a broader spiritual ability to "let go" of even the most compelling personal ties, and seeing it as the most compassionate thing the lama could offer the family.

The Ang Phu story contains several elements of the "higher," more monastic inflected, religious orientation being brought to bear on the death of a young mountaineering Sherpa: the issue of disciplining feelings, or at least displays of feeling, and also the mobilization of that very specific higher Buddhist form of "compassion," which does not sympathize with grief in any ordinary sense, but rather "shows the way" out of it. For some people this dimension of religion is precisely what they want and need; for others, however, it may not be enough, or it may not be the right thing. Thus there was in fact a coda to this episode. As I learned a few days later,

> Ang Phu's cousin, who had come to visit the Rimpoche with the father, went up to Everest Base Camp [and went on a rampage]: he kicked over the dinner table and ruined all the food, screamed that he was going to kill the sahibs, and more. Then he jumped into the river near Pangboche and had to be pulled out.[52]

COMPLICATING THE RELIGIOUS PICTURE

I have thus far been treating Sherpa religion as if it were a consistent presence in Sherpa lives and on expeditions. I have drawn a picture of Sherpas using their religion in a relatively straightforward way to protect themselves from harm, manage the sahibs, and handle their own strong emotions in the face of danger and death. Yet there is always a range of variation in different people's belief in and commitment to religious precepts, and the Sherpas are no exception. Even in the context of "traditional" or "popular" religion, that is, in the context of the local beliefs that were presumably in play before the founding of the monasteries, there is evidence of significant individual variation. For example, on the 1938 Everest expedition, one of the Sherpas, Pasang, had a stroke in a camp at high altitude, and the other Sherpas wanted to leave him there. According to several sahibs' accounts, the Sherpas believed that the gods were angry and had claimed Pasang as a victim. But Ang Tharkay did not invoke any kind of religious interpretation, writing instead that his fellow Sherpas did not want to handle Pasang because he had soiled himself and smelled bad. Apparently unworried about angry gods, and angry with both the sahibs and his fellow Sherpas, Ang Tharkay picked up Pasang and began carrying him down the mountain, whereupon the other Sherpas were ashamed and pitched in to help.[53] Perhaps Ang Tharkay did not subscribe to the prevailing notions about angry gods and mountaineering, or perhaps he did not feel that they applied to this particular situation; alternatively, he simply rejected the possibility of not saving Pasang because of those beliefs. In any event the point is simply that there was always individual and situational variation in the Sherpas' commitment and adherence to their "traditional" beliefs.

A related point is that the religion itself had a good deal of flexibility. Sherpas would often get divinations to forecast the auspiciousness of undertaking some trip or other major activity, including a mountaineering expedition. But if they received an inauspicious reading, it did not necessarily mean that they would not undertake the activity. They might go back for a different divination, possibly done with different stipulated conditions, much as a sick person in the United States might, after a bad medical diagnosis, go to another doctor for a second opinion. Several instances of ignored or redone divinations show up in the mountaineering literature.[54]

The founding of the monasteries opened up new axes of variation and difference among Sherpas concerning their religion. The monasteries began pushing an agenda for upgrading popular religion, pushing it in the direction of a "higher" Buddhism in which the ideal figures would be the monks and the reincarnate lamas. Some people entered into these changes with great enthusiasm, while others had their reservations.

And then there has been "modernization." Sherpas have been exposed to secularist assumptions for almost a century, and these may have opened up skepticism and nonbelief for many of them, causing them to question their religion not so much from an alternative ethical angle, as in the examples above, but simply from a shift into the kind of personal hedonism that modern consumer culture encourages. There is no doubt some of this going on as well. To cite one example, there was the case of one Ang Kami on the 1965 Indian Everest expedition. Whereas most Sherpas going to a summit carry prayer flags or other religious items to place there, or utter prayers to the gods thanking them for their help and protection in the enterprise, Ang Kami was clearly a "modern" young man with few if any traditional religious impulses:

> Ang Kami was reported to have carried a pin-up picture of a film actress with which he wanted to be photographed on the Summit. But C. P. [Vohra, his climbing partner] would have none of it and Ang Kami agreed reluctantly to the advice of C. P., though only after a mild altercation. Later, Ang Kami confessed that he had carried a prayer-flag to plant on the Summit but forgot all about it then and had brought it back with him.[55]

In fact, most contemporary Sherpas still seem very involved in their religion, and this has raised another question: the possibility that the Sherpas are in some sense performing their Buddhism for the sahibs, that as modern subjects they would normally have been secularized but because the sahibs have responded to and desired the Sherpas' exoticness as (Tibetan) Buddhists, the Sherpas have in effect reembraced their religion as a way of fulfilling the sahibs' desires.[56] I think there is no doubt[57] that the sahibs' interest in the Sherpas' Buddhism, for reasons of the sahibs' own fantasies, desires, or inclinations, has further firmed up the Sherpas' commitment to and involvement with their own Buddhist religion. Indeed such shifts of religious commitment in relation to a larger social and political context are quite normal; we saw earlier, for example, that Sherpas were drifting in the direction of Nepali/Hindu practices in the early years of the century, a trend that was reversed by the foundings of the monasteries. But it does not follow from this that Buddhism has been turned (as Adams [1996] seems to argue) into an artifact whose entire meaning is located in its responsiveness to sahib desires. Rather, I would argue that it retains a certain "authenticity," not in the sense of being isolated from the influences of the world around it but in the sense that its beliefs and practices, however much they may fulfill someone else's desires and fantasies, nonetheless continue to be part of agendas and meanings that are based in the Sherpas' community. That community itself, of course, is not untouched by the outside world or by "modernity"; far from it. It nonetheless operates as a continuing site of relationships and meanings that are locally formed and practiced within the community's own everyday life.

That everyday life, however, is not a monolithic "Sherpa culture" but is rather a complex interaction of differences, among men and women, old and young, villagers and urbanites, lamas and laypeople, big people and small people, and everyone else in between. Contemporary Sherpa religion on expeditions is clearly a mixture of all of these tendencies: idiosyncratic individual variation (including variations of secularization and modernization), performances for the sahibs (themselves taking several forms: resistance, identity statements, playing on the sahibs' desires for exoticness), and finally the embodiment of real differences over religious direction that have animated and continue to animate the Sherpa community. Some of this may be seen in yet another religious phenomenon on expeditions, funerals.

THE RISE OF THE BIG BASE CAMP FUNERAL

In earlier years, when there were one or more deaths on an expedition, the sahibs would generally hold some sort of memorial service for the deceased climbers. Bodies would be brought down if it was not too difficult and dangerous to do so; otherwise they would be lowered into a crevasse or, if they had fallen to an inaccessible and invisible location, left where they were. (Bodies often pose a disposal problem, as the ground at these altitudes is frozen, and there is no wood for a cremation). In any event, at the memorial service, there might be personal comments about or individual prayers for the deceased, or someone might produce a Bible and read some passages, or there might simply be a period of silence.

This sort of private memorializing was not traditional for the Sherpas, who in the case of Sherpa deaths on expeditions seem in the past to have simply followed whatever format the sahibs offered in base camp, and waited to get back to their homes for the full-scale funeral rites. In the one pre–World War II example for which we have information, the 1922 Everest expedition on which seven Sherpas died in an avalanche, the bodies were not recovered, but General Bruce (perhaps at the urging of Sherpas, but he does not say so) sent money down to Rumbu monastery for some funeral rites for the men.[58] Throughout this early period, relatives of deceased Sherpas did not come up to base camp, nor were lamas invited up to do funeral rites.

After the war, it became more common for relatives of deceased Sherpas to come up and participate, often very emotionally, in an abbreviated version of traditional Sherpa funeral rites at or near base camp. On the 1970 Japanese ski expedition, the bodies were carried down to a site below base camp (Lobuche, a high grazing area) in order to have funeral rites conducted there. Many Sherpa families came up to the site, and the relatives of some of the surviving Sherpas tried, in some cases successfully, to drag their kinsmen away from the expedition.[59]

On the 1974 Everest expedition, the French leader and five Sherpas were killed. I have been unable to find a detailed account of this expedition,[60] but according to an interview with the sardar, Sonam Gyalchen, a funeral was held below base camp, presumably at the Lobuche site; a lama and several families of the deceased Sherpas came up from Khumjung.

We also have two accounts of the 1982 Canadian Everest expedition. Three Sherpas were killed in an avalanche, and a funeral was held. This event involved extensive rites lasting over several days, with many family members in attendance:

The bereaved relatives began to assemble. Pasang Sona's widow and youngest daughter arriving first, their wailing audible for a great distance. Next came Ang Tsultim's father, a middle-aged man with a limp, leaning on a stick for support and silently weeping. Dawa Dorje's widow was slow to appear—she had one infant and was pregnant with another, and no one had wanted to break the news to her.[61]

One of the widows wept uncontrollably for hours and tried to throw herself into the funeral pyre, but was held back by others. One "very old, wizened little man" grabbed one of the sahibs' arm and said, "Let no more Sherpas die!"[62]

What is going on in the increasing elaboration of these events? Authentic performances of religious rites that are important to the Sherpas at such a time? The same kind of "resistance" that allowed the Sherpas to expand religious practices on expeditions in general? Dramatizations for the sahibs of the terrible cost of their "sport"? Dramatization of Sherpa "identity," including their Buddhism, for both themselves and the sahibs? Authentic expressions of grief? The answer, of course, is all of the above, and it would be foolish to try either to separate these various interpretations or to exclude any of them from the discussion. It would be particularly foolish to try to insist that these rites were either entirely oriented toward the gaze of the sahibs or entirely oblivious of that gaze. Rather it is crucial to try to understand how Sherpas can be deeply shaped by the mountaineering experience and yet sustain their own structures of intentionality, their own projects in life, and their own ways of enacting those projects.

Thus, what I especially wish to call attention to about base-camp funerals is the way in which these events—however much they may address themselves to the sahibs—also play off against, and embody within themselves, long-term historical differences and implicit debates within the Sherpas community itself. The intense grieving of the relatives implicitly stands against the strict discipline of feelings encouraged by the monastic community, and the emotional base camp funerals (and even more, the attempted suicides) implicitly say that the monastic position may be valuable but it is not enough.

Indeed we can see this difference enacted even within one of the funerals. During the extensive 1982 Canadian Everest expedition funeral for Sherpas, in the midst of all the very dramatic expressions of grief and anger, the lama who came up for the funeral took one of the sahibs aback with a comment that I presume was coming from a "high religion" perspective: "Distraught, Stephen talked to the lama about the calamity. But the lama's words caught him off guard: 'This is just one of those things. It just happens.' "[63]

6

MEN

In the late 1940s, a political revolution was brewing in Nepal, partly in reaction to developments in India. In addition, the first major Chinese incursion into Tibet took place in 1950, and Nepal hoped to find some international support against possible Chinese aggression. For a variety of political reasons, then, foreign visitors began to be allowed into the country starting in about 1950. In that year the climbers Bill Tilman and Charles Houston were the first Westerners to enter the Sherpas' home region of Solu-Khumbu, which they described as a virtual paradise.[1] In that year as well, Maurice Herzog, a French climber with a background in engineering and business, and Louis Lachenal, a Chamonix guide, reached the summit of a mountain called Annapurna (26,545 feet), in central Nepal. It was the first time a summit of a peak over 8,000 meters had been reached, and it represented the true beginning of the era of modern Himalayan mountaineering. Three years later a British team finally succeeded in putting a party—consisting of a New Zealander, Edmund Hillary, and a Sherpa, Tenzing Norgay—on the summit of Everest (29,028 feet), the highest mountain in the world.

The fifties and sixties saw several contradictory trends in mountaineering. On the one hand, some of the prewar romanticism persisted in some circles, with some sahibs seeking a kind of mystical communion with the mountains and with the Sherpas. On the other hand, the military approach to mountaineering became much stronger than it had been before the war, and in fact came to dominate mountaineering in this era. This is the period of the mega-expeditions and of the hypermasculine sahib.

Masculinity had always been one of the underlying "sahib games" of mountaineering, but its character changed in the postwar period; the nature of those changes, and the ways in which they informed the sahib/Sherpa relationship, are among the main themes of this chapter. But the Sherpas of course had their own gender patterns, and the sahib/Sherpa relationship with respect to masculinity was more than a question of sahib "influence" on Sherpa patterns. At this point I need to return briefly to the conceptual frameworks that are informing this book.

More on Serious Games

Earlier, I introduced the idea of "serious games" as a way of thinking about the cultural framing of intentions within which people operate at any given time. The idea of the game includes the purposes of the activity, the discursive categories through which it is viewed, the organization and relative power of the players, and so forth. Mountaineering as an activity has been situated within a number of overlapping and intertwining games—the countermodernity game; the romantic, testing-the-existential-limits, game; the masculinity game—and to know this is to begin to understand the kind of language mountaineers speak, the kinds of risks they are willing to take, and the kinds of control they exert over themselves and others.

But there is another very important dimension of serious games that must be emphasized. Games are not just bundles of intentions or fields of language and discourse. Games involve players, differently positioned, differently situated, with respect to those intentions and those discourses. Games are social, indeed intensely social; people play against each other, with each other, for each other. Games thrive on difference; there is no game without difference. Within mountaineering, and at the center of this book, is the Sherpa/sahib difference (and relationship) and its multiple permutations.

But this is only the beginning. For each of the parties there are additional questions of how they are situated and differentiated with respect to the contexts from which they come and to which—this being a game in the ordinary language sense, too—they return. For the sahibs, I have been concerned until now to situate them in relation to their largely educated middle-class backgrounds, which allow and even encourage them to position themselves against the dominant modernity that produced them. For the Sherpas, I have looked at other axes of difference: the differences between big people and others in the Sherpa community, and thus the kinds of economic pressures that drove many Sherpas into mountaineering; the differences between monastic and "popular" religious agendas that began to open up in the early twentieth century and that continued shifting throughout the century; and again—for this chapter—issues of gender difference, here issues of masculinity.

It is all of these differences that come to bear on the Sherpa/sahib relationship at the center of mountaineering. This relationship is not some transparent difference of "power" that needs no further definition; rather, it involves the orchestration of the various differences of the Sherpas and the sahibs, contained within a framework of the relative power of the sahibs. If one of the themes of the book is the ways in which mountaineering allowed the Sherpas to break out of and perhaps even transform their political-economic constraints, if another is the constant transformation and reorganization of religion across the century, a third is the way in which mountaineering actually exacerbated gender differences and inequality among the Sherpas, and set in motion a distinct "dialectic of sex." Among other things I will argue that Sherpas and sahibs used their shared masculinity to establish certain kinds of would-be egalitarian bonds. I begin then with a broad look at egalitarian relations on some mid-century expeditions.

THE EQUALITY CONTRADICTION

THE FANTASY OF EQUALITY

A number of expeditions in the late forties and early fifties made a point of establishing quite egalitarian relations with the Sherpas. This often went farther, in the sense of the sahibs feeling that they and the Sherpas achieved some sort of intense bonding. In some cases the Sherpas reciprocated; in others the equality and the bonding remained more at the level of the sahib's fantasy. Earl Denman in 1947 had claimed to be the first climber to offer the Sherpas full equality on an expedition, and he also imagined that he had achieved a special bond with the two Sherpas who accompanied him:

> Tenzing and Ang Dowa were acting as porters, but I never thought of them in this way, for a climber can only go as far on Everest as the porters, by their own efforts, will permit. Thus there was an ideal bond between us. We were all porters and we were all climbers.[2]

The French on Annapurna in 1950 were intent on treating the Sherpas as full "climbing partners." Some personal friendships were formed, but the main point seems to have been that the French made no distinctions between sahibs and Sherpas in terms of equipment and food (both of which were apparently of extraordinarily high quality),[3] and the leader Herzog also offered Ang Tharkay the chance to come with him to the summit (Ang Tharkay, whose feet were beginning to freeze, declined, but was ashamed of himself afterwards for doing so).[4]

A 1950 English expedition to Nanga Parbat was described by Tenzing Norgay as very egalitarian,[5] as were several Swiss expeditions in the late forties and early fifties.[6] The Swiss expeditions seem to have been genuinely committed to equality at all levels, and to actually have achieved this to an impressive degree. Indeed, it may have been the commitment of the Swiss to treat the Sherpas as equal partners that cost them the summit of Everest in 1952. When several Sherpas said that the wind and bitter cold were beyond endurance and that they were going to turn back, the Swiss felt that they had no right to press them to go on,[7] a situation to be compared with Bauer forcing Dorji to keep climbing on Kangchenjunga in the thirties, after Dorji had become demoralized and did not want to continue.[8]

Moreover, in some cases it does appear that a genuine bond developed between some of the members and some of the Sherpas. Raymond Lambert wrote about an exchange between himself and Tenzing:

14. Tenzing Norgay Sherpa and Raymond Lambert, Swiss Everest
Expedition, 1952.

"Sahib, we ought to stay here this evening." And [Tenzing]
showed me the tent that he had been carrying since we left. I
smiled, our two thoughts having followed the same road. This
is the kind of thing that creates a profound solidarity in the
mountains . . . and perhaps everywhere.[9]

Tenzing and Lambert became very close, in a relationship that lasted
for many years. Tenzing called Lambert, "my companion of the
heights and the closest and dearest of my friends."[10]

Finally, the Indian expeditions in the sixties also seem to have had
a relatively egalitarian view of the Sherpas' roles on the expeditions.
Sherpas were made full members of the climbing party and were
included in every summit party. When the Indians were finally successful on Everest in 1965 (on their third attempt), an Indian (Major
H.P.S. Ahluwalia) and a Sherpa (Phu Dorji) shared the success.[11]
The leader of that expedition, Major Kohli, made the usual dis-
claimer of money motives for the Sherpas, but then called them "our
full companions in adventure."[12]

These relatively egalitarian postwar expeditions represented a shift in some ways and a continuity in others. Before World War II, a figure like Dr. Kellas might establish close relations with "his" Sherpas, but this was very unlikely to happen on the larger expeditions, and in any event all such relations were tinged with a certain amount of condescension and paternalism. Sahib romanticism was largely directed at the mountain, and at Sherpas insofar as they were viewed more or less as part of nature itself. The post–World War II expeditions just discussed remained "romantic" in their quasi-mystical approach to mountaineering, but the paternalistic tone faded somewhat. The Sherpas were viewed more as fellow travelers in this mystical endeavor, and the romantic fantasy shifted to include the idea of bonding with the Sherpas as relative equals and friends.

This pattern became much more important in the seventies, when the counterculture as a recognized cultural movement took shape. In the fifties and sixties, however, it remained a minority style, though very important insofar as it gave the Sherpas their first full taste of equality on expeditions and fueled for them a more general sense that they should not settle for less.

STRIKES AND THE VIOLATION OF EQUALITY

It was in this period (the fifties and sixties) that the Sherpas became much more visibly self-conscious—and occasionally militant—about their role and their rights on the expeditions. By the mid-fifties they were organizing themselves on a formal level, at first in Darjeeling. The British in Darjeeling had run something called the Himalayan Club, which served as a kind of contracting organization funneling Sherpas to expeditions, setting wages, and so forth. With the British presence fast disappearing in India, however, the Sherpas strengthened one of their own urban self-help organizations in Darjeeling and took over the functions that the Himalayan Club had been performing. The Sherpa organization had been founded in the 1920s and had been called the Sherpa Buddhist Association. Both the date and the name suggest links with the founding of the first monasteries in 1916 and 1924 in Solu-Khumbu, and the organiza-

15. Photo captioned "A promising generation," unidentified Sherpas, Swiss Everest Expedition 1952.

tion had been "concerned mostly with religious affairs." But, as Tenzing Norgay wrote,

> During the thirties and the war years it did little or nothing, but recently it has been revived, the word "Buddhist" has been dropped from the title, and it concerns itself not with religion but with all sorts of practical matters that affect our community . . . it has now begun to act as a sort of employment agency and labor union for expedition Sherpas, trying to get a higher wage scale than that set by the Himalayan Club and better compensation for men who are injured and the families of those who are killed.[13]

In about 1961 (or perhaps a bit earlier), an organization called the Himalayan Society (not to be confused with the Himalayan Club) was founded in Kathmandu.[14] Once Nepal had been officially opened to foreigners in the early 1950s, the staging base for Himalayan mountaineering had quickly shifted from Darjeeling to Kathmandu. There seems to have developed a certain competition between Sherpas who lived in Darjeeling and sought to keep the expedition business there, and Sherpas who lived in Nepal and found it more convenient to work out of Kathmandu. The opening of the Kathmandu-based Himalayan Society in the early sixties represented and furthered this shift. Moreover, just as the Sherpas on the early expeditions pushed the sahibs to keep out the Tibetans, so some Kathmandu-based Sherpas seem to have held up the sahibs to keep out the Darjeeling men. The society made a rule that "not more than two non-Nepalese [i.e., Darjeeling] Sherpas could be allowed with any foreign expedition into Nepal."[15] Presumably in response to these developments, another new club was founded in Darjeeling in 1963, again with Tenzing's involvement: the Sherpa Climbers' Association.[16]

These organizations could and did work for such improvements as better conditions of employment and better compensation. What they could do nothing about was the quality of relations between Sherpas and sahibs on the mountains. As noted earlier, there were many reasons for Sherpas to go on strike or otherwise refuse to cooperate on expeditions, but one pattern in particular stood out: resistance emerged when the Sherpas felt that they were being treated as inferiors. This pattern seems to have intensified as a result of the more egalitarian relations of the late forties and early fifties, and most of the major expeditions of the fifties and sixties had serious strikes.

For example, the 1953 British Everest expedition was led by a long-time British Army officer, John Hunt, who seems to have been particularly hierarchical: "Socially conscious though Hunt was (and is) he had a military mind conditioned to a strict class division between 'officers' and 'other ranks.' And the Sherpas were definitely 'other ranks.' "[17] The expedition started off very badly when Hunt arranged for the sahib members of the expedition to stay in the British embassy, while the Sherpas would stay in the embassy garage. This was both problematic at the practical level—the garage had no bathrooms—and symbolically humiliating. The Sherpas were furious and staged a very dramatic representation of their feelings: they urinated in the road outside the embassy.[18] Following this incident, there were continuing conflicts between the Sherpas and the sahibs over various equipment issues.

Another expedition that had major conflicts with the Sherpas over questions of parity was the 1963 American Everest expedition. One of the main arguments had to do with sleeping bags:

> The team members had both outer and inner bags, the Sherpas only outer bags, and even though these were the heavy warm ones—with the sahibs themselves rarely using the others— there was, sure enough, a chorus of protest. For the better part of a day Base Camp became a sort of alfresco courtroom, while assorted "mountain lawyers" (and the Sherpas have some pretty good ones) argued their case and cited precedents from previous expeditions.[19]

Eventually the matter was settled to the Sherpas' satisfaction, and relations between sahibs and Sherpas settled down for a time. But later there were repeated problems with oxygen use at very high altitude. There was a limited amount of oxygen, and the resources were strained by a split within the expedition that resulted in two separate summit assaults by two separate routes. According to the sahibs' accounts, the Sherpas were fairly "selfish" about the oxygen, refusing to give up an oxygen regulator so that the Sherpa designated for one of the summit parties could go, consuming more oxygen during the night than they had been allocated, and then refusing to give up oxygen on their descent so that one of the summit party could go up.[20]

There have been a number of interpretations of what happened. The leader of the expedition thought that much of the Sherpas' uncooperativeness over the oxygen bottles derived from a split between the Darjeeling and Khumbu Sherpas, although others feel that this interpretation has been exaggerated.[21] But another interpretation had to do with issues of equality and hierarchy between

Sherpas and sahibs. At a certain point in the climb, the Sherpas were doing all the carrying, while the sahibs (and the Darjeeling Sherpas who had been designated as "members") lay around in their tents "hoarding their resources for the summit push soon to come."[22] Thus, two all-Sherpa teams shuttled back and forth, carrying loads up from Camp III to Camp IV. It could be argued that letting the Sherpas do unescorted climbing was a mark of the sahibs' confidence in the Sherpas' abilities, and an advance over an earlier paternalistic situation in which Sherpas always had to be escorted by sahibs:

> In earlier days of Himalayan climbing Sherpas were rarely, if ever, permitted to make high carries without an escort of team members. By 1963, however, their general level of climbing competence was so good that, once a route had been prepared, unescorted carries were routine; and on the American Mount Everest Expedition the all-Sherpa parties performed in first-rate fashion.[23]

But a simpler interpretation was that the sahibs were being lazy and selfish about the hard work of the expedition, and using the Sherpas essentially as coolies while the sahibs conserved their energies for the glory of the summit assault. Colonel James Roberts, an Englishman with long Himalayan experience who served as the officer for "Sherpas and transport" for the expedition, noted that there might have been fewer problems between sahibs and Sherpas on the expedition "if the sahibs had undertaken more routine carries with the porters instead of sitting about in the Cwm [a Welsh term for an enclosed valley; the Cwm is one of the established camp sites on Everest] and at Base."[24] Several of the climbers shared this view.[25]

This issue came up again on a later American expedition. Whereas the Sherpas' attitudes toward the sahibs' allowing them to do all the work on the 1963 expedition is not recorded, we get an indication from a similar episode later that they took it in the "coolie" sense just suggested:

> For some time the Sherpas had been complaining that the sahibs weren't sharing the load carrying responsibilities, and they were incensed that now we had the audacity to scold them for

turning back this one time. I had been aware for some time of the Sherpas' discontent over this issue. Some of the sahibs, for example, hadn't carried all of their own personal gear to the higher camps.[26]

It seems reasonable to suppose that the problems with the oxygen tanks in 1963 were as much related to these equality issues as to conflict between Solu-Khumbu and Darjeeling Sherpas.

One more example of the Sherpas' intolerance for being treated as inferiors—and the effectiveness of their powers of resistance by this time—comes from the European Everest expedition of 1972. Despite warnings from one of the British climbers, the German leader Karl Herrligkoffer had not brought enough equipment for the Sherpas, who went on strike at base camp. There were extensive arguments, and several attempts by noninvolved climbers to mediate the conflict, but in the end the Sherpas would not back down, and—in perhaps the most extreme instance of sahib defeat on record—Herrligkoffer was forced to hire a helicopter, fly back to Kathmandu, fly from there back to Germany, and get the additional equipment. Chris Bonington, who provides the one account of this event that I have found, ascribes the essentially total breakdown partly to language barriers, but points especially to "the poor relationship which had already developed between the Germans and the Sherpas [because] the Germans tended to shout at the Sherpas and to bully them."[27]

MEGA-EXPEDITIONS

One of the factors generating hierarchical behavior among the sahibs, regardless of their personal inclinations, was the sheer size of some of the postwar expeditions. As we have seen, from early on the dominant model of the mountaineering expedition was derived from military practice. Expeditions were modeled on army campaigns, in which camps were set up and stocked with supplies at successively higher altitudes, thus forming a supply chain that would support the climbers making the final "assault" on the summit. A success on a mountain was always described as a "conquest."

Although this was the general model, the pre–World War II expeditions were relatively small and technologically simple by postwar standards. After the Second World War, however, the size and complexity of expeditions simply exploded. Partly this was a result of the tremendous validation of the military model, of "militariness," for the victorious nations—the French, the British, and the Americans. The symbols of military organization, technology, and determination in the immediate postwar period were enormously positive symbols. Even the more self-described romantic climbers found themselves swept up in this kind of language and thinking:

> General quarters! Operations! And I who would always smile at this military language when I encountered it in the Himalayan literature found myself using it in my turn! Whether I wanted to or not, the idea of a campaign, a war, imposed itself on me with more force every day.[28]

The defining expeditions of the fifties and early sixties (including the French on Annapurna in 1950, and on Everest the Swiss in 1952, the British in 1953, and the Americans in 1963) were thus enormous military-style operations. They capitalized on technological advances developed during World War II, and took a great deal of high-tech (for that time) equipment, including a full supply of oxygen, which had become more conveniently portable than had been the case earlier. They also took more supplies, as they were more committed than ever to the idea of stocking a chain of camps between base and summit on the model of a military campaign. They even took more climbers, on the theory that they needed to be assured of fresh troops for the final assault. All of this meant more porters. Probably the most strikingly visible aspect of the postwar expeditions of the fifties and sixties was an enormous train of men carrying an expedition's goods up to the mountains.

The French had four and a half tons of equipment, one and a half tons of food staples, and about two hundred "coolies."[29] There were nine sahibs and nine Sherpas. The Swiss expedition in the fall of 1952 was larger:

It was a procession of almost four hundred men—sahibs, Sherpas and Nepali porters—who set off for the mountain; and if I
have talked before of a brigade going off to war, this was like a
whole army.[30]

The successful 1953 British expedition had eight tons of equipment and provisions[31] for a party that at its largest point reached a
size of fourteen sahibs and thirty-eight Sherpas.[32] I cannot find a
specific number of porters, but the porterage for the expedition was
described as follows:

> To give some idea of the numbers involved: the first part of the
> expedition left Kathmandu on 10 March with 150 porters; the
> rest a day later with 200 porters. And they were carrying just
> the bare essentials—the main body of stores left a month later,
> again in two halves.[33]

One can also get a sense of the military nature of the expedition
from the appendixes in the book (1953) by the leader, Sir John Hunt.
There are ten appendixes, including a flow chart of the lines of authority and responsibility, a detailed "basis for planning," which
mapped out every factor to be considered and every stage of the
expedition from Kathmandu to the summit; and rosters of equipment, oxygen (with drawings of the various components of the oxygen equipment and charts of amounts of usage), diet (with menus
and amounts), and physiology and medicine; plus a table of load
contents for the assault stage of the expedition.

Finally, the 1963 American expedition had nineteen sahibs, thirty-
two Sherpas, and more than twenty-nine tons of equipment carried
by a stunning nine hundred and nine porters.[34] The large number
of sahibs was partly due to the fact that the expedition's funding
came from the National Geographic Society, which required that
the expedition have a scientific component. Thus, in addition to the
usual array of climbing sahibs, there was a physiologist, a psycholo-
gist, a sociologist, and a geologist.

There was one more mega-expedition, in the early seventies: the
famous Italian expedition, with sixty-four sahibs and seventy Sher-

pas. No number was given for porters, but loads were ferried up by helicopter. A five-room carpeted tent with leather furniture was provided for the leader.[35] But the heyday of the large, high-tech expedition was undoubtedly the fifties and the sixties, and along with this pattern went a style of masculinity that was very different from the styles that had dominated the earlier era. Where the men of the earlier era were romantic, idealistic, even mystical about mountaineering, viewing themselves and the enterprise with a kind of high seriousness that is hard to recapture today, the postwar sahibs of the fifties and sixties were a new breed that we may label, for lack of a better term, macho: loud, boisterous, jocular, hypermasculine.

Postwar machismo in Himalayan mountaineering had several strands. There was a heightened emphasis on masculine competition as a driving force in the conquest of the mountains. At the same time, there was a heightened raunchiness of interactive style and a heightened sexualization of the mountaineering enterprise (and of mountaineers as men). Both of these tendencies keyed into Sherpa equality issues, but they also had unintended consequences of their own.

POSTWAR MACHISMO I: COMPETITION

Competition is probably the most consistent strand of sahib masculine discourse in Himalayan mountaineering, running right through the entire literature from the 1920s to the 1990s. It is as if it were the base, the core, the—dare one say it—essence of Western masculinity. The only reason I situate it mainly in the fifties and sixties is that it was only in this period that it was thoroughly and totally validated; unabashed competitiveness became acceptable as almost the sole reason for engaging in the enterprise. In earlier and later periods competitiveness was offset by other, somewhat countervailing, discourses, but in the aggressive postwar years it was part of a larger authorized machismo.[36]

One of the key speakers and practitioners of the arts of competition after World War II was Sir Edmund Hillary, who shared with Tenzing Norgay the achievement of being the first to reach the top of Mount Everest. Hillary participated in a virtual lineage of competition, beginning on the 1951 reconnaissance of the mountain. Describing the very promising effort to scout a route to the top, Hillary wrote:

> Delighted with our success we [he and Eric Shipton] turned downwards and descended at great speed—Shipton and I racing each other the whole way. Although Shipton was forty-four years old he was still very fit and strong and highly competitive.[37]

And again on the triumphant 1953 expedition:

> I can remember on the third day's march pounding up the long steep hill from Dologhat and catching up with John [Hunt, the leader] and the way he shot ahead, absolutely determined not to be passed—the sort of challenge I could not then resist. I surged past with a burst of speed, cheerfully revelling in the contest, and was astonished to see John's face, white and drawn, as he threw every bit of strength into the effort.[38]

A decade later, however, Hillary was on the other side of the age relationship in comparison to Jim Fisher, then just out of the Peace Corps and not yet an anthropologist. Fisher wrote:

> The next day Ed [Hillary] and I went back up to the bridge site. Ed set a faster pace than I would normally have done, although it was not as fast as I was capable of going. I wondered what the hurry was and realized only later how competitive mountaineering can be—much more like competitive sports than I had thought. . . . I wondered if he were racing me—no, that would be absurd; why should he bother? Rather he was probably just testing himself, to see what he could handle at that stage of his life.[39]

From Hillary's point of view, in fact, competition was what got you up Everest. He had a disagreement with Shipton over what he perceived as Shipton's excessive caution:

> Shipton was far from happy about subjecting the Sherpas to [the treacherous Khumbu icefall]—it hardly worked in with the deep-seated British tradition of responsibility and fair play.

But, in my heart, I knew the only way to attempt this mountain was to modify the old standards of safety and justifiable risk. . . . The competitive standards of Alpine mountaineering were coming to the Himalayas and we might as well compete or pull out.[40]

And indeed Shipton's caution may have been one of the reasons he was, in a move that surprised many, not chosen to lead the 1953 expedition.[41] In any event, the above passage should not be read as Hillary risking Sherpa lives without risking his own; he basically was willing to do almost anything to succeed.

A figure very much in the Hillary mold, and another excellent example of this postwar machismo, was Willi Unsoeld, one of the climbers on the successful 1963 American Everest expedition. Unsoeld seemed intent on outdoing everyone on the expedition, including his climbing partner, Tom Hornbein. As described by the mountaineering historian Unsworth,

Hornbein and Unsoeld were two exceptional men. They were determined, intelligent and tough. Both were exceptionally hard goers, and when together on the mountain they not only tended to "burn off" everyone else within sight, but tried it on each other as well.[42]

Hornbein wrote in his diary,

I seemed to be going as strongly as any but the incredible Unsoeld, who appeared to have gone manically awry, threatening to demoralize the Expedition by his extreme hyper-activity, hyper-optimism, and seeming indestructibility.[43]

Unsworth continued:

He wasn't demoralizing Hornbein, as Unsoeld well knew. After one particular session when they were roped together with Unsoeld out in front going like a rocket, Hornbein cried in exasperation, "Damn it, Willi, what are you trying to do?" Unsoeld smiled and said, "Just testing you." "For what?" "Bigger things."[44]

Eventually, Hornbein and Unsoeld pulled off the first and most spectacular ascent of Everest since Hillary and Tenzing's triumph, reaching the summit via the previously unclimbed, difficult West Ridge, then crossing over and coming down the Hillary-Tenzing route.

At issue above all in postwar sahib competitiveness was individual physical superiority in relation to all others on the mountain, including the Sherpas. Early sahibs prided themselves on being morally better than the Sherpas, as having both the discipline and the "spirit" that the Sherpas were said to be lacking. While they were not unconcerned with physical strength and endurance, the emphasis on discipline and spirit was very much in keeping with their more romantic approach to the whole enterprise. By the fifties and the sixties, Sherpa discipline and spirit—that is, their willingness and ability to work long and hard, under sometimes terrible conditions, for an expedition—were no longer in question. At the same time the sahibs (the British and the Americans, at least) were less obsessed with discipline and spirit and more with sheer strength, endurance, and a kind of aggressive drive to get up the mountain at virtually any cost.

Sahibs rarely talk about physicality as such. But we do have one unusually interesting text that articulates the centrality of the well-tuned male body for mountaineering in this era. Of course the well-tuned body, male or female, matters a great deal in mountaineering in any era; the point of this text, however, is the way in which the body is both highlighted as the most important thing and linked not only to success on the mountain but also to competitive success with other men.

The text comes from James/Jan Morris, the journalist and travel writer who underwent a sex-change operation in the early sixties. Morris was the reporter for the *Times* of London who covered the triumphant 1953 Everest expedition. He wrote a relatively straightforward book about the expedition (*Coronation Everest*, 1958) as James Morris, but she also wrote about the expedition from the perspective of Jan Morris in the book about her gender transformation (*Conundrum*, 1974). The issue for Jan was precisely focused through the young male body of the climber and the sense of control it provides. We are invited to

> imagine now the young man's condition. First, he is constant against this inconstant background [of mountain weather and conditions]. His body is running not in gusts and squalls, but at a steady high speed. He actually tingles with strength and energy, as though sparks might fly from his skin in the dark. Nothing sags in him. His body has no spare weight upon it, only muscles made supple by exercise.[45]

Because of this strong and reliable body, Morris goes on to say, the male climber has a distinctive sense of control as he climbs:

> It is this feeling of unfluctuating control, I think, that women cannot share, and it springs of course not from the intellect or the personality, nor even so much from upbringing, but specifically from the body. The male body may be ungenerous, even uncreative in the deepest kind, but when it is working properly it is a marvelous thing to inhabit. I admit it in retrospect more than I did at the time, and I look back to those moments of supreme male fitness as one remembers champagne or a morning swim.[46]

And then comes the competitive payoff of all this: "Nothing could beat me, I knew for sure; and nothing did."[47]

Morris is a very interesting reflexive writer, and one could do many things with her text. For my purposes, however, I am concerned with the ways in which it articulates from an unusual angle the spirit of the fifties, when masculinity itself was founded less on things like spirit and more on the strong male body and the competitive advantages it provided against other men. This focus on physical superiority created its own vulnerabilities, however: in the context of Himalayan mountaineering it had the potential for wiping out virtually any difference between the sahibs and the Sherpas. Indeed it established the Sherpas as a source of competitive anxiety for the sahibs, which the Sherpas would occasionally exploit.

COMPETING WITH THE SAHIBS

The Sherpas have their own traditions of competition. Competition is culturally taken to be more or less intrinsic to human nature, and much of their Buddhist religion is designed to work (apparently fruitlessly, for the most part) against it. From the Sherpa point of view, reaching back into their earliest folklore, everyone—men, women, small people, big people, high lamas—competes for status and recognition, for being recognized as superior in some way or other to one's rivals. There is pain and humiliation in losing, and there is enormous pleasure in winning. A Sherpa friend talked about this with me in the sixties:

> M was talking about the fight between Z and U in which U was so badly done in . . . What was the fight about? He didn't know exactly, but anyway they were both sardars, and there was general competitiveness: When one [person] sees the other going higher, he can't stand it. There are at least three different words for competition: *balabenzin* [Nep.], like dancing or running, not very serious, good, fun, play, if you lose it doesn't matter. Then there is *tatok* [jealousy], which is bad, not really fighting, but the parties wish each other ill, if something bad happens to one, the other's happy, if something good happens, the other's depressed. *Chana* is very similar; the two latter types can be said as a single phrase (*tatok-chana*). It means always trying to have as much as the other, not being able to stand seeing the other get ahead.

Another man emphasized, in another context, that competition always takes place between relative equals. Big men always compete with other big men, and small with small; a small person would never compete with a big person. This is particularly relevant for the discussion that follows, in which Sherpa competition with sahibs appears as a way of both affirming and constructing equality.

The sahibs are big and strong; the Sherpas are small and stronger. Thinking back to Jan Morris's point about the male body, therein lies the rub. At one level the sahibs have always appreciated the

Sherpas' strength and endurance, from the earliest years of Himalayan mountaineering to the present. In an overview of Himalayan mountaineering, Cameron described the Sherpas as "a tough, resilient race, with a reputation for courage and physical strength—a Sherpa can carry a load for hours which a European can hardly lift."[48] Here is a sampling of comments from expeditions over time:

- 1924: "As often before I am lost in admiration of the servants, porters, etc., who walk 18 miles in bitter weather, get into camp and work like beavers to get their sahibs (who have ridden much of the way) fed, clothed, and housed."[49]
- 1933: Ruttledge commented on the Sherpas having "a carrying power which has to be seen to be believed."[50]
- 1952: Roch was "amazed" at the Sherpas' performance.[51]
- 1953: "Two coolies from Solu Khumbu offered to carry a double load for double pay. Who would believe, to see them trotting off, that they were each carrying sixty kilos? It's stupefying."[52]
- 1953: "Fit and strong and small in stature, [the Sherpas'] high-altitude performance without oxygen is exceptional."[53]
- 1978: "For my money—the Sherpas are supermen."[54]

Although these quotes are all in a very admiring mode, given the sahibs' extraordinary competitiveness, the fact that the Sherpas were often stronger than they were, and had greater endurance, was occasionally a source of anxiety. The Sherpas' extraordinary abilities—particularly when sharpened with mountaineering training, skills, and experience—threatened to virtually subvert the achievement of climbing the mountain. There was a nagging fear among the sahibs that it was really the Sherpas who were climbing the mountain, and largely humoring the sahibs in allowing them to think that it was their—the sahibs'—achievement. Of the 1963 American Everest expedition, the expedition scribe James Ramsay Ullman wrote:

The real job, during this phase of the climb, was being done by the Sherpas up on the Lhotse Face, and there was a glumly recurrent, though scarcely realistic, vision of their going on all the way to the top of the mountain while the sahibs cooled heels and behinds in the Western Cwm. THIRTEEN SHERPAS REACH SUMMIT OF EVEREST; AMERICANS GREET THEM ON DESCENT WITH CHEERS AND HOT TEA would be a fine message to send out to Kathmandu and the world beyond.[55]

Both the sahibs' competitiveness and their real dependence on the Sherpas thus constituted a weak point that the Sherpas would mischievously exploit from time to time. In most of the cases of outright competition between Sherpas and sahibs that we see in the literature, it was in fact the Sherpas who initiated it. Of the 1921 Everest reconnaissance, Mallory wrote:

> Unconsciously I was led into something like a race by one of the coolies who was pressing along at my side. I noticed that though he was slightly built he seemed extremely strong and active, compact of muscle. . . . I wondered how long he would keep it up.[56]

The author quoting Mallory went on to say, "[He] wasn't used to people who could keep up with him, but presumably the unknown Sherpa did, for he never mentioned the matter again!"[57]

In the 1950s, the sardar of what is thought to be the first all-Western-women's Himalayan expedition found it necessary to establish that he was faster and stronger than the memsahibs:

> There was a certain amount of tacit rivalry between the sirdar and me. He was the fitter of the two, and well he knew it, but he liked to challenge me to races which he always won, to his undisguised pleasure.[58]

On the 1969 Japanese ski expedition, Yuichiro Miura reported—as an unmistakable boast—the only example I have ever seen of a Sherpa losing the race:

One Sherpa, Ang Pema, who used to be a Gurkha soldier,[59] raced with me about halfway down, but I think he gave up, even though my pack was heavier.[60]

And in the 1970s we hear something virtually identical to what we heard from Mallory in the 1920s:

Ang Mingyur [the second cook, or kitchen boy] was carrying 80 pounds, so Langbauer stepped back to let him pass. "After you, sahib," Ang Mingyur said with a mischievous grin. "The little bastard," thought Langbauer. "I'll show him." Langbauer knew he was caught; the rest of the afternoon was a grim competition as Ang Mingyur chased Langbauer up and down hill, neither giving an inch. Ang Mingyur laughed, and Langbauer asked himself why he was racing. On the last hill, Langbauer resolved to rest at the top, competition be damned. They steamed up the trail in lock-step pace, until Ang Mingyur collapsed in laughter at the top.[61]

There is little doubt about what the Sherpas were up to in all these cases. In their own good-natured style, and within a cultural framework that defines winning races as the lightest and most pleasant kind of competition, they established themselves as operating at least in part on an equal footing with the sahibs. And while winning a race or a load-carrying competition does not constitute a transformation of "real" inequality, it is nonetheless one little piece of practice that, along with many others, large and small, was beginning to have some effect.

If one side of heightened sahib machismo in this era was organized around heightened competitiveness, the other was manifested in a heightened sexualization of the mountaineering enterprise. The sahibs moved into a more raunchy, locker-room mode of dealing with the mountain, with one another, and with the Sherpas. Yet this was a period in which, back in Solu-Khumbu, the monastic movement was campaigning for the de-eroticization of Sherpa cultural life. Before looking at the sahibs and Sherpas on this issue, we must go back to Solu-Khumbu.

THE MONKS' CAMPAIGN III: SEX

MORE MONASTERIES

As noted earlier, although mountaineering was reduced to almost nothing in the late thirties and throughout the forties, monasticism in Solu-Khumbu continued to develop. In the 1950s and 1960s there were several additional important foundings. In about 1952, the Thami married-lama community officially converted to being a celibate monastery.[62] In 1959, Serlo monastery was founded above Junbesi by Sangye Tenzing, a Solu man who took monastic vows and training at a monastery in northeast Tibet, then returned to Solu with gifts from his teacher for the purpose of starting a new monastery. As a result of his training, Sangye Tenzing had ambitious plans to institute some even "higher" forms of Tibetan Buddhist practice than were available in the other Sherpa monasteries.

In 1959, the Chinese completed their occupation of Tibet, which had begun in 1950.[63] The monks of Rumbu monastery (among many other refugees) fled en masse over the border to Solu-Khumbu. The head lama, the Zatul Rimpoche, had died in the late 1930s, the reincarnation succession was in some dispute (see Appendix B), and the monastery was operating under the leadership of the Tushi Rimpoche, a very high reincarnate whose immediate "former body" (*ku kongma*) had been the Zatul Rimpoche's teacher. After their flight from Tibet, the Rumbu monks moved several times within Solu-Khumbu, and were living in the empty buildings of a former married-lama community (at Phungmoche, in Solu) at the time of my first fieldwork, in 1966–68. In that period, the local Sherpa villagers donated land and labor to the monks and built them a new monastery in Solu, Tüpden Chöling.

All this religious activism no doubt gave another boost to the monastic campaign to clean up Sherpa popular religion, a campaign that had begun in the teens and twenties. It was through this process of making popular religious practice "higher" that the monastic ideals were moved out of the monasteries and into lay life. Of particular relevance for the present discussion were the moves against any public validation of sex and marriage. I have already discussed

16. Khumjung village elders welcoming the god Khumbila, Dumje rites, 1979.

briefly the campaign against the married lamas, mostly in terms of issues of violence. The campaign to clean up and reorganize certain major rituals presided over by the married lamas brings out further dimensions of the monastic reform campaign, in this case issues related to sex.

CLEANING UP DUMJI

We have seen that the monks viewed the married lamas as not very expert and not very powerful, and thus not very effective in their performance of rituals. A logical consequence of this view was for the monks to take over at least some of the rituals normally done by the married lamas. This was most dramatically the case with the Dumji festivals, the annual exorcisms held in all the larger village temples.

Dumji was considered absolutely essential to the welfare of the community. The gods were petitioned for the community's protection, and they were mobilized to drive all the forces of evil and impurity out of town. According to one informant, it says in the Khumjung temple charter (*chayik*) that "if Dumji isn't performed, or if the charter rules are broken, everything will go badly: people will lose everything, and they will die vomiting blood." According to another man, "The Nepalis want to stop Dumji, because they say it's too expensive, but even the kings can't stop it. If the Sherpas don't do Dumji, then all the crops will fail, everything will go wrong." A third man said that he told one Nepali that the Sherpas would stop Dumji if the Nepalis would stop Hom, the Brahmanic fire sacrifice. The Sherpa said that Hom was very wasteful, since the Hindus burned vast amounts of food. But he said that of course the Nepali said they would not stop performing Hom, just as the Sherpas would never stop Dumji.[64]

Dumji operated through a compounding series of exorcisms. The lamas first presented themselves in their most powerful and dangerous forms, as *ngawa*, or Tantric priests who control the powerful spells (*ngak*, Tib., *sngags*) that enable the defeat of demons. In this guise they did their first round of demon destruction, as they stabbed little anthropomorphic dough effigies called *linga*. In the second round, the lamas danced costumed as the gods, who had been enlisted by the lamas on behalf of the people to help the community. In the guise of the gods, they disposed of another linga. And finally, there was an exorcism in which other receptacles for the demons were prepared and then run out of town. Some of these were chopped up by representatives of the lay community, while others were simply put out with food offerings to satisfy the demons' appetites and keep them at bay. All of this was done with great drama. Some lamas danced as the embodiments of the gods, in striking masks and costumes, while other lamas kept up a steady, intense throb of music. The linga were chopped up or thrown out amidst enormous crescendos of horns wailing, cymbals clashing, and drums pounding. Everyone, from the smallest children to the oldest members of the community, got caught up in the power and excitement of these events.

From early on after the foundings of the monasteries, the monks began to insinuate that they could do a better job of Dumji than the married lamas. This can be reconstructed from later comments, after they had succeeded in taking over several of the village Dumjis. Thus, for example,

> I asked [a senior Tengboche monk] if Dumji changed after the monks took over. It got better, he said, because married lamas drink chang, and therefore the Dumji was a little "dirty" [this usually means "low status"]. The monks don't drink, so the Dumji is "cleaner."

Similarly, a senior Thami monk said:

> At that time [when the married lamas were performing the Dumji] the dancing didn't have much meaning, it was just dancing, but after [the monks took it over] it got better and better.

To say that religious rituals "do not have much meaning," that they are "just dancing," is actually quite a serious charge. These phrases are also used in contexts of discussing lamas who perform rituals that they are not actually empowered to perform, or lamas who have lost their powers through pollution. In such cases the whole thing is a sham, since such lamas cannot really contact the gods, which is what makes the whole ritual effective.[65] The effect of both the general moves to disparage the married lamas, and the specific suggestions that the monks could do a better job with Dumji, was that in the two of the largest Khumbu temples, Khumjung and Thami, the monks wound up taking over the Dumji performances, and put various changes into effect.

As a result of some rather intense politics, which I have discussed elsewhere,[66] the monks did not take over (indeed were actively kept out of) several major Dumjis in the Solu region where I did my original fieldwork, together with Robert Paul. It thus happened that, in the mid-sixties, Paul and I saw several relatively unreconstructed Dumjis.[67] From these, as well as from published accounts of earlier Dumjis in Khumbu, we can see very clearly what the monks removed when they had the opportunity: all public representations, and certainly any celebratory representations, of sex. These had been present in two different contexts of the overall Dumji performance: in several effigies used in the exorcisms, and in several comic dances.

Looking at the effigies, first, the central altar figure for the final exorcism (in the series of three) was a mud-and-dough creature with three animal heads, breasts, and a long ambiguous form hanging down to the ground between its legs. This figure, called *tonak gosum*, or "black *torma* [with] three heads," was run out of town together with some offerings at the end of this segment of the ritual. (A torma is a ritual offering cake).[68] According to some informants (mostly the married lamas), this figure represented a god being petitioned to help in exorcising the demons. According to others (mostly lay people), the figure was actually a demonic receptacle.[69] In any event, it was a powerful form distinguished among other things by having rather explicit (if complicated) sexual characteristics.

Following the exorcism involving the Tonak Gosum, which is the culmination of the Dumji texts proper, there were further exorcisms in the Solu Dumjis. One of these, which was also commonly performed after funerals, involved a mud-and-dough figure of a tiger, represented with an erect tail and two large testicles.[70] The tiger was unambiguously a receptacle into which the demons were conjured; it was eventually run out of town, accompanied by two ritual clown-type figures called *peshangba*, and violently chopped up.

In the Khumbu Dumjis that were taken over by the monks, both of these figures were removed and/or replaced. In place of the black three-headed torma exorcism, involving the figure with breasts and floor-length penis, the Khumbu Dumjis began using a *lokpar* exorcism, in which a plain three-sided offering cake (called a *lokpar torma*) was taken out of town and burned. At the same time, the exorcism with the very phallic tiger figure was no longer performed at all. In other words, all Dumji components involving sexually explicit ritual items were changed or eliminated.

The other major areas of sexual cleanup were the comic skits, which were interspersed between the main stages of masked dancing and ritual. The comic skits, most of which involved some kind of lewdness, were performed by lay people and stood in a complex counterpoint to the main ritual dances.[71] In the Zhung Dumji, the main skit was a masked dance involving a couple called Gawa and Gama, Old Man and Old Woman, who were associated with ancestral beings called Pawu and Pamu. There was also a third figure, said to be their "servant." In the version of the skit I saw in the sixties, the servant several times tried to mount Old Woman when Old Man's back was turned, and she did not seem to mind. But when Old Man turned around and saw them he beat both of them with a stick. Eventually, Old Man and Old Woman mimed intercourse together.

This skit was preceded by several rounds of prancing about by young boys in homemade masks (*tek-tek*) and cardboard phalluses, making lewd pelvic gestures. The boys were said to be (among other things) the children of Old Man and Old Woman. The whole set of performances was taken to be hilarious by the audience. In the Khumjung Dumji, after the monks took over, these acts were stopped. There was no Old Man and Old Woman dance at all, and no little boys prancing about in their *tek-tek* and jerking their hips back and forth.[72]

At the same time, new rituals, called Mani-Rimdu, were launched in the monasteries. In many ways these were very similar to Dumji, but there were important monastic changes, especially involving the representations of sex and marriage. Instead of lewd, sexually active Old Man and Old Woman and their exuberantly hip-jerking children, there were people dressed as skeletons dancing with a rag doll "baby" that appears to be sexually wounded, and that is subjected to various threats and abuses.[73] In a performance at Chiwong, there was a human couple said to be a husband and wife; their performance consisted mainly of fighting with and beating one another and, at another point, conducting funeral rites for their dead "baby."[74] There are important religious messages here, related in large part to the issues of attachment, strong feelings, and inner discipline discussed earlier, and I do not mean to reduce these rituals to violent caricatures. But the point is that there was a very dramatic campaign on the part of the monks, on several fronts, to both devalue and revalue sex, to remove it from contexts of pleasure, laughter, and the continuity of life, and to associate it with pain, loss, and death.

Yet while the monks were pushing Sherpas in this more ascetic, countererotic direction, the sahibs and the mountaineering experience were going just the other way. The sahibs in their macho, post-war mode were precisely into a more exuberantly sexualized masculinity, which took several different forms.

POSTWAR MACHISMO II: RAUNCHINESS

THE RAPE OF THE MOUNTAIN

There have always been several sexual discourses in play in mountaineering. One involves the feminization of the mountain, and the sexualization of the climber's relationship with the mountain. Here the "conquest" of the mountain is situated within an explicitly sexual, even violently sexual, scenario. The sexualization of nature, and of a certain kind of (male) relationship to nature, is a theme that can be traced quite far back into the nineteenth century, and it can be picked up in accounts of some of the earlier expeditions. For example, in the 1930s the German climber Paul Bauer had written allusively about "many a night under canvas [i.e., in tents, where] we had wrung from nature her inmost secrets."[75]

But the metaphor of climbing-as-sex, sometimes forced, appears much more frequently after World War II. Thus the historian Walt Unsworth complained of the triumphant 1953 expedition, "There might have been a more sporting ethic about the conquest of the world's highest mountains: less rape and more seduction."[76] British climber Dougal Haston wrote about climbing in the sixties on Ben Nevis in Scotland:

> If the Ben was a lady she was a true courtesan. Only practised lovers were allowed to explore her fully. Competent and enthusiastic young searchers were drawn in and taught invaluable lessons. The ignorant and fumbling were totally rejected. We went and paid our homage with old favourite lovers and were slowly accepted and became lovers ourselves.[77]

The discourse continued—and indeed often became more forceful—thereafter, and I will present a few more examples, even though they move beyond the time frame of this chapter. About the 1973 American Dhaulagiri expedition:

As for the female character of the mountain, the anthropomorphism has become automatic, its roots found in a tangle of male psychology and mountaineering tradition. The usage varies, the climbers' approach to the image is personal. [Ron] Fear's sweet lady and delicate lover is [Jim] Morrissey's siren, whore, and bitch: only the eyes of the beholder are different.[78]

The passage goes on with more of the same, culminating with:

When Roskelley started up the spur, sighing "Well, let's climb this pig," he was calling on an image not of the barnyard but of a college freshman mixer."[79]

And from the eighties:

From the beginning, Everest was a classical, mythical heroine. She was discovered from a distance by the Grand Survey of India in 1852 to be the highest mountain in the world. Once she was seen, it was her fate to suffer the human [*sic*] compulsion to find a way close to her, to touch her, then, by almost any means, to touch her summit. A casual period followed, during which other relatively easy paths were explored, until that paled; then the determination arose to probe her deeper, find secrets, test oneself against her, dare her to resist; to find her strengths, her truest, most powerful qualities.[80]

BAWDY JOKING BETWEEN SAHIBS AND SHERPAS

I will note before launching into this next part of the discussion, because I am almost always asked about this, that there is very little—as far as I know—actual sexual relations between sahibs and Sherpa women, or sahibs and Sherpa men, or among male sahibs, or among male Sherpas.[81] Some of this may, of course, have been (and may still be) going on, but there does not *appear* to be much in practice (though I did not pursue the subject in great depth), and whatever there is does not come "into discourse." What we do hear about, and what will be central to this discussion, are reports (by

17. Four climbers (*left to right*: Robert Anderson, Paul Teare, Ed Webster, and Stephen Venables) with the naked "expedition snow woman" carved in ice, American-British Everest Kangshung Face Expedition, 1988.

both sahibs and Sherpas) of male Sherpa dalliances with local (mostly Sherpa) women, and—to be discussed in chapter 7—male Sherpa dalliances with memsahibs. It is the (claimed or real) Sherpa sexual liaisons with local women, to be addressed here, that form the basis of bawdy joking between sahibs and Sherpas.

From early on, some Sherpas apparently sought sexual adventure as expeditions trekked through villages on the way to the mountain. For example, Ang Tharkay wrote of some of the Sherpas, on the walk-in to Everest in 1938, going off for the night with some "ravishing" village girls in the Tibetan town of Shekar.[82] But the fact of Sherpa sex enroute to the mountains became much more common in the fifties and sixties as the routes through Nepal allowed many more women to join up as porters, and the mega-expeditions needed so many porters that they were not picky about gender or age. Indeed, John Hunt thought that women porters were a definite bonus: they added "colour and gaiety" to the expedition, and they carried loads "as stoutly as their menfolk."[83]

Leaving aside the question of whether or not expedition Sherpas have actually been engaging in sexual relations, either with village women or female porters, there has nonetheless been a steady stream of sahib-Sherpa joking about the matter, joking that was initiated by either party on different occasions. Again, some of this dates from the prewar years. For example, on the 1938 Everest attempt, one of the climbers, Noel Odell, got lost briefly.

> The Sherpas . . . unkindly suggested that [Odell's] afternoon had been spent at a neighboring nunnery or ani-gompa, as they are called. Henceforth he was known to them as the "Gompa La Sahib," for it was in the direction of that place he had strayed. When, as not infrequently happened, he again took the wrong path, their advice to him about the right one was always accompanied by the assurance that were no nunneries in that direction.[84]

In the mid-fifties Norman Hardie trekked from Kangchenjunga to Solu-Khumbu with some Sherpa porters, both male and female. Hardie overheard some bawdy banter among the porters of a sort that traditionally took place between young, flirting; Sherpa men and women:

> Our new recruit called out a phrase frequently heard in male company, "Likpa sirki dorje." I waited to hear the women's retaliation, as I knew the meaning of the phrase, "adorned with a thunderbolt penis," applied as a nickname to a sahib on a previous expedition. A stronger remark came back from one of the women. There was general laughter.[85]

Also in the fifties the Annapurna sahibs teased Ang Tharkay about being a ladies' man,[86] and in the seventies Chris Bonington wrote about engaging in phallic banter with Sherpa men, much as Hardie heard men and women do among themselves in the fifties:

As I passed one group [of Sherpas] I yelled out, "Likpadello" (a Sherpa sexual boast meaning "my sexual organ is big"). My remark was received with roars of laughter and accompanying calls of "Likpadello" and other sallies in the Sherpa language.[87]

THE MACHO SHIFT

My overall impression as a female fieldworker in the sixties was that Sherpa men were relatively respectful of women and nonpredatory about sex. Rape, as far as I could tell, was virtually unknown, and I never heard of a Sherpa woman being either pressured or forced to have sex, or in some other way being "taken advantage of."[88] As a female fieldworker I felt perfectly safe, protected in part no doubt by my status ("person from powerful nation with official state permission to be doing research"), but also clearly by the Sherpa men's own nonpredatory attitudes.[89]

The Sherpas were hardly prudes. There was plenty of bawdy banter of the sort noted above, plenty of flirtation between appropriate partners, and plenty of sex between unmarried young men and women, although ideally it was a prelude to marriage. But all of this was supposed to be, and generally seems to have been, quite mutual. The bawdy banter was conceived of as an exchange, and the sex was always (ideally, and as far as I know, in practice) by mutual consent. Sherpa men did not seem to have a Don Juan view of women as so many notches in the belt. Starting in about the sixties, however, there seems to have been what might be called a "macho shift," an increasing tendency to view women and sexual encounters as conquests, suitable for boasting about. Although this is difficult to establish with any certainty, we can perhaps catch a glimpse of it if we look at the changing meaning and role of sexual fines on expeditions.

The fifties and sixties created what were at times coed expeditions for the Sherpas (coed sahib expeditions would not begin until the seventies). For the Everest expeditions in particular, all the local—mostly Tamang—porters would leave the expedition at the 12,000-foot-high Sherpa village (now town) of Namche Bazar, and all the portering from there to base camp (17,600 feet) would actually be done by any able-bodied Sherpa person, including large numbers of women. Some women might spend the night at base camp before returning; on some expeditions some women returned later to base camp to sell provisions and the like. The sahibs tried to establish some rules: the women were not to sleep in the men's tents. The leader of the 1965 Indian expedition, for example, felt that having women in the tents was bad for expedition discipline, and in consultation with the sardars imposed a fine of thirty rupees on any woman entering a Sherpa man's tent without justification.[90]

Yet side by side with this disciplinary model about sex on expeditions, there was another one that carried a rather different tone, one in which the men collectively rewarded themselves for sexual adventures. Thus Lt. Col. N. Kumar reported, without remarking on the contradictions, about this same Indian expedition:

> There were many other laws which [the sardar] included in the code and the funniest one was that if any Sherpa was seen mixing with any girl other than his wife he will have to pay a fine of Rs. 10/-, and if the [Sardar] or the Deputy [Sardar] was seen doing the same, he will have to pay a fine of Rs. 20/-. This had a tremendous effect in sobering the behavior of Sherpas and also built a common fund which rose to over Rs.500/- and was spent on various celebrations.[91]

This in fact became the model: have (or boast of) a series of sexual "conquests," collect a lot of "fines" (which were less punishments than public declarations), and use the money for "various celebrations." Thus on the 1969 Japanese ski expedition, the group stopped at a village where the Sherpa "girls" danced for and with the members of the expedition.

> If they didn't get back to camp by ten o'clock at night, the expedition team members had to pay twenty rupees . . . , and the Sherpas had to pay ten rupees . . . for punishment. There was a lot of payment that night.[92]

The leader, Miura, had lamented earlier that the expedition was drinking too much, stopping at every opportunity to buy the chang. Now they spent the fines on more chang and rakshi:

The men crawled out of their tents at the sound of the breakfast whistle. They all looked as if the morning were too bright. The money that was collected as a penalty was saved to buy more *chang* and *rakshi* for everybody—a vicious circle.[93]

By the mid-seventies, Chris Bonington at least had given up on the rule against women in the tents:

> Our porters [in Khumbu], most of them women ranging in age from 13 to 70, were camped in the open in the woods around us. . . . The lucky ones shared a tent with our high-altitude porters.[94]

Bonington reported as well the now familiar pattern about "fines," this time explicitly tied to sexual boasting:

> The previous night we had heard a great commotion in the cook tent, which was also the meeting place of the senior Sherpas. Purna, forever the natural leader, was organising the funding of the Sherpas' end-of-expedition party. Each Sherpa had to pay a certain amount into the kitty for every Sherpani he had slept with on the approach march. This was a sure way of making plenty of money, for very quickly the Sherpas were having to pay for their boasts of sexual prowess.[95]

In sum, relations between Sherpas and sahibs in the fifties and sixties were particularly complex and contradictory. Some expeditions were relatively egalitarian while others were not; the Sherpas sought equality through various means, and staged some major strikes when at least minimum demands for decent treatment and recognition as fellow human beings were not met.

The postwar sahibs also moved into a very macho mode of masculinity, and for both Sherpas and sahibs sexual teasing and joking became another mode of "making equality." This tended to push young Sherpa men in a more macho direction themselves, which was at least implicitly at odds with a major cultural movement at home—the monastic reform campaign, which was moving in precisely the opposite direction: toward a sharply de-eroticized ideal of life. I am inclined to think, though I certainly cannot prove it, that without the monastic counterweight, the "macho" model might have had even more impact on the Sherpas than it did. But there is no question that for some Sherpa men a kind of "conquest" model of masculinity became an option that had not been culturally salient before; monastic asceticism and Don Juan sexuality would henceforth constitute the (extreme) poles of masculinity between which Sherpa men negotiated. Few fully embraced either position, but the possibilities were clearly rewritten in this era.

COUNTERCULTURE

One of the points of this book has been to chronicle Sherpa "resistance" within the framework of the sahib game of mountaineering. I put resistance in quotes because the term seems to signal nothing more than a negative reaction—a refusal, or a demand for more of whatever is already on offer, primarily material benefits. And indeed it is the nature of power relations that the less powerful party in a relationship may not be able to do much more than try to maneuver within the established terms of the situation. Yet even the simplest act of resistance carries a deeper question about the legitimacy of the terms of the relationship between the parties. Thus, within the context of seeming to accept the general rules of the mountaineering game as set by the sahibs, the Sherpas have actually been able to accomplish much more than gaining improvements in their material circumstances (although that is not to be belittled). They have, as I will argue in this chapter, made significant advances in actually reshaping the game of Himalayan mountaineering itself, in the sense of achieving a redefinition of the terms of the sahib-Sherpa relationship. The old version of the game cast the sahibs as, precisely, "sahibs"—officers, leaders, bosses—with the Sherpas as some form or other of underlings—peons, load carriers, support troops. The new version cast sahibs and Sherpas as something closer to partners, equals, or collaborators. This shift emerged dialectically from the interplay between Sherpa resistance and sahib self-questioning. We start with the sahibs.

Seventies Sahibs

The 1970s saw the birth of the vast popular movement in the United States and Europe that came to be known as "the counterculture." As part of this, starting in the late 1960s, Nepal became probably the single biggest magnet in the world for the countercultural lifestyle.[1] Hippies from virtually every nation flocked there for the cheap living, "Eastern religion," and legal marijuana, and mountaineering itself was strongly influenced by these changes. Some individual climbers in the 1970s went further than others in identifying with the counterculture as such (Al Burgess later referred to his own "countercultural past" in talking about "Freak Street" in Kathmandu;[2] Doug Scott underwent a major lifestyle change),[3] but most were affected to some degree.

Some sahibs in the seventies became interested in the "Wisdom of the East." In earlier eras, although there was a great fascination with things "oriental,"[4] the idea of actually engaging with Asian religions in a serious way was confined to scholars and certain religious figures (such as Annie Besant, president of the Theosophical Society, who spent most of her life in India, or Alexandra David-Neel, who became deeply steeped in Tibetan mysticism and traveled in Tibet in the 1930s).[5] In the seventies counterculture, on the other hand, Asian religions became widely accepted as antidotes to the ills of Western modernity, and some of the more countercultural sahibs brought this perspective to Himalayan mountaineering. Probably the most influential of the seventies countercultural climbers was Doug Scott, who had been on a number of major Himalayan expeditions. On the 1979 Kangchenjunga expedition, for example, Pete Boardman wrote that Scott was quoting the *Chinese Yellow Emperor's Medicine Book*, and "was reading *Journey to Ixtalan* by Carlos Castenada (*sic*), underlining parts in red and clutching it like a Fundamentalist with his Bible";[6] Boardman jokingly teased Scott about being an "aging hippie."[7] Scott later used "eastern religion" language in talking about the entry of women into mountaineering, arguing that the change required expeditions to take a new approach, to "allow the feminine aspect (*yin*) to balance the male (*yang*) principle."[8]

There were also some striking continuities between the earlier romantic sahibs and the hippie sahibs of the seventies.[9] One concerned questions of bodily purity. Thus, where Maurice Wilson had fasted almost literally to death in the forties, Doug Scott in the seventies became a vegetarian,[10] and Yuichiro Miura went on a "Simian Diet" of fruits and nuts that was so austere that he began losing energy and had to give it up.[11]

We also see a resurgence and indeed an intensification of a highly romantic discourse of mountaineering similar to that heard earlier. One dimension of this was a mystical construction of the enterprise, as in Yuichiro Miura's book, *The Man Who Skied Down Everest*, in which Miura wrote of being advised in his dreams by Musashi, a "wandering philosopher-warrior of the seventeenth century."[12] Miura was in fact one of the most mystical of the great seventies climbers, writing further in a vein that could almost have come from no other era:

> I am a child of the earth, I feel a great root in the earth. I feel that I'm living proudly, and from my roots set deep in the soil, my mind expands into galactic space, predicting a quiet self-revolution within me.[13]

Or there is this from Cherie Bremer-Kamp, writing critically of the American K2 expedition in 1978, which was organized in the old "militaristic" style:

> We set out in the manner and style of old British attempts on Everest—to conquer the mountain. Or, as put more succinctly by the leader, "to knock the bastard off"—an attitude I found rather distasteful. There was no talk of probing investigation to establish a rapport with the mountain to see what she might give us in return. . . . For others more comfortable with such things, one is "in tune" with the mountain and often tempted to give it human or godlike status.[14]

Another form of the romantic discourse, reminiscent of earlier texts, stressed how the mountains allowed one to commune with one's inner self, or forced one to confront one's inner self. Miura again:

Only when I'm poised on the edge of life and death do I
fully appreciate the wonder of the human experience, the
beauty of humanity and the spontaneous pleasure of my
inner self.[15]

Similarly, the Austrian Reinhold Messner wrote in that same era:

I don't climb mountains simply to vanquish their summits.
What would be the point of that? I place myself voluntarily into
dangerous situations to learn to face my own fears and doubts,
my innermost feelings.[16]

The epigraph of his book reads: "I wanted to climb high again in
order to be able to see deep inside myself."

COUNTERCULTURAL MOUNTAINEERING

One did not have to be a hippie in one's personal lifestyle to participate in the seventies countercultural transformations. The reaction
against both prior and ongoing dominant—basically "macho"—cultural forms swept across a wide range of mountaineering culture.
First and most prominently, there was a reaction against the rape-
of-the-mountain mentality as embodied in the large military-style
expeditions. Second, some of the men sought to downplay the tremendous competitiveness we saw earlier, and some of the expedition
leaders sought to adopt a more collective, or at any rate less top-
down, style of leadership. Third, as more women began to get involved in mountaineering in this era, became self-conscious about
sexism in their attitudes toward women. And finally, the countercultural sahibs became more open to the Sherpas' point of view, and
the Sherpas were able to make some significant changes in the terms
of the Sherpa-sahib relationship.

DOWNSIZING EXPEDITIONS

The issue of how much technology was too much, how many porters
were too many, and whether or not it was sporting to use oxygen,
were subjects of debate from the very beginning of Himalayan

mountaineering.[17] Those on the side of the small and the low-tech tended to be in the minority, however, and the use of technological aids of every kind, including oxygen, proved to be irresistible up through the sixties. Expeditions took more and more equipment, and more and more porters to carry the equipment, culminating in the huge mega-expeditions of that era.

Some of the reactions began almost immediately, which is not surprising since the low-tech position had always been one strand of mountaineering culture. Thus, Steven Marcus, reviewing Sir John Hunt's account of the 1953 British Everest expedition, was appalled at the heartlessly impersonal and technologized approach to the mountain, which he saw as having been influenced by American technoculture.[18] At the same time Ed Hillary, who was of course part of that expedition, viewed the later Italian mega-expedition—that of the helicopters and the five-room carpeted tent—as having much more egregiously sinned on the technology question. He called the expedition "the height of the ridiculous."[19] With the seventies, however, came a much broader shift of discourse and, more importantly, of practice in the matter of technology. So-called Alpine-style mountaineering, in which equipment was reduced to a minimum, virtually all of it carried by the climbers themselves, and in which the effort was essentially to sprint up the mountain as quickly as possible, began to come in, championed particularly by the Austrian Reinhold Messner.[20] Messner rocked the mountaineering world by taking a very small and lightly equipped expedition to Everest in 1978, and reaching the summit for the first time without oxygen, thereby setting standards for a kind of purity of climbing from which there was no turning back.[21]

In that same decade some Norwegian mountaineers founded a "school of thought . . . called Frijluftsliv, which called for . . . a more environmentally sensitive approach to the mountains."[22] One of the Norwegians told Peter Boardman,

> We have only natural fibre equipment—we have no nylon clothing, and very little steel or aluminium. We want to get away from the techno-culture. . . . The gap between man and nature is getting wider, and we want a reunion.[23]

THE REACTION AGAINST
COMPETITION

In the seventies, some reaction also emerged against the macho competitiveness among climbers that was so prevalent in the fifties and sixties. For example, the Norwegians of the Frijluftsliv school "called for a less competitive attitude to climbing."[24] And Pete Boardman was clearly upset by competitiveness among his fellow climbers on expeditions. With reference to the 1979 Kangchenjunga expedition, he wrote rather bitterly:

> Outward Bound, and other outdoor-education philosophies would have one believe that mountain climbing develops character, courage, resourcefulness and team work. That may be so, but it is also true that mountaineering expeditions can develop selfishness, fanaticism, glory-seeking and cunning. At Camp I we played the opening rounds of a half-serious game that was to develop throughout the expedition—"High Altitude Manoeuvring." The main aims of this game are personal survival, self-image survival, personal success and personal comfort. The first rule is not to be seen playing by the others.[25]

Boardman's reaction was clearly in a seventies mode: he disapproved of competition in principle. His criticism was thus different from Hornbein's complaints about Willi Unsoeld in the sixties, where the problem with Unsoeld's competitiveness was that he always won and thus demoralized the other men.

These kinds of reactions to competitiveness were not widespread, at least in the literature that I have been able to find.[26] In fact it does not seem that competition on the large expeditions noticeably decreased, which is why these few critics were complaining about it in the late seventies and early eighties. What does seem to have happened is that those climbers who disliked the competitive atmosphere of large expeditions increasingly had the option of withdrawing to smaller, Alpine-style climbs, composed of groups of friends with much better prospects for mutual support and cooperation.

MORE COLLECTIVE LEADERSHIP STYLES

Although there was always a good deal of variation in the personal style of individual expedition leaders, at the same time there was general acceptance that an expedition, especially a large one, needed relatively clear-cut lines of authority and relatively firm leadership in order to have any chance of success. It was part of countercultural thought in the seventies, however, that any kind of hierarchical structuring of authority relations was problematic, and that if at all possible decisions should be reached democratically and even collectively. Thus we see a more collectivist or at least "sensitive" type of leadership in the seventies, with very mixed results in the mountaineering context.[27]

On the 1973 American Dhaulagiri expedition, for example, a "loose easy relationship of general participation and accountability was evolving under Morrissey's leadership, and we wanted to keep it that way."[28] The authors also later described the Sherpas as being "baffled by our lengthy discussions; in their experience, expedition leaders did not tolerate collective decision making."[29]

On the 1978 Annapurna women's expedition, collectivist leadership worked less well. The expedition had a great deal of trouble reaching decisions, and there were endless meetings that, for anyone who remembers this sort of thing from political activism in that era, are very painful to read about. The leader, Arlene Blum, felt trapped: "Here was the essential paradox again. I was supposed to be the leader and decide what was going to happen, yet everyone wanted decisions to be made democratically."[30] At the same time, she found it hard herself to exercise firm leadership, which she attributed to her female socialization: "Although my upbringing and experience had taught me to be moderate and soothing, I was learning the hard way that these traits are not always compatible with effective leadership."[31]

One of the most effective expedition leaders of the 1970s was Chris Bonington. Bonington led many important expeditions in that era, but the most famous was probably the 1975 Everest expedition to the hitherto unclimbed Southwest Face. At one level this was still a mega-expedition; there were eighteen sahib members, four more sahibs on a BBC television team, and "a Sherpa team of 82 including Tamangs and Gurkha soldiers."[32] Yet Bonington, who in many ways stood on the cusp between the two eras, knew the old forms of authority were no longer likely to be effective: "I don't think the old military style of leadership can possibly work."[33] He thus described his leadership style as a kind of high-wire act between firm leadership and collective decision making. On the one hand, he wrote, "I don't think there's any danger of us ever having leadership by committee." On the other hand:

> Of course, though, if there is a strong consensus against what I say, this is going to emerge in a troublesome sense later on, and I think this is where I've got to be very receptive to the feelings of the team so that I can effectively sell them my ideas and make them feel and believe that these are ideas they have taken part in forming.[34]

Finally he noted, "At the same time I must draw ideas from their combined experience and not be afraid to change my own plans if other suggestions seem better."[35] Aside from the unfortunate death of one of the members, the expedition was considered a model of good planning, organization, and relations and did in fact succeed.

It is worth looking for a moment at an expedition in that era where relatively hierarchical and relatively collective styles of leadership clashed. The 1976 expedition to Nanda Devi split over a whole range of issues salient in that era. One party, led by John Roskelley, felt the mountain was too difficult, and the range of talent in the group too mixed, to have anything but a traditional military-style expedition. (He said he would personally have preferred an Alpine-style ascent with a small group of friends of equal abilities, but this was not the situation of the expedition.) The other party, headed by Willi Unsoeld, by that time about fifty years of age, wanted a more Alpine-style expedition, with relatively small amounts of equipment and a more aesthetic approach to the mountain. The group as a whole wound up compromising on the amount of supplies and equipment they took—not enough for a big expedition, but more than was needed for an Alpine-style ascent—which created bad conditions (both material and interpersonal) almost from the outset.

In addition the group included several women, including Marty Hoey, a strong and experienced climber, and Nanda Devi Unsoeld (named after the mountain), Willi's daughter, who was relatively inexperienced. Roskelley objected to both women—to Hoey because she was part of a couple and he felt that couples subverted the group, to Nanda Devi Unsoeld because she was inexperienced. Roskelley was viewed as extremely sexist,[36] which was another element in what turned out to be the ongoing conflict on the expedition.

And finally there were issues of leadership. The expedition was originally supposed to have had two coleaders, Ad Carter (by then sixty-two years old), who had been on the first successful climb of the mountain, and Willi Unsoeld. For reasons that are unclear in Roskelley's account, Carter left the expedition early and Unsoeld became the sole leader. Unsoeld, however, despite his highly competitive style in 1963, turned out to be an ambiguous leader. Although he was not exactly collectivist in a seventies mode, he was nonetheless a rebellious individual who was resistant to both taking and giving orders.[37] Roskelley complained early on that the team was disunified and that no one was taking responsibility for basic organizational needs. Unsoeld replied:

"I don't feel strong leadership is essential with a group of people as experienced as this. We're not two-year-olds who need a mother, but adults capable of making our own decisions. I don't feel that we should have to hold your hand." He recalled the 1963 Everest Expedition where he felt the leadership had been too overbearing and there had been some conflict because of it.[38]

Yet it was Unsoeld's lack of firm leadership, Roskelley strongly implies, that caused serious, and ultimately fatal, problems on the expedition. For example, Marty Hoey became extremely ill with altitude sickness, and the expedition doctor said that her life was in danger if she did not immediately descend. Unsoeld, however, would not make the decision to order her back down, and instead insisted that he wanted her to make the decision on her own, which she was in no condition to do. She almost died before having to be carried down the mountain; she did survive in the end.[39] On the other hand, Unsoeld's daughter, Nanda Devi, did die later of altitude sickness in a high camp, and Roskelley implicitly blamed Unsoeld's poor judgment and weak leadership. Though Roskelley and two climbing partners eventually summitted, in what was considered a brilliant piece of climbing,[40] Roskelley was later ostracized by the climbing community for what was considered his gross insensitivity about the Unsoeld tragedy.[41]

Willi Unsoeld did not actually speak any seventies-style rhetoric about collective decision making. His casual leadership style, which evidently grew out of different convictions, nonetheless fit easily in with various new trends in mountaineering: the participation of women on expeditions, and a desire for a more aesthetic approach to climbing. One has the feeling that he backed the Alpine-style group not only because it included his daughter, but because his sympathies could so easily link up with the seventies countercultural issues. Roskelley, on the other hand, was very much in the fifties and sixties macho mode—antiwomen in the man's world of climbing, focused on his own physical strength and skills, and highly competitive. The clash on the mountain in the mid-seventies was virtually inevitable.

THE ENTRY OF WOMEN: SEVENTIES SEXISM AND SENSITIVITY

Although there had been women climbing in the Himalayas earlier, it was only in the seventies, in relation to the emergence of the feminist movement, that women entered the sport in significant numbers. There were both coed expeditions, like the Nanda Devi one just discussed, or the 1976 American Bicentennial expedition; there were also all-women's expeditions, like the 1975 Japanese women's expedition that put the first woman, Junko Tabei, on the summit of Everest, or the 1978 Annapurna women's expedition led by Arlene Blum, discussed briefly earlier. (I will have much more to

say about all this in the next chapter, which will be entirely devoted
to the "woman question," but I introduce it here to consider the
ways in which it entered into the sahibs' countercultural perspectives in the seventies.)

In some cases, the reactions of male climbers to the entry of
women were largely negative—resistant, hostile, threatened. Indeed, the seventies produced some of the most intensely sexist rhetoric of the whole century—something I was at first surprised to dis-
cover in the reading and then realized that it made sense: women
seemed to be, and in many ways were, challenging the whole social
contract of gender relations, and this was indeed very provocative
at the time.

At the same time a more "sensitive" discourse also began to appear
in the mountaineering literature. By sensitive discourse in the gender arena, I mean a discourse that recognizes the importance of men
monitoring their own machismo, and of making a conscious attempt
not to slight women. Two climbers who spoke a relatively "sensitive"
language about women in this era were Peter Boardman and Ned
Gillette. Peter Boardman, who was critical of the competitiveness
among male climbers, also wrote about struggling with his own traditionally gendered impulses, in the context of climbing with his
wife, Hilary:

> I was becoming angry with Hilary, the mountain, the rain and
> wind and myself. I tried to rationalise and channel my frustra-
> tion into energy. . . . "Why does she always seem to move so
> slowly when the going gets rough? Why do I shout at her and
> long for an equal? I'd never do that to any other climbing part-
> ner—it's unfair, it's not that serious a situation."[42]

Ned Gillette and his wife, Jan Reynolds, were former Olympic
cross-country skiers. They undertook a major trek/climb/ski expedition around Mount Everest in 1982, and wrote a joint book about
it.[43] Their book was clearly an attempt to create even textual equality, consisting of excerpts from both of their diaries and sections
alternately written by each of them. Reynolds was explicitly feminist
in her expectations of equality on the expedition, and critical of dis-

plays of male dominance.[44] And Gillette struggled, as Boardman did, with his own tendencies to either dominate his wife or to slight her. The couple had met an old (male) climbing friend, and Ned started to move ahead with him:

> "Hold on," Jan shouted. "No way can I move that fast in this light."
>
> "Just stay on the stream," I yelled back. "If we head off it, I'll wait." I took a couple of steps forward. Craig was moving on rapidly.
>
> "Okay, big man. Go with Craig."
>
> I stopped, frozen in place by Jan's desperately disappointed tone. She came closer, and I could see that her face was set and pale. Those were more than words of complaint; they were words that asked for simple consideration and companionship. I shut down my adrenaline pump and walked beside her.[45]

Nothing like this kind of gender reflexivity had appeared in the earlier mountaineering literature; it must be said, however, that one does not find much more in this vein. The point is not that "machismo" disappeared, but that it became problematized in this period.

Summarizing the counterculture of the seventies within the mountaineering context, we may say that, in a wide range of ways, the sahibs pulled back from the unalloyed machismo of the fifties and sixties. Some sahibs underwent real personal changes characteristic of that era—engaging with (some usually imaginary version of) "Eastern religions," taking up (mostly soft) drugs, or adopting vegetarianism or other bodily purification regimes.

With respect to the actual practice of mountaineering, the most visible and durable change was the decline of the large, military-style expedition, and the rise of Alpine-style climbing in the Himalayas. This kind of climbing had its own macho implications, but at the same time it clearly arose at the time it did from a reaction to the technologism and militarism of the earlier expeditions, which appeared to have thrown in their lot with modernity after all.[46]

We may characterize sahib culture in the seventies as relatively more "sensitive" than in the preceding era, and in some ways closer to the romanticism and mysticism of the prewar sahibs. All of this in turn resonated through the sahib-Sherpa relationship. Before we get to that, however, we must consider the situation of the Sherpas themselves, within their own home contexts.

THE DEVELOPMENT OF SOLU-KHUMBU

Starting in the early sixties, and continuing up to the present, the Sherpa region of Solu-Khumbu began to undergo a set of changes specifically linked in one way or another to the Sherpas' involvement with mountaineering. This is not to say that the region would have otherwise remained unchanged, but that both the form and the pace would have been different.

The first visit by Westerners to the Solu-Khumbu region was the so-called Houston-Tilman expedition in 1950. Houston wrote:

I remember vividly walking with Bill [Tilman] through the autumn gold, reflecting on what we had seen [in Khumbu], and what damage we and others like us might have set in train for this innocent, backward, beautiful country. We were all sad, knowing we were witnessing the end of something unique and wild, and the beginning of a period of great danger and immense change.[47]

The author, Ian Cameron, who quoted this passage in his history of mountaineering, described the Houston-Tilman expedition as "like a walk through Eden before the fall."[48]

Up through the early sixties, there were very few foreign visitors to the area. However, Sir Edmund Hillary had returned to the region several times after the 1953 expedition, and in 1960 he was back with a group interested in solving the mystery of the *yeti*, or "abominable snowman." Hillary wanted to borrow the "yeti scalp" in Khumjung village and take it back to the West to be studied by the scientific community. The villagers requested some sort of compensation for risking its loss, and Hillary asked them what they would like.[49] As the story is always told, a climbing Sherpa named Urkien said that what they needed above all were schools.[50] Hillary

18. Sir Edmund (Ed) Hillary on the 1963
Schoolhouse expedition.

went home and founded a nonprofit organization called the Sherpa
Trust (later the Himalayan Trust), and set about raising funds for
building Sherpa schools. The first one was in the village of Khumjung, where most of the climbing Sherpas had come from. It was
built in 1961.[51]

Hillary was immediately besieged with petitions from other
villages with requests for more schools, as well as for other local
needs such as new roofs for temples. In 1963 there was a second
"schoolhouse expedition," which built the schools at Thami and
Pangboche, and in 1964 a third. Present on the 1964 expedition was
Jim Fisher, on loan from the Peace Corps, who has since written an
invaluable book about that expedition and the subsequent unfolding
of changes in the region. These changes were many and varied, in-

cluding the spread of literacy as a result of the schools; the elimination of goiter and cretinism as a result of the introduction of iodine into the diet; a drop in the birth rate as a result of the introduction of contraceptives and surgical sterilization; and various changes in the national political system that brought the Nepali state more intimately into Solu-Khumbu than had been the case before.[52]

Of special importance for the present discussion was the building of an airstrip, at a site called Lukla in 1964, which "shortened the travel time from Kathmandu to Khumbu from two weeks to forty minutes."[53] According to Fisher, who essentially organized the project from beginning to end, the airstrip was originally built to make it easier for Hillary to bring in supplies for building the hospital in Kunde. But as Fisher goes on to say, "Our hardheaded intention . . . seems naive in retrospect. Neither [Hillary] nor I had the remotest inkling that the airstrip would soon become a major conduit for tourists and would spark a burgeoning, radically new industry in Khumbu."[54]

The number of foreign visitors to the region went from twenty in 1964, when the airstrip was built, to thirty-five hundred in 1974.[55] And here we connect with both my own field experiences and the issues of this chapter. Robert Paul and I first worked in the lower Sherpa valley of Solu in 1966, and saw only a handful of foreign visitors.[56] When I went back with a crew to make a film for Granada television in 1976, one field note entry reads (with all underlines in the original): "We trekked from Thami to Lukla in 2 days. There were a *million* tourists. Both the trail and Lukla itself were *awful*, essentially *polluted* with tourists."[57]

The impact of tourism on Solu-Khumbu has been enormous, and has sparked an industry of research and recommendations.[58] In particular, there has been great concern about the impact of tourism on the environment, including especially issues of deforestation, as the tourists burn large amounts of firewood.[59] It was in response to these problems that a decision was implemented to have the Solu-Khumbu region declared a national park, which could then be environmentally regulated. The Sagarmatha (Everest) National Park was created amidst a swirl of local rumor and politics, with some complex and highly contested participation of Hillary and the Himalayan Trust, to which I was privy in 1976 while on the Granada film expedition. Subsequent scholarship has examined not only the impact of the tourists but of the National Park itself.[60]

Less noted, at least in a positive vein, was the enormous economic boom that the influx of tourism created in Khumbu. Fisher describes the ways in which tourist and mountaineering expeditions have created spectacularly large incomes for the many Sherpas who have worked for them;[61] he points out as well that "incipient class differences are emerging as a new 'tourist Sherpa' class begins to develop. This nouveau-riche group is distinguished by the novel source of wealth at its disposal . . . and the ostensibly different life-style it can buy."[62] This class, in fact, is a "class" in a stricter sense as well, since in addition to a difference of lifestyle, there is actual exploitation involved in maintaining its position:

> Beginning in the spring of 1974, Khumbu Sherpas began hiring Solu Sherpas in large numbers to work their fields while they themselves went off to pursue more lucrative trekking jobs. In 1978 a majority of the households in Khumjung-Khunde had at least one servant, paying them Rs 6 per day plus food for their labor while they themselves earned trekking wages and pocketed the difference.[63] By 1988 the vast majority of load carriers in Khumbu were from Solu, as Khumbu Sherpas, typically keeping one step ahead, opened more lodges or worked in managerial, or "front-office," trekking jobs.[64]

All of this points to the fact that for at least some Sherpas involved in climbing and trekking there was a major economic takeoff. In addition, there was the development of an industry catering to tourism within Khumbu itself. Hundreds of little, and some big, tea shops, lodges, hotels, rest houses, and the like sprang up. A few were started by foreign investors, who no doubt took most of the profits out of the country with them, but most of them were owned and operated by Sherpas, and some of those were quite large and profitable. Reporting on conditions in 1978 in the town of Namche Bazar, Fisher wrote that about twenty-five shops and hotels had been opened by "Namche entrepreneurs," and that "more establishments [were] springing up all the time."[65]

In addition, certain kinds of infrastructural enterprises developed to support the lodge industry. One particularly welcome development was the emergence of commercial farming of fruits and vegetables for the tourists. Another of my field notes from 1976:

> Yesterday afternoon [we trekked] along the rocky *Pharak* area [the middle area, along the Dudh Khosi, between Solu and Khumbu] of Chaunrikarka. It seems to be doing very well economically, probably since the Lukla airstrip got going. Many new big houses, more into colored painted window frames and designs—very pretty ... And flowers ... And the biggest change—vegetable gardens, as cash crops. Cauliflower, cabbage, carrots, peas, beans.

When I returned in 1979 to do the fieldwork for *High Religion* (1989a), I lived (mostly) in Khumbu but had a vegetable *teka* ("contractor") from Pharak who delivered fresh vegetables to me on several occasions.

My point again is that Khumbu in the seventies was booming, and climbing Sherpas had a strong sense of there being far more money in circulation, and particularly an enrichment of people who formerly would have been "smaller", thus leveling off wealth differences in the area to some extent (even if new differences were emerging). One man who worked for us on the Granada film expedition in 1976 was talking about this casually one day:

> Phu Tharkey said Namche has gotten very rich. But he made a point of saying that anyone can get rich now—everyone is *khamu* ["expert," literate, educated], everyone goes to school— so who's rich, who's poor, we don't know any more. Before there were a few big people and everyone knew who they were, and you bowed and scraped to them, but now it's more equalled out.[66]

This, then, is the context—of rising wealth, rising education, and more widespread opportunity for economic advancement—from which Sherpas in the seventies were participating in expedition

work. Between the softening of the sahibs as part of the counterculture, and the real successes of the Sherpas both on expeditions and
in their home context, the way was paved for major shifts in at least
some of the terms of the Sherpa-sahib relationship.

A Crack in the Discourse

I began this book with the sahibs' "Orientalist" views of the Sherpas,
including the idea that the Sherpas were simple, natural, and childlike. Part of this view was the notion that the Sherpas, as innocent
natural people, were not primarily climbing for money. It will be
recalled, for example, that the leader of a 1929 expedition wrote that
the Sherpas "followed us to the last man in desperate places, with
. . . no thought of payment, but . . . purely from ethical motives,
from noble natural instincts."[67]

After the Second World War, there was still an insistence that the
Sherpas were not climbing primarily for money, although this was
based less on the kind of paternalism prevalent among the early sahibs,
and more on the idea that Sherpas actually shared the sahibs' motives
and desires about climbing. About the Sherpas on the 1963 American
Everest expedition, for example, James Ramsey Ullman wrote:

> *It was not primarily for pay* that they were on that march. No
> less than the Western mountaineers who employed them, they
> were doing what they wanted to do, what they were born to
> do. They were not hired help but *companions in adventure.*[68]

In that same era, the leader of the 1962 Indian Everest expedition
wrote:

> Naturally, they had joined us to earn money, but as member
> and Sherpa got to know and understand each other, *money took
> a secondary place*: there was team-spirit, love and understanding.
> Looking back at one's Sherpa rope-companions grinning up
> under any condition, one cannot help but feel that *mountains
> matter to these people as much as money.*[69]

Summarizing somewhat schematically, early sahibs believed that
Sherpas were willing to take the risks of climbing largely because of
loyalty to their sahibs; fifties and sixties sahibs believed that Sherpas

climbed because they shared the sahibs' romantic and adventurous desires to climb. Both minimized the Sherpas' interest in money or questioned what money might mean to the Sherpas. No one seems to have considered the possibility that money might mean something different to them, carrying more positive values than it did to upper-middle-class sahibs who did not need to worry about it, or who indeed rejected the "materialism" of modern life. Here, then, we must return to questions of the "real."

THE SHERPAS CLIMBED FOR MONEY I:
ETHNOGRAPHIC REALISM

I have already indicated that early Sherpas, in spite of what the sahibs thought, climbed largely for reasons of money. Not all of them were poor, or as they would say, "small," but their traditional economic system made it difficult to get rich and easy to get poor. Moreover, climbing mountains had no indigenous value whatsoever, and indeed was religiously problematic.

I state all of this flatly as objective fact. Yet, if we acknowledge that anthropologists can be as biased as mountaineers or any other observer, why should this "fact" be accepted as such? Here I must make a brief case for "ethnographic authority." The reason for accepting a relatively strong truth value for anthropological claims can only be in terms of the practice of ethnography itself, a practice committed to understanding the point of view of another, and— more importantly—a practice organized to gain such an understanding. There can be, of course, no guarantees that such understanding is achieved in any given case. But it is the conditions of ethnographic fieldwork—long periods of time living with people; speaking, however, imperfectly, their own language; engaging with them in the things that matter in their lives—that significantly enhances the chances of actually knowing something "real."

This is not the place for a long disquisition on the epistemological foundations of knowledge gained through ethnographic fieldwork. Nor am I making a claim that one should believe everything anthropologists write; far from it. But I would still insist rather strongly that fieldwork makes a difference, and thus that there is still a good reason why anthropologists are more likely to say something real or true about the people they study than more casual observers. At issue are both the length and the depth of the relationships established, as well as the relative openness of the perspective with which those relationships are approached.

But there is one particular difference between older and newer ethnographic work that must be emphasized here: the contemporary insistence on the importance of social differences in the community under study. Older ethnographies tended to genericize, to override social difference in favor of cultural homogeneity: in such accounts, what was interesting about the Sherpas (or any other group treated that way) was all the ways in which they were different from "us" (i.e., the presumed Western reader). In contrast, while I remain committed to fieldwork in the classic sense, and to the hopefully rich understanding of the point of view of other people that such fieldwork is designed to produce, it is a fieldwork that is attuned to social differences within the community, and to the sense that there is in fact no single "Sherpa point of view." Within the position I am taking here, then, what further enhances the truth value of ethnographic claims is their specificity in terms of the subject positions and the historical moments to which they are attached: Men or women? Old or young? Rich or poor? Now? When?

Armed with all this, then, let us return to some ethnographic claims about the Sherpas and money. Anthropologists first began to do ethnographic work with Sherpas in the 1950s and 1960s. Where the mountaineers had been saying that the Sherpas did not primarily climb for money, anthropologists constructed a very different picture of the situation. In conversations with Sherpas, and in looking into the structures of inequality in Sherpa life, it was immediately clear that the primary reason Sherpas went into mountaineering and related work was for the money it paid, and the entailments of that money: material satisfactions, freedom from dependency relations, participation in a wider and more cosmopolitan world. The first ethnographer of the Sherpas, Christoph von Fürer-Haimendorf, tended largely to downplay differences and difficulties within the Sherpa community. Nonetheless, he clearly recognized that many young Sherpas went into climbing because their alternative was to enter into debt and local dependency relations.[70]

19. Mingma Tenzing Sherpa holding a sun reflector for interior filming at Thami monastery, Granada Film Expedition, 1976.

The theme was sounded again in my 1977 film, *Sherpas*. In this the sardar Mingma Tenzing spoke of the financial hardship caused when he was not able to get climbing work, and of how working for anthropologists (including myself) did not pay well enough to compensate for the loss of mountaineering wages:

And then for a number of years I didn't go climbing. . . . I did a lot of trekking work and anthropology work. And after that I went back to climbing. Because when I went to do anthropology work, they didn't give any clothes, and they didn't pay very much. And I had a wife and children, and so I went back to expeditions. On expedition work, one makes more money, and so I went back to climbing.[71]

His wife also said in the film, "Expedition work is very difficult, but Sherpas have no other way of making money. There's no trade. If they don't go on expedition work, they don't earn any money."[72]

Shortly after that film was made, Jim Fisher interviewed climbing Sherpas in more detail, and heard the same story yet again:

> Eight of Khumbu's most experienced and illustrious sardars unanimously agreed that virtually the only reason they climb is that they need the high income they cannot earn any other way.... Sherpas see no intrinsic point in climbing: neither fame (though that is welcome since it helps them get their next climbing job more easily; it also accounts for the multiple ascents of Everest), nor challenge, nor adventure. Climbing is simply a high paying job. (Fisher 1990, 129)

Finally, my own 1990 interviews with climbing Sherpas did little to change this picture. Although I found a handful of individual Sherpas who had occasionally climbed for sport (mostly when they went abroad to visit sahib friends), in general most Sherpas still said they would not carry loads or risk their lives if they had better ways to make the same kinds of money.

Of course, there have always been individual exceptions to these assertions. Tenzing Norgay was one such exception, which may have fueled the fantasies of the fifties sahibs about the Sherpas sharing their romantic motives. From all accounts, including his own autobiographies, Tenzing had a certain burning drive to get to the top of Everest that was similar, if not actually identical, to the sahibs'.[73] More recently, some other Sherpas, who expressed enthusiasm for climbing for sport, have moved in this direction as well. But the numbers are tiny, and these Sherpas tend to come (like the sahibs) from the relatively privileged sectors of Sherpa society, who do not need to make a living from climbing.

As I have stressed throughout, money has a certain range of meanings. Many of these meanings are common to both the Sherpas' and the sahibs' understandings of money, including things like security, freedom, comfort, status, power, and generosity. Perhaps the biggest difference historically, and the one most relevant to the present discussion, is that for many Sherpas, money largely carried a positive charge, as a means of buying into modernity-as-freedom, while for many of the more romantic or countermodern

sahibs, money was largely—if ambivalently—negative, part of mo-
dernity-as-corruption.

Two points are being made here. First, to say that money has a
range of meanings is to say that the Sherpas' motives are not "materialist" in any simple sense; the need for money embodies complex
desires, and the Sherpas do not seek money merely to eat or to get
rich. Indeed this is true for most people in most times and places:
money as a motive is never a simple one. At the same time, the
structure of the sahib-Sherpa relationship, and the degree to which
the Sherpas served as a field of Orientalist projection for the sahibs,
has meant that the Sherpas' motives with respect to money have
remained particularly obscure.

Starting in the mid-seventies, however, the sahibs (and not just
the anthropologists) began to assert that the Sherpas were in it for
the money. These assertions took different tones—the sahibs were
saddened, or disillusioned, or simply realistic. But the idea cropped
up very consistently in the mountaineering and trekking literature,
and represented a noticeable shift in the discourse.

THE SHERPAS CLIMBED FOR MONEY II:
SAHIB PERCEPTIONS

The idea that the Sherpas climbed largely for money was often represented with some anguish. For example, Rick Ridgeway, on the
1976 American Bicentennial Everest expedition, had a series of almost desperate conversations with Sherpas on the expedition, hoping to find that the rumors were not entirely true, and that most
Sherpas were not climbing largely for money after all. The Sherpas
were polite but honest. Ridgeway wrote:

> Several times I had asked Ang[74] why he had such a desire to
> climb Everest, and each time he only laughed at the question,
> as if he didn't fully understand it. . . . I would not completely
> dismiss the possibility of self-seeking and even perhaps a pecu-
> niary element in Ang's motives. . . . I was still hoping, though,
> to find, if not in Ang, then at least in some of the Sherpas . . .

love for Everest... Did not some of the Sherpas these days have these feelings for the mountains?[75]

Ridgeway asked another Sherpa the same questions, still hoping to find some who loved what they were doing, but again he was disappointed:

"Nima, do the Sherpas like working on expeditions, or if you could get it, would you guys prefer some other kind of job?"

"Oh, I think if Sherpas have money, they prefer to stay home with wife and children. Expedition job very dangerous, but that is why we get paid much money."

The conversation went on:

"Nima, if climbing is so dangerous, why do you think we like to do it?"

"I don't know. You know, Sherpas talk about that a lot. Maybe you people have too much money, and you don't know how to spend . . ."

"But doesn't it seem strange to spend your holiday, and a lot of money, doing something very difficult and dangerous?"

Nima laughed. "Well, if you want to know what we think, we think it is kind of silly. But you people seem to like it."[76]

Ridgeway's framing of the point in terms of "Sherpas these days" signals a larger theme (to which I will return in chapter 9), the idea that present-day Sherpas have been spoiled or corrupted by modernity. Many of the sahibs, however, took a much more factual tone in the matter of recognizing the Sherpas' money motives. One American trekker wrote:

So why do they climb? Every Sherpa I asked gave the same answer. "I like going climbing. Well, if you get killed it's not good, but if you don't, you make a lot of money, more money than you can make anywhere else."[77]

In this same matter-of-fact mode, other sahibs in the seventies described the Sherpas with adjectives that almost never appeared in the earlier mountaineering literature. The Sherpas were said to be very "practical,"[78] "astute and business-minded,"[79] and "innovative [and] adaptive."[80]

Much of this discourse may have originated with Chris Bonington, who in addition to being a brilliant climber, leader, and expedition entrepreneur, seems to have read some of the anthropology of the Sherpas, and to have spent some time talking to his anthropologist-climber friend Mike Thompson, who himself had studied the Sherpas. Thompson is the one who had talked about the link between the Sherpas' involvement in trade and their friendly outgoing style. In 1976 Bonington wrote:

> Living close to the passes into Tibet, the Sherpas have always been traders as well as farmers. As a result they have a shrewd business sense and entrepreneurial spirit. . . . They understand the worth of money. . . .[81]

Later in the book he asserted that the Sherpas' primary motive in climbing was to make money:

> This might sound very mercenary, but then it must be remembered that in helping the expedition in return for payment, the Sherpas are no different from any other employees on a daily wage, though—in common with an ordinary factory worker in Britain—they need more than just money to command their enthusiasm as well as obedience.[82]

While we may quibble with parts of Bonington's views—the Sherpas are probably more petty entrepreneurial than proletarian; and there is a goodly whiff of paternalism in the idea of "command[ing] their . . . obedience"—his ideas nonetheless represent a major departure from the orientalism of the earlier era. The Sherpas are deromanticized; Bonington clearly hears what they are saying; and in fact he followed the practical implications of his talk: he always paid them very well.

Let me be clear about the point here. The idea that emerged among climbing sahibs in the seventies, that the Sherpas climbed for money rather than for love of sahibs or of mountains, represented—I am arguing—an accurate recognition of a Sherpa point of view that had not been heard earlier. (It was distinct from the idea that the Sherpas had become spoiled and materialistic *as a result of* mountaineering, a view that will be discussed later.) My question here has been, what allowed the sahibs to hear more accurately or, to turn the point around, how did the Sherpas finally make themselves heard? The answer has been at least partly in terms of countercultural transformations in the seventies. Although this counterculture subsequently collapsed, and although there has been a great deal of rewriting of seventies cultural history, it is worthwhile recalling that in that period young, educated, middle-class people—the same class that gave us the sahibs—did open up questions of hierarchy and domination on a broad scale, and did in fact try to be "sensitive" to those less powerful than themselves. Many mountaineers were clearly affected in one way or another by the cultural changes of the era, and I am inclined to think that at least some sahibs became genuinely open to hearing "the Sherpa point of view."

This is not to negate the effects of fifty years of Sherpa resistance in Himalayan mountaineering—the strikes, the arguments, the demands, the tactful management of sahibs—that I have been at pains to document. It is only to say that such resistance in the 1970s fell on particularly receptive ears. We can see in the expedition reports far more reflexivity on the part of the sahibs about the question of equality and hierarchy in relation to the Sherpas, and far more frequent and varied egalitarian interactions between sahibs and Sherpas. The Sherpas in turn responded strongly to this changed climate, and moved beyond "resistance" to practical assertions of equality: younger Sherpas in particular began to drop the term "sahib" altogether.

THE END OF THE SAHIB

There was a tendency in the fifties and the sixties toward equality between sahibs and Sherpas on some expeditions, but such egalitarian expeditions were in a minority. In the seventies the idea of equality with the Sherpas became much stronger, as part of the general antihierarchical sentiments of the era. In writing about his 1970 Annapurna expedition, Bonington reported, "We certainly always treated [the Sherpas] as fellow-climbers and never allowed a Sherpa-sahib relationship to creep in."[83] And on the 1973 American Dhau-lagiri expedition, the one in which the relatively collective leader-ship worked fairly well,

> The expedition team gained the strength of Sonam Girmi and his Sherpas by accepting them with the same trust and respect with which the climbers treated each other. Morrissey [the leader] was one of the last to arrive at Cornice Camp; looking around for a place to sleep, he found room in Sonam Girmi's tent and asked if he could move in. Morrissey saw nothing special in his request; a tent is a tent, and we recognized no particular distinctions between the sahibs and Sherpas on the team, but to Sonam the request was unprecedented. He had been on 18 expeditions and had never before been in the same tent with the leader, the bara-sahib. If our team functioned at all, it was in large part because the Sherpas worked with us, not just for us.[84]

On the 1983 expedition to Everest, one of the "Seven Summits" efforts of Bass and Wells, there was a similar sense that success de-pended on a relative level of equality with the Sherpas:

> [Ershler, the leader] had listened carefully to Gerry Roach tell about the 1976 expedition when the Sherpas had refused to carry more oxygen to the high camps after the first summit attempt; Roach felt the problem stemmed from the Sherpas' feeling of being nothing more than hired hands. Sonam [the Sherpa sardar] had also warned Ershler that if the Sherpas felt they were only beasts of burden, with no real hand in the climb-ing, they might quit early.[85]

In fact, the question of equality with the Sherpas was not simply one of abstaining from setting oneself above them. Given the sahibs' occasional competitive anxieties about the Sherpas—the sense or fear that the Sherpas were physically stronger and also often more experienced than the sahibs—the question of equality was some-times a matter of struggling against *Sherpa* superiority. As Burgess wrote, "I wanted to feel that I was on equal terms with my Sherpa companions, not a client in the hands of guides."[86]

Elsewhere in the Burgess and Palmer book (1983) we see a situation reminiscent of the earlier competitions between sahibs and Sherpas. But the discourse takes a different turn at the end, for the sense of wanting to keep up with the Sherpas is taken as a refusal of neocolonial superiority. This from Pete Boardman in the mid-seventies:

> I sense a tinge of guilt about this expedition. Nobody ever thinks that it is right that a foreign power subjugates another; and so it is that I feel guilty about being waited on by the Sherpas and having all the appendages and contrivances of the Western world carried on the backs of a string of Tamang porters. . . .[87]

And a similar expression of sentiment, also cast in an anticolonial frame, came from the early eighties:

> I was a little embarrassed by the fact that the Sherpas could carry so much weight day after day and still go faster than most of the climbers. I felt that they were actually taking us up the mountain. To gain back at least some respect, and maybe to make a point to some of the other Westerners, I decided to carry one of the large propane bottles. This is classed as a load-and-quarter at this altitude. It went into my rucksack to a sudden round of cheers and applause from the Sherpas. The image crossed my mind of a colonial bwana being applauded by the natives for successfully picking a banana.[88]

All of these examples demonstrate the delicate interplay between the sahibs' seventies sensibilities and the Sherpas' careful but unmistakable communication of their withdrawal from, or evasion of, the old hierarchical relationship. Expedition Sherpas that I interviewed in the nineties were very clear that by the seventies they had felt entitled to be recognized and treated as equals, and also that they had felt they were in a position to demand it, even if not in so many words. One Sherpa, Pema, talked to me about an unsuccessful joint Japanese/Nepal expedition to a peak called Ganesh III in 1976. In the early seventies, the Nepal government's Ministry of Tourism, which issues climbing permits, had passed a rule that the first ascent of every peak in Nepal had to be made jointly by foreign nationals

20. Pema Sherpa, 1990.

and Nepali nationals, which effectively meant, for the most part, Sherpas. This meant that both the foreign climbers and the Sherpa climbers were equal "members." Pema said:

> There was a problem between the Japanese and Nepali [Sherpa] members. Most of the time the Nepali members made the route, and the Japanese didn't help much. The Japanese kept adding their stuff to the Sherpa loads. The Sherpas said, we are all the same, this is a joint expedition. One day he [Pema] wound up carrying 40 kilos and he got very tired. After that he was unhappy and didn't want to work with the Japanese, and also he wasn't feeling well. He went back to Base Camp. . . . [He said he] *tsera lasung*—he became annoyed, fed up.[89]

Many Sherpas viewed the kind of equality they expected not simply in terms of formal equivalence, but—harking back to the discussions of Ang Tharkay and Tenzing Norgay—in terms of real friendship. Ang Karma, who has done high-altitude Sherpa work and is also a practicing journalist, was talking about nationality differences among foreign climbers. For various reasons I will leave out the specific nationality categories (the Sherpas do not like to see this sort of backstage talk published; it may have the tone of an ethnic slur; not all Sherpas would agree on these characterizations anyway, etc.), but his point is well worth quoting:

21. Ang Karma Sherpa, 1990.

[X nationals] and [Y nationals] have bad tempers. He has refused to join some of their expeditions. [Why are they like
that?] Maybe they suffer from an inferiority complex. They
come to Nepal and want to be masters. Also maybe those people have too much hierarchy in their home countries—respect
those above, kick those below. Sherpas don't like this, they work
with Europeans and Americans where they are treated as
friends.[90]

Similarly, I had a conversation in 1990 with Pertemba, who featured so prominently in Chris Bonington's expeditions, and made
many other important climbs as well. Pertemba was talking about
Sherpas having more opportunities since the early seventies to join
in the summit attempts on expeditions. He said:

Before 1973, few Sherpas were allowed to go to the summit.
After that there was more opportunity to share. [Why?] Well,
before that it depended on the leader, but now anyone with
experience can have a chance. The most important thing is
communication—there was more of a communication gap with
the early climbers.[91]

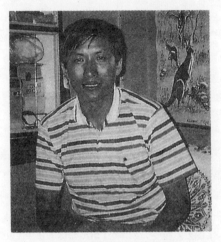

22. Pertemba Sherpa, 1990.

I kept pressing for more of an explanation:

> [So why did it change? Did the Sherpas push for more summit opportunities?] Well, the Sherpas pushed, but also the climbers realized it was better—the Sherpas are strong, their presence provides more safety, and also now there is simply more—he paused—*friendship* between climbers and Sherpas.[92]

Putting these Sherpa feelings together with the somewhat greater sensitivity of the sahibs in the seventies produced the quite dramatic change noted by many observers: the Sherpas stopped calling the sahibs "sahib." I had a strong awareness of this in my own fieldwork, which spanned the period from the mid-sixties to the 1990s. In the early years sahibs were universally referred to and addressed as "sahib," while by 1990 only older Sherpas used the term (and even then not entirely consistently), but younger Sherpas almost never did. The point showed up in the mountaineering literature starting in the mid-seventies:

> The Sherpas, as professionals, performed their tasks efficiently but without subservience, rarely using the traditional term "sahib" in addressing us, preferring the more egalitarian "member."[93]

After that the practice became quite established. A trekker in the eighties said this about her sardar Lhakpa:

> Although he still looked fairly young, Lhakpa gave the impression of having worked with Westerners for some time. His clothes were smart by Solu-Khumbu standards, and I noticed that he addressed Julie and me by our first names as soon as we were introduced.[94]

Jim Fisher, whose work with the Sherpas covers much the same period as my own, summarized the situation with some tongue in cheek:

> A number of the more successful [Sherpas] in recent years have dropped the suffix saheb [sic] and address their Western clients by their first names—something no house servant, hotel servant, or tour guide in Kathmandu would dream of doing. Westerners often react favorably to being treated as equals, even by someone waiting on them hand and foot. But some of them, accustomed to or expecting more traditional hierarchical relations between servant and master, are taken aback by the I'm-just-as-good-as-you-are Sherpa personality.[95]

Although I have been using the language of "resistance," I have also been trying to say that the idea of resistance carries much more complex desires. Acts of resistance both question the assumptions of superiority at the basis of hierarchical relationships and demand respect in addition to whatever specific benefits are at issue. Going further, acts of resistance are claims for a certain kind of cultural or symbolic power, the power to define, or to share in defining, the situation and the relations in question. Categories matter. The point is crucial for understanding why it was important that sahibs no longer be sahibs, but simply employers and occasionally "friends."

8

WOMEN

Himalayan mountaineering until the 1970s had been an overwhelmingly male sport. It was engaged in almost (but not quite) exclusively by men, both Sherpa and "first world;" it built on male styles of interaction derived from other all-male institutions, especially the army; and while it was about many things—nature and nation, materiality and spirituality, the moral quality of the inner self, and the meaning of life—it was always in part about masculinity and manhood.

Starting in the 1970s, women, both international and Sherpani, began to enter the field. Given the masculine character of the sport, any woman who engaged in Himalayan mountaineering was in some sense what I will call a "gender radical." To say that someone is a gender radical is to say that they are questioning or breaking gender rules, although there are many ways of doing this, and many ideological frameworks within which it may be done. The feminist movement that took shape primarily in Europe and the United States in the 1970s was only one specific historical example of gender radicalism, and it itself encompassed a variety of styles and positions. At the same time it did not—as many minority and Third World feminists have argued—encompass all forms of gender radicalism even in the West, no less in other parts of the globe.

The entry of women into Himalayan mountaineering in the seventies (and the growth of trekking and tourism in this era, which brought even larger numbers of memsahibs onto the scene) had numerous and very diverse effects. Most obviously, it produced the kinds of successes for women that the feminist movement sought—the first female ascent of Mount Everest, the first Sherpani summit achievements, and greater overall representation of women in the ranks of climbers and high-altitude Sherpas. But the situation was much more socially, politically, and in some cases sexually complex than these kinds of records would even begin to indicate. For one thing, the social movements of the seventies went in a number of different, and not entirely consistent, directions with respect to gender and sexuality. For another, there were multiple gender combinations and permutations in the context of mountaineering: memsahibs vis-à-vis both sahibs and Sherpa men; Sherpanis vis-à-vis Sherpa men and sahibs; memsahibs and Sherpanis together within a globalizing feminist movement; and more.

In this chapter, then, I continue to follow some of the twists and turns of what I earlier called "the dialectic of sex," that is to say, the complex tangle of gender dynamics as they were played out in Himalayan mountaineering. As with the men, so with the women, we must begin by trying to understand the "serious games" in terms of which they entered the sport. Broadly speaking, for both memsahibs and Sherpanis, these were games of "liberation," but from what, for what, and in what ways one sought to be liberated varied significantly, both between memsahibs and Sherpanis, and among the memsahibs. Before getting to that, however, a brief "prehistory" of women in Himalayan mountaineering.

Gender Radicalism in Himalayan Mountaineering before the 1970s

Before World War II, there were scattered examples of individual women, both "memsahib" and Sherpa, climbing in the Himalayas. Some of the Western women active in this period were explorers like the explicitly feminist Fanny Bullock Workman or, in a more spiritual mode, Alexandra David-Neel.[1] But in 1930 a Swiss climber named Hettie Dyhrenfurth was part of an expedition to Kangchenjunga,[2] and in 1934 she reached the top of Queen Mary Peak (24,370 feet) in the Karakoram Himalaya as part of an expedition exploring and mapping the Baltoro Glacier region.[3] It is more difficult to find traces in the prewar period of Sherpa women climbing, beyond "local portering," that is, carrying loads to the base of the mountain. But there was a woman whom the sahibs called "Eskimo Nell" who evidently climbed at least part way up Everest:

> And there was Eskimo Nell. I had heard tremendous stories of her efforts as a porter to Everest in 1933, when she had been the driving force among the Sherpas and her caustic tongue had spurred the others on to carry to even greater heights.[4]

The period between the fifties and the seventies saw an intensification of Himalayan mountaineering in general, and a slightly more visible presence of women. Among the memsahibs were those on "the first expedition composed entirely of women ever to explore and climb in the high Himalaya," in 1955;[5] the Women's International Expedition to Cho Oyu led by the French climber Claude Kogan in 1959;[6] and the group of women led by Josephine Scarr who climbed in the Kulu area in 1961.[7] Again it is harder to find traces of Sherpa women climbing, but there is a record of two daughters and a niece of Tenzing Norgay climbing with Claude Kogan on Cho Oyu in 1959.[8]

With such small numbers and scant information it is difficult to generalize about the social positioning of these women. In general, the memsahibs who climbed in the Himalaya up to the 1970s were fairly similar to the sahibs. They—at least the ones who left records—were Western European and American; they were all—as far as one can see in the published accounts—white, and, for the most part, broadly middle class. Some were married or in long-term relationships with men; some had children; and some were unmarried and/or single.[9] Most seem to have had at least some higher education, and most expressed some form of awareness or consciousness about breaking barriers for women in this quintessentially man's world. As a generalization it is probably safe to say that these women were, like the sahibs, part of the more liberal, sometimes verging on the bohemian, or countercultural, edge of the middle classes.[10]

As for Sherpa women, there is even less information available. They, too, probably came from the "middle" levels of Sherpa society. In the pre-1970s, daughters of "big people" who were gender radicals would have been more likely to enter a nunnery than to join a mountaineering expedition, while daughters of "small people" would have been unlikely to have the necessary contacts or confidence to achieve any position higher than local porter. Concerning familial status, it is known that "Eskimo Nell" was the wife of one of the Sherpas on the 1933 expedition,[11] and that the Sherpa women on the 1959 Cho Oyu expedition were, as noted, related to Tenzing Norgay. These examples signal a pattern that held true until very recently: Sherpa women had to climb under the sponsorship of, or in partnership with, a related male, whether kinsman or husband. Sardars—the Sherpa foremen of expeditions—were, and still are, generally unwilling to take an unrelated woman on a climb; and for women who wanted to climb, a relative or husband who was a sardar was generally the only way in.

Sherpas and Memsahibs

Among other things, the seventies counterculture in the United States and Europe produced the sexual liberation movement. This movement in turn took several different forms, but one of them was simply a general loosening of rules and inhibitions about sex: sex outside of marriage came to be considered morally acceptable, basically healthy, and meant to be fun for all concerned. To a great extent, the double standard in which it was acceptable for men to both seek and enjoy sex, while women should not be observed to be doing much of either, was at the very least demoted from dominant ideological status.

Sexual liberation intersected with, but was not coterminous with, the women's liberation movement. Most (though not all) feminists were sexual liberationists, but sexual liberationists were not necessarily feminists, and for some women inviting and enjoying more frequent or more casual sex was simply an enhancement of a more traditional gender stance.

Nepal was one of the earliest sites of the counterculture in the mid-1960s, in part because of the countercultural fascination with "the East," and in part because marijuana and hashish were cheap and legal there at that time.[12] Apparently dating from that period,

23. Donna and Phurba Sherpa, ca. 1990, who married after meeting on a trek.

Western women coming to Nepal on treks, and to some extent on climbs, were inviting and engaging in sex with Sherpa men. It is not known for a fact, of course, who was inviting whom, but the general view among both Western observers and Sherpas was that it was primarily the memsahibs—at least in the earlier years—who initiated the encounters. This is plausible on several grounds: because of the Sherpas' traditionally unpredatory attitude toward sex; because memsahibs have often not been thought by them to be particularly attractive; and because memsahibs were definitionally (at least in the early years) of high status, and the Sherpas were quite careful about transgressions of status and power.

Although for obvious reasons it is hard to get data on these sorts of phenomena, the fact of sex between male Sherpas and memsahibs on many treks and on some climbing expeditions is widely known in the streets of Kathmandu.[13] James Fisher reported "many . . . informal liaisons, primarily between trekking sardars and their Western female clientele," as well as "forty or so cases of marriage between Westerners and Sherpas, almost all relatively uneducated villagers from Solu or Khumbu."[14]

In addition, both Sherpas and Western observers often discussed the sexual goings-on from specific expeditions. What follows must of course be classified as gossip; I report these things not as true stories (though they may indeed be true) but as examples of what observers believed was going on. With respect to a certain women's expedition in the 1980s, for example, it was said that one of the women wanted one of the Sherpas to go home with her, but he did not go. In addition it was said that the Sherpa leader of the expedition had a son by one of the women, now living in America. The Westerner relaying these stories to me was of the opinion that it was the women who made the advances, the Sherpas being "too shy."[15]

One of the Sherpa women climbers I interviewed told me the story of another women's expedition, from a different country:

> There was a problem when [a certain man's] son got together [had sex] with the leader. After the expedition succeeded, there was a big party and the Sherpas got drunk. The father [of the Sherpa boy got very angry and] broke all the tent poles. He said he would put it in the papers that [climbers of this nationality] should never come to Nepal again.[16]

The father's reaction illustrates the point that the issue of young Sherpa men's sexual connections with memsahibs are not unproblematic for other Sherpas, who in fact express a range of attitudes on the subject. For the most part there are relatively mild and benign jokes about the whole thing. For example, some Sherpas were quoted as joking with a writer about the Annapurna women's expedition of 1978:

> There is one other way to go to foreign countries. There was one American Women's Expedition this year and some Sherpas they marry [actually, one married and one had a sexual relationship] with some of those women. Now Sherpas say, "For Women's Expedition you not have to pay, I work for free." We both laughed.[17]

But there were also less benign attitudes in play, and one occasionally heard a kind of contempt for memsahibs, coupled with a relatively calculating attitude about sexual relationships with memsahibs, that link up with the "macho shift" discussed earlier. That is, along with the bawdy banter between sahibs and Sherpas on expeditions, and the boasting of conquests accompanying the sexual "fines" on expeditions, the pattern of some memsahibs looking for "adventure sex" with Sherpa men seems to have added another

dimension to that shift. It is worth stressing that the more preda-
tory, "macho," attitudes are not by any means characteristic of all
Sherpa men. Nonetheless they represent an emerging tendency that
has clearly been disturbing to many observers, Sherpa as well as
Western.

One example is from one of my field trips, in this case with a
Granada television crew to make a film on the Sherpas in 1976.[18]
While filming in one of the villages, I met a young mountaineering
Sherpa who had gotten involved with a Swiss woman on a trek. He
was supposed to follow her back to Switzerland where they would
get married. Even at that early stage, however, he seemed a good
deal less interested in her than she in him. Later, I was visiting
Sherpa friends in Kathmandu when this same young man (R) came
in the house:

> R came in with his Swiss girlfriend—very surly [toward her]—
> he seems to be sick of her. She's leaving day after tomorrow
> and I said to him, "You must be sad." [Of course I was fishing
> to see what he would say.] He said, "Well, I've got plenty of
> friends here." [The woman I was visiting, RJ] said to him, "But
> you can't sleep with your friends." And he said—fast, hoping I
> wouldn't understand—"Well, there's plenty of women here [to
> sleep with]."[19]

On another level, here is a crude "joke," attributed to "a Sherpa,"
that was making the rounds in Kathmandu in 1990:

> Did you hear the one about the Sherpa who said trekking work
> is very easy? You only need one word of English: "Yes." Sherpa
> climb high? "Yes." Carry load? "Yes." Cook dinner? "Yes."
> Memsahib wants to fuck? "Yes."[20]

If this really is a joke that originated with a Sherpa, it illustrates
several things: first, the perception that memsahibs would initiate
sex; second, that the Sherpa was not in a position to refuse; and
third, that a Sherpa in this position might become callous toward
and openly disrespectful of women, or at least of memsahibs. This
was the sort of thing that put some Sherpa men on a collision course
with feminist, and decidedly antimacho, expeditions in the seventies.

SEVENTIES FEMINISM

It should be clear that gender boundaries were in some sense under challenge (and in other senses not) both within and across cultural borders, even before the onset of feminism as a political and cultural movement in the 1970s. But the rise of the feminist movement had some dramatic effects within Himalayan mountaineering.

It is worth pausing here to note that, from the perspective of Himalayan mountaineering, the seventies feminist movement had a completely transnational character. Women from virtually every "developed" country, including by that time virtually every country in Asia, came into Himalayan climbing within that decade. There was thus a great deal more ethnic and national diversity, although not necessarily class diversity—my general sense is that the women, whatever their nationality, remained largely middle class.

In any event, feminism produced first of all a large influx of women into Himalayan mountaineering. Not only did the women come, they conquered. In 1975 Mount Everest was climbed twice by women, first via the traditional southern route by Junko Tabei, who was coleader of a Japanese all-women's expedition,[21] and second, via the difficult north face by Phantog, a Tibetan woman who was part of a coed Chinese expedition (actually composed mostly of ethnic Tibetans).[22]

But the feminist movement was about a lot more than making gains of this sort for women. For many women, it was also about problematizing presumptions of male superiority and boundaries of gender difference. At the least it took the form of a heightened consciousness of, and sensitivity to, "sexism," which itself took a variety of forms in mountaineering, some more and some less familiar. Generalized disrespect and dismissal by fellow male climbers was probably the most common.[23] Beyond that there was more active sexual harassment:

This morning Jeff [one of the French men] called me into the mess tent where a little group of them were sitting. They had obviously just been smoking "strong cigarettes" [marijuana] with the cook, and were laughing raucously. "Come in, Julie," Jeff encouraged, "Gelaal [the Pakistani policeman/guard with the expedition] says he wants to f—— you!" . . . "Well, what do you say?" Jeff, our supposedly responsible doctor, giggled. "I would say that it was typical of you and your friends, you all seem to keep your brains in your balls," I retorted and walked out.[24]

There was also a question of "paternalism," which was a particularly thorny issue among women mountaineers. There was the sense that, in climbing as in other areas of life, men would tend to take over and that had to be resisted. Thus, many women argued against mixed-gender expeditions, taking the position that the only way to maintain leadership and independence for women in mountaineering was by not climbing with men at all.[25]

This was by no means a fully shared position. Many women who were in other ways gender-radical continued to climb ·in mixed groups and/or with a strong male climbing partner. Julie Tullis, the English climber who told off a group of men on Nanga Parbat in the quote just above, nonetheless identified single-sex women's expeditions with a kind of "feminism" that she was not interested in. She always climbed in mixed groups, often as the only woman on the expedition, and she commented about an all-women Polish expedition on K2: "The four girls [sic] got on well together and were very strong and extremely determined in their climbing, but I could never see myself as part of a 'feminist' expedition."[26]

And Junko Tabei, one of the first two women to reach the summit of Everest, had no qualms about acknowledging that she relied heavily on her male Sherpa climbing partner, Ang Tshering. Ang Tshering led the whole way on the final summit attempt, keeping up the momentum (if one can talk about "momentum" at that altitude) for the effort:

Ang Tshering was climbing faster and often urged me to move on by pulling my hand. I was tired and we progressed slowly towards the summit, sometimes on our elbows. It was a very hard climb.[27]

24. Junko Tabei, the first woman to reach the summit
of Mount Everest, with her climbing partner,
Ang Tshering Sherpa, 1975.

Yet for many of the women, climbing without men was an exhila-
rating experience. They expressed a sense of "liberation," a sense of
being independent, grown-up, on one's own. As the American
climber and leader Arlene Blum put it,

> I had taken part in a previous all-woman expedition—an ascent
> of Mt. McKinley in 1970—and it had been my most satisfying
> climb so far. . . . We felt as though we were climbing our moun-
> tain "without the grownups," and we successfully handled some
> difficult problems.[28]

Similar sentiments were expressed by Stacy Allison, the first American woman to reach the summit of Mount Everest:

> Being together gave Ev [her female climbing partner] and me the energy to do whatever we wanted. We had male friends, male teachers, male climbing companions. We didn't avoid climbing with men, but climbing together meant we didn't have to rely on them, to worry one might question our strength or our ability to climb where only men had gone before.[29]

In these cases,[30] what was being resisted was not men as sexual partners, lovers, or husbands, but quite specifically men in the mode of "patriarchy," men as "fathers," men who would take over and make women feel childish.[31]

The question of whether to climb with men or not would be relatively unproblematic if women climbers could simply choose between mixed-gender and all-women's expeditions. But in the context of Himalayan mountaineering, with its tradition of Sherpa support, the choice was not so simple, as became apparent in the famous Annapurna women's expedition of 1978.

FEMINISM, SHERPAS, AND THE ANNAPURNA WOMEN'S EXPEDITION

Intercultural relations are never gender-neutral. Although Junko Tabei was happy to accept the Sherpa Ang Tshering's help, in fact one of the effects of the women's movement, combined with the sexual liberation movement, was to problematize relationships between memsahibs and Sherpas. Both movements brought to the fore new ways in which "the Sherpas," hitherto seen primarily as generic, function-performing human beings, were actually MEN.

In the context of all-male expeditions, Sherpa masculinity was played upon by both Sherpas and (male) sahibs as a way of "making equality" between them.[32] At the same time, contradictorily, the Sherpas may well have been coded metaphorically as female. This gendering of difference is probably true of many forms of Western "othering," that is, of rendering cultural differences as both absolute and inferior: the Western self is construed as male, the "Oriental" or "Primitive" Other, regardless of gender, is construed as female. But in the Sherpa case the linkages were perhaps more specific. The Sherpas' job could be seen as basically mothering the sahibs— cooking, cleaning, carrying their loads, and occasionally even carrying them. Indeed it may in part be because Sherpas were coded female, as well as because of their smaller size, that their frequently superior physical strength, speed, and stamina were so disturbing to the sahibs.

It took the women, then, to truly notice Sherpa male climbers' maleness. More precisely, it took this particular, historically shaped cohort of women—producers and products of both sexual liberation and feminist politics—to construct Sherpas as "male." By "construct" I mean not simply noticing that the Sherpas were physically men, but endowing this maleness with a range of meanings with practical and political implications. Thus, there was the pattern of constructing Sherpa men as sexual males and getting involved with them sexually. But there was also the amplification of feminist awareness: constructing Sherpa men as political males, in all the senses that feminists were trying to get away from or change: men who would view themselves as superior to women, who would want to tell women what to do, or who would not be willing to take orders from women leaders. Thus, when explicitly "feminist" expeditions were put together in the seventies, there was a real question for some women about whether to take Sherpas at all. If the expedition was a success, but Sherpa men had assisted, would it still be a success as a women's expedition?

Both of these issues—sex with Sherpas, and the question of excluding men from the climb—came together in the 1978 Annapurna women's expedition, as described in one of the most extraordinary mountaineering books ever written, Arlene Blum's *Annapurna: A Woman's Place* (1980). I want to trace some of the ways in which this expedition manifested the points just discussed.

The expedition was organized by Blum, an experienced climber who had previously participated in the (mixed-gender) American Bicentennial Mount Everest expedition, among other climbs. At the time she and some friends began to think about an all-women's climb, no woman had ever reached the top of an over-8,000-meter peak.[33] The Annapurna women's expedition received enormous publicity from the outset, at least in part because of its double-entendre slogan, "A Woman's Place Is on Top," which was printed on tens of thousands of T-shirts that were sold (very successfully) to raise money for the expedition.

The party consisted of thirteen women, all American, ranging in ages from twenty-one to fifty. The group had the upper-middle-class, high-education profile of most Himalayan expeditions. Blum herself had a Ph.D. in biochemistry, and one of the women was a medical doctor. There was also the usual mix of marital/relationship/sexual statuses—some of the women were married, some in long-term relationships with men, and one was a mother; the sexual/marital statuses of others was not stated.

One aspect of the feminism of the expedition was that the group had asked to have it arranged that some Sherpa women be brought along to be trained as "Sherpas." This was largely unheard of at the time, and the women felt that the Sherpa sardar, Lopsang, was resistant to the idea. He did, however, hire two of his female relatives to act as kitchen girls in base camp. But this appeared to be just the opposite of what the American women wanted, and it produced— like everything else about this star-crossed expedition—irresolution and conflict. It is not clear from the book what happened. but according to a Sherpa friend of mine, one of the Sherpa women got sexually involved with one of the Sherpa men. Whatever the case, Blum wound up firing the women, who in turn became very angry. There was an ugly confrontation, which left Blum very shaken.

In addition, right from the beginning there was an incipient split in the expedition over whether to use Sherpa support or not. Alison Chadwick-Onyszkiewicz and some others were in favor of not using Sherpas, echoing the theme of independence expressed by other women climbers. The Sherpas "may turn out to be a bloody nuisance," Chadwick-Onyszkiewicz warned. "This is a women's climb, after all. We don't really need Sherpas. We should do it on our own."[34]

But they did take male Sherpas, and everything that everyone had feared came to pass. Although the expedition had a rule ("no romance during the climb"),[35] one member of the group fell in love with and began sleeping with the Sherpa kitchen boy.[36] This was not terrible in and of itself, but it did put the question of "sex with the memsahibs" on the table for the expedition as a whole:

> The Sherpas were very conscious of the relationship between Annie and Yeshi and apparently couldn't understand why the rest of us were not similarly inclined. Marie complained that the Sherpas kept looking at her in a way that made her feel very uncomfortable.[37]

Evidently another member of the expedition got involved later with a Kami (blacksmith/"untouchable") porter, which the Sherpa telling me the story (in 1990) found to be completely beyond his comprehension. The collective feeling about the expedition among large sectors of the Sherpa community was that "the whole expedition was looking for husbands" (a polite Sherpa way of saying they were looking for sex).

The fallout of this came later, when the expedition began to break down in various ways. Some of the women were clearly hostile to the Sherpas, and some of the Sherpas—in another example of the macho shift—began to engage in a form of sexual harassment:

> "Besides, they're getting awfully obnoxious," Liz added. "They keep pointing at us and giggling all the time. I know they're making obscene comments."
> . . . .
> "How do you know?" [Blum] asked.
> "Well, for one thing, they keep drawing phallic symbols in the snow," Liz said. "And when Vera W. asked them to stop, they just said, 'Yeti [the "abominable snowman"] make pictures in snow—not Sherpas.' "[38]

Generally, the women felt either disrespected or patronized.[39] And while all the women felt, to some degree, these problems with the Sherpas as men, there was nonetheless a split between those who thought it would be enough of an achievement for women if they reached the top of Annapurna, even with Sherpa support, and those who did not. In the end the bitter weather on the upper reaches of the mountain, combined with Sherpa insistence, produced a summit party composed of two memsahibs and two Sherpas. They were successful in reaching the top.

Normally, if one party reaches the summit, the entire expedition is deemed a success. However, on most expeditions, regardless of gender composition, other members want a chance at the top, and this climb was no exception. Left in the second party were Alison Chadwick-Onyszkiewicz and Vera Watson. Chadwick-Onyszkiewicz had been one of the most vociferous in arguing that if one went to the summit with Sherpa support, it would not count as a success for women. There was one remaining Sherpa who might have accompanied these two to the summit, but he came down with altitude sickness on the final day (Blum had had doubts about him all along), and went down. Blum tried to talk Chadwick-Onyszkiewicz and Watson out of trying for the summit with no Sherpa support, but they took off anyway. They never came back.

The deaths of Alison Chadwick-Onyszkiewicz and Vera Watson seem almost a parable of the pitfalls of the women's movement, a just-so story that implies the conclusion, "You can't fool mother nature." At one level this would be an absurd interpretation. Death on the mountains respects neither gender (hundreds of men die as well) nor ideology: Julie Tullis, who always climbed with men and never thought of herself as a feminist, died of altitude sickness on K2. At another level, however, one must conclude that the deaths of *both* male and female climbers are the effect of what may be called bodily politics, a risking of the body in the name of, or for the honor of, the gendered self.

SHERPA WOMEN: A BRIEF OVERVIEW

Memsahibs were not the only women to enter mountaineering in the 1970s. The feminist movement that began in that decade had an almost instantly global character. Despite the failure of the Annapurna women's expedition's attempt in 1978 to recruit Sherpa women as "Sherpas," in fact by that year a small number of Sherpa women had begun climbing with other expeditions. In order to understand how they got there, it will be useful to take a quick look at what used to be called "the status of women" in Sherpa society and culture over the course of the twentieth century.

Sherpa gender culture was in many ways disadvantageous to women. The ideology favored men as "higher"; men were viewed as capable of greater spirituality, and as being less mired in selfish and worldly sorts of concerns. In addition, menstruation was said to be offensive to the gods, and harmful to male spirituality. Femalehood was thus a bad rebirth; a woman who worked hard on her spiritual improvement would hope to be reborn as a man.[40]

In the practical realm, girls were generally given less education than boys,[41] not only because of prejudice but because mothers felt they needed their daughters' help at home. In addition, the structural rules of the society favored men—residence after marriage in the traditional village setting was virilocal, with the woman having to move to her husband's village or homestead, and with men inheriting and owning most of the real property in the society, land and herds. Men also did the trading, the source of major wealth, and men occupied such few political positions as existed.

At the same time, this society would not be described as a heavily sexist or male-dominant one. There was virtually no segregation of sexes, and in secular life there were no arenas in which men regularly congregated and participated simply as men. Virtually all economic production and social life took place in households. The domestic group, normally coterminous with the nuclear family, was a very tight unit. Husbands were defined as having ultimate authority in the husband-wife relationship, but as economic producers, and as social actors (especially as cohosts) in relation to the rest of the community, the husband and wife were partners.[42]

Within this cultural and institutional context, Sherpa women's own position was somewhat contradictory. Some of the ideology represented women as weak, self-indulgent, and unreliable.[43] On the other hand, there was no ideology or practice of special protection of women. Sherpa women were encouraged to be outgoing and independent actors who could take care of themselves and operate in almost any capacity in the world. In particular, they were seen as capable domestic managers who could be counted on to operate the household as an economic enterprise for long periods of time, while husbands were away on extended trading or climbing expeditions.

Starting in the 1970s, an increasing number of Sherpa families began moving from their villages and settling permanently in the capital of Nepal, Kathmandu. The moves had multiple effects on women. Because of the prevalence in the capital of Hindu models of family, and also because of the absence of agricultural work, Sherpa women found themselves more confined to the home than they would have been in a village. Contradictions about the independence and autonomy of women were thus heightened in this context.[44]

At the same time, daughters were much more likely to get a full education in the city than they were in the villages. My data suggest that, interestingly enough, it was often Sherpa fathers who pushed harder for the education of their daughters, partly because it would be useful to the family economy, and partly because it would stand the daughter in good stead in her own life. But Sherpa mothers in the city also had fewer objections to their daughters going to school, as the work of a Kathmandu housewife was much less demanding than that of a householder in a farming village. In 1979 a village woman told me that she had to keep her very bright and lively daughter at home to help her, though her husband, an expedition Sherpa, really wanted the two daughters to go to school. And in the film *Sherpas*, the sardar Mingma Tenzing talked about educating all of his children, girls as well as boys. He said he did not know what they would do later on, but education would be useful for anything they might want to do.[45] At the time of my last visit in 1990, one of his daughters was a nurse in a Kathmandu hospital, one was a bilingual secretary for the French embassy in Kathmandu,[46] and one was a student in a private school in Darjeeling.

Also, in the mid-seventies, a gender "equalization" law had been put on the books in Nepal: for every eight male district leaders, there had to be one woman.[47] In the village where I did my original fieldwork, the daughter of one of the big men of the village was appointed. As I wrote in my field notes in 1976:

C. F. [the father] stressed the woman's lib [*sic!*] aspects of all this. So does he think it's a good thing? Yes. Why? Because before if he didn't have a son, and only daughters, who would inherit the property? Now, his daughters can inherit. . . . Before men were *che* (higher/senior) and women *tua* (lower/junior), but now they're *chikparang* (equal/identical).[48]

And while it was—and still is—hardly true that Sherpa men and women, or the male and female citizens of Nepal in general, are "equal," clearly a law like this did have some impact.

Behind a number of these developments for Sherpa women was a broader kind of economic and cultural pragmatism among the Sherpas that linked up with aspects of Sherpa gender ideology. Although there were certain prejudices about women, most of them did not have implications for women's freedom of movement, or for their assumed ability to learn, excel, and make money if they could. Thus, when conditions opened up for various kinds of personal advancement for women, women themselves were predisposed to take advantage of them, and "their culture" (whether in the hands of husbands, parents, or "men") was not disposed to hold them back.

SHERPA RELIGION AND WOMEN'S INDEPENDENCE

There was one other major arena of Sherpa society in which women's independence was given a major boost over the course of the twentieth century: religion. One piece of the monastic reform movement was the institution of a ritual called Nyungne, in which lay people embarked on extended fasting, silence, and prayer, and became, as the Sherpas say, monks and nuns for a day. The Nyungne ritual was supposed to bring to its practitioners an especially high level of religious merit.

Nyungne in turn was said to have been brought to the world by a female bodhisattva (a kind of Buddhist saint) called Gelungma Palma. The story of Gelungma Palma is told every year during the Nyungne ritual and is well known, at least in its general outlines, to most Sherpas. In the story, a young princess is unhappy with all the sins committed in her father's kingdom. She resolves not to marry, and when she learns that marriage arrangements are being made on her behalf, she runs away from home and takes vows of celibacy. She becomes a brilliant and learned religious practitioner, and is appointed head of a male monastery. But she becomes ill and the monks, thinking she is having a baby, throw her out of the monastery. She wanders about for many years achieving greater and greater levels of spirituality, until finally she becomes a bodhisattva. She goes to the heaven of the god Chenrezi, who sends her back to the world with the text of the Nyungne ritual, to bring enlightenment to the ignorant and suffering creatures who remain in the world (for a fuller version, see Appendix A).

The Gelungma Palma story was given a good bit of prominence in the monastic cleanup campaign and in the annual observance of Nyungne that was one of its manifestations. The story must be taken in turn as part of the context for the founding of the first Sherpa nunnery, Devuche, in 1928. Devuche was founded by a group of young women from "big" or high-status families, who ran away from home without parental consent, took vows at Rumbu monastery across the border in Tibet, and then returned to study and eventually found the nunnery in their home Sherpa region. The women knew that their parents would not be happy about their running away from home and, in some cases, foiling marriage arrangements already in progress. But they hoped that the legitimacy and cultural value of the act was such that the parents would accept it as a fait accompli and back them up in the end, and this is indeed what happened.[49]

Other nunneries (like other monasteries) were subsequently founded. Female monasticism in turn apparently had a consciousness-raising effect for some women about the privileges of men and the constraints on women in Sherpa society. For example, one nun commented about men's privileged religious status:

As a woman one is always inferior . . . however much one learns one is never given as much respect as a lama. Even corrupt lamas are still treated with some respect; a man can lead a sinful life, and yet later become a lama and be considered superior to any woman.[50]

Other young women of my acquaintance at least toyed with the idea of becoming nuns; the idea that there were alternatives to marriage gave them a sense of options. They might get married in the end, but this no longer had the status of inevitability and naturalness it might otherwise have had.

In much the same period (the first half of the twentieth century), opportunities for wage labor opened up in Darjeeling, under the "development" efforts of the British Raj in India. Here again, women "ran away" from home to take up these opportunities. They did so in fewer numbers than the men, but there is no question that they did so. The framing of the process was similar to that for becoming a nun: that one's parents would not let one do it if they knew, but that they would probably ratify it and go along with it after the fact. Whereas running away to join a nunnery was something largely engaged in by women from wealthier families, running away to work in Darjeeling or—later—Kathmandu was done more by women from poorer (but also middle-status) families.

Sherpa Women Mountaineers

There was (and still is) resistance on the part of many Sherpa men to having Sherpa women join expeditions. The question of women menstruating on the mountain (this applies to memsahibs as well) is worrisome, as offending the gods whose favor many Sherpas still believe is important to the success of the expedition. (The status of this "belief" among contemporary Sherpas may be changing, but there is no doubt that for many individuals it continues.) One sardar in the early nineties told the story of the 1979 French Dhaulagiri expedition on which one Sherpa died and the French leader lost both hands and feet to frostbite. The leader and his girlfriend, according to this account, stayed too long at high altitude because the woman was "personally sick."[51] This sardar felt that the woman should not have been climbing at the time of her period and that she caused much misfortune as a result. Many Sherpa sardars also feel that women as (climbing) "Sherpas" among the male "Sherpas" will cause discord and conflict among the men. Most still say they would not hire women, and it is the sardar who is in charge of the hiring.

25. Pasang Lhamu Sherpa, 1990.

As early as 1977 my friend Pasang Lhamu joked in the film, *Sher-pas*, that her husband had had many chances to go on mountaineering expeditions, and now it was her turn. "Next year," she said with a twinkle in her eye, "I'm going to Everest."[52] In 1990, I asked Pasang Lhamu—who never did go climbing—what she thought of Sherpa women climbing:

> She said many women want to go but they don't get the chance. Her second daughter would like to climb, but probably sardars won't give her jobs. Sardars feel that women are weak, won't carry, and also if you mix boys and girls you'll have problems.[53]

Yet there were always exceptions to these points, and the exceptions grew more frequent over time. From the early days, as Sherpas wished to keep mountaineering jobs within the Sherpa community in general and within their own families in particular, it became the practice to use Sherpa women, and even children and old people, as "local porters" if not as actual climbers. Somewhat later, women began moving into the kitchen jobs, as cooks and kitchen helpers.

The sardar Lopsang had recruited some of his female relatives into these jobs on the Annapurna Women's Expedition, and although the memsahibs evidently took this to be "traditional" women's work, and essentially nonliberatory, in the past the expedition cooking had been, like all expedition jobs, men's work. It was a step up from local portering, it paid a bit more, it got one onto the mountain proper, and for many men it was and is the route to more skilled "Sherpa" work in mountaineering. For women too, it could serve these functions.

Starting in the 1970s, then, some Sherpa women did indeed seek to get involved in the more difficult, dangerous, but also more highly paid and prestigious role of "Sherpa," involving high-altitude portering and expedition support. And most recently some women, as well as some Sherpa men, have sought simply to be mountaineers in their own right, with or without sahib or memsahib partners.

How can we understand this history? We cannot necessarily assume that Sherpa women entered high-altitude mountaineering for the same motives as "first-world" women.[54] But we also cannot assume that their motives were entirely different; that would simply reinscribe the hard "self/other" boundary. Rather, we need an awareness that difference comes as much from different histories and politics as from different "cultures." In order to see this I will examine the only material currently available on Sherpa women mountaineers: interviews that I conducted in 1990 with two women who started climbing in the seventies, as well as various secondhand accounts about a third woman, slightly younger, who became the subject of intense public debate in Nepal following her success and death on Mount Everest in 1993.

ANG RITA

The first of the woman I interviewed was named Ang Rita, and she came from Pangboche village in Khumbu. In about 1976 she and two other Sherpa women took and passed a training course at the Nepal Mountaineering Association.[55] One of her early expeditions was a joint Italian-Nepali Everest expedition in 1980, on which she

26. Ang Rita Sherpa, 1990.

had a conflict with the Nepali coleader of the expedition about how
high she would be allowed to climb:

> She and [one of the other women] wanted to go all the way to
> the summit but the Nepali [leader] didn't support her. The
> leader was an officer in the Nepal army. She got to Camp 2 but
> the men wouldn't support them. They went as far as just below
> Camp 3 without the leader's order. The leader got very angry,
> said why did you go without permission? He didn't give her a
> chance.[56]

In 1981, she climbed with a Japanese expedition to Langtang Ri,
and reached Camp 3. She had a chance to go to the summit, but
at that time she received word that her brother had been killed on
Annapurna, and the liaison officer told her not to go because she was
upset about her brother. She participated in at least four more climbs,
of which the last was the Japanese women's expedition to Changla
Himal in 1983. She concluded the interview by saying that she would
still like to climb but apparently had no other opportunities.

Ang Rita was quite shy throughout the interview, and did not offer any general reflections on women climbing. However, a few points may be noted here. First, although she never mentioned it, I knew from other sources that she had been married to a sardar in her younger years and that all of her climbs had been on expeditions on which he was the sardar.[57] In fact, in all three cases that I will discuss, the women climbed with their husbands. Partly this was because men as sardars would not take unrelated women on climbs, but there may be something else at work, to which I will return shortly.

Second, it is worth noting that Ang Rita's confrontation with the Nepali co-leader of the expedition took a distinctive form: she did not argue or talk back; she simply pushed the limits with her behavior (climbing to Camp 3 without permission) and hoped to create a fait accompli. This is perhaps another variant of running away to a nunnery or to Darjeeling, and hoping or assuming that others would go along with the act after the fact.

ANG NYIMI

The second woman climber I interviewed was called Ang Nyimi (or just Nyimi), from Zhung village in Solu (the lower Sherpa valley). Her husband, Lhakpa Norbu, was a sardar. They met in 1977 when she was sixteen, and were married shortly thereafter. She began trekking with him and enjoyed it very much, and they have operated pretty much as a team ever since.

Her first real expedition was the French expedition to Ama Dablam in 1979. This was her husband Lhakpa Norbu's first expedition as a sardar. Ang Nyimi was the second cook and was a bit daunted as there were twenty-one French members, but she did it. The expedition was successful, and she has remained friends with some of the French women of the group. She was the cook again on the French/Nepal Police joint expedition to Dhaulagiri, and again on the 1983 French expedition to Ama Dablam. In the interim she also led many trekking groups, and was in those contexts herself the sardar.[58]

In 1984 she joined a French expedition to Nuptse, and for the first time actually reached a summit.

27. Ang Nyimi Lama, 1990.

At first she was not a "Sherpa." But the French offered some training and then chose four boys and her. (The leader had asked her if she was interested and she had said yes.) After about four days of training she asked the leader and the Liaison Officer [if she could go], and they said, we'll see how you do. If you do well you can go to the summit. At that time there was no insurance for her because she wasn't supposed to be a "Sherpa." And she didn't really become a "Sherpa," they just let her go.[59]

She said the climbing had not been bad until after about 7,000 meters (the mountain is 7,865 meters). They were climbing without supplementary oxygen, which made it much more difficult. Sometimes she became afraid when it was very steep. It took twelve days to make the round trip from base camp to the summit and back.

There were four people in the first group—one member and three "Sherpas" including herself and her husband Lhakpa Norbu. Her husband kept telling her to go down, she only had single boots, he said her parents would be angry with him if she had an accident. Even just below the summit he said go down—she got a little angry with him. But each time he said go down she said "just a little more."

And she made it to the top.

Nyimi had obviously thought a great deal about the implications of what she had done and why. When I asked her why she began climbing, she said that because she was not educated, she was not equipped to do much else, and that it was important to do *something* with one's life.[60] She said other women were equally strong—if they wanted to they could do it too, but they would not try, or their families would not let them. She repeated this dual theme of how others held women back, but also that women themselves were too timid:

> There's a problem for Sherpa women because if they go out and do things people think badly of them. People are "very conservative." Also women's psychology is a problem—they are too retiring. She doesn't care what other people think—she lets it go in one ear and out the other (which she illustrated graphically with a gesture). Otherwise you'll never do anything.

Nyimi's story illustrates a number of things. We hear in it the same kind of independence that we heard from Ang Rita—a sense of capability and autonomy that tends to be characteristic of Sherpa women in general. We also see in Nyimi's story the same silent but active resistance that we have come to recognize as something like a cultural script for Sherpa women: she did not argue with her husband when he told her to go back, but she just kept climbing.

But let us focus here for a moment on Nyimi's partnership with her husband. It will be recalled that there were a variety of ways in which mountaineering was destabilizing the Sherpa gender system. Young men were being encouraged in a kind of machismo that had not been common in the culture. Memsahibs offered many attractions, up to and including marriage and long-term residence in Europe and the United States. At the very least there was a tendency for men to stay away for longer and longer periods of time, both on expeditions and in Kathmandu, and to have very attenuated ties with their families back in the villages.

Nyimi's very committed partnership with her husband then could be read as an active move against these developments in Sherpa gender relations. In the next example, too, the climber Pasang Lhamu and her husband worked in a literal partnership with one another.

Not only did they climb together, they were partners with some other relatives in the ownership of a trekking agency. All of this contrasts rather sharply with the need expressed by some Western feminists to climb without men in order to feel independent. Yet far from being "traditional," as it might appear in the Western context, Sherpa women's pattern of climbing with their husbands may be read as gender-radical in this historical moment; that is, it may be read as an attempt to work against some of the creeping machismo of the younger generation of men, and to establish or reestablish more mutually respectful gender relations.

Nyimi was probably the most famous of the small number of Sherpa women mountaineers in the 1970s and 1980s. She was invited to Europe, where she climbed Mont Blanc, and she and her husband made a film about Sherpas and Himalayan mountaineering with a French filmmaker. But as she told me in the interview, she still wanted to climb Mount Everest. If she were to do so—although she did not say this—she would be the first Sherpa woman to achieve that distinction. Equally important from the point of view of ethnic and national politics, she would be the first Nepali (in the sense of citizenship) woman to do so. But that was not to be. Instead a woman called Pasang Lhamu (not the same Pasang Lhamu as my friend in the film) reached the top in 1993 as part of an expedition that she herself had organized and led. She also died, along with another Sherpa, on the way down from the summit.

THE PASANG LHAMU STORY

The story of these events—the narrative of what happened and of people's motivations—is tremendously contested. The following version, which is also consistent with most published accounts, comes from a conversation with some Sherpa friends, a husband and wife, who were visiting with me in Ann Arbor, Michigan, shortly after Pasang Lhamu's funeral.

Pasang Lhamu, a native of Pankongma village in the Pharak region of Solu-Khumbu,[61] had climbed as a "Sherpa" on a number of previous expeditions with the French. In 1991 she had been on a French Everest expedition and had reached the south col (one of the highest camp sites before the summit), but then the leader had not chosen her for the summit party and she had been angry. She subsequently went on another Everest expedition, but it was canceled because of bad weather. She was now determined to make it to the top.

In 1993, an Indian women's expedition was being planned. The organizers contacted Pasang Lhamu, but she wanted to be named coleader with the Indian leader, with a guaranteed place in the first summit party. The Indians would not agree, so Pasang Lhamu refused to participate. They then asked Nyimi, who agreed. According to this informant, as well as to a number of published sources, Pasang Lhamu and Nyimi were very *chana* (competitive).

Meanwhile Pasang Lhamu determined to go ahead on her own. She formed a Nepal women's expedition with herself as the leader, and with two other women, Lhakputi Sherpa and Nanda Rai, as members. She applied to the government for a waiver of fee (as a citizen of Nepal), but for complex reasons, which became the subject of debate later, the government refused. So she went about fundraising herself to get the $50,000[62] that was the fee for Everest at that time. She was able to persuade San Miguel Beer/Nepal to put up half of the money, and she raised the other half by the sale of T-shirts and the like.

So they went. She took five male Sherpas on the expedition, including her husband, an experienced climbing Sherpa. She and four of the men, not including her husband, reached the summit. (Her husband had wanted to go, but they had agreed that it was better for their three small children if they not go together.) Bad weather started coming in, and they all bivouacked[63] at the south summit one night. Then, when two Sherpas went down to get help, the weather closed in; they had no radios and no way to get back up. Within a day or two Pasang Lhamu sent down another Sherpa for help, but there were no further communications. She died on the mountain with one male Sherpa (Sonam Tsering), whose body was never found, only his rucksack. They think he stayed with her until she died, then tried to get down, and fell. Her body was not found for twenty-one days.

Pasang Lhamu became a great heroine. While she was missing, the situation had been a front-page story in the papers, day after day. Appeals were put out to pray for her safety. When it was confirmed that she had died, the government announced that it was awarding her the Nepal Tara award, of which only two had been given before, one to Tenzing Norgay. Her body was brought all the way back from just below the summit of Everest to Kathmandu (an enormously difficult and completely unprecedented feat), and she was cremated in the national stadium, with a national flag over her coffin, and tens of thousands of people in attendance.

Pasang Lhamu's intentions, motives, and self-representations have been almost impossible to recover, at least from the kinds of reports that have appeared thus far. Several reporters portrayed her as highly competitive and self-promoting, while others charged that this description was sexist and ethnically or nationally prejudiced.[64] She certainly must have had impressive drive, energy, and persuasiveness. And it is important to remember that she not only died on Mount Everest, but had raised the money, organized the expedition, and climbed to the top of it first.

There are many things going on in the Pasang Lhamu story that cannot be explored in detail here. There was the alleged rivalry with Nyimi, which articulates with Sherpa cultural patterns of competition usually involving men.[65] There are the echoes of the Annapurna women's expedition, involving everything from the entrepreneurial sale of T-shirts to the excessively risky bodily politics. There are divisions of opinion and feeling over whether Pasang Lhamu as a mother of three small children should have been taking such risks.[66] And there is the play of transnational capital in the background, with the sponsorship of San Miguel Beer/Nepal.

Again, I can only attend briefly to a small number of points. The first concerns a question that arises here more clearly than it did in the other women's stories: the intertwining of gender issues on the one hand and ethnic and national issues on the other. The linkage of gender with other political issues and identities is a major point of difference between various forms of "first-world" feminism and various forms of minority and/or "third-world" feminism.[67] It is clear in the Pasang Lhamu case that questions of gender were from the very beginning tied up with questions of Sherpa ethnic politics in relation to the dominant Nepali state, and with questions of Sherpa-Nepali nationalist solidarity in relation to larger, stronger, and more "modern" nations.

In some contexts, Pasang Lhamu joined the two discourses. For example, when she had the falling-out with the French climber in 1991, she "went public accusing [him of] discrimination against a woman and a native climber."[68] But in contexts where the gender issue was equalized, as in her conflict with the Indian women's expedition, Pasang Lhamu framed the issue purely as a national one: "She felt that since the joint venture was envisioned at a national level and patronised by the Prime Ministers of the two countries, the question of co-leadership was very important."[69] The counterpoint between frames of gender and of nation continued in the journalism following her death. When a Nepali journalist suggested that the heroization of Pasang Lhamu had been greatly blown out of proportion,[70] the angry responses from letter writers included charges of both "sexism"[71] and national divisiveness.[72]

The second point on which I will comment briefly, is that, as in the other two cases, Pasang Lhamu climbed with her husband. Not only did they climb together, but they were business partners as well. I noted earlier that it was plausible to suggest that Sherpa women climbed with their husbands not only because they could not get climbing jobs without them, but because it was part of a more active and intentional move to reestablish some solidarity and relative equality with Sherpa men. This may seem to beg the question of why Sherpa women wanted to climb in the first place, to which several answers have already been suggested: that they came from a tradition of independence that had been enhanced by various religious changes over the course of the twentieth century; that they had been chafing in the more housewifely role they were forced to take up in Kathmandu; that climbing was both well paying and charismatic in Nepal; and that, given the role of tourism and climbing in the Nepal economy, climbing was virtually the only game in town for young people without formal education (and even for some with it).

None of these points exclude the possibility I am suggesting here: that climbing with one's husband was an act of gender-radical politics in this context, an attempt to intervene in, and counteract, a situation of growing inequality. And in fact it is my impression, though only at this point an impression, that the various aspects of Sherpa women's gender politics seem to be paying off. Following a period in which Sherpa society seemed to be splitting between men in the cities getting caught up in the national and transnational "flow," and women in the villages remaining "backward" and "traditional," the number of husband-and-wife teams in this story is at least suggestive of a shift.[73]

Along with this shift a certain self-reflection in the matter seems to be coming in. For example, at the conclusion of the conversation in Ann Arbor mentioned above, the discussion moved from Pasang Lhamu's death to gender politics more generally:

> I asked, do you think more Sherpa women will climb, because in my interviews with sardars most of them said they wouldn't take a woman, it causes trouble on the expedition. And Rinzi [not his real name] said yes, most people do not feel comfortable taking someone else's wife on an expedition.
>
> And he also said, you know, we Sherpas are still kind of "male dominant." I said well yes, but the Sherpas seem to me relatively egalitarian compared to some of the Hindu groups [in Nepal]. And he said yes, our wives don't have to wait till we finish eating. And I said, or wash their husbands' feet. And he said yeah, a Sherpa wife would just say, wash them yourself! And we all cracked up.

9

RECONFIGURATIONS

If the Sherpas have been defined by mountaineering, they have also defined it. And if they have been defined by their own cultural background, they have also redefined it. It has been my position throughout that the Sherpas' engagement with mountaineering was always at the same time an engagement with their own culture. Returning to the metaphor of serious games, we can say that the Sherpas have always played several games at once. They sought to do well in the sahib's game of mountaineering, a game that over time became part of their identity and thus one of their own games as well. But success in mountaineering was always also for them in the service of other games, games defined by their own history, their own politics, their own culturally shaped desires. In this chapter, I bring this argument up into the present. I begin again with sahib representations.

Has Success Spoiled the Sherpas?[1]

Starting in the 1970s, the view of the Sherpas and their motives for climbing began to shift, and it became much more common for climbers to see the Sherpas as climbing for money. This discourse, however, could go in several directions. On the one hand it embodied a kind of deromanticizing and, ideally, deorientalizing of Sherpa culture. But it could also begin from the assumption that the Sherpas were once very different from "us," innocent and nonmaterialistic, and thus that the "discovery" of their interest in money was a discovery of their corruption, of their being spoiled by having been drawn into a wage economy at all, or by having been paid too highly and given an inflated sense of their worth.[2]

The idea that the Sherpas had been "spoiled" by their relative fame and high (in the local context) wages has appeared from time to time in the mountaineering literature,[3] but it has become a more insistent theme since the 1970s. In a 1981 article, Tom Laird, a long-time resident of Nepal with a strong countercultural perspective,[4] was tremendously saddened by what he called the "new Sherpa," the young man who had been swept against his will into modernity because of the lure of or need for money. Laird also wrote of the "subtle, gradual changing of the Sherpa will, the bending of it with money, that is the costliest result" of Western mountaineering.[5]

The idea that the Sherpas had been corrupted by the kind of work they did and the world they lived in also began to show up in the anthropological literature in the late seventies. Mike Thompson argued then (1979) that a set of new options had emerged for the Sherpas.[6] The first was what he called a relatively "together" option, in which the individual was able to do well in the contemporary games of tourism and mountaineering and yet retain the older values in which there was always time for kin, old friends, and traditional practices. The second was what he called the "frantic entrepreneurial option," which itself took two forms: one in which the individual was very successful but was too busy running back and forth between expeditions, trips to Europe and Japan, and his lodges and restaurants in Khumbu and Kathmandu to spend time with friends or simply to enjoy life; the other, in which a young Sherpa man became a kind of bottom-feeder on the tourist market, desperately hanging out around tourists, trekkers, and agencies, hoping for the crumbs of jobs and connections. Thompson's point was that fewer and fewer Sherpas were able to take the easygoing, culturally "together" option. Instead there were an increasing number of type-two Sherpas, economically successful but losing their cultural bearings, and also an increasing number of the type-three Sherpas, who would abandon a dying porter or fleece an unsuspecting sahib with little conscience if the occasion arose.[7]

The deterioration of Sherpa culture under the onslaughts of modernization was also the subject of a major book by Christoph von

Fürer-Haimendorf that came out in 1984. Haimendorf had begun his first ethnography of the Sherpas (1964) with an extremely positive account of their culture, admiring them for "their spirit of independence, their ability to cooperate smoothly for the common good, their courtesy and gentleness of manner and their values which are productive of an admirable balance between this-worldly and other-worldly aims."[8] Even in that book he had noticed certain instances where people were not upholding the traditional virtues, largely as a result—as he saw it—of contact with sahibs in Darjeeling.[9] But in the 1984 book he described major negative changes among the Sherpas, resulting from the growth of tourism and extensive involvement with "an economic system which encourages individuals to consider acquisition of money their first priority."[10] Thus, he asserted (with only very slight anecdotal evidence) that there was a "change in the attitude of Sherpas, who used to be renowned for their honesty and loyalty to their employers."[11] He commented as well that "the old values of a society virtually free of competition and rivalry" had gone into decline.[12]

The most recent variant of this position appeared in Vincanne Adams' 1996 book *Tigers of the Snow (and Other Virtual Sherpas)*. Adams drew on a variety of contemporary theoretical perspectives that would in many ways differentiate her views sharply from those of these other writers. In particular, she would argue strongly against the notion of an authentic Sherpa culture that had either existed in the past or that exists in some sense "backstage" in the present; from her perspective "the Sherpas" have always only existed in dialogue with Western desires. Partly as an offshoot of this argument, and partly in contradiction to it, there is another discussion running through her book: a decline-through-modernization narrative that is in many ways parallel to those of von Fürer-Haimendorf and others. Within this line of discussion, Adams identifies a certain cultural pattern that is embedded in many traditional Sherpa practices (especially religious ones), a pattern of "mimesis and seduction," in which a person makes him- or herself desirable to powerful others (including gods) in order to gain their affection and assistance. The Sherpas have applied this dynamic to modern relationships—with mountaineering sahibs, tourists and trekkers, and anthropologists—and in these contexts it has exacted a terrible cost. As they have tried to make themselves into what they think the sahibs desire, they have wound up in effect sacrificing their bodies and souls on the altar of modernity. Adams reported high rates of ulcers among the Sherpas; she also summarized the appalling record of mountaineering deaths. But beyond that, there is throughout the book, and especially in the chapter on the costs of "staying Sherpa," a picture of a people who have sold out every part of their culture and identity to please the sahibs and enact the Sherpa-ness of the sahibs' desires.

Within this book, in contrast, I have emphasized the social, and especially political, complexities of both "traditional" and "modern" Sherpa society. In the early chapters I have emphasized the problems of the inheritance system, the economic inequalities captured in the idea of "big" and "small" people, and the ways in which the Rana state intensified some of those inequalities. I have also tried to show that the emergence of monasticism, while extraordinarily important for the Sherpa community, was not without its ambivalent aspects. Without denying some admirable, and even enviable, dimensions of an earlier Sherpa society and culture, then, I sought to recognize its multiple and contradictory dimensions.

In this chapter, I bring these questions up into the 1980s and 1990s. Like most people on the planet, Sherpas have been changed, even enormously changed, by their experiences in the twentieth century. But it is important to be specific about the nature of those changes, and about the agents of those changes; we would be wiser to speak not a language of corruption but a language of remaking and reconfiguration. In this chapter, then, I want to look at several key areas of change. I begin with some of the bad stories that seem to be at the root of the corruption narrative.

BAD STORIES

Stories of bad Sherpa behavior go back to some of the earliest expeditions. They are distinct from stories of "resistance" in that they usually concern Sherpa relations among themselves, or with other porters, and are not directed against the sahibs in a political sense (although as they sometimes involve cheating or robbing the sahibs, the "resistance" issue may get blurred). Normally, these are stories of Sherpas mistreating people who are in some way less powerful than themselves—cheating and/or beating other Sherpas or the local porters, or abandoning a sick or injured porter. For example, the sardar on the 1922 Everest expedition was thought to be cheating the other Sherpas; the sahibs found this a problem as it fomented constant ill feeling and resistance in the ranks, but they did not generalize from the individual to the Sherpas as a whole.

Recently, however, it has become more common to treat such cases as indexes of a general decline in Sherpa morality due to their being spoiled or corrupted by money, success, or other features of the modern world. One of the key cases concerned the abandonment of several Tamang porters on a tourist trek in the late seventies:

> Last year some Sherpas (on a "safe" tourist trek not a "dangerous" mountaineering expedition) were caught in a storm. . . . The well-equipped clients and the well-equipped Sherpas survived but several of the local (non-Sherpa) porters, who had only cotton clothing and were carrying heavy loads, died. Some Americans also happened to be crossing the pass and they did all they could, and tried to get the Sherpas to help the exhausted porters. One porter who had collapsed in the snow had just been left there and they tried to persuade the Sherpas to go back up to help him. They refused, saying "He is not a member of the party."[13]

This incident is one of the things behind Michael Thompson's discussion (1979), sketched above, of the effects of modernization on the Sherpas.

More generally, the notion has got around that more and more Sherpa sardars are cheating the Tamang porters. In an interview with trekking-agency owner Mike Cheney in the late seventies, Cheney told me about this incident of abandoning the porters, and also said that Sherpas were "cheating the Tamang porters by dismissing them the day before the destination so the tourists won't tip them and will have more baksheesh [tips, bonuses] for the Sherpas."[14] Anthropologist David Holmberg, who has worked among the Tamangs for many years, has suggested recently that Sherpa cheating and abusive neglect of Tamang porters has become a widespread pattern, especially on the more comfortable tourist treks as opposed to the mountaineering expeditions. I quote here from unpublished comments by him:

> In recent years, Sherpa sardars in attempts to avoid savvy, organized, resistant porters have shifted their bases and draw porters from more naive (and thus underpaid, underequipped, underfed, and overexploited) communities. Organized treks thus bring Sherpas into contact with other ethnic groups whom they often treat in quite exploitative (and there are a whole host of ruses sirdars use to rip off porters to enrich themselves), demeaning, and dangerous ways.
>
> . . . .
>
> Deaths of porters both on the approaches of major expeditions and on treks, many of which cross passes and arrive at base camps well above 5,000 meters, over the years probably number more than [those of] high-altitude Sherpas—but this is a prejudiced, unconfirmed guess. Porters die silently, unnamed, and almost always unrecorded from exposure during storms—never having the equipment or experience of Sherpas or sahibs—from acute mountain sickness, and from disease.[15]

I certainly join in condemning any abuses that have taken place, as indeed would most Sherpas. But I am also inclined to try to understand what is behind them, to look—as I have tried to do throughout this book—at the structures of inequality within which "bad behavior" takes place. Holmberg has suggested, in another part of his comment, looking at long-term patterns of exploitation between Solu Sherpa landlords and Tamang sharecroppers, and this would certainly be an important context to examine. For present purposes, however, I will look briefly (extensive data are not available) at the new forms of inequality emerging within the Sherpa community, and between the Sherpas and other groups, in the context of the emergence of mountaineering and tourism.

New Forms of Inequality

I began this book with an account of the structure of political-economic relations in Solu-Khumbu that drove some of the early Sherpas into mountaineering. In the past, very poor or landless Sherpas had very few options for acquiring economic resources, both for survival and to improve their situation in life. Poor people borrowed from rich people; when they could not repay the loan, their only option (other than running away) was to tie themselves to the lender as servants or tenant farmers and hope to work off the debt. Even for those who were not very poor, the rules and realities of property and inheritance were such that the prospects of success in life were always somewhat risky. Some families had too many sons; even when this was not so, some sons were structurally favored over others, and some sons were simply done out of their inheritance by an ambitious brother. The prospect of "smallness," in terms of both poverty and dependency, was always real.

The wages from mountaineering began to rectify the situation, and the income from tourism had a further leveling effect. The rich might still be rich, but the poor were no longer forced into dependency relations, and the more feudal aspects of the old system were significantly undermined. However, new forms of inequality among the Sherpas have begun to emerge.

There is first of all a new class of "big people"—not the old traders and landowners but a few fabulously successful sardars who have been able to retire early from the dangerous and hard work of climbing and from the social stress of the sardar position. They have gone into various forms of business, mostly hotel and restaurant ownership. They may be contrasted with less successful climbing Sherpas, who for whatever reason have not achieved the position of sardar, and who continue to carry loads at high altitudes into a relatively advanced age (into their fifties) because they cannot afford to stop.

There are also significant differentials between Sherpas who live on the tourist-and-expedition routes and those who do not; the former are profiting disproportionately from the tourism trade.[16] Some individuals who live away from the tourist routes—mostly, but not entirely, Sherpas from Solu—have come to form a kind of internal proletariat among the Sherpas, working in the tourist lodges and doing agricultural work for Sherpas who are too busy with their expedition work or who have too much land to work themselves.[17]

In addition, a significant number of nonethnic Sherpas—mainly Tamang and Gurung—have gone to work for mountaineering and trekking sardars. One observant climbing sahib noted:

> Nima, our kitchen boy, was one of two young Tamang brothers whom Ang Phurba had adopted in his house in Khumjung. Joe [Tasker] was perceptive about hierarchies and often teased Ang Phurba that he, a member of the Sherpa super-race, exploited Nima like a slave—and Ang Phurba laughed for he, also, had just read some short stories by James Lester about black slaves in America.[18]

Whether the workers are Solu Sherpas or members of other ethnic groups, the relationship is exploitative in standard terms, yet there seems to be a particular local/Sherpa inflection on the pattern. That is, many of these relationships are set up, by mutual understanding, so as to serve as stepping-stones into the mountaineering and trekking labor market for the disadvantage party. The employees agree to work at little or no pay in exchange for a promise to be given climbing and trekking opportunities. In these cases, the climbing and tourist Sherpas themselves have become *zhindak*s (patrons, protectors) in relation to less advantaged groups. Whether or not this mitigates the exploitation is another question.

The new forms of inequality represent one of many reconfigurations of "traditional" Sherpa society, a society that was not some pristine site of egalitarianism, but that had its own forms of inequality. The new forms will, presumably, set in motion resistances and transformation as did the old ones, and thus lead to a future that we do not yet see. Without minimizing their significance, however, we must set these changes alongside other, more positive, changes that the Sherpas have both experienced and brought about, in two major areas: reconfigurations of Sherpa "identity" and reconfigurations of Sherpa religion.

RECONFIGURING IDENTITY: TRANSFORMATIONS
OF THE "SHERPA"

We saw, early in this work, how early climbing Sherpas succeeded in consolidating the category "Sherpa" in such a way that the ethnic category became virtually isomorphic with the work role of high-altitude porter. One way to approach the reconfiguration of identity for contemporary Sherpas is to consider how this consolidation is coming apart. I will put the question in the form of a word game: As we reach the end of the twentieth century, the climbing Sherpa may no longer be an ethnic Sherpa, and vice versa. Let me unpack this little puzzle.

OTHER GROUPS AS "SHERPAS"

There are several senses in which a person labeled "Sherpa" may not in fact be a Sherpa. First, it appears that the Nepali state has forced the category "Sherpa" on several Tibetan-derived northern-border groups in eastern Nepal.[19] Second, members of other ethnic groups who are working in tourism sometimes call themselves Sherpas because the tourists want "Sherpas."[20] In both cases, the matter is a source of some irritation to the non-Sherpas, who feel constrained to accept or adopt an alien identity.

On the other hand, in high-altitude mountaineering, a number of non-Sherpas have achieved success without pretending to be Sherpas, and this has been a source of ethnic pride for the groups in question. The first non-Sherpa Nepali to reach the top of Mount Everest was a Tamang, Sambhu Tamang, with the Italian expedition of 1973. He was also at that time the "youngest Chomolongma [Everest] summitteer,"[21] and he summitted again in 1985.[22] On that second expedition, a young man by the name of Narayan Shrestha became the first Newar to reach the top of Everest.[23] The French Everest expedition of 1988 included one Gurung and one Tamang among the high-altitude Sherpas.[24]

Here we may reconnect with the questions raised earlier about relationships between Sherpas and other ethnic groups. While in some contexts there is evidence that some Sherpas are exploiting (and even abusing) non-Sherpas, in the case of non-Sherpas working as high-altitude Sherpas it seems clear—given the Sherpas' virtual monopoly on this work—that ethnic Sherpas must be facilitating, or at the very least allowing, the non-Sherpas' gaining access to these jobs. In a recent article in the popular regional magazine, *Himal*, some Sherpas were asked whether there was friction between Sherpas and non-Sherpas as the non-Sherpas came into the high-altitude jobs. Ang Tshering Sherpa, described as a trekking executive, was quoted as saying, "There is always a demand for people in this profession, so there is no friction between Sherpa and non-Sherpa."[25] Similarly, former sardar Pertemba Sherpa was quoted as saying, "It is good that non-Sherpas are getting involved."[26]

In fact, in Pertemba's case we know from another source that he actively helped get jobs for non-Sherpas on expeditions. As a young sardar in the mid-seventies, it was he who had proposed including four young Tamang men among the high-altitude Sherpas on Chris Bonington's Everest Southwest Face expedition. Although there was some resistance among the ethnic Sherpa Sherpas at first, in the end Pertemba prevailed, the Tamangs were hired, and they and the Sherpas worked together "in perfect harmony."[27]

SHERPAS IN OTHER PROFESSIONS

If Tamang high-altitude porters and climbers represent Sherpas who are not ethnic Sherpas, Sherpas working in professions other than mountaineering represent Sherpas who are not climbing Sherpas. Sherpas in this sense occupy an increasingly wide range of jobs and professions in the contemporary world, and it is important to recognize this fact. These Sherpas succeed not by doing well in or changing the game of mountaineering, but by using the institutional fallout of mountaineering—especially education—to move in entirely new directions.

The construction of the Lukla airstrip, in the sixties, for the purpose of bringing in supplies to build hospitals and schools in Solu-Khumbu, and to service the hospitals thereafter, produced at that time an unintended consequence: the massive influx of tourism. But in fact, the schools and hospitals were built as well. James Fisher,

28. The late Ang Gyelzen (A. G.) Sherpa and Pemba Tsering Sherpa in the office of their trekking agency, Journeys Nepal, 1990.

who was involved in the building of both the airstrip and the schools, reminds us of the importance of those schools, alongside the more dramatic "impact of" tourism: "While tourism knocked the Sherpa economy off center, the schools brought change but also gave Sherpa society the tools to maintain its cultural equilibrium. Coming before tourism, the schools bought the Sherpas time."[28]

Educated Sherpas, and indeed many without a significant amount of education, have gone on to do a wide range of things, and it is here that the Sherpa is not necessarily a "Sherpa"; that is, that ethnic Sherpas are not simply mountaineers. Many Sherpas have gone into business, operating trekking agencies and other enterprises.[29] Sherpas now own about thirty percent of the trekking agencies in Kathmandu, and about fifty percent of the largest ones.[30] Other educated Sherpas work for various government and nongovernmental agencies, including Sagarmatha National Park and the Himalayan Trust. And finally, a small group of Sherpa professionals is emerging. Four Sherpas, including a close friend of mine, A. G. (Ang Gyelzen) Sherpa, have been pilots for Royal Nepal Airlines,[31] and there were at last count three Sherpa physicians.[32] The recognition of the growing numbers of Sherpa professionals provides a positive counterpoint to the spoiled-by-modernization argument. To take one small but telling example, at one point I had read an article in the *New York Times* on how the Sherpas were being "spoiled" by tourism, and one of its key examples was how tourists had introduced candy to the Sherpas, bringing about a rise in tooth decay.[33] Later I came across another article that told another part of the story: "A Canadian-trained Sherpa woman has opened a dental clinic" in Namche Bazar.[34] The Canadian-trained Sherpa woman dental practitioner represents both a creative response to a small but unwelcome pitfall of modernity, and a nicely compounded example of a Sherpa who is not in virtually any sense a "Sherpa."

THE SHERPAS AS MOUNTAINEERS

In the context of mountaineering, the question of Sherpa identity takes another turn. Here the question is one of being *more than* just high-altitude support staff; it is a question of their being recognized for their mountaineering achievements as such. In this context, the Sherpas quite actively engage in a kind of high-altitude identity politics. Like the Sherpas of the 1920s who reconfigured the category of Sherpa in the context of mountaineering in the first place, the Sherpas in the late-twentieth century seek to both expand and reconfigure the category yet again.

The issue of recognition—the idea of not being merely a climbing Sherpa—has been amplified in recent years. There is fairly widespread discontent among Sherpas at the lack of recognition for individual Sherpas and their feats in mountaineering. Sherpas have expressed annoyance that they were often not named in sahib climbing accounts, being listed instead as an undifferentiated mass of "Sherpas." Even a hero like Ang Rita Sherpa, who has reached the summit of Mount Everest multiple times without oxygen, may be slighted; when he made his record ninth ascent, the Russian party he was working for did not mention this accomplishment at their press conference.[35] Sherpas have noted as well that the sahibs often take innumerable photographs or extensive film footage of the Sherpas on an expedition, yet little or none of this appears in the final book or film. I have heard these complaints consistently in my fieldwork since the

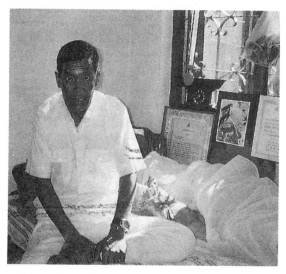

29. Ang Rita Sherpa, who had at last count reached
the summit of Everest 11 times, with some of
his awards, 1990.

1970s, but they have become more public and audible in recent
years. The issue was laid out in some detail in a 1995 article entitled
"Fame Still Eludes Sherpas."[36]

The most clear-cut example of the Sherpas demanding recognition
as climbers and not just as "Sherpas" has been the rise of the all-Sherpa
climbing expedition. At an earlier point in mountaineering history,
when climbing was nothing more and nothing less than a job from the
Sherpa point of view, such expeditions would have been considered
absurd. Even at the present time, most Sherpas see little point to climbing mountains, risking lives, and spending time better spent on other
pursuits if they do not get paid to do it. Nonetheless, in the early eighties, the first all-Sherpa expedition ever—as far as I can tell—made the
first winter ascent of a lesser-known peak called Tilicho (7,132 meters).
The organizer, Sarkey Tshering Sherpa, explained that the point of the
expedition was to "change the Sherpa attitude toward mountaineering
which we approached more as a sport."[37]

In 1991 the Sherpas put together the first (and, as far as I know,
only) all-Sherpa Everest expedition. The expedition had first been

conceived in the mid-eighties by Lopsang Sherpa, who had worked for American climber Peter Athans on a successful 1990 American Everest expedition. Athans and some other Americans helped raise funds for the project and, in a nice twist on the usual arrangements, worked for the expedition as supporting members with virtually no recognition. After some difficulties in which it appeared that the unthinkable—the failure of an all-Sherpa Everest expedition!—might happen, the expedition was successful, with Sonam Dendu, Ang Temba, Apa Sherpa, and the American Peter Athans getting to the top. And the language, at least on the part of the leader, Lopsang, was pure identity politics: "We want to take pride as a people apart."[38] Sonam Dendu was quoted as saying, "This is *our* expedition. . . . It is for all the Sherpas"[39] We even hear some of the kind of splitting that operates in identity politics generally, as subgroups within subgroups sought recognition. One of the two Sherpas on the expedition from the lower Sherpa valley of Solu, which has traditionally supplied far fewer climbing Sherpas than the upper, Khumbu, area, said that he was "climbing for Solu pride too."[40]

In sum, late 20th century Sherpas have reconfigured the identity of "the Sherpa" in multiple ways. Some have avoided or moved out of "Sherpa work," while allowing and even fostering members of other ethnic groups moving into the work, thereby beginning to break the link between the role and the ethnic identity constructed in the early 20th century. Even when Sherpas have stayed within mountaineering, they have sought to move out of the ranks of "Sherpas," and into the ranks of "members," whether together with other nationals (as on joint expeditions) or on all-Sherpa expeditions where in fact all Sherpas are members.

INTERNAL TRANSFORMATIONS:
RECONFIGURING RELIGION

Another major arena of cultural reconfiguration has been religion. At one level, religion has simply been a given of Sherpa life. Sherpas have "taken refuge" in their religion in relation to fundamental issues of security and identity—for protection from harm, for providing the bases for the good things in life, for comfort and meaning, for the very core of who they were. They have used religion in this sense on expeditions: to protect them from danger and death, to give them some power over their own fears, over their own grief and shock when there was an accident, over the sahibs with their reckless ideas and their real power.

At the same time, with the rise of the monasteries, there was a sense in which "Sherpa religion" had itself became a form of internal "difference." I have thus treated the monastic movement, even though it was internal to Sherpa society, much as I have treated mountaineering: it was initially a new, and even somewhat alien, game on the Sherpa scene, with which ordinary Sherpas had, willy nilly, to engage. Over the course of the century, the monks reshaped the religious landscape of Sherpa society just as mountaineering reshaped the economic landscape. In fact, the parallel between mountaineering and monasticism can be pushed further: the relative alienness of monasticism, and its disciplinary stance in relation to ordinary Sherpas, made monasticism, like mountaineering, an object of a kind of low-key resistance and reconfiguration.

In this section, then, I summarize first the impressive overall success of the monastic campaign in making Sherpa popular religion "higher." I then review briefly the state of monasticism among the Sherpas today, which—despite its successes—is very mixed. And finally I look at some ways in which Sherpas seem to be reconfiguring monastic religion itself, bringing it more into line with their contemporary concerns.

MAKING LOW RELIGION HIGHER

At the end of the twentieth century, it is possible to see that there have been an enormous number of changes in Sherpa popular religion, changes that embody the higher religious ideals embodied in monastic Buddhism. "Low" practices have either been eliminated or revised; "high" practices have been institutionalized. A quick summary:

- The Nupki Gyelwu rites, oriented toward gaining wealth through animal sacrifice to a violent and bloodthirsty god, were the first things to go.

- The annual family *lha-chetup*, or offering rituals conducted in the household for the well-being of the family, apparently included the worship of gods with characteristics similar to Nupki Gyelwu, and for similar purposes. Many Sherpas in recent years have cleaned up their family lha-chetup rituals as well, getting rid of a lot of the "smaller" gods.
- The married lamas, denigrated for their drinking, their lack of ritual expertise, and their (whispered) involvement in sorcery on behalf of private clients, are, with one or two exceptions, almost entirely gone in Khumbu.[41] Most village ritual work is now performed either by monks invited down from the monasteries, or by fallen monks now serving as village lamas. (Just to be clear on the difference, the original "married lamas" [*banzin, choa, ngawa*, or simply *lama*] saw no incompatibility between marriage and spiritual practice, and indeed believed that religious powers were enhanced by descent from a long line of married lamas. Fallen monks practicing as "village lamas" have become "married lamas," too, but they usually view this as the result of a failure, and not as part of a positive alternative to monasticism.)
- There had been at least four religious communities in Solu-Khumbu composed entirely of married lamas and their families, but only one (Kyerok) now remains. This one, moreover, has been upgrading its practices, to bring them more into line with higher monastic ideals.[42]
- The major village rituals that remain—especially Dumji, the annual village exorcisms—have been transformed. Most of the bawdy elements have been cleaned up, and the violence has been toned down.[43]
- The shamans are almost entirely gone in Solu;[44] in Khumbu some shamans are still said to be practicing, but there has been a tendency to translate their purpose into monastic terms. Thus, instead of curing a sick person, they are now "helping all sentient beings." [45]
- The ritual of Nyungne, in which the lay people practice an abbreviated version of monastic discipline for several days,

has by now been instituted in virtually every village temple in Solu-Khumbu. These rites are explicitly said to bring the experience, and the spiritual benefits, of monastic practice to lay people on a regular basis.

- All of these shifts in the direction of "higher" monastic ideals have been reflected in the iconography of Sherpa temples and chapels. Virtually all of the religious artwork done before the foundings of the monasteries had the (married) Guru Rimpoche, the founder of Tibetan Buddhism, as the central idol or image, usually flanked by his two wives. All of the monastic art, as well as all of the temple art done (or redone) after the foundings of the monasteries, has the celibate Buddha in the center, flanked by Chenrezi (the god of compassion) on his right and the Guru Rimpoche on his left.

I think it is fair to say that Sherpa religion has been "monasticized," cleaned up, and shifted—as the monks intended—in a "higher" direction. The outward features of the religious landscape—the specialists who are available to be called, the rites that are available to be participated in—have changed considerably. And for at least some lay Sherpas, these outward shifts of religion have been accompanied by personal transformations.

The case I knew best in this regard was that of Nyima Chotar, who worked for me in the late 1970s. He was one of many Sherpa men I knew who said they wished they had become monks, but in his case, as in many others, circumstances had pushed him in other directions. Nyima Chotar became an expedition Sherpa, and although he did a few mountaineering expeditions, he came to specialize in scientific expeditions: botanical, medical, and—in my case—anthropological. Two brief anecdotes convey his personal move to "high religion."

Nyima Chotar lived for many years in Darjeeling. His father was a famous early mountaineering Sherpa, Dawa Tenzing, but he had lost a younger brother in mountaineering, and his mother had committed suicide over that death. The first story concerns his decision to clean up the family *lha-chetup* rituals, to get rid of the low gods and spirits:

> After his mother died, when he was still in India, he decided he didn't want all the *lu* and *gyelwu* and *gyabtak* [various local spirits] that his family and all the others had. You have these to help make you rich, but he was thinking he didn't need them. He wrote his father and told him to call the Tengboche lama and the monks, and they came and did a ritual and threw them all out. . . . Nothing happened to him as a result of doing this. His father feels the same way.[46]

The second story concerns his rejection of shamanism:

> He said he really wasn't very interested in *lhawa* [shamans], only in *payin* [Buddhist merit, the opposite of *dikpa*, sin] and high gods. . . . One time he had been a little sick and his sister had commissioned a *lhabeu* [shamanistic trance-curing ritual] in his absence. The shaman said the cause of his illness was the *lu* [locality spirit] of a certain rock where he had once sat. He got angry at the lu and he went to the rock and hit it with a hammer and shat on it. Nothing bad happened to him, and indeed within two days he got better.[47]

Nyima Chotar is an example of the fullest possible effects of the shift to higher Buddhism that the monks could have desired. He accepted for himself virtually the whole of the monastic agenda for lay people, orienting his religious practices almost entirely toward the avoidance of sin (not always successfully; he battled a drinking problem) and the accumulation of merit toward a good rebirth.[48]

But not all Sherpas were as clear in their own minds as Nyima Chotar about a commitment to "higher" Buddhist practices. Indeed, I want to suggest that, while the move to higher Buddhism among the Sherpas certainly had powerful effects, it was itself an object of some ambivalence and, over time, reconfiguration. The first indicator of this is the state of the monastic system among the Sherpas today.

FALLING LAMAS AND LANGUISHING MONASTERIES

The Sherpa monastic system today is in a very mixed condition.[49] Although some new monasteries are being built, others are clearly in decline, and yet others are flourishing not because of Sherpa support but because of foreign support. The decline of the monastic system may be yet another negative effect of "modernization," and certain aspects of contemporary life have undoubtedly played a role in this process. Yet I would argue that these changes must also be viewed as responses to internal Sherpa wishes about the shape of their religion. I begin with a quick survey of the state of the monasteries. (Fuller stories, some involving local scandals, may be found in Appendix B.)

- The first (1916) Sherpa monastery, Tengboche, is active and doing well. Its head lama, the Tengboche Rimpoche, has maintained his vows and remains a vigorous leader. But the monastery is heavily dependent on foreign donations.
- The second (1924) Sherpa monastery, Chiwong, has been languishing since the late 1950s. Its first head lama broke his vows with a nun and left; its second head lama accepted another offer in Tibet and then died there, and after that its *geken* or teacher left, too. No new head lama has been found. Without a head lama to ordain new monks, and without a teacher to train them, there cannot be any further growth of the monastery.
- Devuche nunnery, founded in 1928, was reduced to six nuns in the late 1970s, and had not had any new recruits for a long time.
- Takshindo monastery, founded in 1946 by a former Tengboche monk, has been unable to continue its line of leadership. When the head lama died in 1960, a reincarnation was found, but the family refused to turn the child over to the monastery.
- The monastery at Serlo was founded in 1959 by a Sherpa monk, Sangye Tenzing, who had been trained in Tibet and

had plans for making the monastery even "higher" in its ritual practices than the other Sherpa monasteries. But he broke his vows with a nun in the mid-eighties, and subsequently died. The monastery shut down completely.

• The monastery at Thami had seemed to be the other big success of the Sherpa monastic movement. Originally a local, and very old, temple headed by married lamas in a long and powerful descent line, it converted to celibacy in the early 1950s. When they old head lama died in the late 1950s, his reincarnation was found and successfully trained and ordained. But he broke his vows in 1990, and the monastery was for a time thrown into disarray.

Sherpa monasticism, or perhaps I should say monasticism among the Sherpas, is not dead, but its place in the overall configuration of Sherpa religion has shifted quite a bit, in several different ways. As the Sherpa monasteries have declined, the Sherpas have come to use Tibetan refugee monasteries when they have needed monastic services. The Tibetan refugee monastery in Solu, Tüpden Chöling, under the leadership of the revered Tushi Rimpoche, is still vigorous, and the Tushi Rimpoche and his monks even perform the annual Mani Rimdu festival for the Sherpas at the languishing Chiwong monastery nearby. The Sherpas have also, until recently, used the Tibetan monasteries in Kathmandu in similar ways.

At the same time, the Sherpas have been happy to accept Western support for their monasteries. Tengboche monastery has received extensive funding from Western donors, including Sir Edmund Hillary's Himalayan Trust, the American organization Cultural Survival, and the American Himalayan Foundation. Other examples include Kopan Gompa (*gompa* can be used narrowly as a term for a temple, and more broadly for a whole monastery) on the outskirts of Kathmandu and its related monastery in Khumbu, Laudo Gompa, both of which are said to be supported by American Buddhists.[50] And most recently, a former Serlo monk began to build a new monastery in the Solu valley, with his funding coming primarily from an American sponsor.[51]

Sherpa Buddhism, like the Sherpas themselves, has become part of a set of Western desires and Western "serious games." Despite the foreign funding, however, the monasteries retain certain specific kinds of value for Sherpas: their rituals are powerful, their practitioners are well trained, and, most importantly, they produce reincarnate lamas, who are still tremendously valued. But from a broader perspective, they have done their work of injecting a higher Buddhism into Sherpa religious life, and have now moved into a somewhat more marginal position in the Sherpa community.

The major exception to this point would seem to be the new Sherpa monastery in Kathmandu, founded in the early 1980s. This monastery is not funded primarily by foreign donors, and it is quite central to urban Sherpa community life. But it is also a new kind of monastery, and its changes reflect other ways in which Sherpas have been reshaping their "high" Buddhism. First, there has been the problem of the removal of monks from the community, their social detachment. Although in standard Buddhist terms this is fundamental to the idea of the monk, from the viewpoint of many lay Sherpas (and many other Buddhists), such detachment has often been construed as "selfish." There has thus been a gradual tendency—however contradictory—to tighten the bonds between the monasteries and the lay community. Second, although the monasteries brought into Sherpa religion a greater emphasis on "compassion," contemporary Sherpas seem to have made compassion even more central to popular religiosity than it was to monastic religiosity. I begin with the tightening of the linkages between the monasteries and the lay community.

TALOK (FALLEN MONKS) AND THE "WORLDING" OF HIGHER BUDDHISM

When I first did fieldwork among the Sherpas, in the mid-sixties, I was told that monks or nuns who broke their vows (talok, from tawa lokpa, monk-undone; also ani lokpa, nun-undone) incurred great sin and also great shame. They felt compelled to leave the community, usually for Darjeeling, or at least for another part of the Sherpa area. There were very few fallen monks and nuns in Solu (although possibly somewhat more in Khumbu) at the time of my first fieldwork.

They were not totally absent, however. A few remained in the area and became, in effect, agents for spreading "high religion" further throughout Solu-Khumbu. In the 1920s, Sangye Lama, who eventually single-handedly sponsored the founding of Chiwong monastery, had a son by the name of Dawa Tenzing who was a monk in a monastery in Tibet. Sangye is said to have decided that he wanted the son to marry after all, and thus recalled him from the monastery to enter into an arranged marriage. The son dutifully returned and married, but remained committed to monastic ideals, and it was said that it was he who not only prompted Sangye to build Chiwong, but also was very active in the fund-raising. Similarly in the 1940s, it was said to be a fallen Tengboche monk who invited Tolden Tsultim from Tengboche to found Takshindo monastery.

Over time, the number of fallen monks and nuns grew, and more and more stayed in the area. Many became village lamas, occupying the niches vacated by the declining numbers of the married lamas (*banzin*) who came by their powers by virtue of descent from a line of married lamas. Many of the fallen monks felt tremendous regrets about their lapse, and remained strongly committed to the "high religion" of the monasteries. Much of the reform of popular village religious practice, especially the cleanup of the Dumji festivals, took place in their hands. They also have tended to send their own sons into the monasteries, and thus have served as a significant source of new monk recruits. Thus, fallen monks have increasingly constituted a kind of invisible bridge between the monasteries and the villages, both bringing their training to the villages and sending their sons back to the monasteries.

Even more strikingly, some monks who had broken their vows were reintegrated in limited ways into their original monasteries. In the late 1960s, a Tengboche *talok* whose wife had died was participating again in the life of the monastery. When he was a monk he had been a central figure at Tengboche as the *geken*, or teacher. He had also been the dancer for Mi Tsering, one of the key roles in the Mani Rimdu dances. In a conversation in 1967 with Lama Tenzing, the head of the Kyerok married-lama community,

Lama Tenzing asked about Tengboche [from which we had just come]. Mingma told him about the *talok* or *domshur* (*domba shorup*, vows breaker) whom they continue to allow to work in the monastery (his wife died) because he's so *khamu* (expert).[52]

There was a similar case in Khumjung in the late seventies. At Tengboche I met a former monk who continued to spend time around (though he did not actually live at) the monastery. The story gradually emerged:

> The talok is actually in the process of being reintegrated. His wife died. He was evidently drinking heavily but now has stopped completely.... Rimpoche evidently wants to take him back and it is his doing to send the talok on many assignments [to do rituals for lay people]. Before he was a senior *gelung* [fully ordained monk], but now of course he sits at the bottom [of the row of monks]. Nyima Chotar noted how *hard* he works [during rituals]. Other monks periodically go to sleep, or just space out, but he's in there chanting every word, making every gesture.[53]

The most recent example is the fallen *tulku* (reincarnate head lama) of Thami monastery. In a brief lapse of sobriety and judgment in 1990, the lama broke his vows. As far as I know, no fallen head lama has ever previously been taken back by his monastery. And in the cases of reintegration noted above, the reintegration took place only after the wives had died. Yet according to the gossip in Kathmandu in 1990, the monks at Thami were discussing the possibility of having the Thami tulku stay on as the head of the monastery. In fact I learned much later that the monks "forgave him for his mistake" and he has stayed on.[54]

These various levels of traffic in talok (fallen monks), suggest a more complex two-way process of adjustment between monasteries and lay Sherpas, rather than the simple "impact" of the monasteries. On the one hand, the process had the effect of bringing high religion into the villages, and this was extremely important to the success of the monastic campaign. But on the other hand it gradually brought about a more general reconfiguration of the boundary between monasticism and lay life. In the late seventies there were so many fallen monks staying in Khumbu that I asked a friend whether I had been right in reporting earlier that breaking monastic vows was felt to be very shameful. He said, yes, but the large numbers had more or less normalized the pattern, and people no longer felt *ngotza* (shame). My sense is that this process has continued and become even more routinized, that the whole notion of "falling," or breaking vows, has been softened up, and that—in the fashion of Buddhism in Thailand or Burma—monasticism is becoming a temporary stage of life, rather than a permanent vow, for many young Sherpas, while at the same time monasteries are becoming part of, rather than opposed to, the community.

It is in light of this discussion that we may consider the new Sherpa monastery in Kathmandu. In the early 1980s, the Sherpa Sewa Kendra, the Sherpa community-affairs organization in the city, organized the founding of a new monastery under the leadership of the Tengboche lama.[55] Although there are said to be a few monks studying there, the *gompa* (again, the term can be used narrowly for a temple and more broadly for a whole monastery) seems to be operating primarily as a cross between a traditional village temple and a community center, a place where the Sherpas hold both traditional religious rituals (such as the celebration of the New Year, or *Losar*) and newer religio-community events.

For example, one of my friends in Kathmandu told me about the use of the temple for funerals. Funerals have been an issue of some friction between Sherpas and their Nepali neighbors and landlords. A Sherpa funeral normally was conducted in the home of the deceased, and normally entailed keeping the corpse in the house for an extended period of time, while the requisite rituals were performed. According to Kathmandu Sherpas, however, Hindus do not want people even to die in their houses, no less have the corpses in extended residence, so the funerals are now held at the gompa.

In a more festive vein, the temple is also used for a large Sherpa gathering on the holiday of Phangnin. Phangnin was not, as far as I know, traditionally celebrated in Solu-Khumbu, and appears to be a new urban holiday (possibly of Tibetan origin) that has been taken up by the Sherpas. It is an occasion for picnicking, and apparently also for slightly more licentious forms of fun. Vincanne Adams reports a 1987 celebration with skits involving cross-dressing, a mock marriage, and the showering of the mock couple with condoms.[56] Here indeed is an example of the "worlding" of monastic Buddhism. Where the monks had once cleaned all pleasant or funny representations of sex out of village Dumjis, the urban Sherpas seem to have brought those back into the Kathmandu gompa, one more piece of the reconfiguration of the relationship and boundary between monasteries and lay life.

MORE COMPASSION

Issues of compassion, selflessness, and generosity are in theory central to Tibetan Buddhism. As part of the Mahayana tradition, it is precisely the centrality of these concerns that distinguishes Tibetan Buddhism from various Buddhisms of the Theravada schools. Yet from a Western point of view it is a peculiar kind of compassion. It is defined from within a framework that privileges monastic discipline as the most effective way to achieve transcendental salvation. It involves recognizing that others are in pain, but it offers them as a solution the model of the monk—disciplined, disengaged from social ties, free of pain because of being free of those ties.

This "high" model of compassion certainly continues among the Sherpas. It is fundamental to Buddhist theories of dealing with strong and potentially overpowering feelings, and it is valued by many for precisely this reason. This kind of compassion was evident earlier in the case of several mountaineering deaths. The increasing popularity of the monastic-inspired Nyungne observance, in which the ritual acquisition of great compassion is closely linked to ascetic practices, is another indicator of the continuing value of "high" compassion for the Sherpas. Thus, although both von Fürer-Haimendorf in the mid-fifties and I in the late sixties had reported that Nyungne was not very popular, and was mostly observed by old people,[57] by the mid-eighties it was being more enthusiastically celebrated than ever, and not just by the old and the pious.[58]

At the same time, and as important, there is a more ordinary model of compassion, stressing giving and generosity to others, with no hought of reward for the self. This is, ideally, the spirit in which one makes offerings to the gods, and the spirit in which one gives charity to monks. My sense is that this kind of compassion—more relevant for everyday life, more positive for ordinary social relations—has become increasingly central to popular Sherpa Buddhism.

A major indicator of this shift to what might be called everyday compassion is to be seen in the continuing, and indeed intensifying, popularity of the reincarnate lamas, the *tulku*, who are especially associated with "compassion" in several senses. Some tulku are said to be gods, who take human form in order to help a suffering humanity. Others are said to be *bodhisattva*s, humans who have achieved enlightenment and who could enter nirvana if they wished, but who chose to stay in the world in order to show others the way. In both cases, their mere presence in the material world is a living and continuing act of compassion.

Many tulku are also quite kind and warm in their personal styles, but whether they are or not, there is always some sense in which they are, or seem to be, more giving and generous than the monks. This generosity may include practicing acts of personal kindness to individuals; being institutionally generous (making "grants" to other monasteries, for example); or being inclusive and integrative rather than drawing boundaries and divisions as the monks do (for example, my data show that the tulku were much more willing to keep a place for the shamans in the religious life of the Sherpas after the foundings of the monasteries, unlike the monks who constantly denigrated the shamans).

Whatever ambivalences people may have felt about the monks did not apply to the tulku, whose popularity has been sustained, and even intensified, up to the present time, even in urban, "modernized" contexts. James Fisher has remarked that he has "yet to find [even] a university-educated or tourist [-guide] Sherpa who does not believe in reincarnation or prostrate himself before the rimpoche to receive his blessings."[59] To this day, probably no expedition involving Sherpas leaves Kathmandu without the blessings of the Tengboche head lama or some other rimpoche.[60]

In addition to the popularity of tulku, there are other ways in which an emphasis on compassion, in the sense of ordinary kindness and generosity, has become more prominent in contemporary Sherpa Buddhism. In particular, there is the increased popularity of *tso* rituals. *Tso* are defined as "parties" for the high gods of Buddhism, in which one gives the gods offerings with no expectation of return, purely for the goodness of giving. Whereas offerings to lower gods are done with assumptions of reciprocity (we keep them happy, they protect us in return), offerings to the highest gods of Buddhism do not have this reciprocal character and, like donations to monks, are meant simply to cultivate selflessness and thereby generate merit.

Tso are the all-purpose collective merit-generating rituals. Whereas any individual can perform merit-making practices on his or her own behalf, collective merit-making is most often done through tso; everyone shares in contributing to the offerings, and everyone shares in the benefits. A tso can be commissioned on any occasion, but some have also been added to the regular ritual calendar. For example, after the Sherpas stopped worshiping the blood-thirsty Nupki Gyelwu, they added a tso on the occasion of the Nepali Dasain. Dasain is a holiday on which numerous animals are sacrificed, and the tso is meant to counterbalance all the sin brought to the world by the animal sacrifices. Again, tso are meritorious because they are acts of pure giving with no expectation of return.

Recently, and in line with the present argument, Vincanne Adams reports that the urban Sherpas of Kathmandu have "reinvented" a ritual called "Bumtsho," which means "10,000 Tso." According to Adams, it was first performed in the early 1980s in Kathmandu, and has since been taken up in many Khumbu temples. Some time in the early 1990s, some Sherpas paid for a famous tulku, the Khentse Rimpoche, to be flown up to Khumbu to preside over a Bumtsho, which he did. He also gave an extended sermon (sermons are not traditional among the Sherpas, although they occur from time to time) in which he emphasized the importance of generosity, giving, and compassion. He said among other things,

> You cannot take [your wealth] with you. When you have that money now in your hand, while living, let's share with other human beings. Give alms. Help poor people. You give one time

and, after, you get more compassion and you can give more and more. Your compassion gets stronger and then you don't mind giving away your wealth. Don't waste wealth, don't save wealth. Realize between right and wrong.[61]

The importance of the reincarnate lama, the religious emphasis of this particular kind of ritual, and the lamas' very words all embody the shift to a more "compassionate" form of Buddhism. Thus, although contemporary Sherpas are actively seeking "high religion," they are also choosing (and thereby inflecting) the version of high religion that they are going to support. While they continue to support monasteries, they have been willing to destigmatize the "falling" of monks and nuns, making for a more active communication between the disengaged monasteries and the engaged world. And while they have been willing to drop a good deal of "low" religion— the married lamas, the shamans, the "lower" gods in their lha-chetup rituals—they support a warmer and more generous version of high religion than that originally offered by the monasteries, a high religion centered on the figure of the tulku and the ideal of compassion as generosity.

THE CONTINUING KINDNESS
OF THE SHERPAS

The language of von Fürer-Haimendorf and others on the decline of Sherpa culture is very strong. Haimendorf saw a rise of individualism, competitiveness, and rivalry, and a decline of loyalty and honesty. Thompson saw an increase in Sherpas "frantically" pursuing business and profits, and a growing number of a kind of despicable Sherpa who would do anything to "make a buck" from the games of tourism and mountaineering. Finally, Adams has discussed the many ways in which contemporary Sherpas are "virtual"; that is, little more than mirrors of the sahibs' desires for authentic Sherpas. One way or another, the Sherpas seem to have lost most of their traditional fine qualities.

Yet if one looks again at the sahib literature from mountaineering and trekking, this simply does not appear to be true. Although sahibs have lamented, and continue to lament, that the Sherpas have been

"spoiled" by money and modernity, if one looks at the actual accounts of expedition behavior, or descriptions from tourists of treks,
one finds virtually no difference between contemporary and earlier
accounts of Sherpa kindness, generosity, and good nature, not to
mention occasional outright heroism. Starting in the late seventies:

> Talking to a German woman schoolteacher just back from a
> trek. Raving about her Sherpa. She kept saying, in wondering
> tones, he was so *nice*, so *kind*, so *gentle* (but not, she added
> quickly, effeminate.) She was really rather knocked over.[62]

The early eighties:

> We had a superior lot of Sherpas to work with: cheerful, selfless,
> and proud of their jobs. . . . [The cook, Phutashi] was . . . ex-
> tremely sensitive and giving . . . our Sherpas treated us like roy-
> alty. Each morning we were awakened by a soft voice offering
> us sweet, warm tea as we lay muffled in our snug bags. . . . I was
> quietly astounded to see that it seemed to please the Sherpas to
> serve us so well.[63]

And into the nineties:

> The most delightful part of our trek . . . was the friendship we
> developed with our crew. The Sherpas were endlessly cheerful
> and pleasant, caring for us with a constant courtesy and atten-
> tion, and singing and whistling half the day. They taught us
> Nepali songs; we taught them "Old MacDonald Had a Farm,"
> which had them rolling with laughter.[64]

By the eighties most sahibs had read or been told that many Sherpas had become very modernized or mercenary about their work.
Sahibs were thus doubly impressed when a seemingly slick and modernized Sherpa turned out to be as nice as the legendary Sherpas of
old. Elaine Brook accompanied a blind friend, Julie, on a trek to
Solu-Khumbu in the mid-eighties. Their sardar was a young man
named Lhakpa Sherpa, about whom Brook at first had some doubts:
"I was beginning to perceive Lhakpa's Western manners and clothes
as indicative of opportunist motives."[65] The idea of the pragmatic
Sherpa had by then become so established that Brook was surprised

to find that the Sherpas had any aesthetic sensibility at all: "Slowly the full moon rose, throwing shadows of the mountains onto the whiteness of the cloudbank, and making the frost sparkle with a cold light. *Even the usually pragmatic Sherpas* came out to gaze at it in wonder."[66] It gradually became apparent that Lhakpa was not the cold and uncaring "modern Sherpa" Brook had feared. Lhakpa, as well as the cook, Jangbu, and the kitchen boy, Dawa, became enormously invested in having the trek work out well for the women. Julie was having a great deal of trouble along some parts of the trail, and they thought about hiring a yak to carry her. But Lhakpa knew they had little money, and he carried her for long stretches of the way himself:

> I had already told them all at the beginning that the equipment they had been given was all the baksheesh they were going to get. . . . In spite of that, they had gone out of their way to give us extra help along every step of the journey—even to the point of carrying Julie rather than have us spend money we could ill afford on a riding yak.[67]

Some of the more recent examples above come from tourist treks rather than mountaineering expeditions, and it does appear that the more gentle, caring, parentlike forms of Sherpa kindness have remained more common on these smaller, more intimate expeditions.[68] Yet kindness and other forms of Sherpa good nature continue to manifest themselves on the big mountaineering expeditions as well. On the 1988 British/American North Face Everest Expedition, there was a sardar named Pasang, who became "a father figure" for some members of the expedition, "pampering" the members at base camp and showing great concern for their welfare.[69] The climber who wrote this account in 1989 summarized his view of the Sherpas in language that could have been written in the thirties:

> The remarkable thing about the Sherpa people is that, in spite of constantly witnessing the incomparably greater wealth of foreign tourists, most of them have managed to retain their legendary dignity, humour, efficiency and generosity.[70]

Pasang was forty-nine years old at the time, a veteran of an earlier era of climbing. It might be thought, then, that he was simply an anachronism, one of the increasingly rare "old-school" Sherpas. Yet we hear "good Sherpa" stories about even highly modernized, young, upcoming Sherpa climbers as well. On the Norwegian Everest expedition in 1985, for example, Chris Bonington described Sundhare Sherpa as apparently corrupted by modernity:

[Sundhare] appeared to be very westernised, loved pop music and disco dancing and cultivated the fashions of a smart young man about Kathmandu, with a trendy shoulder-length hairstyle and tight jeans. [Bonington compared him unfavorably to] Ang Rita ... [who] was very different from Sundhare. Stolid and very much a farmer, one felt he had a firmer hold on his own heritage and background.[71]

Yet it was Sundhare who in 1978 had performed heroically on the German Swabian Expedition on Everest, in the manner of the early feats of heroism of Gaylay or Pasang Kikuli. He bivouacked overnight near the summit with the exhausted Hannelore Schmatz; he went down to a lower camp the next day to get additional oxygen for her; he returned and stayed with her when she collapsed again; and he did not descend, despite his own frozen feet, until she died.[72]

Starting in the mid-eighties, commercial climbing expeditions, in which paying clients are led by a paid guide, began to come into Himalayan mountaineering. These expeditions have been quite problematic (I will have more to say about them in chapter 10). But even on these, it was often the Sherpas who come through when the sahibs were taking care only of themselves. On the partly commercial 1988 American Everest expedition, a climber named Geoff Tabin and some Sherpas had been heading for the summit and had left one of the women, an inexperienced climber named Peggy, resting alone at the Hillary Step, the last difficult technical piece of the climb before the top. On the way back—in perfect weather, it might be added—they met her again, struggling up toward the summit alone:

Geoff looked at the Sherpas. "I'm heading down," he said. "You can come along or wait for Peggy." The Sherpas looked at each other, looked at themselves. Finally, one spoke up. It was Dawa Tsering, one of the two younger Sherpas who had climbed with Peggy all the way from Camp 2.

"I wait Peggy," he said. Geoff nodded. *Good man!*[73]

There were also the notorious 1996 commercial expeditions, when so many people died. The sardar for one of the commercial groups was a Sherpa named Lopsang Jangbu, described like Lhakpa or Sundhare above as highly modernized, wearing a ponytail like his "idol," the leader Scott Fischer, being "extremely cocky," and having a "flashy manner."[74] Yet Krakauer also described Lopsang Jangbu as "kind to a fault," and in another account of the disaster he was described as trying to stay with the dying Fischer, in the manner of Sundhare with Hannelore Schmatz, although Fischer threatened to throw himself off the mountain if Lopsang Jangbu did not go down, which he did.[75] Krakauer encountered him after Fischer's death, "half-crazed with grief and exhaustion," repeating over and over that it was his fault.[76]

I close this discussion not with a story of either great tenderness or great heroism on the part of a Sherpa but of simple common decency. On the mountain at the same time as Krakauer's group was a South African expedition that was troubled by enormous internal conflict. The leader had thrown a reporter and a photographer out of base camp, but their newspaper, the Johannesberg *Sunday Times*, was a major sponsor of the expedition, and their editor had ordered them to return. When they returned, the leader again ordered them to leave. As the reporter later wrote about his experience:

Ms. O'Dowd [one of the members] walked to the team's Sherpa leader, Ang Dorje, and said audibly: "This is Ken Vernon, one of the ones we told you about. He is to be given no assistance whatsoever." Ang Dorje is a tough, nuggety rock of a man and we had already shared several glasses of Chang, the fiery local brew. I looked at him and said, "Not even a cup of tea?" To his credit, and in the best tradition of Sherpa hospitality, he looked at Ms. O'Dowd and said: "Bullshit." He grabbed me by the arm, dragged me into the mess tent and served up a mug of steaming tea and a plate of biscuits.[77]

These "good Sherpa" stories have not been presented in order to cancel out the "bad Sherpa" stories told earlier. Nor are my accounts of some of the more positive changes in Sherpa religion meant to cancel out the sketch of the new problematic forms of inequality relations presented earlier. The Sherpas' lives in the late-twentieth century are just as contradictory as anyone else's, which was precisely—as against the modernization-decline view—the point of this chapter.

EPILOGUE

In chapter 7, I discussed the changes in sahibs and in mountaineering that were part of the broad social and cultural movement called "the counterculture." The movement of that name was a phenomenon particularly of the 1970s, linked in complex ways to political movements of the same era (civil rights, the antiwar movement, and feminism, more or less in that order). It involved young middle-class people dropping out of the "rat race," getting off the success track toward a standard lucrative, respectable middle-class career. This might have been temporary or permanent, it might have been literal, or it might have been largely symbolic, but in any event it involved a rejection of the dominant cultural values of both "modernity" (bureaucracy, technology, hyperrationality) and the middle class (money, comfort, security, propriety).

One could argue that there has been some form of counterculture for as long as there has been capitalist modernity, that the regimentation of modern life and the materialism of a capitalist middle class produce, almost of necessity, an ongoing opposition. In part this would be true because of the simple variability of personal tastes and styles. But it would also be true because not everyone can succeed in the capitalist games of life; there is not "room at the top" for all the children of the middle class, which thus always produces its own "excess" children.[1]

The idea would be, then, that there has always been a countercultural game waiting for the less successful, more marginal, or simply more critical children of the middle class, and mountaineering has been part of it. Although the styles and issues of the game have varied with changing definitions of "modernness" and "middle classness," the general idea that the dominant culture is in some way stifling is always at the core of it. This is not to say that every climber has been recognizably "countercultural," or that mountaineering has had no resonances with both the modern and the bourgeois. On the contrary, like the historically specific counterculture of the 1970s, this more enduring countercultural game of Euro-American culture has operated in a very delicate and symbiotic relationship with modern institutions and middle-class values. But its, as it were, official stance has been largely oppositional and critical.

I had originally planned to push this counterculture argument through this entire book. I have already suggested that the romantic culture of climbing in the 1920s and 1930s, and the hippie culture of climbing in the 1970s, shared many aspects of worldview and values—both countermodern and antibourgeois. The problematic era for making this argument was the 1950s and 1960s, in which the dominant style of the sahibs was hypermacho, and the dominant style of expeditions was highly technologized and rationalized. One might argue, however, that although modernity had triumphed at the technological and organizational levels, the machismo of the sahibs was nonetheless in some extended sense countercultural. The sahibs viewed themselves as operating against the conventionality of that era, as embodied in the figure of the "organization man" and in the bourgeois blandness of suburban life. But this argument must remain largely conjectural at this point.

The 1980s and 1990s raised different questions about these issues. The cover on the Sunday *New York Times Magazine* for 26 July 1998 carried one word in giant font, "Explornography," the teaser for an article about wealthy, successful people going on extremely difficult and dangerous adventure expeditions, including mountaineering. Were these people being in any way "countercultural?" Indeed, is there anything left of either the 1970s counterculture or the longer-running oppositional game that, I am suggesting, has been a more or less permanent undercurrent to modernity and capitalism? Again

I would argue against a decline-and-fall view, and in favor of some
more complex and optimistic sense of transformation and recon-   *sahibs*
figuration. With this in mind, a closing look at the sahibs at the end   *also*
of the twentieth century.   *reconfigured*

YUPPIE MOUNTAINEERING

Starting in the mid-eighties, Himalayan mountaineering took a new
turn with the explosion of "adventure travel," the idea of paying
to participate in difficult high-risk activity in faraway places. The
tremendous growth of the adventure-travel industry in this era was
one offshoot of the enrichment and other transformations of the
professional middle class that started in the 1970s, the emergence
of the so-called "yuppies." One form of adventure travel in turn was
high-altitude mountaineering, in which anyone with enough money
and a desire for adventure or risk-taking could pay a very hefty sum
to climb with more skilled and experienced climbers, who in turn
began evolving into commercial "guides." Whereas Himalayan expeditions had previously consisted mostly of groups of friends, or
of climbers who knew one another by word of mouth, commercial
expeditions put together a set of people on the mountain whose only
connection with one another was that they were wealthy and had a
desire to climb.

The commercialization of climbing has had many consequences.
One very obvious change is related to the tastes and lifestyles of this
new clientele. Two of the earliest practitioners, Dick Bass and Frank
Wells of the Seven Summits project, were both corporate executives
and millionaires. Bass had an oil business in Texas, a ski resort—
Snowbird—in Utah, and coal interests in Alaska. Wells was president of Warner Brothers Studios and later became president of Dis-
ney Studios. The cost of the project was about a quarter of a million
dollars per expedition, and they went to Everest twice, so the entire
cost was about two million dollars, most of it financed out of their
personal resources. The general cultural style of these and similar
climbers in this era was far from the countercultural positionings of
many of their seventies predecessors. Rather, it was a sort of master-

of-the-universe approach: money was no object, and anything was possible with enough will, drive, and weight-throwing. Take Frank Wells:

> Frank also continued single-handedly figuring out how to get the DC-3 to Antarctica, and Dick realized that even if he had more time to spend on the Seven Summits he wouldn't have been able to match Frank's performance with a challenge like Antarctica where Frank's background as a corporate executive was essential. He was indomitable; whenever he encountered a new hurdle, he just found a solution, refusing to accept from anyone an opinion that something was impossible.[2]

The physical lifestyle on the commercial expeditions also came to reflect the lifestyles to which such individuals were accustomed. One of the commercial climbing firms was a company called Adventure Consultants, founded and owned by a New Zealander, Rob Hall. The 1996 Adventure Consultants commercial Everest expedition, led by Hall, included four doctors, a lawyer, a publisher, and a corporate manager, among others. This was, once again, the professional middle class,[3] and the material trappings of the expedition were consistent with their expectations:

> In striking contrast to the harshness of our surroundings stood the myriad creature comforts of the Adventure Consultants camp. . . . Our mess tent, a cavernous canvas structure, was furnished with an enormous stone table, a stereo system, a library, and solar-powered electric lights; an adjacent communications tent housed a satellite phone and fax.[4]

A climber on another commercial expedition, Sandy Hill Pittman, was widely ridiculed in the press for, allegedly, bringing her cappuccino maker to base camp, but it seems perfectly consistent with the material life of such expeditions.

In addition, there was some reversal of the anticolonial values of the seventies: "Continuing a Raj-era tradition established by expeditions of yore, every morning Chhongba and his cook boy, Tendi, came to each client's tent to serve us steaming mugs of Sherpa tea in our sleeping bags."[5]

In terms of the actual climbing, the commercial nature of the expeditions had a number of effects. Jon Krakauer (1997), the writer who chronicled the 1996 Everest disaster, complained that the top-down organization of these climbs, in which the guide was defined as the absolute leader and authority, encouraged passivity in the clients, who were told that their best chance of success lay in doing only what they were told.[6] More importantly, Krakauer emphasized again and again that the absence of prior social relations among the clients meant that the group was simply a collection of unrelated and self-interested individuals. Krakauer himself wrote in the language of the earlier counterculture; for him, "climbing provided a sense of community. . . . To become a climber was to join a self-contained, rabidly idealistic society, largely unnoticed and surprisingly uncorrupted by the world at large."[7] He was thus enormously saddened by the lack of bonding and interpersonal connectedness in the commercial group:

> [At the South Col] In this godforsaken place, I felt disconnected from the climbers around me—emotionally, spiritually, physically—to a degree I hadn't experienced on any previous expedition. We were a team in name only, I'd sadly come to realize. Although in a few hours we would leave camp as a group, we would ascend as individuals, linked to one another by neither rope nor any deep sense of loyalty. Each client was in it for himself or herself, pretty much.[8]

commercial / no community

The lack of social connectedness among the climbers produced a noticeable increase in selfish behavior among the sahibs, at least as reported in the literature. The rescue ethics in climbing are very unclear, and it is always hard to tell when the rule of *sauve qui peut* is operative or when one has a duty to help another climber. Especially under extreme conditions, climbers are reluctant to blame one another for saving their own lives and failing to help another climber; most climbers realize that they themselves might not be heroic under similar conditions. Nonetheless, there were some instances of strikingly selfish behavior among sahibs on expeditions in the 1980s and 1990s that did not appear in the earlier literature. In the case of the 1987 American Everest North Face Expedition, which was a mixture of group or team organization and self-paying clients, for example, perhaps the first sign of something amiss was the fact that only two of the members had the curiosity to go up to Rumbu monastery on the way to the North Face.[9] Throughout the expedition, small groups began peeling off and pursuing their own agendas. Toward the end, wrote Stacey Allison,

> We had all jettisoned whatever dedication we once had to the better interests of the expedition. We may have started our journey as a cohesive group of friends, but as we positioned ourselves for the summit, we were little more than a group of mercenaries.[10]

The expedition failed, but Allison went again with another, part-team, part-commercial, group in 1988.[11] This one also got off to a bad start, as the leader attempted to charge another group two thousand dollars for the use of the route for which Allison's group had already paid (in equipment, porters, and Sherpas) to be established through the Khumbu Icefall. In many ways it seemed fair, but it was the first time anyone had charged a fee (which is now standard) for using a route on Mount Everest, and it represented another dimension of the commercialization of the enterprise. The leaders of the two groups had a nasty argument over it.[12] There was a series of incidents on the expedition that raised questions about the leader, including the fact that he had put himself on the first assault team (very bad form), and that, according to Allison, he lied to the press about how she (Allison) came to make the first summit bid. As the group began to seriously unravel at the end, individuals were engaging in private negotiations for scarce transportation resources, and the leader himself picked up and left the group before the expedition was actually off the mountain, something virtually unheard of in the annals of mountaineering.[13]

It was also in this period that encounters with dead bodies on the mountain began to be treated as commonplace, and even light-hearted, matters. No one expects climbers to risk their lives simply to give a body a respectful burial, and the mountain is in such constant motion that even buried or otherwise properly disposed of bodies may later appear on the surface. But there appears to be a certain hardening of attitudes toward encounters with frozen corpses. In 1978, Hannelore Schmatz had died on her way back from the summit, and her body remained in the place where she had died for more than a decade. (Her husband later paid for the recovery of her body; a Nepali and a Sherpa climber died trying to bring it down.)[14] Allison wrote about the 1988 expedition, "When the snow recedes off [Schmatz] in the springtime, descending climbers leave empty oxygen tanks [around her] or pat her head for good luck."[15] Also on the mountain at the same time was a French expedition during which two Sherpas died, and the French—possibly trying to be more respectful in not leaving the bodies lying about—rolled them off the mountain. But one of the bodies flew past a group of American and Sherpa climbers from Allison's expedition:

Sherpa body

> [The Sherpas] knew it was a body, and they watched open-mouthed, saw it falling like a comet past them, down past the *bergschrund* [a giant crevasse] and then onto the flat surface of the cwm, where it somersaulted, cartwheeled, then rolled to a stop.
>
> When he leaned over the body, Steve knew the Sherpa had been dead for at least twelve hours. He was frozen solid. Someone, it appeared, must have thrown him down on purpose.... Next to him the Sherpas were crossing and uncrossing their arms, their faces gloomy and clouded. No one, they knew, would ever throw a white climber's body down the Lhotse face.[16]

Jon Krakauer recounted several encounters with abandoned bodies on the 1996 Adventure Consultants expedition, as well as the quickness with which he developed emotional numbness:

> At 21,000 feet, dizzy from the heat, I came upon a large object wrapped in blue plastic sheeting beside the trail. It took my altitude-impaired gray matter a minute or two to comprehend that the object was a human body....
>
> Feeling slightly better on Saturday, I climbed a thousand feet above camp to get some exercise and accelerate my acclimatization, and there, at the head of the Cwm, fifty yards off the main

track, I came upon another body in the snow, or more accurately the lower half of a body. . . .

The first body had left me badly shaken for several hours; the shock of encountering the second wore off almost immediately. Few of the climbers trudging by had given either corpse more than a passing glance.[17]

The very idea of yuppie mountaineering suggests that mountaineering is no longer part of a countercultural stream within Western, bourgeois, "modern" culture, but rather has become part of the dominant culture. Climbers bringing their cappuccino makers to Mount Everest, tents in base camp with fax machines and telephones in a "communications annex"—none of this seems even remotely conceivable as countercultural. Yet the situation is actually more complex, mirroring the confusing complexity of cultural politics in the last decades of the twentieth century. Another dimension of those cultural politics is identity politics, which appears in Himalayan mountaineering as in most other arenas of contemporary life.

HIGH-ALTITUDE IDENTITY POLITICS

Depending on how one defines them, identity politics have always been a feature of Himalayan mountaineering. Although nationalism was not a strong feature of Himalayan mountaineering, it did become an issue in some cases. But identity politics in a more contemporary sense—that is to say, identities constituted by subnational categories like "race," gender, age, ethnicity, and sexuality—probably started with the feminist movement in the seventies; indeed gender is still probably the biggest identity divide in the sport. Stacey Allison, the first American woman to reach the summit of Mount Everest, translated George Leigh Mallory's reason for climbing the mountain—"Because it is there"—into an identity value: "Because I'm here."[18]

Identities in mountaineering have continued to multiply in the eighties and nineties. Again, the story probably began with Dick Bass, the Texas millionaire who set out to climb the "seven summits," the highest peak on every continent, and successfully completed the enterprise in 1985 by reaching the summit of Everest. Besides all the fanfare over the "seven summits," however, an identity issue came to the fore in the Everest climb: Since Bass was fifty-five years old at that time, age identity became an issue: Bass became briefly (the record was soon bested) the oldest man to stand on top of Everest.

Then there was Geoff Tabin, a member of the 1992 American Everest expedition. Tabin's "life's ambition [he] told everyone, was to be the first Jew to stand on top of Mount Everest. He delivered the line as if it was a joke, but [the author] could tell [he] was absolutely serious."[19] Tabin made it.

And one more example. During the ill-fated 1996 season, one of the expeditions on the mountain was a South African group, which included both a black man and a black woman. The man was "a soft-spoken black paleoecologist and a climber of international renown" named Edmund February, who had been named by his parents after Sir Edmund Hillary.[20] February is not represented as phrasing his aspirations in terms of representing his "race" (although he could have; if he had succeeded he would have been the first black person to climb Everest), but rather in terms of making a statement about the newly integrated nation of South Africa. The woman, Deshun Deysel, was a "black physical-education teacher with no previous climbing experience."[21] Deysel's views about her presence on the expedition are never quoted; it emerged later that the leader, Ian Woodall, who was white, had not listed her on the climbing permit, and there was suspicion in some quarters that he had used her presence as a black woman merely to raise money.[22]

Identity politics can have a wide range of significance—anything from relatively harmless *Guinness Book of Records* distinctions to genocidal "ethnic cleansing." The book has not yet been written on the long-term implications for the shape of political action during the past two decades, and into the future. In mountaineering and elsewhere, however, they do signal the changing role of minority groups in relation to what we think of as the "dominant culture," which brings us back to the question of the counterculture.

New Forms of Counterculture?

The counterculture in one of its classic forms—antimodern and antibourgeois—still exists in mountaineering, but it is no longer as visible as it used to be. Climbers who are countercultural in this sense tend to climb nowadays in very small groups, or solo, on difficult but little known peaks, out of the spotlight of the media. They rarely write books, or they write books with highly ambivalent titles such as David Roberts' *Moments of Doubt* (1986) and Greg Child's *Mixed Emotions* (1993), which are highly reflexive and critical (albeit in an affectionate way) of many aspects of the sport.

One could argue that the growing presence in mountaineering of (in the current jargon) previously underrepresented groups—women, racial and ethnic minorities, and climbers from small or poor or postcommunist nations—represents another form of the countercultural game today. This may not appear countercultural in the classic sense—antimodern or antibourgeois—yet this trend implicitly or explicitly questions other dominant models of the sport: male, white, Western, and individualistic.

The implications of these new countercultural trends may be illustrated by a fascinating article by Greg Child on Polish climbers. The Poles have produced some great Himalayan mountaineers in the last decade or so; Child singles out three. One is Wanda Rutkiewicz, "probably the world's leading female high-altitude alpinist" [23] and a strong champion of all-female expeditions as a way of developing women's sense of independence and decision making;[24] another is Jerzy Kukuczka, who began as a relatively "pure" climber but was seduced by the high-visibility track;[25] and the third is Wojciech (usually Anglicized as Voytek) Kurtyka, who remains in the mold of the classic counterculture, "the last of a breed of mountaineering romantics" who climb a mountain "for its geometric beauty and for the promise of adventure that it may hold."[26]

The three represent a good part of the spectrum in contemporary mountaineering: the woman/feminist, the superstar, and the old-fashioned climbing romantic. But in addition, for all three, there is a "Polish" factor at work, which places all of them in a somewhat oppositional position in relation to the sport as it has been historically constructed. For one thing, many of the Polish expeditions are tremendously underfunded, but the Poles' solution to this is very different from the kinds of fund-raising and sponsor-finding engaged in by the Western Europeans and the Americans. Thus, they often trade and barter their way overland between Poland and Nepal. They do this so successfully that they raise far more money and equipment than they need, and take the surplus back to Poland where they use it to finance a higher level lifestyle than would otherwise have been possible.[27] Voytek Kurtyka also considered that the historical oppression of the Poles has made them better climbers:

> Under the Germans and the Russians we've lived between the hammer and the anvil. Because of the struggle in Poland for freedom at home, most Poles feel a sense of being tough. The sense of defeat on a mountain is greater for a Pole, so the last thing a Pole wants is to fail on an expedition. In the end we are better at the art of suffering, and for high altitude this is everything.[28]

Finally, a third contemporary countercultural scene might be identified, and labeled, with an extreme sense of paradox, the "yuppie counterculture." This is a set of wealthy and powerful people who are, even more clearly, neither antimodern nor antibourgeois, but have nonetheless brought with them from the seventies certain classic countercultural values: environmentalism, feminism and other forms of social egalitarianism, and fascination with other cultures in a mode of relativism and appreciation for diversity. The most visible example of this style today would be Ted Turner, with his marriage to former political activist Jane Fonda, his support of environmentalist causes, and his billion-dollar contribution to the United Nations. Within the Himalayan context, the most prominent figure is the wealthy investment banker Richard C. Blum, husband of the Senator from California, Dianne Feinstein, and founder and chairman of the board of the American Himalayan Foundation. The AHF, begun in the 1980s, raises funds for projects in environmental and cultural preservation, and in health and social welfare, throughout the Himalayas. Among other things, the foundation has been a major funder of Tengboche monastery.[29]

The board of the foundation brings together (at least on the mast-head of the newsletter) wealthy and socially prominent supporters with big-name mountaineers, such as Ed Hillary, Maurice Herzog, and Jim Whittaker. The foundation stages fund-raising events at which the star attractions are famous climbers and reincarnate lamas, among others. At a gala sixtieth-birthday party for the chair-man, Dick Blum, "President Clinton, [star mountaineer] Reinhold Messner, and Sharon Stone offered birthday greetings. . . . Sir Ed-mund Hillary and the Rimpoche of Tengboche Monastery were among the 450 distinguished guests."[30]

One could be cynical about an organization like the American Himalayan Foundation, but there are certainly worse things they could do with their money. It may also usefully be viewed as part of an emerging world of transnational nongovernmental organizations (NGOs) that operate outside existing nation-state structures. Here again the book has not yet been written about the changing forms of political action in the late-twentieth century, and the ways in which organizations like this may—or, of course, may not—be part of major political transformations.

And where is anthropology amidst all this? This entire book has not only chronicled a certain kind of encounter, but has also been an attempt to answer this question. If I had to summarize the pieces of answers that have been given along the way, I would say this.[31] In the 1960s and 1970s there was a revolution in anthropology—associated most prominently with the name of Clifford Geertz—that redefined the field as an enterprise concerned with "meaning"; that is to say, concerned with what people in different times and places wanted from their lives, and with the ways in which the worlds they lived in both reflected and constituted those desires. A bit later, there was another intellectual revolution, this one closely connected with the political and culturally critical movements of the 1970s, and associated especially with the names of Edward Said and Michel Foucault. This revolution brought to the fore issues of power, of the ways in which the worlds that people live in are distorted not only by political and economic domination, but by cultural categories and images that construct people as inherently different, inferior, and deserving of their own domination. For many scholars, the second revolution displaced the first; but although I strongly embraced the second, I could never renounce the first. I could never let go of the idea that, however profoundly power, violence, and sheer difference may form and deform the world, people still try, wherever they are and whatever they are doing, to construct meaningful worlds from their own point of view. The strongest kind of anthropology today, in my view, is the kind that attempts to keep walking the tightrope between the two perspectives. Falling off on either side gives up the game.

A RECENT issue of the *American Himalayan Foundation Newsletter* contains a photograph of the Tengboche Rimpoche throwing "a bundle of sacred objects" into the Pacific near California's Big Sur. The photograph made me smile. I know the Rimpoche. I have stood on beautiful stretches of the California coast like that one, and it seemed nice to have the Rimpoche come into "my" space as I came into his. Yet one must be careful with such images. It stands as a sign—moving toward the status of a cliché—of "globalization," a real-enough phenomenon but one that carries a certain set of meanings: It emphasizes the spread of capitalism and Western culture "out" to other parts of the world, and the displacement and circulation of people from other places into Western sites. Either way, the West remains the point of reference.[32] The image of globalization in this sense systematically slights the local worlds and local histories that are still profoundly meaningful to many people, and that undergird their identities as they engage with others. In the case of this photograph, it has the effect of enclosing the Rimpoche, as Sherpas have long been enclosed, within yet another sahib narrative, and rendering invisible the degree to which he is, after all, a figure with a world and a history of his own.

APPENDIX A

TALES

All of these tales were told to me by the senior Tengboche monk, Au Chokdu.

THE *NUPKI GYELWU* TALE

Long ago in Lhasa, King Tisen Detsen's queen, Sai Markyen, bore a son. The son was born with goat horns on his head, a dog's mouth, and a human body. The father was greatly ashamed, and pronounced a curse. He had the child carried to a place where nobody was, to Khembalung in eastern Nepal. Actually, there were people living there, of the Kiranti Rai tribe, and he became their king—King Kikha Ra-sa (Dog-mouth Goat-horn).

[According to a story told separately by another individual, when Kikha Rasa was king of Khembalung, he killed a young maiden every day.]

Later, King Tisen Detsen invited the great Tantric adept, Guru Rimpoche, to Tibet to found Buddhism there, and to build the first Tibetan monastery, Samye. Guru Rimpoche wanted to use Khembalung valley as a *beyul*, a secret hiding place for religious texts. [Or—my notes are not clear—he knew that it was a beyul, and wanted to get at the texts that were there.] So he devised a trick to get King Kikha Rasa out of Khembalung. First he caused him to become ill, by sending a spirit of the dead (a *nerpa*) against him. Then the Guru Rimpoche traveled from Tibet to Khembalung disguised as a religious beggar. The sick king asked the beggar if he knew how to do a divination for him, to determine the cause and cure for his illness. Guru Rimpoche did the divination and informed the king that he would have to make offerings to the gods. Otherwise he would die.

When the time came to perform the offering rituals (*lha-chetup*, the usual periodic rites of giving hospitality to the gods), the Guru Rimpoche told people to take all the infants out of the village to do the ritual. Then he closed the village, hiding it in clouds, so that the king could not find his way back. The king then wandered from place to place, looking for a new location in which to build his palace. He went to Chukung, Dingboche, Zonglo, Maundzo, Changma, and finally Dolakha, where he died.

King Kikha Rasa then reincarnated as Nupki Gyelwu, Western King. He proclaimed that people must make sacrifices to him, or they would be afflicted by *nerpa*, illness-causing ghosts. Every month [or every year?] an unmarried young person was to be killed, and the blood offered to the god/king.

This state of affairs became known to Guru Rimpoche. He came to Dolakha. Disguised once again as a beggar, he approached the house of the boy who was to be killed the next day. He stood outside for a long time, but no one came out to give him alms. So he went in and asked why nobody had come out. The father said, "My son is to be sacrificed to the god tomorrow, I'm upset about my son, I can't give you alms." Guru Rimpoche said, "Where is this god? Show him to me." The father took him and showed him, and the Guru Rimpoche cast a spell upon the palace, causing it to fly apart in all directions. Then he said to the father, "Now you don't have to sacrifice your son."

Later a Limbu trader came through the area seeking to buy pigs' hair. He and his friends took lunch together out in the open. A large rock in the area where they were sitting kept moving about. Two or three times it overturned the trader's food. Then some water came out of the stone. The trader took his *kukuri*, his large curved knife, and slashed the rock, whereupon blood came out of it. The trader asked the rock what was going on.

The rock said, "I'm King Bimshing. I was in my village when some yogi came along and closed my village. Then he followed me down here to Dolakha. I was getting fed lots of children but I lost all of that. Now I don't get any more, so I just stay here as a rock." Then he told the trader, "if the Gorkha [i.e., Nepali] king will sacrifice to me and to the goddess Pashupati, we will help him. He won't have to sacrifice people, just female buffalo calves, little goats, and pigeons, and I'll be satisfied." The trader told everyone, and the Gorkha king and the Newar king and all the Newars heard about it and began to worship Bimshing. This is the origin of Dasain [the holiday on which thousands of animals are slaughtered throughout Nepal].

THE GELUNGMA PALMA STORY

(I was given a brief summary, virtually a synopsis, of this text in 1967.[1] This version provides much more detail, and also changes the emphasis of that synopsis somewhat.)

In India there were a king and queen. Their kingdom comprised half the world, and they had much wealth and many subjects. [The king and queen had first a son, and then a daughter. The night after the daughter was born,] the queen had a dream in which many flowers were blooming, and on each flower sat a *kangdoma* [a goddess]. When the daughter was three years old, she went upstairs in the palace to look around at the town. She was with her servant, Samdema. Two butchers came along with many sheep and killed the sheep one by one. The girl said, "These sheep are ours, why are they killing them?" The servant said, "The day after tomorrow all the subjects and chiefs will be having a party, all these sheep are ours." The girl said, "All this killing and eating [I cannot stand]. I won't be a lay person, I'll go to *cho* [religion]."

When the girl was seven years old, she asked her parents if she could go to cho. They said, "No, just as water can't flow under a dry landslide, so girls can't do cho. We won't send you to do cho." When she was eleven, four kings came to ask for her hand. Her father tentatively agreed to give her in marriage, but he couldn't decide on which king to bestow her. He came to ask his daughter which one she wanted. She said, "I won't be anyone's wife. I'm going to do cho. If you had four daughters you could give one to each. But

I am only one, and if you give me to one the other three will harbor a grudge against you. So you must send me to cho." [Her father, through divination, decided to give her to one of the non-Buddhist kings.] She went to the [figure of the god] Eleven-headed Pawa Chenrezi and said, "My parents won't let me go to do cho. They are trying to marry me to a king. I am too good looking. [She pronounced a curse, saying] Let me get leprosy."

Later, she went to her mother and asked again to be sent to do cho. Her mother said, "I can't send you, you must ask your father." Then she asked her father, but he said, "I cannot decide, you must go to your brother [who had earlier been crowned and] who is now king." She went to her brother. Not speaking, she sat down in front of him. He said, "You have something to say. What is it? Tell me!" [She said] "I'm going to do cho. My father said [I could] 'go,' my mother said 'go,' now I need your permission." He said, "You've been saying you want to do cho since you were seven years old. Every day between the ages of seven and eleven you've been talking about cho. You go then and do good cho." And he gave her an elephant and two loads of gold. Samdema, her servant, held the elephant's bridle, and the girl walked behind, going off to do cho.

They walked and walked a long way. They saw a *gelung* [a fully ordained monk] plowing. The gelung had hung his shawl in the tree. He had a leather bag of *chang* [beer] and there were some small children at his side. The girl thought to herself, "This is bad for a gelung, this is no gelung." The gelung [read her mind and said] "Don't think like that, you must hear my story." Then the girl prostrated herself before the gelung [because he had read her mind] and said "Please give me cho [here, religious teaching]." "I can't," he said, "but up there, there is a very big *gonda* [monastery] with a very powerful lama," and he showed her the way to the monastery.

They reached the gonda near sunset. The servant said, "Now it's nearly sunset. This is a monastic gonda, and since we are women we cannot sleep there. Tonight we'll stay here and we'll go in tomorrow morning." The king's daughter agreed . . . and that night they slept outside on the dancing platform. When the sun rose the lama's servant came out carrying a kettle to collect water. He asked them where they came from . . . and of which king was the girl the daughter. [She answered these questions and then said] "This is my servant and I came to seek cho. Go and ask the lama [for me]." The king [her brother] had sent with her a gold *mendel* [a ritual object, symbol of the cosmos] one forearm tall, together with a letter. Samdema said, "We should send the mendel and letter by this boy's hand to the lama." But the girl said, "We'll give it to him ourselves when we meet him." The lama's servant went to the lama, saying, "Some people are here to see you." The lama said, "Why are you coming to me so early?" [The lama's servant replied] "The daughter of King Dharmapala and Queen Domo Hlazen has come from [an Indian kingdom] to seek cho. Our gonda has a big reputation. You should give religion to the two women." The lama said, "That girl was promised to four kings. They will attack our gonda. You think it's good news that they came, but I don't think so. Get out!"

The servant brought them a kettle of tea and served it, saying, "Now it's early. Have some tea. The lama won't give you cho, he has yelled at me. You must leave." Samdema said to the girl, "I told you to send the gold mendel and the letter. Whether he gives cho or not, you must send them by the lama's servant's hand." They sent them. Then the lama agreed, and said they could come in. Under the lama the princess did much religion. She learned many texts and became very learned.

Her brother, the king, heard about this and came to the gonda. He saw the lama sitting on his throne and only a little lower his sister [now called] Gelungma Palma [Ordained Nun Illustrious Woman] and on the other side of the lama the seat of the *geshe* [a monk of advanced degree]. She and the geshe were debating. The lama was the witness: Gelungma Palma won the debate. There was a powerful *tolden* [Tantric ascetic] and she debated him and won that debate too. Also one *gomjemba* [meditation master], who was very powerful, but again she won. Then the king believed [that she was a skilled religious practitioner] and went home. She stayed at the gonda.

After doing much cho, the lama gave her one bowl made from a human skull, full of *chang* [beer]. He said, "Do not give it to anyone else because I have put a *molom* [spell, blessing] on it. Only drink it yourself." She took it home and drank a little more than half. Then she thought, "*Nyingje* [pity], I'll give some [as] *chelap* [religious medicine] to the servant." So the servant drank the rest, a little less than half. The lama [later] asked Gelungma Palma if she had drunk all the chang herself. She said, "I drank a little more than half, and Samdema drank a little less than half." The lama said, "If you gave some to Samdema, then you can't stay with me any more. It won't be good for us. You go down to the village below, and I'll stay up here and give you cho. But you and I can't stay together any more." She asked him, "If you're not dying or I'm not dying, why can't we stay together?" He said, "Because you gave half the chang to someone else." She said, "If I'm staying down there, how will I hear your cho?" He said, "You have a god's ear, and I have a god's voice. You'll be able to hear." Samdema and she went down the hill and there they did cho.

One day, the *khembu* [head lama] of a big monastery died. One monk said, "I'm rich. I shall be khembu." Another said, "I'm learned [*khamu*] and brilliant [*yenden chemu*], I'll be khembu." Another said, "I'm older, I'll be khembu." Between them there was much conflict. Then one more clever monk gave tea to all the others, and said, "There is no real khembu among us. Gelungma Palma is very powerful and very khamu. We'll call her and make her our khembu. The others said, "All right, we will go and ask her lama." They discussed whether to go with respect scarves [*kata*] or not, and one monk said, "No, we'll just take her." Ten monks went to the lama and said, "Our khembu died, we need a khembu." The lama at first said, "No, she is my heart lama (*tsawa'i lama*, literally 'root lama')." But then he sat with his eyes closed for a few minutes. Behind the gompa many monks were waiting for a fight. The lama thought, "This is no good." Then he said, "All right, I will send her." He called her up to the gonda and said, "Go and be their khembu." She cried, and said, "I don't want to go." He said, "If you don't obey my orders, it's like tearing my words/writing in half, they become worthless. You'll go to hell." He asked her many times to go there. Finally she agreed.

Many people carried her. The lama had said, "Down there, you must take a rest, and pray to me, and offer a mendel." But when they carried her they were so happy they ran very fast, and didn't

stop at the place the lama said. She said, "I have the lama's order.
You must take a rest. The lama is up there thinking, 'I gave the order
for you to rest down there. She's not very good. Not even giving
[me] one prostration. Women are no good, they don't pay attention,
they don't care.' " Later they took a rest and she did her prostrations
to the lama.

Then she went to the monastery and became its khembu. For the
small monks she gave [one particular] cho; to the head monk she
gave [another], to the old ones she gave [another]. Then with
Gelungma Palma as khembu the gonda fared very well, and all the
monks became very accomplished.

Many years later, Gelungma Palma got sick. She told the monks,
"I'm going for three years of meditation. You must teach well and
do good cho." The monks said, "Three years is too long, do one
year." So she agreed. She stayed one year upstairs in the upper room
of the temple. Earlier she had cursed herself to Chenrezi, and asked
him to make her ugly. Now she was sick with leprosy. From the
upper story drops of blood fell. The little monks said, "Our lama is
not meditating, she's having a baby." All the little monks went to
look in at her. She was still sleeping and they couldn't see anything.
One little monk called loudly and she started up a little bit. He saw
that her face was all disfigured. He said to the other, "Our khembu
has a bad sickness." They talked very badly and they took up sticks.
The old monk said, "Gelungma Palma, you should not stay here,
because all the boys are threatening violence. Stay on the porch."
Then the servants carried her down to the porch and gave her a mat
to lie on, and she stayed there. But later they said she couldn't stay
on the porch, that she must move farther away to a small woodshed.
"If she stays on the porch, no patrons will come to our gonda."

Not stopping at the woodshed, her servant carried her far far away
to a high summer pasture area. Gelungma Palma thought she remembered the place from her last life, and told the servant to ask a
shepherd what the name of the place was. He told the servant and
Gelungma Palma said that she remembered and that, "This is a good
place. Down there are three water mills. Go and beg some flour,
and I'll stay here." The servant said, "If you stay here, the monks
will come to beat you." Gelungma Palma said, "They won't do any-

thing. Go and beg the flour." The people from the highest of the three mills gave the servant some flour. Then she went to the middle one and they gave her a little too. Then she went to the lowest one. A little boy was there and he said, "My mother and father aren't here. I don't have any flour. But you take this turnip." The servant thought, "I'll take this up and burn it in the fire. The smell will calm Gelungma Palma's bad humors."

The servant saw a *tolden* (a Tantric ascetic). The sound of his chanting was very good [to her ears]. She went before him. They asked each other, "Where are you coming from?" She told him what happened and learned that he had previously been the king's chamberlain. She said to the tolden, "You were the king's chamberlain. We have been away a long time. How are my mother and father?" She said, "My lama is quite sick. She is up there in the cave." The tolden said, "Your parents' house collapsed and they were killed. The king has died, the queen has died. Gelungma Palma's older brother [the king] went to western India to do cho and there is nobody there [at the palace] now." She went back to Gelungma Palma and Gelungma Palma asked her, "Did a dog bite you?" "I wasn't bitten by a dog, but my father and mother are no longer alive," she said, and she cried a little. Gelungma Palma said, "You have [more] things to say. Tell me." The servant said, "The king has died, the queen has died, my parents are dead, and your brother has gone to western India to do cho." Gelungma Palma said, "Well, if he went there to do cho, that's good. We won't stay here, we'll go somewhere else to do cho."

They went to another place, the servant carrying Gelungma Palma on her back. They went a long way. Gelungma Palma said, "Before, we left our gold and the elephant in a rich man's house, we will go and get them." The servant brought the gold and elephant and they went off and came to a very big river. The servant said, "We cannot cross. Shall we turn back, or what?" Gelungma Palma said, "I'll pray. You must not worry. Close your eyes tightly, take hold of the elephant's bridle, and go down into the river." The lama prayed, the servant went into the river holding the elephant, the river parted and a road opened up. Gelungma Palma asked, "Now can we cross the river?" She couldn't see because of the leprosy. "Are we on the other side?" and the servant said, "Yes." Gelungma

Palma asked, "What is the state of the river?" [The servant said] "Before, the river was running. When we went in, a road opened up. Now it's running again." Gelungma Palma said, "Running water is good [i.e., a good omen] for us, and good for cho. We'll go down. There's a nice cave. Carry me to that place." Once again Gelungma Palma thought she remembered the place, and the servant confirmed that it matched her description.

Gelungma Palma told her servant, "Now we two won't stay together. You must take one load of gold and the elephant and go to cho. It doesn't matter. You go to cho." And she gave her the gold and the elephant. The servant said, "I won't go till you die." Gelungma Palma said, "If you disobey a lama's orders, it's like tearing up words, you'll go to hell, you must go."

So the servant went to collect the two loads of gold. The householder's wife said, "We have plenty of land and sheep and cows, horses and much wealth. You have much gold. Stay here and marry." The servant said, "I have the lama's orders, I'm going to cho. Give me my gold. But if you won't give it, I'll go to cho anyway. I won't marry." The house-mistress said, "Your lama is Gelungma Palma with leprosy." The servant threw dirt in her face and took the gold and went off. She traveled from village to village and finally came to a retreat hut, and stayed there meditating for a year.

One day in the cave Gelungma Palma was in very bad pain. She sat doubled over. She couldn't sleep stretched out on her back because her body was covered with sores. She was sitting doubled over, crying, and she went to sleep. All the little sores on her eyes got wet, and she could open her eyes a little. She saw Eleven-headed Pawa Chenrezi in front of her, with her eyes a little open. She went to embrace him, "I'm praying all day, all night, so many years. Why haven't you come looking for me?" He said, "I'm with you all the time, day and night, but your le [karma] is full of clouds, you can't see me, I'm with you all the time. Now your sins are finished, your bad karma is finished." Then he said, "Pawa Zhembi Yang [another god] has sent you a rilwu [a pellet, used in long-life rituals] as chelap [religious medicine], and Sangye Mela [another god] sent another medicine." She took the two and ate them, and Pawa Chenrezi disappeared. Three days later the leprosy was completely gone, her face was once again beautiful, and everything was good.

One day Pawa Chenrezi came again. "Don't stay here. We'll go to Takbi Shingkam [one of the heavens]. So they went to [Takbi] Shingkam. She didn't die, she went to [Takbi] Shingkam alive. There were *kangdoma* [goddesses] there talking among themselves: "Here there are only dead people, but she is not dead, she's alive." Others said, "Some will believe it, others won't." Gelungma Palma heard, and said, "Tomorrow all you kangdoma come to see an entertainment." The next day they all came. She had cut off her head with a sword, put her head on the point of the sword, with her body staying to one side. Her head was singing and her body was dancing. Then all the kangdoma believed it. They said, "You've come alive to Takbi Shinkgam, now we believe." She did something with her hands, her head rejoined her body, and she was the same as before.

One day Pawa Chenrezi spoke to her: "Tomorrow your servant is coming to the cave. You must go back down there." Gelungma Palma said, "She has enough for food. I'm not going back." Pawa Chenrezi said, "She is going because she is faithful to you, she [religiously] adores you. She wants to see how you are. You must go there." Then Pawa Chenrezi gave Gelungma Palma the prayers for the Nyungne ritual in Takbi heaven, and giving his words/voice [*sung*, i.e., the texts] he directed her: "Go to the secular world, and give this to everybody. It is very powerful. It is Chenrezi's words/voice. Give it to the lay people." All sects of Tibetan Buddhism—Nyingmawa, Gelugpa, Kadyupa—all say it's Gelungma Palma's precept/commandment, she brought it from heaven. From that time we have Nyungne. He gave her all the Nyungne texts, and she went back to the cave and did some meditation.

The servant arrived. The servant was thinking, "Maybe my lama died. If so, I'll collect her bones and make *tsawar* [molded forms made from clay and the ground bones of the deceased, with impressions of holy things on them—a way of making merit for the deceased]. But if she's alive, I'll rejoin her as her servant, to help her." The lama was meditating. The servant saw how beautiful and well she looked. They embraced one another, and kneeling, facing one another, touched heads. The servant asked, "Who gave you medicine?" Gelungma Palma said, "I met Pawa Chenrezi, and Pawa Zhembiyang gave me chelap, and Sangye Mela gave chelap, and then after three days I was completely cured. I went to the Takbi heaven and then Pawa Chenrezi told me to come here, so I came today to the secular world. He gave me the Nyungne cho, the Nyungne observances, and we two will go to give it to the secular people."

The servant said, "Before, when you were very sick, they threw you out of the gonda. Now we'll go back there and show them." Gelungma Palma said, "I won't go there, there is too much conflict. I wouldn't even go there to pee." The servant urged, "You're a Buddha now. We'll go to the monastery. Go up to the sky and speak three words of cho—just that, no more." Gelungma Palma agreed.

[At the gonda] the servant was on the ground, while the lama levitated and gave her cho. She said from the sky above the gonda, "I'll give the old men their cho, and the young men their cho, and the little monks their cho. Then there must be no more conflict. You must do good cho from now on." All the monks prostrated themselves before the lama. But a few of the little monks did not believe her, some saying that a doctor had given her medicine. All of them are still in hell. All the monks did prostrations, and the lama came back to the gonda, and she gave them the Nyungne cho. In India she gave it to everyone, and it went very well. Then she went to Tibet, and it went very well. . . . Nyungne is what . . . Chenrezi gave Gelungma Palma in heaven to bring to the world. . . . Nyungne is very powerful. She brought it from heaven.

THE STORY OF THE *DÜ* MOTHER

(The story of the *dü* mother was cited by von Fürer-Haimendorf[2] as the primary precedent for Nyungne in Khumjung. According to Au Chokdu, however, it is primarily associated with *sozhung*, a day of ascetic practices that is both contained within Nyungne and can be observed on its own. The story resonates with both the Nupki Gyelwu story and the Gelungma Palma story.)

Once there was a nun, very very poor, and all alone, living in Waranasa [Benares]. She went around begging food. Everyone gave her leftovers. Some young monks—small boys fooling around—put dirty things in her begging bowl. The nun uttered a curse, saying "In my next life, I'll have 500 sons and I'll have plenty to eat." So in her next life [she became a demoness and] she had 500 sons, and they all went around eating people.

The Buddha heard about this and he stole her youngest son. The dü mother was distraught, and not knowing the Buddha had taken her son she went to the Buddha for help. He said to her, in effect, "If you are so upset over losing just one son, think how all the people must feel whose children your sons have eaten." He promised that if she and her sons stopped eating people he would give her son back and make sure she and all her sons had enough to eat. Now at sozhung people squeeze their leftover food into a small wad that they leave for her. *Gelung* [fully ordained monks] do this every day. Later the dü mother and her sons became gods.

APPENDIX B

MONASTERIES

I include here brief histories of the five Sherpa monasteries I knew best. Much of the data on Tengboche has been previously published and I include it (briefly) for the sake of completeness. Much of the rest has been previously unpublished unless otherwise noted; it is pulled together from Robert Paul's field notes in the mid-sixties (with permission and thanks), from my own project on monastic history in 1979, and from later communications from Sherpa friends.

The main point of the stories is to convey the fates of the monasteries up into the present, most of which (Tengboche is the major exception) have had serious problems, especially at the level of leadership. The stories also illustrate the complex interconnections between various lines of descent and reincarnation among the head lamas, and I will conclude the appendix with an account of the history of the Zatul Rimpoche succession, and a chart of all the interconnections of which I am aware.

TENGBOCHE

The early history of Tengboche has been covered in detail elsewhere, including both the founding of the monastery in 1916[1] and—in chapter 4 of this book—the discovery of Lama Gulu's reincarnation, the present head lama of the monastery. The monastery did well for a long period of time, but it was losing monks and declining in the late 1960s. This trend was reversed in the late 1970s, and the monastery was flourishing with both new monk recruits and lay students when von Fürer-Haimendorf revisited it in 1983.[2] In the interim it had received funding from the American organization Cultural Survival for a "culture center" and a monks' residence; from the Nepali government's Department of Parks and Wildlife for a library and museum building; and from the Himalayan Trust for salaries for monk-teachers.[3] It was also apparently taking in substantial donations from tourists and from mountaineering expeditions.

In the late 1980s, at the request of the head lama, or Rimpoche (as he is generally referred to), the San Francisco–based American Himalayan Foundation (AHF) funded a project to build a mini dam and bring electricity to the gompa. In April 1988, the project was begun, and an optimistic spread in *National Geographic* magazine said that the electricity would "ease the austere existence of [the] 50 monks" at the monastery.[4] At the bottom of the page a man in a red sweater (only monks and ex-monks wear red in Sherpa society; it is not clear what the man was) is shown holding up and gazing at a glowing space heater.

Less than a year later, on 19 January 1989, the large main temple and the galleries surrounding the courtyard of Tengboche monastery burned to the ground, the most likely culprit being an unattended space heater.[5] No one was hurt,[6] and a few of the most sacred relics of the monastery were apparently saved, but otherwise the losses were great. In addition to the extensive fresco work that had covered all of the interior (and some of the exterior) walls, the majority of Tengboche's texts and artifacts did not survive the fire. Included in these losses were the Mani Rimdu costumes and masks, some of which came originally from Rumbu monastery; a complete 108-volume set of the Kengyur and Tengyur, the sacred texts of Tibetan Buddhism; and "some rare texts that the present abbot had been importing from Tibet for many years."[7]

Little more than a year after the fire, on 27 April 1990, the Rimpoche presided over and blessed a ceremony at which Sir Edmund Hillary placed foundation stones at the four corners and inaugurated the rebuilding of Tengboche. The estimated cost for the completion of the rebuilding, not including frescoes, statuary, books, and other interior furnishings, was about \$160,000,[8] over half of which was already in hand, evidently also from the AHF.

The building, which the Rimpoche designed based on the design of a gompa in Bhutan, is now complete, larger than before and very impressive.

CHIWONG

The second Sherpa monastery, Chiwong, was founded in 1924 by Sangye, the younger brother of the founder of Tengboche. Sangye recruited a monk called the Kusho Tulku, a brother of the (married) head lama of Thami gompa, to be the head of his newly founded monastery. The Kusho Tulku was the reincarnation of a powerful married lama of the Solu Sherpa village of Chalsa. At Sangye's invitation, the Kusho Tulku came to Chiwong with his younger brother, Kusho Mangden, also an ordained monk, as well as several senior monks who had been living at Thami temple, even though it was still a married-lama community.

After about five years of successful leadership at Chiwong, however, the Kusho Tulku became sexually involved with a nun, by one account a daughter of the clan of the founder of the monastery, the Lama clan.[9] The founder, Sangye, and other Lama clan members were extremely upset about this, and the Kusho Tulku and the nun, Ani Galden, left the area and went to Kathmandu. But that was not the end of it. A member of the Lama family, possibly the girl's father, subsequently beat up the Kusho Tulku, either (in one version) near the Lamjura pass on the trail to Kathmandu, or (in another) in the streets of Kathmandu. The Kusho Tulku's days as head of Chiwong were over.[10]

Chiwong was now without a head lama. Many of the Khumbu monks gradually drifted back to Thami. As one informant put it, "When a mother [sic] leaves a place, her children go with her." Despite its huge endowment, Chiwong began to go downhill. This was seen by many to be a result not only of the Kusho Tulku's sin in breaking his vow of celibacy, but also of the almost equally serious offense of the beating of the Kusho Tulku.[11]

As long as the Kusho Tulku was alive, no attempts were made, apparently, to replace him in the headship of Chiwong. The monastery was run by the esteemed *geken*, or teacher, from Thami, Lowen Woser, but this was not the same thing as having a fully empowered (and reincarnate) head lama. Chiwong probably further lost cohesion after the death of the founder, Sangye, in 1939. In the same period, however, the lama who in a sense started this whole history, the Zatul Rimpoche, died, and a few years later he was reincarnated. Actually, there were two (claimed) reincarnations—one in a Tibetan child, in Lhasa, and one in a Sherpa child of Solu parents. The Sherpa child was the illegitimate son of a fallen Devuche nun, herself a daughter of the Chalsa lama who had reincarnated in the Kusho Tulku.[12] After the Lhasa claimant was recognized as the "official" reincarnation, and given the abbotship of Rumbu monastery,[13] the Sherpa claimant—called the Kumdul (a contraction of Khumbu Tulku) Rimpoche—was asked by the Chiwong monks to fill the vacant headship of Chiwong monastery, which he did.[14]

Chiwong was somewhat revived for a time by the presence of fresh leadership of high spiritual status, and when the Tibetologist David Snellgrove visited the monastery in 1955, the reincarnate lama, then seventeen years old, was in residence, and was pursuing his studies with an energetic and talented monk from a Zhung family. Snellgrove cited the monastery "for the excellence of its religious practice" at the time.[15] Within a year or two, however, the Zatul Rimpoche *tulku* traveled to Tibet for study, and while there was invited to head a larger and more prestigious monastery. He accepted the offer, and then died suddenly in 1958 without ever returning to Solu.[16] His excellent teacher, Ngawang Yenden, also left Chiwong at about the same time.[17]

Since the late fifties, Chiwong monastery has had no official head lama. It is still supported handsomely by the Lama family, and there are still a handful of monks in residence at the monastery. For a time they stopped doing the biggest annual ritual, the Mani Rimdu festival, with its masked dances, exorcism of demons, and ritual conferral of long life on the lay people who attend. Mani Rimdu has since been restarted by the refugee Tibetan reincarnate lama, the Tushi Rimpoche, who comes down from his monastery nearby with a group of Tibetan monks to do the ritual in the Chiwong temple.[18] The collective ritual life of the monastery has been much diminished, and there have been few if any new monk recruits for many years.

TAKSHINDO

Takshindo monastery was founded in the Year of the Ox (about 1949) in the Solu region, not far (as Sherpa distances go) from the site of the languishing Chiwong gompa, and in a sense picking up the slack from Chiwong. It was founded by a Tengboche monk, Tolden Tsultim. Although it was defined as a branch or a "daughter" of Tengboche monastery, Tolden Tsultim was apparently a strong individual and the general view was that he wanted to create (and head) a new monastery in the region that he had originally come from, in eastern Solu. The monastery flourished in its early years, attracting some ordained monks from Tengboche who had, like Tolden Tsultim, originally hailed from Solu, and attracting as well some young new recruits.[19]

In addition, it was discovered that a boy from a village in the region was the reincarnation of a local married lama, and he was brought to Takshindo for training; this *tulku* (reincarnation) became known locally as the Takshindo lama, though he was not in fact the head of Takshindo monastery as the label would suggest. And finally there was an excellent teacher, an extremely learned Sherpa who had studied for fifteen years in Khams, in northeast Tibet, and had attained the degee of *geshe*, roughly equivalent to a Ph.D.

Tolden Tsultim died in the late 1950s, and the monastery was ambiguously headed by the young reincarnate lama (even though he had no official position there) and the geshe. About three years later, however, it was discovered by the Takshindo monks that Tolden Tsultim had reincarnated in a child of a Lama clan family in Phaphlu. The monks approached the family, but they were apparently not interested in turning their son over to the monastery, and the situation has remained in limbo.[20]

THAMI

Thami monastery had originally been a married-lama community, one of the three oldest temple communities in Solu-Khumbu.[21] Around the time of the foundings of the first Sherpa monasteries in the teens and twenties of the 20th century, the head lama of Thami (who was a married lama from the powerful founding descent line of the temple) had three sons, two of whom took monastic vows at Rumbu, and one of whom took training as a married lama. The middle son was none other than the Kusho Tulku, who has already appeared in the story of Chiwong monastery. A number of celibate Sherpa monks were living at the Thami married-lama community, and there were moves around this time to convert the temple to celibacy, with the celibate Kusho Tulku as head lama (passing over his noncelibate older brother for the succession). The Kusho Tulku evidently did take over for a short time, and oversaw the rebuilding of the main temple in a new location, with a larger courtyard, in order to begin to stage the monastically central Mani Rimdu rituals. This was in the early 1920s, after the founding of Tengboche but before the founding of Chiwong.[22]

If events had unfolded as planned, the conversion of Thami temple into a celibate monastery at that time would have made it the second monastery in Solu-Khumbu. But events did not unfold as planned. On the one hand, the Kusho Tulku was said to have been having trouble with some of the Thami sponsors. On the other hand, he was lured by Sangye Lama to take over as head of the newly built Chiwong monastery in Solu. When the Kusho Tulku left Thami, most of the celibate monks went with him to Chiwong, and he is said to have taken the Mani Rimdu costumes as well. This would have been around 1923. The initial attempt to convert Thami to celibacy thus collapsed. The Thami leadership was taken over after all by the Kusho Tulku's older brother, the married Lama Tundup.

The Kusho Tulku broke his vows at Chiwong in the late twenties or early thirties, and the monks began to drift back to Thami, where they once again made moves to upgrade the temple to a monastery. They restarted the Mani Rimdu festival in the 1940s, although, since

they did not have the costumes, they at first performed a much reduced version of it.[23] But the numbers of celibate monks living in
the community continued to grow, and the temple was finally converted to a celibate monastery in about 1950.

The married, and much beloved, Lama Tundup continued to preside over the community until his death in 1958. (The anomaly of
a married lama presiding over a celibate monastery was resolved
through some set of ritual arrangements.) Within a few years his
reincarnation was found in a young boy from the remote Sherpa
area of Rolwaling, northwest of Thami. The boy was brought to
the monastery and was carefully trained and raised by the monks,
including especially his regent/tutor Ngawang Samden (who was a
biological grandson of Lama Tundup).[24] He grew up to be a bright
young man and a dutiful lama, and Thami monastery continued to
thrive up through the 1980s. Along with Tengboche, Thami was
one of the major successes of the Sherpa monastic movement, and
the Thami Rimpoche was, along with the Tengboche Rimpoche,
the other major Sherpa tulku.

And then disaster struck. In February of 1990, the Rimpoche went
back to Rolwaling to visit kin and preside over some rituals. His
tutor, Ngawang Samden, usually traveled with him, and always kept
him under very close watch. In this case, however, Ngawang Samden
did not accompany the lama, who is said to have had too much to
drink, and he went to bed with a woman of the household in which
he was staying. Everyone was stunned, including this ethnographer,
who learned of this shortly after it had happened.[25] Subsequently,
the monks "forgave" the lama for his breach of vows, and he continues today as head of the monastery.

SERLO

One of the last monasteries founded indigenously in Solu-Khumbu
was Serlo gompa, established on the hillside above Zhung (Junbesi)
village in Solu in about 1959. The lama, Sangye Tenzing, was a
young man from Solu who had gone off to Khams in northeastern
Tibet for ordination and training and stayed for many years. He
returned to Solu at the time of the Chinese invasion, and his teacher

gave him a great deal of money and many religious objects with which to found a new monastery. Sangye Tenzing was, along with the Takshindo geshe, probably one of the best educated monks in Solu-Khumbu, and he became something of a local authority on Tibetan Buddhist practice and Sherpa religious history. He worked with the Tibetologist Alexander W. MacDonald[26] and with theology student Kurt Schwalbe,[27] and he himself published a religious history of the Sherpas.[28] He had ambitions to make Serlo gompa even more "high" in terms of scholarship and advanced religious techniques than the other Sherpa monasteries. At the time of my first fieldwork (1966–68), the main temple was partially completed, and the lama had attracted a small but devoted coterie of young monks, as well as a group of children there for elementary teaching.

In the 1970s, several of the key monks broke their vows, which was perfectly normal, but the monastery was tiny to begin with and this took a major toll on the morale of the monastery—especially, I think, on the morale of the head lama.[29] And then some time in the 1980s, the lama himself became sexually involved with a nun, and that was the final blow to the monastery. The lama continued to reside at the monastery, but he was not on good terms with the local villagers, with whom he had a series of property disputes. He had five children in quick succession after his fall, and then died suddenly in 1990. The monastery closed down completely.[30]

THE FATE OF RUMBU MONASTERY AND THE ZATUL RIMPOCHE SUCCESSION

The Zatul Rimpoche died in about 1940. After he died, there were two claimants to the status of his reincarnation, one a Tibetan child, and one a Sherpa child of Solu parents. It is culturally possible to have up to three reincarnations of a single individual, one each for the three components of his person: body, speech, and mind. Despite the fact that the Rumbu monks were said to prefer the Sherpa candidate, the Tibetan claimant was recognized by the central government in Tibet as the official reincarnation, and was installed as abbot of Rumbu monastery. The Sherpa claimant (who was called the Kumdul [a contraction of Khumbu and Tulku] Rimpoche) remained in Solu-Khumbu, where according to some accounts he served as head of the Nauje village temple for a while. Eventually, as we have seen, he became head of Chiwong monastery for a few years, then traveled to Tibet for study, accepted an offer to head up a monastery in Tibet, and died suddenly there at the age of twenty.

Meanwhile, the Tibetan reincarnation (the individual recognized by the Lhasa government as the official Zatul Rimpoche reincarnation) was installed at Rumbu. But some monks began to gravitate toward an alternate source of leadership. Living at the monastery was the reincarnation of the Zatul Rimpoche's teacher in a former existence, a tulku by the name of Tushi Rimpoche.[31] His mother, an unmarried former nun, had brought him from his home in central Tibet to Rumbu monastery in 1926, when he was five years old. At the time of the death of the Zatul Rimpoche in the late 1930s, he was in his teens. Many of the monks began to drift into his orbit, away from the Rumbu tulku, and by 1950, at the time of the first Chinese invasion, it was the Tushi Rimpoche rather than the Rumbu Tulku who led a large group of Rumbu monks over the border into Solu-Khumbu into temporary exile from the Chinese. The group stayed for about a year in the environs of Thami gompa, and it was apparently at that time that the Thami monks received the Tushi Rimpoche's advice on the conversion of Thami temple to celibacy.

The group returned to Tibet after the threat subsided, and the Tushi Rimpoche apparently began to build his own monastery not far from Rumbu (and presumably to be filled in part with Rumbu monks), but the project was interrupted once and for all by the Chinese invasion of 1959. Again the Tushi Rimpoche led the monks out of Tibet into the Solu-Khumbu region, this time permanently. The monks at first returned to the Thami area in Khumbu, but then moved down to Solu. The group split up and lived in several different locations; they also moved around quite a bit. The Tushi Rimpoche built a monastery at Senghe Puk, and many of the monks lived there, but some also lived at Churung Kharka. At one point the Tushi Rimpoche and some of the monks moved into Chiwong, which should have been ideal for all concerned, since the monastery lacked a leader and the Rimpoche and his monks lacked a monastery. But for some reason things did not work out (all that could be

30. Four tulku. *Left to right*: Ngawang Samden (tutor and guardian of the Thami tulku), the Thami tulku, the Tushi Rimpoche, the Chiwong tulku, the Zatul Rimpoche tulku (called the "Napta tulku") in his father's arms, and one of the Tushi Rimpoche's personal attendants, 1967.

learned was that the Rimpoche felt the water was not good). When I first arrived in Solu in 1966, the group was living at Phungmoche, at the site of a former married-lama community that was no longer operating.

During the period of my fieldwork, a Tibetan refugee family in Solu came forth claiming that their son was showing signs of being another reincarnation of the Zatul Rimpoche. (Classically, the child says things like, "This [its natal house] is not my home; my home is at such-and-such monastery," and so forth.) The child was brought to Phungmoche to be tested for his authenticity. The test would normally focus on the child choosing "his own" objects (from his past life) from among a set of similar objects. I was present at the ceremonies, but the test was never administered. According to Sherpa informants, this was because the Tushi Rimpoche had been able to ascertain, through supernormal mental feats, that the child was authentic.

In the picture I took on that occasion, the small child in his father's arms is this particular Zatul Rimpoche's reincarnation, called "the Napta tulku." The Tushi Rimpoche is in the center. To his right is the eight-year-old Thami tulku, who happened to be visiting the monastery at the time of this occasion, accompanied by his tutor and guardian, Ngawang Samden, at the far left of the photo. On the Tushi Rimpoche's left is a young monk who was identified as the "Chiwong tulku," though my notes are not clear as to who his "former body" is supposed to have been. At the right side of the photo is a monk who was the Tushi Rimpoche's long-time personal attendant. The photograph is considered very sacred and powerful by many Sherpas, since it has four tulku in the one picture.

In 1967, with both money and labor from the Solu Sherpas, as well as from Tibetan refugees, the Tushi Rimpoche built a monastery for himself and his monks not far from the village of Zhung. It is the Tushi Rimpoche, then, who in practice has filled the Zatul Rimpoche's shoes from about the midcentury on, playing the kind of strong role in Sherpa religious developments that the Zatul Rimpoche had played in the early decades of the century.

The Tibetan Zatul Rimpoche reincarnation apparently escaped to Dharamsala at the time of the Chinese invasion. He then led a group of Tibetan refugees to settle in Switzerland, and has recently resettled in Sydney, Australia.[32]

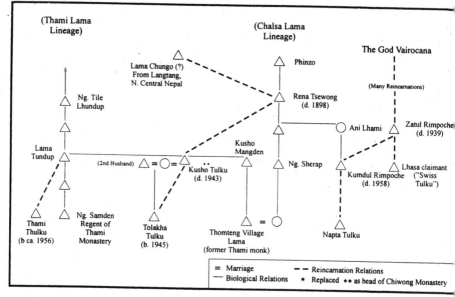

Fig. 1. Interrelations between selected descent lineages (*lami gyudpa*, or *largyu*) and reincarnation lineages of lamas in the greater Solu-Khumbu region. (Note: There are many uncertainties in this chart, and I welcome corrections.)

NOTES

CHAPTER 1

1. One Sherpa died of altitude sickness earlier in the expedition.

2. Doug Scott complained about the lack of good information on Himalayan climbing accidents: "Magazine editors have a responsibility to publish details and statistics of accidents as well as success[es] so we would all know what to expect." (1985, 32).

3. Blum 1980, 20.

4. Fleming and Faux 1977, 40.

5. Allison 1993, 206.

6. Morrow 1986, 63.

7. Dowling 1996, 42.

8. Fisher 1990, 146.

9. Carrier 1992, 82.

10. Bonington 1987, 246.

11. It sometimes seemed as if every time I sat down to work on the discussion of "risk," a fatal accident in Himalayan mountaineering would appear in the international news. As I was working on the first draft in 1995, the death on K2 of Alison Hargreaves, the first woman to climb Mount Everest without oxygen, was reported on the radio; as I was working on the second draft in 1996, I heard about the Everest disaster with which I opened this chapter.

12. Quoted in Tilman 1983, 487.

13. Blum 1980, 91.

14. The term "Sherpa" has become a metaphor in Western vocabulary in a variety of ways: there is a British van called "sherpa" presumably because it carries large and heavy loads over long distances; a certain kind of fleecy lining in coats is called "sherpa," presumably drawing on the idea that Sherpas live in a cold climate and know how to keep warm; and support staff in corporate and political negotiations are sometimes called "sherpas" with the idea that they support the higher status parties to the negotiations in their difficult efforts. The figure of speech works particularly well for high-level political meetings, since the idea of mountaineering is also invoked by calling them "summit" meetings. Adams (1996) discusses metaphoric Sherpas, and the impact of Western metaphors on Sherpas.

15. Ortner 1989a.

16. Hansen (n.d. a).

17. Thapa 1997.

18. Barcott 1996, 65.

19. Ang Tharkay 1954; Tenzing Norgay 1955. Tenzing Norgay wrote another autobiography, published in 1977. Most of the material on his early life is repeated from the 1955 autobiography; most of the newer material pertains to his life after he stopped climbing. I draw on it occasionally, but it is less relevant for the present study than the earlier book.

20. I never learned Nepali, the national language. Many Sherpas are bilingual in Sherpa and Nepali, or trilingual in Sherpa, Nepali, and English. My lack of Nepali was not much of a problem when I was working primarily in the villages of Solu-Khumbu, because people rarely used Nepali except for conversations with the occasional government official who came through. It was more of a liability in Kathmandu, where Sherpas were more likely to conduct casual conversations, even among themselves, in Nepali.

21. E.g., Greenblatt 1993; Sahlins 1981.

22. E.g., Said 1978; Guha and Spivak, eds., 1988.

23. E.g., Appadurai 1990; Clifford 1997.

24. Spivak 1988.

25. For similar arguments pertaining to closely related issues, see Hansen 1997.

26. Clifford and Marcus 1986.

27. Said 1978.

28. See Ortner 1995b, where I have discussed these issues in greater detail.

29. Geertz 1973; see also Ortner 1997.

30. Sahlins 1981.

31. Ortner 1996d.

CHAPTER 2

1. Cameron 1984,110.

2. Ibid., 111–12.

3. Mason 1955, 76.

4. Thanks to Harka Gurung for the translation.

5. Cameron 1984, 111; Mason 1955, 75.

6. When they could not go themselves, the British sent Indian explorers. The Sherpa region of Solu-Khumbu was first explored (from the British point of view) by an Indian named Hari Ram, working for the Survey of India in 1885–86 (*Survey of India 1915*).

7. See especially Hansen 1996a and 1996b.

8. The Gurkha regiments were "loaned" and/or hired out to the British in India by the rulers of Nepal. For recent treatments of the British views of the Gurkhas,

see Caplan 1991, 1995; Des Chene 1991. For notes on Gurkha presence in early mountaineering, see Gurung 1985, 1991.

9. Herrligkoffer 1954, 11.

10. Ibid., 7.

11. Collie, quoted in Herrligkoffer 1954, 14.

12. Ibid., 15.

13. I use the term here in the sense of professional and amateur scholars who were fascinated with "the Orient" and studied it for what Westerners could learn for their spiritual improvement. Although south Asia was the object of a certain amount of Christian missionization, the attitude of many Westerners from early on seems to have been that Buddhism in particular was a superior religion and could be used to counter the growing materialism of Western civilization.

14. See Mason 1955.

15. Hooker 1854.

16. E.g., White 1909.

17. Waddell 1888.

18. Freshfield 1979 [1903].

19. Cameron 1984, 144–52.

20. Hansen 1996a and 1996b; Unsworth 1981, 16.

21. See Ortner 1989a, ch. 7, for the story of the great financial success of Sangye Lama and his wife in Darjeeling.

22. Dash 1947, 72; Ortner 1989a,160.

23. Rubenson 1908a, 67.

24. C. G. Bruce 1910, 28.

25. Quoted in Cameron 1984, 161; see also Kellas 1913, 144–46.

26. Cameron 1984, 161–12; Noel 1927, 60.

27. Peter Hansen (personal communication) has indicated that he thinks the views of Rubenson/Monrad-Aas and Kellas of the Sherpas were not widely circulated until later. But Bruce was repeating the report of Rubenson in 1910, as we saw, and traveled with Kellas to Everest in 1921.

28. Unsworth 1981, 163; see also Hansen 1995.

29. Unsworth 1981, 24. Fifty years later similar sentiments can be heard from one climber concerning another, again apparently too elite: " 'We didn't think much of him at first. . . . I suppose he was too much of the posh private school type, but when we got to know him, we realised he was a good bloke.' " Quoted in Bonington 1976, 37.

30. Unsworth 1981, 163.

31. Bauer 1937, 6.

32. Tilman 1983 [1948], 465.

33. See also Hansen 1995 on the middle-class origins of mountaineering. Hansen and I differ over the "countercultural" stance of mountaineering, but we share a sense of the critical role of class.

34. Simmel 1959, 243. Thanks to David Koester for the Simmel reference.

35. Unsworth 1981, 23; see also French 1995.

36. Unsworth 1981,100; Morrow 1986, 63.

37. In Chevalley et al. 1953, 48.

38. Tilman 1983 [1948], 502.

39. Denman, 1954, 230.

40. Tilman 1983 [1948], 502.

41. Desio 1956, 3; see also Miura 1978, 40.

42. Singh 1961, 140.

43. Quoted in Ullman 1964, xvii.

44. Ridgeway 1979, 149. Peter Hansen (personal communication) has told me that Sir Edmund Hillary considered titling one of his books *Escape from Boredom*.

45. Younghusband 1926, 17.

46. Bauer 1937, xiv.

47. Unsworth 1981, 237–46.

48. Denman 1954. There were virtually no large expeditions from the mid-thirties to the early fifties because of the disruptions of World War II, and then the Indian independence movement. The absence of expeditions for almost two decades caused great economic hardship for those Sherpas who had come to rely on the income from this kind of work. See Tenzing Norgay's autobiography (1955, ch. 6).

49. Unsworth 1981, 237.

50. Tilman 1983 [1948], 505.

51. Ibid.

52. Ibid., 508.

53. Ibid., 509.

54. Younghusband 1926, 196–97; see also Norton et al. 1925, 39.

55. Beetham 1925, 189–90.

56. Younghusband 1925, 5.

57. C. G. Bruce et al. 1923, 23.

58. Norton et al. 1925, 39.

59. Northey and Morris 1976 [1927].

60. Ibid., 253.

61. Finch 1923, 238.

62. J. G. Bruce 1925, 229.

63. Herrligkoffer 1954, 47.

64. Morris 1958, 60.

65. Dias 1965, 16. See Peter Bishop (1989) on the Western imaginings in this region, as these came to be summarized in "the myth of Shangri-La."

66. Kohli 1969, 7.

67. Miura 1978, 77.

68. Bauer 1937, 83.

69. Smythe 1931, 93.

70. Ruttledge 1935, 85.

71. Eiselin 1961, 140.

72. Ullman 1964, 67.

73. A few pre-1920s fatal expeditions should also be noted: In 1895 the British attempted to climb Nanga Parbat, a very difficult mountain in the western Himalaya. The leader of the expedition, A. F. Mummery, and two Gurkha soldiers (Ragubhir Thapa and Gaman Singh) disappeared, "probably destroyed by one of the avalanches that raked the route." (Gurung 1985, 2; see also C. G. Bruce 1910) In 1905, the Swiss attempted to climb Kangchenjunga. One sahib and three porters were buried in an avalanche (Mason 1987 [1955], 126). Climbing was interrupted by the First World War, from 1914 to about 1920.

74. Unsworth 1981, 489; Mason 1955, 157ff.

75. Macdonald 1973, 231; C. G. Bruce et al. 1923, 280ff; Unsworth 1981, 490.

76. Unsworth 1981, 490.

77. Noel 1927, 157ff; Norton et al. 1925, 88ff.

78. G. O. Dyhrenfurth 1931, 84.

79. Bauer 1937, 146; Bauer 1955, 137; Mason 1955, 199.

80. Tenzing Norgay1955, 32, 137; Bechtold 1935, 27ff. (obituary); Mason 1987 [1955], 159, 229ff; Herrligkoffer 1954, 56–57.

81. Unsworth 1981, 237–46. Tenzing Norgay was very critical of Wilson's Tibetan porters, who he thought should have done more to help him; Tenzing also believed that they had taken Wilson's money after he did not return (Tenzing Norgay 1955, 40).

82. Ang Tharkay 1954, 75; Tenzing Norgay tells a different version of this story (1955, 45).

83. Brown 1936, 312; Mason 1987 [1955], 210.

84. Pfeffer 1937, 210.

85. Bauer 1939, 103.

86. Tilman 1948, 95ff.; Ang Tharkay1954, 82ff.

87. Hunt 1978, 58; Tenzing Norgay1955, 122; Desio 1956, 40. This expedition has been subjected to heavy criticism (see Mason 1955, 263; and also a recent reappraisal [D. Roberts 1986a, 161ff.]).

88. Roch 1947, 150ff.

89. Tilman 1946, 37.

90. E.g., Somervell and Mallory, quoted in Unsworth 1981, 97–98.

91. Noel 1927, 157. This was, however, one of the occasions when the sahibs were very upset.

92. Bauer 1955, 137, 155; Mason 1955, 199.

93. Bauer 1955, 157. Frank Smythe, however, said, "The Sherpas may be the prey to superstitious fears, but they are men enough to be able to conquer them" (1931, 84).

94. Bauer 1939, 103.

95. Quoted in Unsworth 1981, 253.

96. Bauer 1955, 156. Tenzing Norgay describes himself roughing up another Sherpa in order to get him moving (Tenzing Norgay 1955, 179), and Reinhold Messner beat and kicked a Sherpa to make him keep moving in bad weather on the 1978 first ascent of Everest without supplementary oxygen (Messner 1979). The Sherpas of that expedition collectively complained about Messner's behavior, but Messner felt he had saved the Sherpa's life (Faux 1982, 24).

97. Some of the discipline was physical: one can find instances in the literature of a porter being smacked with a cane, or threatened by a fist shaken at the face, or punished by being made to carry extra loads. (Sewell n.d., *passim*). These instances were not trivial, but they were much less frequent and less relied upon than the forms of authority that sought to establish consent.

98. J. G. Bruce, 1925, 192, 348.

99. Norton et al. 1925, 20.

100. Bauer 1937, 83, writing about the 1929 Kangchenjunga expedition.

101. J. G. Bruce, 1925, 69.

102. Norton et al. 1925, 107–8.

103. Unsworth 1981, 107. One of the Sherpa awardees may have been Narbu Yishe, who also worked on the 1924 expedition (Norton et al. 1925, 153). I cannot find any clue in the published literature to the identity of the other porter.

104. Tilman 1983 [1946], 281.

105. Tenzing Norgay 1955, 57.

106. Ruttledge 1935, 128–29.

107. Ruttledge 1934, 52.

108. Ruttledge 1935, 128–29.

109. Tilman 1983 [1948], 489.

110. Ortner 1989a.

CHAPTER 3

1. E.g., Guha and Spivak, eds., 1988.

2. Althusser 1971.

3. Fisher 1990.

4. C. G. Bruce 1910.

5. Barnes, in Tenzing Norgay 1977, 20.

6. See also Dias 1965, 13; Kohli 1969, 7.

7. Hillary and Hillary 1984, 208.

8. Burgess and Palmer 1983, 135.

9. In Hagen et al. 1963, 5.

10. Hillary 1975, 151.

11. Ullman 1964, 170–71.

12. Kohli 1969; Roch 1952.

13. Sonam Gyalchen, interview by author, 1990; Kohli 1969, 121.

14. Herzog 1987 [1952]; Lhakpa Norbu, interview by author, 1990.

15. Allison 1993, 262.

16. Ang Nyima, interview by author, 1990; Harvard and Thompson 1974.

17. Blum 1980, 74; G. O. Dyhrenfurth 1963, 113; Unsworth 1981, 422, 289; Harvard and Thompson 1974, 172; Tilman 1983 [1948], 485.

18. Unsworth 1981, 440, and other references too numerous to list.

19. Hillary 1955, 207.

20. Sherpas have not risked their lives to rescue just anyone, and they have been reported to have walked away from a non-Sherpa porter who was down in the snow (Thompson 1979, 48), and from a Sherpani porter with frostbite (Dingle and Hillary 1982, 56–57). I will come back to these cases in chapter 9.

21. Tenzing Norgay 1955, 122; Hunt 1978, 58.

22. G. O. Dyhrenfurth 1963, 120.

23. Younghusband 1941; Tenzing Norgay 1955, 32.

24. Sungdare later died falling off the Pangboche bridge. He was drunk at the time, and was rumored to have become an alcoholic at a young age as a result of being overwhelmed by fame.

25. Dowling 1996, 36. Lopsang Jhangbu was killed in an avalanche on Everest in September of the same year.

26. Tilman 1935, 25.

27. Yaks were used to carry loads for long-distance trade into Tibet. They were rarely used for purely local carrying, and they cannot be taken down to lower altitudes as they do not do well in warmer climates.

28. Houston 1987, 224. Arlene Blum has written that "the actual physical structure of the hemoglobin in [Sherpas'] blood is different from ours" (1980, 84), but she does not present evidence or sources for this statement.

29. For more on the traditional political economy of Sherpa society, see Ortner 1989a.

30. In all fairness to the sahibs on this point, it is probably the case that Sherpas successfully hide this side of their culture from them. Thus, several observers have argued that the Sherpas are good at "impression management" (Thompson 1979; Zivetz 1992). Moreover, the Sherpas themselves make a distinction between the outside manners and self-presentation of a person, and what that person is really like inside (see especially Paul 1970). There is no doubt, then, that "bad" Sherpa individuals and "bad" Sherpa interactions may be kept out of sight of the sahibs.

31. See also March 1979; Brower n.d.

32. Ortner 1989a.

33. See Ortner 1973.

34. Thompson took his Ph.D. in anthropology with Mary Douglas at University College, London, and also did extensive climbing in the seventies, including the Bonington-led ascent of the difficult Southwest face of Everest in 1975.

35. Ortner 1989a.

36. Thompson 1979, 46. In *Habits of the Heart*, Robert Bellah et al. briefly discuss the historical emergence of "friendliness" in the cultural style of the American mid-

dle class. They speak of the strains placed upon people by the emergence during the nineteenth century of a less locally based social system combined with an emphasis on individual achievement: "In the new, mobile middle-class world, one autonomous individual had to deal with other autonomous individuals in situations where one's self-esteem and prospects depended on one's ability to impress and negotiate. Social interactions under these conditions were often intense, but also limited and transient. 'Friendliness' became almost compulsory as a means of assuaging the difficulties of these interactions" (Bellah et al. 1985, 118).

37. Two traditional solutions to the parcellization problem were monasticism (one or more sons went off to a monastery and did not take their shares of the estate) and fraternal polyandry (several brothers married one wife and jointly owned the undivided estate). But neither option was a major solution for the Sherpas. Until the twentieth century, there were no Buddhist monasteries in Solu-Khumbu, and a young man had to go off to Tibet. This was a major undertaking, and the numbers that went were very small. Even after the foundings of the monasteries in Solu-Khumbu, the monastic option was not really possible for a poor person (as will be discussed in the next chapter). As for polyandry, this was an option among all the Tibetan-speaking peoples in the area, but the Sherpas have (always, apparently) had one of the lowest rates among these groups. Why this is the case has not, as far as I know, been examined.

38. Ortner 1989a, ch. 6.

39. Ortner 1989a; Regmi 1978.

40. Ang Tharkay 1954, 15–16. Although in theory there is an equal inheritance rule, in practice—especially if the younger brother is relatively unscrupulous—he may wind up with all of it.

41. Ibid., 22.

42. Tenzing Norgay 1955, 21.

43. Ang Tharkay 1954, 33.

44. Ibid., 46.

45. Ibid., 182.

46. Tenzing Norgay 1955, 22.

47. Ang Tharkay 1954, 47.

48. Knowlton 1933; Brown 1936; Shipton 1938; Tilman 1937; Herrligkoffer 1954.

49. Herrligkoffer 1954, 249.

50. Ibid., 25.

51. Ibid., 119.

52. Ibid., 126.

53. The same interpretation may apply to the frequently bad relations with Tibetan porters, both under the traditional "feudal" political system in Tibet, and (more clearly) under the Chinese Communist regime. More research would be needed to see if, and how, the comparison would hold up.

54. Ang Tharkay 1954, 64–65.

55. J. C. Scott, 1985. I discuss new directions in the study of resistance in Ortner 1995b.

56. Norton et al., 1925, 97, 106ff.

57. Bauer 1937, 146; Bauer blamed the sardar.

58. Ibid., 155.

59. There were also questions of insurance for the families of Sherpas killed on expeditions. This was rarely addressed in strikes that took place on the mountains, but it has been the focus of activism in various Sherpa organizations off the mountains since the 1950s. (See Mason 1955, 192; Tenzing Norgay 1955, 120). Expeditions are now required by Nepal law to carry a fixed amount of insurance per Sherpa, but according to Sherpa friends there are sahibs and expeditions that do not comply, and Sherpas have had to bring lawsuits in some cases to get the sahibs to pay up.

60. Howard-Bury et al. 1922, 47.

61. For whatever it's worth, Bruce took the same sardar on the next expedition, and there were no strikes.

62. Bauer 1937, 51.

63. Ibid., 117. Unfortunately, I do not know the outcome of the case.

64. Ang Tharkay 1954. 58.

65. Ibid.

66. The Sherpas enjoy competition (within limits, and especially when they win), pretty much like many Western men. Thus, competing with Tibetans, among themselves, and even with sahibs, probably added another dimension to the cheerfulness. The subject of competition will be taken up in chapter 5.

67. Bauer 1937, 51.

68. Ibid., 117.

69. Unsworth 1981, 112.

70. Tilman 1983, [1948] 450.

71. Ibid. Pack animals were available for the walk-in' on the early expeditions going through Tibet. They were not available, for a long time, for later expeditions going in through Nepal. Starting in the eighties, however, Sherpa entrepreneurs began keeping yak for rental to tourists and expeditions once they reached Khumbu.

72. Tilman 1935, 25.

73. Ibid.

74. Ortner 1989a, ch. 4. The original Horatio Alger stories had a similar structure. The hero goes out and finds a rich patron, and this patron gives him a leg up, a chance to show his high motivation, cleverness, and willingness to work hard. The patron has dropped out of Americans' memory of the tale. Americans generally think that the hero made it by hard work alone (see, e.g., Alger 1962).

75. Adams (1996) discusses the zhindak relationship extensively in her book, situating it within the argument about the making of "virtual Sherpas."

76. Quoted in Laird 1981, 127. For a discussion of a similar dynamic in an Indian case, see Appadurai 1990.

77. James Fisher recently reported a Sherpa analogy from the tourism business: "Tourists are like so many cattle, representing highly mobile, productive, and prestigious, but perishable, forms of wealth. Like cattle, tourists give good milk, but only if they are well fed" (1990, 123). This analogy maintains the idea of reciprocity but inverts the status relations among the parties. It is, of course, rather less respectful than the zhindak idea, but it maintains the sense of the necessary reciprocity of the relationship.

78. Samuel 1993, 14.

79. In Chevalley et al. 1953, 74.

80. Eric Shipton, recorded 16 September 1969, National Sound Archive, London, recording LP32593. Thanks to Peter Hansen for the careful research that turned this up, and for generously passing it on to me.

81. Ang Tharkay 1954, 149.

82. Ibid., 139. This may be an example of a passage in the autobiography that has been heavily infused with sahib fantasy. But it still seems to contain a trace of Ang Tharkay's point of view.

83. Ang Tharkay did not learn to speak any European language with any fluency. The process of writing the autobiography is never described in the book, but one can tentatively piece together the following: The autobiography seems to have been told orally to a Nepali (or Hindi) speaker. It is worth noting that Nepali (which is close to Hindi) was not Ang Tharkay's first language; he grew up as a boy speaking Sherpa, which is a dialect of Tibetan and is totally unrelated linguistically to Nepali. But Nepali was the lingua franca of the region, and he probably came to speak it reasonably well over time. In any event, the Nepali or Hindi speaker to whom he told his story then translated it orally into English, telling it to the editor, Basil P. Norton, who wrote it down as he saw fit. Finally, the ethnographer Christoph von Fürer-Haimendorf is thanked for "reading the first chapters of the book . . . and clarifying (préciser) numerous details." To complicate matters further, it does not seem that Norton's English version was ever published. Rather, it was translated into French by one Henri Delgove and published in Paris; the French version is the one I used, the only one I could find. A thousand thanks to Peter Hansen for telling me of the existence of the autobiography.

84. Ang Tharkay 1954, 9.

85. Ibid., 148.

86. Tenzing Norgay 1955, 21.

87. In Chevalley et al. 1953, 74.

88. Tenzing Norgay 1955, 268.

89. Ibid., 267.

90. Ibid., 204.

91. Ibid., 135.

92. Ibid., 142.

93. Ibid., 119; emphasis added.

94. The Tiger medals went out of use after the British pulled out, and after the labor recruitment scene shifted from Darjeeling to Kathmandu. The Nepali government later began awarding medals as well, but these never carried the same charge. See Dixit and Risal 1992, 18.

CHAPTER 4

1. All information on the history of political-economic trends in Solu-Khumbu in the early-twentieth century, and on the foundings of the monasteries, condensed (radically) from Ortner 1989a.

2. Ibid.

3. The photograph was given to me by his grandson, Tsering Tenzing Lama, which I gratefully acknowledge. It appears in Ortner 1989a,106.

4. For a fuller account of Sherpa popular religion, see Ortner 1978. Although the fieldwork for that book was done in the 1960s, and the monasteries had been around for some time at that point, the fieldwork was done in Solu where the monastic movement had somewhat less impact. I discuss possible explanations for that lesser impact in Ortner 1989b.

5. There were also whole communities of married lamas (who in this case called themselves *ngawa*) and their families in Solu-Khumbu. These included Pangboche (which had become the nucleus of an ordinary secular community by the time any ethnography was done in Solu-Khumbu), Kyerok (which is still functioning as a married-lama community today), Thami (which upgraded to being a celibate monastery in the fifties), and Phungmoche, which was defunct by the time of my first fieldwork in the sixties, and the buildings of which were occupied by the refugee Tibetan monks under the Tushi Rimpoche while their own monastery was being built. Married-lama communities are like monasteries in that their raison d'être is to serve the religious life as much as possible, but the lamas (unlike monks) have wives to take care of their secular work. These communities have never been studied among the Sherpas, but see Aziz (1978) on *serkim gompa* in Tibet. Unless otherwise specified, my discussion of "married lamas" in this book refers entirely to the married lamas who live in secular villages and serve the needs of the villagers.

6. Shamans were not considered "religious" specialists, and their work was not "religion work." They were, however—except for their particular technical specialization—ordinary members of the community and Buddhists like everyone else.

7. The most complete treatment of the relationships between "high" and "low" religion in the context of Tibetan Buddhism is Geoffrey Samuel's excellent *Civilized Shamans* (1993).

8. Robert Paul (1976a, 1979, 1982) has written extensively on the contrast between the "wildness" of popular Sherpa religiosity and the disciplinary stance of high Buddhism, and in many respects I follow his lead in this discussion.

9. Ortner 1995a; see Paul (1977) on the importance of not revealing "truth" if it might cause discord in the community.

10. There is yet another line of criticism that radiates from the issue of marriage: the question of the value of biological descent for defining status. Married lamas and shamans gain status from being born into lineages that have produced (powerful) married lamas and shamans before them. For a married lama in particular (the situation with shamans is more complex), descent from a long lineage of married lamas (largyu) was considered to make one more powerful and of higher status than a "self-made" (rangjung) lama. The monks, in contrast, emphasized learning and spiritual achievement, and descent was denigrated as a principle of status and/or social identity. Lay people were sometimes called "descent people," or "lineage people" (gyudpi mi).

11. Ortner field notes, 1967.

12. Ortner 1989a.

13. Ortner field notes 1979.

14. Ibid.

15. Everything that follows applies to a nun (ani) as well, but the figure of the nun does not have the same charisma as the monk, and I will use the monk as the primary model of the religious ideal here. Nuns will be discussed more fully in chapter 8.

16. I am reluctant to even begin to provide general sources on Buddhist doctrine. The list is enormous and also the subject of contention. For sources immediately relevant to this book, see footnotes and citations attached to particular discussions.

17. The privatization of the monk's life is in one respect even more extreme among the Sherpas than in the Tibetan monasteries. Unlike the major Tibetan monasteries, Sherpa monasteries are not supported by the state, and each Sherpa monk is supported mainly by his own family.

18. Ortner 1977, 47.

19. Quoted in Downs 1980, 21.

20. See Ortner (1973, 1978) for a full discussion. Sherpas also think that too much intellectual work can disorder the mind. Prolonged mental work can make one ill, or even crazy, and monks who work hard at their studies are admired for risking this outcome in the name of religious devotion. Similarly, too much mental work can cause one to get body lice, or to lose weight. Here is a field note from 1979: "I comment that I seem to have come down with lice again. Nyima Chotar (my assistant) says 'thinking people' tend to get lice and to get thin: [This includes] people who have too much mental stress (sem dukpa), like businessmen, thinking about how to get their money, or how to call in their loans, or people like me [qua anthropologist], thinking about what should I ask people tomorrow, etc."

21. Ortner field notes 1967.

22. Ortner field notes 1979.

23. The Dorsem at Thami monastery was filmed in 1976 for the film *Sherpas* (Ortner 1977).

24. Quoted in Brook 1985, 37.

25. Here is an analogous example from a lay man: "Nyima Chotar said that when his sister [who was a nun] fell, he felt *rulwa*, rotten, inside, although on the outside he laughed it off saying, 'Well, if she needs a husband let her go.' " We will see later that Nyima Chotar identified strongly with the monastic perspective (Ortner field notes 1979).

26. There is a kind of practice-theory model here (Bourdieu 1977) in which outer bodily practices achieve an effect on the inner state. Similarly, the Tengboche lama often talked about the relationship between human beings and gods in a practice-theoretical way. He once explained the process of developing a close relationship with a god as follows: "If you have a small picture of the king, it's really nothing, just paper, the king isn't really there. But if you clean it every day and pay attention to it, pretty soon you start wanting a bigger picture, and eventually you start wanting to meet the king himself" (Ortner field notes 1967).

27. Ang Tharkay 1954, 17.

28. Ibid., 58.

29. Ibid., 63.

30. Ibid.

31. Ibid.

32. Ibid.

33. Ibid., 65.

34. Apparently some Sherpa families were also worshiping a god of the Gelugpa sect of Tibetan Buddhism, Shunden (or Shugden), also for the purpose of getting rich. The Zatul Rimpoche said people should not do this either, also on the grounds that the god was "bad," requiring meat, and meat fat instead of butter.

35. Ang Tharkay 1954, e.g., 77–78.

36. Tilman 1983 [1948], 473.

37. Weir 1955, 104–5.

38. This is not to say that the end of killing was the end of all forms of violence among the Sherpas. As discussed briefly in the last chapter, there is still plenty of fighting, and a certain amount of domestic violence as well. But the end of killing was virtually absolute.

39. There were rumors among Khumbu people that Solu people did not entirely forswear murder. I have the following field note from 1967, but since Khumbu people were often quite prejudiced against Solu people I would be very careful about taking it as fact without further confirmation: "About 10 years ago [this would have been the mid-fifties] Solu had a bad reputation for much killing, especially around Takto, where rich passersby were waylaid, robbed, killed, and thrown in the river. [One woman's] first husband was jailed for stealing and killing, and died in

jail. Currently in Darjeeling eight Solu Sherpas are under arrest in connection with a murder of some official on the Indian road project."

40. There were poor monks, but I do not have data on how they were supported. In Tibet, in the non-state-supported monasteries, or where a monk simply needed additional funds, a poor monk could work as a servant for a better-off monk, but this was not common among the Sherpas. I can only assume that a poor Sherpa monk had to have some sort of sponsor, perhaps a distant relative who took on the obligation to support him and thus to gain merit. Monks also made some money doing ritual work for lay people.

41. Paul field notes, 1967.

42. Monks do help out their families with agricultural labor from time to time; this is undesirable, but it does not represent a major breaking of vows. Monks also do a fair amount of trade, both for themselves and for their monasteries; this is evidently not considered "work."

43. Ortner film transcript, 1977.

44. There is a long history of debate over whether Buddhist ideals are "selfish." The Mahayana school of Buddhism, to which Sherpa/Tibetan Buddhism belongs, originated in charges that the established school of Buddhism, called Theravada, promoted a selfish orientation in monks, who were encouraged to pursue their personal salvation while doing nothing about the suffering of others. (See especially Conze 1975 [1951]). With respect to Sherpa/Tibetan Buddhism, Snellgrove (1957) and I in an earlier work (Ortner 1978) supported this view. Other scholars have dissented, and have presented a view of Buddhism as much more socially oriented and "compassionate" (see Obeyesekere 1980, Ling 1976, Collins 1982). Yet others have emphasized its dual character (e.g., Dumont 1960; Tambiah 1976). The discussions in the present book modify my earlier position in various ways.

45. Tenzing Norgay 1955, 18.

46. Ibid., 19.

47. Ibid., 24.

48. He never gives the name of the head lama but at one point says that "a great lama from Rongbuk" bestowed the name Tenzing upon him, which was also the name of the lama himself (ibid., 18). The Rumbu lama's full personal name was Ngawang Tenzing Norbu.

49. See especially Hansen 1997, Stewart 1995.

50. Tenzing Norgay 1955, 99; emphasis added.

51. See Ortner 1978, 1989b.

52. The year of death is not known exactly. From a range of different kinds of information I would place the year of death between 1936 and 1940.

53. Actually, there are three kinds of tulku within Sherpa/Tibetan Buddhism. One is a god who takes human form. The Dalai Lama, for example, is a reincarnation of the all-compassionate god Chenrezi, mentioned above in conjunction with Nyungne. The second type of tulku is, strictly speaking, a bodhisattva, a human

being who had attained enlightenment but chose to stay within the world to help others achieve enlightenment too. The third type—rather less exalted but still very high—is that of a great religious leader or practitioner who has not quite reached enlightenment, but who is well on his way. He reincarnates in order to complete his spiritual work. All Sherpa tulku are said to be of the last sort, although the Zatul Rimpoche, the spiritual ancestor of the Sherpa monastic system, was actually a bodhisattva, and the Tushi Rimpoche, his teacher, who settled in Solu with his monks as refugees from the Chinese invasion of Tibet, is a reincarnation of a god, possibly Vairocana.

54. Sometimes more scholarly monks will voice some mild complaints about the elevation of (some, "smaller") tulku above all other monks regardless of the level of their learning. As noted earlier, personal achievement is central to the monastic career, and this may be contrasted with both the biological-descent basis of status among married lamas (see note 9 above) and with the spiritual-descent basis of tulku.

55. The Sherpa trader was Tsepal, the former Gembu, or head tax collector, of Khumbu, who had fled to Lhasa after he had allegedly committed a murder. Tsepal was one of the big financial sponsors of Tengboche. This murder was the one mentioned earlier as the last known killing in Solu-Khumbu. See Ortner 1989a for the details.

CHAPTER 5

1. See Regmi 1978; Ortner 1989a, ch. 6.
2. Regmi 1978, 68–69.
3. Ibid., 74.
4. Von Fürer-Haimendorf 1964, 119.
5. See Miller 1965, 245–46; von Fürer-Haimendorf 1964, 121.
6. Von Fürer-Haimendorf 1964, 126.
7. See especially Tenzing Norgay 1955, 78.
8. Denman 1954.
9. Tenzing Norgay 1977, 134–35.
10. Ibid., 118.
11. Tenzing Norgay 1955, 61–62.
12. All the information we have about this event comes from von Fürer-Haimendorf's account (1976); see also March 1979, 128. The headman donated both land and money for the support of the nuns, and also persuaded the villagers to donate their labor to the construction of the temple. He invited a Bhutanese lama, who had earlier passed through the village on pilgrimage, to head up the temple.
13. Jerstad 1969; von Fürer-Haimendorf 1964, 211.
14. The head lama and early monks of Takshindo went to Darjeeling to do some fund-raising for the new monastery, and apparently they did quite well.

15. Von Fürer-Haimendorf 1964, 159.

16. Ortner field notes, 1979. Early in the century, Karma and Sangye Lama had sponsored the construction of a residence for Sherpa and other Himalayan monks in Tashilhunpo (Ortner 1989a, 129).

17. Noel 1927, 160. It is difficult to know, without seeing it, whether the mural meant what Noel thought it meant. In standard Tibetan Buddhist iconography, there is often a naked, human-looking figure being trampled under the foot of a god in his powerful (takbu) aspect, but the figure in such cases is normally said to represent a demon being subdued by the god. (Why demons are represented in human form in these contexts in another question.) But Noel's interpretation is not utterly implausible from a cultural point of view.

18. Tenzing Norgay 1955, 24.

19. Ang Tharkay 1954, 180.

20. Laird 1981, 127.

21. See Kohli 1969, 188; Curran 1987, 84; Brook 1985, 37.

22. MacDonald 1973.

23. C. G. Bruce et al. 1923.

24. Cameron 1984, 188; Ruttledge 1952, 159.

25. Harvard and Thompson 1974, 96.

26. Ortner field notes, 1990. See also Boardman 1982 for several examples of the Sherpas trying to teach the sahibs not to offend the gods on the mountains.

27. Boardman 1982, 116.

28. Bass and Wells 1986, 116.

29. Ang Tharkay 1954, 154.

30. Hillary 1955, 90.

31. Harvard and Thompson 1974, 101.

32. *Puja* is the Nepali/Hindi term for any kind of religious ritual. It is now in general use among urban, if not village, Sherpas (replacing various Tibetan/Buddhist terms). It is often written the British/colonial way, with an "h" at the end.

33. Herrligkoffer 1954, 47.

34. Jackson and Stark 1956, 152.

35. Bonington 1976, 76. This was an interesting event, as Bonington describes some of the Sherpas reading seriously, while others were joking around. Many possible interpretations spring to mind, but there is not enough information to choose any particular one.

36. Blum 1980, 89–90; see also Bass and Wells 1986, 118.

37. Allison 1993, 206. The good effects of the "pujah" on the "team effort" were very short-lived. According to Allison, the expedition broke down later into very nasty and self-serving individual behaviors. See chapter 10.

38. C. G. Bruce et al. 1923, 76.

39. Ullman 1964, 111.

40. Ibid. In that same period, there was a Sherpa death on the first Indian Everest expedition (1962). Apparently the Sherpas did not show a strong reaction, but the

Indian leader did not invoke any kind of Oriental fatalism line: "Death in mountaineering is an occupational hazard. In its constant proximity and threat lies the great fascination of all dangerous endeavors. Members and Sherpas knew this and responded valiantly by taking it in their stride" (Dias 1965, 33–34).

41. Bonington 1976, 78.
42. Messner 1979, 86.
43. Hillary 1975, 136–37.
44. Singh 1961, 109.
45. Ang Tharkay 1954, 109.
46. In Scott 1985, 31.
47. Ortner field notes 1990.
48. Blum 1980, 233.
49. Ibid.
50. Ortner field notes 1979.
51. Ortner 1997.
52. Ortner field notes 1979.
53. Ang Tharkay 1954, 82ff.
54. E.g., Kohli 1969, 188; Ridgeway 1979, 83–84.
55. Kohli 1969, 170.
56. Adams 1996.
57. See also Fisher 1990.
58. C. G. Bruce et al. 1923, 74–75; Macdonald 1973.
59. Miura 1978, 117
60. It is summarized in Unsworth 1981, 460–61.
61. Morrow 1986, 71.
62. Burgess and Palmer 1983, 95.
63. Morrow 1986, 73.

CHAPTER 6

1. Tilman 1952.
2. Denman 1954, 222.
3. Ang Tharkay 1954,143.
4. Ibid., 162.
5. Tenzing Norgay 1955, 142.
6. Ibid.
7. Chevalley et al., 1953, 162.
8. Although the Swiss were in many ways quite egalitarian, one still comes across passages like the following: "[The Sherpas] have a certain kind of divination of our desires, of our needs, and they anticipate them. No need for many words, they have something of the marvelous intuition of infants" (ibid.).
9. Ibid. 168.
10. Tenzing Norgay 1955, 165.

11. Ahluwalia 1978.

12. Kohli 1969, 50.

13. Tenzing Norgay 1955, 120.

14. According to the late Mike Cheney, there were many problems with this society; see his article (1978), which he also discussed with me in an interview in 1990. More research would be needed in order to evaluate his various charges.

15. Kohli 1969, 13; see also Eiselin 1961, 49.

16. Tenzing Norgay 1977, 85.

17. Unsworth 1981, 315.

18. Ibid.

19. Ullman 1964, 116.

20. Ibid. 170–79.

21. J.O.M. Roberts, personal communication.

22. Unsworth 1981,155.

23. Ibid., 156.

24. Ullman 1964, 339.

25. Ibid., 159. The historian Unsworth (who is English) thought that the Americans were too egalitarian rather than too hierarchical (Unsworth 1981, 372), but he gave no evidence that this was the issue for the Sherpas, and the interpretation seems to be his own.

26. Ridgeway 1979, 179.

27. Bonington 1973, 51.

28. Chevalley et al. 1953, 81.

29. Herzog 1987 [1952], 10–12.

30. Tenzing Norgay 1955, 188.

31. Hunt 1993 [1953]. This information appears in a photo caption that may not be present in all editions.

32. Ibid., 232 n. 1.

33. Unsworth 1981, 316.

34. J.O.M. Roberts 1964; Ullman 1964, 56.

35. Unsworth 1981, 461–62. Unsworth later said there were a hundred Sherpas (1981, 501).

36. This was especially the case for the British and Americans, and one might speculate that it grew out of the military successes of World War II. Others have suggested other speculations: a tie-in with the nationalist machismo of the Cold War, or an effect of the entry of more working-class men into the sport. One would need a lot more data to make any of these arguments.

37. Hillary 1975, 137.

38. Ibid., 145.

39. Fisher 1990, 48.

40. Hillary 1955, 54.

41. Unsworth 1981, 298ff.

42. Ibid., 374.

43. Quoted in Unsworth 1981, 374.

44. Ibid.

45. Jan Morris 1974, 81.

46. Ibid., 82.

47. Ibid. Morris pulled off an extraordinary feat himself on the 1953 Everest expedition; it was he who set up the system of runners and radios that brought the news of the success back to Kathmandu and thence to London in time for the Coronation of Queen Elizabeth. And, in fact, "nothing beat him"; other newspapers were trying to get the scoop as well, but Morris bullied and terrorized his messengers into secrecy, and the *Times* of London (which was not only paying his salary but financing a good part of the costs of the expedition) was able to break the story first (James Morris 1958).

48. Cameron 1984, 232.

49. Norton et al. 1925, 32.

50. Ruttledge 1935, 49–50.

51. Roch 1952, 158.

52. Chevalley et al. 1953, 36.

53. Hillary and Hillary 1984, 208.

54. Messner 1979, 96.

55. Ullman 1964, 159. It is also worth noting that the Sherpas are often, on average, younger than the sahibs, being in their teens and twenties as against the sahibs generally being in their twenties and thirties.

56. Quoted in Unsworth 1981, 54.

57. Ibid., 55.

58. Jackson and Stark 1956.

59. A tiny handful of Sherpas have joined Gurkha regiments. One of the climbing Sherpas I interviewed for this book had been a Gurkha and had found it very "boring," emphasizing that one had to wait in endless lines, especially for meals.

60. Miura 1978, 64.

61. Harvard and Thompson 1974, 71. I do not mean to suggest that the idea of using competition to "make equality" is some exclusively Sherpa notion; John Roskelley reports a very similar race initiated by a non-Sherpa porter in the Karakoram (1987, 115,117).

62. Ortner 1989a.

63. The Chinese occupation of Tibet had numerous consequences for the Sherpas that cannot be pursued here. One very important one was the closing of the trans-Himalayan trade, which has been discussed elsewhere (von Fürer-Haimendorf 1984; Fisher 1990).

64. Quotes from Ortner field notes, 1967.

65. Part of the problem in the Thami case was that some of the dancing was actually done by lay people, in which case it really was "just dancing," without any particular ritual effectiveness. But the charge was ambiguously directed against both the married lamas and the lay dancers.

66. Ortner 1989b.

67. I do not mean to suggest that the founding of the monasteries had no effect on popular religion in Solu as opposed to Khumbu. As I have discussed elsewhere, the impact simply played out differently in the two regions (Ortner 1989b).

68. See Ortner 1975, 1978.

69. See Nebesky-Wojkowitz (1956, 514) and Waddell (1888 [1959], 531–33) for variants of what seems to be the same ritual figure.

70. See Ortner l978, ch. 5.

71. See especially Paul (1979) for a detailed interpretation; for descriptions, see von Fürer-Haimendorf 1964; Kunwar 1989; Funke 1969.

72. There is little doubt that these elements were present before. See Hardie 1957, 79; von Fürer-Haimendorf 1964, 202.

73. Paul 1982, 109ff. Actually, the "Old Man" figure seems to be split into several figures in the Mani Rimdu transformations. On the one hand there are the skeletons; on the other hand there is an old man figure called Mi Tsering, or Long Life Man, who tries to teach various cultural practices to someone taken from the audience. Where the skeletons (or a married couple in the Chiwong version) with their wounded or dead babies illustrate the negativity of biological reproduction, the Mi Tsering figure illustrates the positivity of teaching, i.e., of cultural rather than biological reproduction.

74. Deepest thanks to Kathryn March, who gave me copies of her field notes on several Chiwong Dumjis of the mid-seventies.

75. Bauer 1937, xiii.

76. Unsworth 1981, 196.

77. Haston 1997 [1972], 18.

78. Harvard and Thompson 1974, 139.

79. Ibid.

80. Burgess and Palmer 1983, 5.

81. The question of gay male climbers and/or male homosexual relations on expeditions has come up frequently when I have given talks. There are a number of male climbers who have been frank about their homosexuality (e.g., John Morris 1960, Jan Morris 1974), but I have never seen or heard anything about homosexual relations between sahibs and Sherpas.

82. Ang Tharkay 1954, 79.

83. Hunt 1993 [1953], 58.

84. Tilman 1983 [1948], 455.

85. Hardie 1957, 49.

86. Ang Tharkay 1954, 157.

87. Bonington 1976, 91.

88. James Fisher (personal communication) told me that Tom Laird has written about a gang rape of a Sherpa woman by several Sherpa men. I have not heard about it directly, I am not sure when it was supposed to have happened, and Laird has not published his account. I have tried to contact him about the story but have

been unable to do so. Similarly, David Holmberg has indicated (personal communication) that Sherpas have been somewhat sexually aggressive with Tamang and Rai women when expeditions have passed through villages of those groups, but again I have no further information on this subject.

89. I was also part of a married couple the first time I was in the field. This certainly had an effect. When I went back as an unmarried woman on my second trip, there was a definite rise in the level of flirtation; the men in question were not expedition Sherpas and the change seemed related to my being unmarried and alone, rather than to changes in Sherpa male sexual attitudes under discussion. Nonetheless, I still felt completely physically safe. My biggest fears were of being bitten by a dog, which did happen once, and of falling off some of the more terrifying bridges (a major cause of accidental deaths in the area and throughout Nepal).

90. Kohli 1969, 132.

91. Kumar, in an appendix on "Sherpas" in Kohli 1969, 303.

92. Miura 1978, 65.

93. Ibid.

94. Bonington 1976, 72.

95. Ibid., 85.

CHAPTER 7

1. It is relevant that airfares dropped significantly in this era. Thanks to Peter Hansen for this point.

2. Burgess and Palmer 1983, 13.

3. See Child 1993.

4. See, e.g., Hansen 1996b.

5. Besant 1893; David-Neel 1932.

6. Boardman 1982, 111,133.

7. Ibid., 133–34.

8. Scott 1985, 32.

9. Climbers in the seventies continued to come largely from the educated middle classes (e.g., Ridgeway 1979, 7), which had been true throughout the entire twentieth century. (I have already sketched this for the early period; for the fifties, see e.g., Herzog 1987 [1952], 2; for the sixties, see e.g., Ullman 1964, 29.) There was however something of an increase of working-class climbers in this era. It is not clear whether this affected the larger "sahib culture" in any significant way.

10. Boardman 1982, 111.

11. Miura 1978, 27.

12. Ibid., 4.

13. Ibid., 56.

14. Bremer-Kamp 1987, 21.

15. Miura 1978, 5.

16. Messner 1979, 9.

17. See Tilman 1983 [1948].

18. Marcus 1975.

19. Quoted in Unsworth 1981, 462.

20. Messner 1979; Scott 1984.

21. Messner 1979, 1981; Faux 1982; Child 1993.

22. Boardman 1982, 181.

23. Ibid., 183.

24. Ibid., 181.

25. Ibid., 114.

26. Frank Wells made a few ambiguously critical comments about the competitiveness of expeditions (Bass and Wells 1986, 56, 95), but Wells was highly competitive in other contexts, and his remarks seem related to the fact that he had little mountaineering experience and felt himself to be one of the weaker members of the expeditions. Wells died in a helicopter crash while on a skiing trip in the Ruby Mountains of Nevada in 1994.

27. In earlier eras, a notably democratic leader was often considered weak, and was subject to criticism from many quarters. See, e.g., various discussions about Norman Dyhrenfurth's leadership on the 1963 American Everest Expedition (Ullman 1964, 75; Unsworth 1981, 378) and the International Expedition in 1971 (Unsworth 1981, 410).

28. Harvard and Thompson 1974, 33.

29. Ibid., 147.

30. Blum 1980, 116.

31. Ibid., 36.

32. Unsworth 1981, 503.

33. Bonington 1976, 62.

34. Ibid.

35. Ibid.

36. See also the quote earlier about "climbing this pig," and the discussion in D. Roberts (1986a) about his views on "absolute authority" in his marriage.

37. See Leamer 1982 for a very "countercultural" portrait of Unsoeld. Thanks to Jim Fisher for the reference.

38. Roskelley 1987, 36. Others have argued that the leadership on that expedition was weak and indecisive; see note 27 above.

39. Marty Hoey later died in a fall on Everest in 1982 (Bass and Wells 1986).

40. D. Roberts 1986a.

41. Ibid. Willi Unsoeld later died in a storm while leading a group of students (one of whom also died) on Mount Rainier in 1979.

42. Boardman 1982, 59.

43. Gillette and Reynolds 1985.

44. E.g., ibid., 103.

45. Ibid., 108; see also p. 65 in Gillette and Reynolds 1985.

46. As an aside, it is worth noting that the shift to Alpine-style climbing, requiring far fewer Sherpas, had less economic impact than might have been thought, because the number of expeditions coming to Nepal each year was growing so rapidly that there were always more jobs than Sherpas.

47. Quoted in Cameron 1984, 193.

48. Ibid.

49. The scalp was eventually studied and found to have come from a "serow, a member of a rather rare goat-antelope family" (Bishop 1962, 527).

50. Hillary 1964, 1–2. Kalden, a successful Sherpa businessman in Kathmandu, claimed in a 1990 conversation with me that it was not Urkien but his father, Lama Ongju, who had made this request. According to Fisher, Lama Ongju did write the formal petition to have the first school in Khumjung (Fisher 1990, 68). This, however, does not rule out the original story about Urkien, whose interest in getting an education for his children was apparently very strong; in the fifties he had told Norman Hardie that "he would be [Hardie's] foreman for no wages, anywhere in the world, if [Hardie] would send two of his sons to an English or a New Zealand school" (Hardie 1957, 69).

51. Hillary 1964. This was not actually the first school in the area. There was a school operating in Namche Bazaar when Shipton went through in the early fifties (Shipton 1952a). It makes sense that Namche, a village of relatively wealthy and cosmopolitan (by local standards) traders would organize the first school in the area. Apparently it was short lived, collapsing when—according to Hillary—someone "absconded with the school funds" (Hillary 1964, 35).

52. Fisher 1990, *passim*.

53. Ibid., 66.

54. Ibid., xxii.

55. Ibid., xxiii.

56. I can only remember one American trekker—an African-American ethnomusicology student from Wesleyan; I have often wondered what happened to him—and two Swiss nationals who were running a Tibetan refugee camp in Chalsa for SATA, the Swiss Association for Technical Assistance.

57. Of course I wished they weren't there, but it is a tribute to the film producer, Leslie Woodhead, that he realized they were part of the story, and there is an excellent segment on tourism in the film for which I can take no credit (Woodhead 1977).

58. Burger 1978; Bjonness 1983.

59. The deforestation problem had already begun in 1959, when huge numbers of Tibetan refugees came over the border and camped for months in various parts of Khumbu. People in Thami in 1976 claimed that the refugees had stripped the hillsides for firewood.

60. Brower 1991; Stevens 1993.

61. He also emphasizes that much of it gets eaten up by inflation, and further-more that many Sherpas have little experience with saving and investing and tend not to wind up with very much in the end (Fisher 1990, 115–17).
62. Ibid., 118.
63. See Bjonness 1983.
64. Fisher 1990, 122.
65. Ibid., 111.
66. Ortner field notes 1976.
67. Bauer 1937, 83.
68. Ullman 1964, 67; emphasis added.
69. Dias 1965, 31; emphasis added.
70. Von Fürer-Haimendorf 1964, 4.
71. Ortner 1977, 69. This was the period, 1966–69, of the Great Cultural Revo-lution in China. The Chinese were extremely sensitive about border violations in this era, and in response Nepal closed all the border peaks to climbing. Climbing work became very scarce for Sherpas.
72. Ibid., 3.
73. Tenzing Norgay 1955, 1977; Hillary 1955.
74. Ridgeway evidently did not realize that "Ang" is not a name. It is a term that, when attached to a name, means "young" or "junior." Some children just pick up an "Ang" when they are young (Ang Tenzing, Ang Purwa, etc.) and it sticks, so that they cannot shake it off when they get older even if they want to. It is perhaps analogous to an American child being called by a diminutive—"Bobby"— and then wanting to be called "Bob" or "Robert" when he gets older, but every-one keeps calling him Bobby. In any event no Sherpa, child or adult, is simply called "Ang."
75. Ridgeway 1979, 229–30; sentence order rearranged.
76. Ibid., 142–43.
77. Brook 1985, 36.
78. Cameron 1984, 233.
79. Morrow 1986, 63.
80. Burgess and Palmer 1983, 13.
81. Bonington 1976, 48.
82. Ibid., 88.
83. Bonington 1971, 87.
84. Harvard and Thompson 1974, 81.
85. Bass and Wells 1986, 119.
86. Burgess and Palmer 1983, 188.
87. In Bonington 1976, 58.
88. Burgess and Palmer 1983, 138. The Swiss climber Dittert did something similar in the fifties: "Out of curiosity I tried the load of a coolie, only sixty kilos. . . . I would not be able to go very far, my shoulders cut by the straps (two cords), my back killed by the trunk and the muscles of my neck stretched to breaking by the

brow-rope. So I was forced to set it down heavily, to bursts of laughter from the Sherpas, enchanted by this paltry demonstration" (in Chevalley et al. 1953, 44).

89. Ortner field notes 1990.

90. Ibid.

91. Ibid.

92. Ibid.

93. Harvard and Thompson 1974, 65.

94. Brook 1987, 56.

95. Fisher 1990, 137.

CHAPTER 8

1. Blum 1980, ch.1; David-Neel 1932.

2. Smythe 1931; H. Dyhrenfurth 1931.

3. Blum 1980, 6. Hettie Dyhrenfurth was the wife of one of the men on these otherwise all-male expeditions. In that same era, an American named Elizabeth Knowlton went along as a nonclimbing member with the all-male German-American expedition to Nanga Parbat in 1933. Knowlton was an experienced climber who had "made many ascents," but joined this expedition "to handle the English-speaking newspaper work" (Knowlton 1933, 15).

4. Bourdillon 1956, 203. According to the flap of her book, Jennifer Bourdillon "spent many weeks entirely alone among the Sherpas—the first white woman ever to do so." Her husband, Tom, was at that time climbing on Everest. He later died in an accident in the Alps (Unsworth 1981, 341).

5. Jackson and Stark 1956.

6. Birkett and Peascod 1989; see also Lambert and Kogan 1956.

7. Scarr 1956.

8. Birkett and Peascod 1989, 211. Kogan was killed along with three male Sherpas in an avalanche on this expedition.

9. As I am often asked, in this era of heightened awareness of sexual identities, about the sexual orientation of climbers, I will note that explicit statements about sexual orientation of women climbers have not been made until very recently, and then only in passing, in the mainstream literature (see da Silva, ed., 1992, "Introduction," xv–xx, and essay by Maureen O'Neill, 233–50 in that volume). The details of personal lives of both male and female climbers are of variable relevance, depending on context, although they tend to be more significant for women climbers since women's participation in mountaineering violates cultural gender assumptions and thus seems to call for explanation or justification.

10. For a very bohemian example, see Moffatt 1961. Gwen Moffatt climbed in Europe in the late forties and the fifties.

11. Shipton 1952a, 172, 174.

12. I have been unable to get firm information on the legal developments in Nepal relating to marijuana and hashish. According to one respondent who an-

swered my query on the World Wide Web (1996), "Hashish and marijuana were outlawed in Nepal in the spring of 1973." According to another respondent, "Only the sale of marijuana and hashish is outlawed, not possession or consumption." Thanks to my Web Wallah, Tim Taylor, and to the responders.

13. See also Adams 1996, 56ff.

14. Fisher 1990, 127, drawing in part on von-Fürer-Haimendorf 1984. For a remarkable first-person account of one of these marriages, see D. M. Sherpa 1994; see also F. Sherpa 1997.

15. In this case and others I do not name the expedition or the individuals when the stories had been told to me in confidence and/or when they had been unpublished or unconfirmed.

16. Ortner field notes 1990.

17. Laird 1981, 124.

18. Ortner 1977.

19. Ortner field notes 1976.

20. Ortner field notes 1990.

21. Birkett and Peascod 1989.

22. *Another Ascent* 1975. The year 1975 was in fact International Women's Year. Junko Tabei later said she did not realize it at the time. The invention of things like "International Women's Year" by global agencies like the United Nations clearly has, at least in a case like this, more effect than might cynically be expected.

23. See Ridgeway 1979, 119ff, about Arlene Blum's problems on the mixed American Bicentennial expedition; see also Bremer-Kamp 1987; Gillette and Reynolds 1985.

24. Tullis 1986, 150.

25. See Rutkiewicz 1986.

26. Tullis 1986, 227.

27. Quoted in Unsworth 1981, 463; see also Birkett and Peascod 1989, 99–111.

28. Blum 1980, 9.

29. Allison 1993, 46. I chose to go to a women's college, and in retrospect I think it was for essentially these kinds of reasons—getting away from an evaluative and patronizing male gaze at that stage of my life. Perhaps this is the place to thank Bryn Mawr College, without which I am quite sure I would not be here, doing what I am doing, today.

30. See also Johnson, in Gardiner 1990, 91.

31. In some cases there are more disturbing issues involved than personal independence and freedom to be the best. Two major women climbers, Cherie Bremer-Kamp and Stacy Allison, describe leading lives of outward gender radicalism (including, in Allison's case, getting to the top of Mount Everest), yet enduring deeply abusive relationships with men in their private lives (Bremer-Kamp 1987, Allison 1993).

32. Again, although there is often a good deal of personal affection in some individual Sherpa/sahib relations, I am not convinced that calling them "homoerotic" adds much to what is going on. Physical homosexual relations seem not to

be practiced among Sherpa men, as far as Robert Paul (1970) or I could ascertain in earlier fieldwork. But there is fairly well documented male homosexuality in some Tibetan monasteries (Goldstein 1964).

33. By the time the expedition took place in 1978, however, Everest had been climbed twice by women, as noted earlier.

34. Blum 1980, 27.

35. Ibid., 38–39.

36. They eventually got married.

37. Blum 1980, 179.

38. Ibid., 110.

39. E.g., ibid., 111, 169, 171.

40. James Fisher also reports on "the great joy expressed at the birth of a boy and the distinct lack of enthusiasm shown at the birth of a girl" (Fisher 1990, 79).

41. Fisher 1990, 79.

42. Ortner 1978; March 1979.

43. Ortner (1996a) (1983); March 1979.

44. Thanks to Vincanne Adams for emphasizing the Hindu factor to me.

45. Ortner 1977.

46. She now spends part of each year in Switzerland, where her Sherpa husband is a climbing and ski instructor.

47. This according to a Sherpa villager. I have tried to learn more precisely what the law actually said, but have been unable to do so. And by now, in fact, it has apparently been changed again.

48. Ortner field notes 1976.

49. Ortner 1989a, ch. IX; 1996a (1983).

50. Quoted in von Fürer-Haimendorf 1976, 148.

51. The words he used in Sherpa were *metsenga ten*, which translates literally as being "dirty." Another individual present translated it into English as "personally sick."

52. Ortner 1977.

53. Ortner field notes 1990.

54. Mohanty 1991.

55. Unfortunately, I have no further data on the other two women. One of them was called Ang Maya, and I was told that she was the younger sister of an expedition Sherpa, but that is all I know. I did not get even a name for the other woman.

56. Ortner field notes 1990.

57. At the time of the interview she and the sardar Sangye were divorced. She had remarried, and was running a tea shop on the road between Kathmandu and Baudha.

58. For an account of another Sherpa woman trek leader, see Mitten 1992, 205ff.

59. There was no taped transcript. The extracts are verbatim quotes from my field notes, while the rest of the story is summarized from the field notes (1990).

60. Ang Nyimi may not be "educated," but she speaks at least four languages fluently—Sherpa, Nepali, French, and English. The interview was in English.

61. Her village of origin did not appear in any of the published accounts, although for Sherpas—and for me—it is a crucial item for placing people, given the many identical names among the Sherpas. This information came from Vincanne Adams (personal communication); Adams extensively discusses Pasang Lhamu as a personal friend, and as a public-cultural phenomenon (Adams 1996, *passim*).

62. Adams gives the figure as $38,000 (1996, 5). Either way it is not a negligible amount of money.

63. Slept out in the open, or in a snow cave. Climbing on the upper reaches of Everest is so difficult that most climbers leave anything they can spare behind, including tents.

64. See the debates in *Himal*: Risal 1993; Sharma 1993; Acharya 1993; Lieberman 1993a and 1993b; Sherpa-Padgett 1993; Sangroula 1993.

65. According to Vincanne Adams (personal communication), Pasang Lhamu and Lhakputi Sherpa were said to have been very competitive as well.

66. Laura Ahearn, then a doctoral candidate in anthropology at the University of Michigan, was in the field in a Magar village at the time of the Nepal women's expedition. She wrote in a letter to me: "It's been interesting for me to talk to Nepali women about Pasang's death; all the (educated) Kathmandu women I've spoken with strongly support Pasang's efforts and seem inspired by her achievement, despite the tragedy that followed it. Women in my own Nepali family (educated as well as uneducated), however, consider Pasang's desire to climb mountains at best folly, and at worst, especially when considering her three children, criminal" (letter to author, 25 May 1993; quoted with permission).

67. Mohanty 1991; Johnson-Odim 1991.

68. Risal 1993, 43.

69. Sangroula 1993, 7. It appears that the Indian women's expedition, and Nyimi Lama, did reach the summit of Everest. This went virtually unreported.

70. Risal 1993.

71. Acharya 1993.

72. Sharma 1993.

73. A famous historical husband-wife partnership was that of Sangye, the founder of Chiwong monastery, and his wife, in the early decades of the twentieth century (Ortner 1989a). Tenzing Norgay's third wife did some climbing with him, and also led treks on her own; he was quite supportive of this (Tenzing Norgay 1977, 39).

CHAPTER 9

1. Fisher used this question as the title of his 1991 article.

2. Another area in which the Sherpas have been seen as experiencing major degradation is in the environment of Solu-Khumbu. The sense that the region was being despoiled by tourists and tourism-related economic practices led to the creation of Sagarmatha National Park in the mid-seventies, turning the Sherpas'

homeland into a state-regulated area. Subsequently both Brower (1991) and Stevens (1993) have questioned whether the environmental threat may have been exaggerated, and even if it was not, whether the creation of a national park was the solution.

3. E.g., Streather 1954, 80; Kohli 1969, 51; Bremer-Kamp 1987, 54.

4. Laird was described as follows at the beginning of his article: "Author Laird has lived on and off in Nepal since 1972, when he was 18, and speaks Nepali. He spent a year and a half with the Sherpas in eastern Nepal, near Mount Everest. At this moment he's on his way back there to live. He invited one of us to visit: 'I could get you a house on a cliff beside a waterfall where ravens steal your potatoes while you scrub them. Besides the noise of the waterfall all the time falling over the 1000 foot cliff the noise and glare of the Milky Way at night is deafening, blinding' " (Laird 1981, 116).

5. Ibid., 125.

6. Thompson 1979.

7. See also Lively 1988, 52ff.

8. Von Fürer-Haimendorf 1964, xix.

9. Ibid., 70.

10. Von Fürer-Haimendorf 1984, 12.

11. 14. Ibid., 68.

12. Ibid., 112.

13. Thompson 1979, 48. See also Dingle and Hillary (1982, 56–57) for the story of an encounter with some Sherpa men who were refusing to help a Sherpa woman with frostbitten feet. Like the early sahibs, the authors in this case avoid generalization.

14. In an article published the previous year, Cheney explained bad Sherpa behavior on expeditions with reference to certain deals that had been made between the Nepali state and some Solu Sherpa business interests (Cheney 1978). But at the time of this interview he seemed to have a more general view that the Sherpas had gone downhill.

15. Comments on the manuscript for this book, 1998. Quoted with permission.

16. Brower 1991, 85–87.

17. Stevens 1993, 370ff.; Fisher 1990, 122.

18. Boardman 1982, 166; see also Brower 1991, 85.

19. Parker 1989, 12.

20. Ibid., 13.

21. Dixit and Risal 1992, 17.

22. Fisher 1990, 123.

23. Ibid., Dixit and Risal 1992. Narayan Shrestha was killed in an avalanche on the Spanish Everest expedition in 1992 (Allison 1993, 267).

24. Fisher 1990, 123.

25. Dixit and Risal 1992, 16.

26. Ibid.

27. Cheney appendix ("Organisation in Nepal"), in Bonington 1976, 180.

28. Fisher 1990, 173.

29. The least savory enterprise is drug transportation, in which a small number of Sherpas have become involved. See Brower 1991, 90.

30. Fisher 1990, 115; see also Kunwar 1989.

31. Ang Gyelzen, who had reached the rank of captain, and was about to return to flight school to qualify to pilot advanced jet planes on international routes, was killed in a small-plane crash in Khumbu in November 1998.

32. Carrier 1992, 87.

33. Crossette 1991.

34. Carrier 1992, 82.

35. Thapa 1995, 50.

36. Thapa 1995; see also Fleming 1988, 10.

37. My only source on this, which is frustratingly vague, is Scott 1985. The quote from Sarkey Tshering Sherpa is on page 31. It is not stated whether the expedition was a success.

38. Quoted in Carrier 1992, 74.

39. Ibid., 70.

40. Ibid., 85. Sherpa identity politics in the contemporary sense are central to issues beyond mountaineering, particularly to ethnic and national politics in Nepal. I do not have the data to pursue this question here.

41. I have explained elsewhere why they seem to have survived better in Solu. See Ortner 1989b.

42. The point about Kyerok upgrading its practices is from von Fürer-Haimendorf 1984, 93.

43. I was also told that the Tengboche lama was reducing his practice of "*takbu* work;" that is, rituals that mobilize gods in their ferocious/violent forms.

44. Ortner 1995a.

45. In Kathmandu there are no Sherpa shamans; on the theory that the illness-causing spirits in Kathmandu are likely to be Nepali spirits, Sherpas may go to local *dhami*, Nepali shamans (or to Western doctors, or both).

46. Ortner field notes 1979.

47. Ortner field notes 1979. Nyima Chotar never told me (and perhaps he never knew), but one can reconstruct from von Fürer-Haimendorf's account that his mother was considered to be a *pem*, or witch, in their village. The fact that his mother was thus the target of local hostility, as a result of popular beliefs, may have been the impetus for his own hostility to "low" popular religion.

Belief in pem may be declining among younger Sherpas. When I asked a group of young mountaineering men if they were ever bothered by *pem* (witches) and *nerpa* (ghosts) in Kathmandu, they said, basically no, that in any event there weren't many pem and nerpa in Kathmandu, and then they began joking around—"Yeah, pem can't afford the plane ticket," "Yeah, and it's too far to walk."

48. Nyima Chotar and his wife were two of the twenty-eight Sherpas killed in a bus accident on the way back from a pilgrimage to see the Dalai Lama in Dharamsala in 1982.

49. The Sherpa monastic system was never very large in terms of numbers of monks and nuns, who made up only about 2 percent of the population (see Paul 1970, 1990). This is quite low compared to Tibet (see Samuel 1993, Appendix 1, for the best estimates on Tibet to date), but many of the Tibetan monasteries were state supported, and monks were actually drafted into those, where the Sherpa system was mostly privately supported and entirely voluntary.

50. Both Kopan and Laudo were founded in the 1970s, at the height of the counterculture. Kopan's monk population is primarily made up of Sherpa monks from the Thami side of Khumbu, and its head lama is a Sherpa reincarnate. But it is affiliated with the Gelugpa sect of Tibetan Buddhism (the Dalai Lama's sect), whereas the Sherpas have always practiced the Nyingmapa-sect version of Tibetan Buddhism. The monastery conducts classes in various aspects of Buddhist thought and practice for Western tourists and anyone else from the general public who wishes to sign up. Laudo is the Khumbu "branch" of Kopan, situated on the slopes of Khumbila, high above the trail between Namche Bazar and Thami. Laudo was said to have a population of Sherpa monks as well as several American monks and nuns. (Not much is known about either Kopan or Laudo. I have visited Kopan several times, as I have a monk friend there. I have never been to Laudo, and as far as I know nothing has been written about it. I picked up incidental information in the course of my various trips. James Fisher also provides a few notes on both places [1990, 91–95]).

51. Lively 1988.

52. Ortner field notes 1967.

53. Ortner field notes 1979.

54. Personal communication (E-mail) from Ang Rita Sherpa of the Himalayan Trust, October 1998.

55. Von Fürer-Haimendorf 1984, 99; Adams 1996, 63.

56. Adams 1996, 102.

57. Von Fürer-Haimendorf 1964, 182; Ortner 1978, ch. 3.

58. See, e.g., Brook 1987, 112.

59. Fisher 1990, 150.

60. There are many reasons, in addition to their association with compassion, for the continuing and even growing popularity of tulku. They combine the training and discipline of the monks with the more intuitive and "magical" powers of married lamas and shamans, and those two dimensions in turn are infused with the "compassion" of the boddhisattva. Tulku are, in effect, all of Tibetan Buddhism embodied within a single figure.

61. Quoted in Adams 1996, 131.

62. Ortner field notes 1979.

63. Gillette and Reynolds 1985, 23.

64. Lieberman 1991, 14. David Holmberg (personal communication) has suggested that the reason the Sherpas might have been rolling with laughter is that "chick" means "fuck" in Nepali, and thus "with a chick chick here" might have been heard as "with a fuck fuck here."

65. Brook 1987, 71.

66. Ibid., 103; emphasis added.

67. Ibid., 201.

68. I have not separated discussions of trekking from discussions of climbing. Trekking in Nepal is distinguished from mountaineering as referring to any walking under 18,000 feet, and as not involving any technical equipment or skills. "Trekking" is the way in which tourists see the country, which has very few roads. Leading treks generally pays less than climbing, and does not produce the large bonuses in equipment that mountaineering does, but it is a lot safer. Sherpas have a variety of views about the relative advantages and disadvantages of each type of work. But both involve extended contact with sahibs, and I have kept them together for that reason.

69. Venables 1989, 80, 108, and *passim*.

70. Venables 1989, 38.

71. Bonington 1987, 215.

72. See, e.g., Morrow 1986, 89.

73. Allison 1993, 262; emphasis in original.

74. Krakauer 1997, 130.

75. Dowling 1996, 36.

76. Ibid., 260.

77. Quoted in Krakauer 1997, 98. One interpretation of the continuing kindness of the Sherpas is that they are good at "impression management" (Thompson 1979,49; Zivetz 1992,109). While some specific instances may certainly have this quality, many—I would say most—come across as "authentic." In the end, of course, authenticity is a subjective category, yet the weight of the details in the anecdotes is highly persuasive, as well as the frequency of the anecdotes.

CHAPTER 10

1. These comments point toward my new project on the American middle class. See Ortner 1998.

2. Bass and Wells 1986, 80.

3. See also Venables 1989.

4. Krakauer 1997, 59–60.

5. Ibid.

6. Krakauer went with Rob Hall's Adventure Consultants group as a paid journalist for *Outside* magazine. The magazine was itself a product of the emergence of

the Yuppie market. It "targeted an upscale, adventurous, physically active audience [which was also] the core of [Hall's] client base" (Krakauer 1997, 66).

7. Krakauer 1997, 20.

8. Ibid., 163.

9. Allison 1993, 138. Rumbu had been destroyed and disbanded during the Great Cultural Revolution in the 1960s, but by this time it was again partly inhabited and functioning.

10. Ibid., 157.

11. Allison gives a good account of how the organizers were tempted into taking paying clients, even if they were less skilled, and/or less collegial, than another possible member. See also Ullman on the difficulties of expedition fund-raising, which he characterized as "only slightly less difficult than, say, soliciting funds for a statue of Karl Marx on the White House lawn" (1964, 21).

12. Allison 1993, 215–17.

13. Ibid., 272.

14. Bass and Wells 1986, 295.

15. Allison 1993, 235.

16. Ibid., 269.

17. Krakauer 1997, 107.

18. Allison 1993, ch. 8.

19. Allison 1993, 189.

20. Krakauer 1997, 95.

21. Ibid.

22. As a result of serious problems with the leader, February left the expedition early. It is not clear who, if any, in this party, reached the summit.

23. Child 1993, 173.

24. Cain n.d.

25. He competed with Reinhold Messner (probably the highest visibility climber today, partly because he won the competition) for the distinction of climbing all fourteen over-8,000 meter summits in the world. He was killed in an accident on Lhotse in 1989.

26. Child 1993, 174.

27. Ibid., 177.

28. Ibid., 187–88.

29. The American Himalayan Foundation's funding of projects at Tengboche is actually quite a dramatic story, which I have had to omit in the interests of space. Among other things the foundation funded a hydroelectric installation to bring electricity to the monastery. Less than a year after the lights were turned on, the entire monastery temple and the galleries surrounding its front courtyard (where major ritual dances are held) burned to the ground, evidently caused by a faulty or carelessly handled space heater. The AHF then financed a good part of the reconstruction of the monastery. See Sassoon 1988; Adams 1996.

30. *AHF Newsletter* (Summer 1996): 6.
31. The following was discussed more fully in Ortner 1997.
32. See especially Taylor 1997.

APPENDIX A

1. See Ortner 1978, 51.
2. Von Fürer-Haimendorf 1964, 181.

APPENDIX B

1. Ortner 1989a, ch. 7.
2. Von Fürer-Haimendorf 1984, 91.
3. On the Culture Center and the Monks' Residence, see Leon 1984. On the Himalayan Trust, thanks to Ang Rita Sherpa for information by E-Mail, October 1998.
4. Kohl 1988, 643.
5. Sassoon 1988.
6. One reason no one was hurt or killed was that the head lama and all but one of the monks (the poor caretaker on whose watch all this happened) were not then leading an "austere existence" in the monastery, but had taken off for the warmer climes of Kathmandu.
7. Sassoon 1988, 8.
8. Ang Rita Sherpa 1990, 10–12. This is not the Ang Rita Sherpa who climbed Mount Everest nine times (nor the woman climber Ang Rita discussed in chapter 8). The Ang Rita who wrote this report as secretary of the Tengboche Monastery Reconstruction Project worked with Jim Fisher on the book *Sherpas* (1990) and can be seen in a photograph with Fisher on the dust jacket of the book.
9. Von Fürer-Haimendorf 1964, 158.
10. He was later invited by the villagers of Tolakha, in western Solu, to found and head a village temple, which he did. He and his younger brother Kusho Mangden designed, built, and ran the temple. Kusho Tulku died fairly young, in his early or mid forties. His widow, the former nun, remarried, and had a child, which she proclaimed to be his reincarnation. This is considered somewhat unusual by Sherpas—no other cases are known in which a lama was reincarnated in a son of his own widow—but it is accepted. The brother, Kusho Mangden, also broke his vows and married in Tolakha. He continued to run the temple, and trained the young reincarnation of his brother. The young tulku married and stayed on in Tolakha. Kusho Mangden ultimately had friction with his Tolakha sponsors, and retired to the meditation retreat (Charok) in Khumbu, which he inherited as the youngest son of the previous Thami head/married lama. (Our interview took place at Charok). His own son became a Thami monk after Thami converted to celibacy. But the son broke his vows, and is now a village lama at Thomteng, where

he is considered quite *khamu*, expert. He married the daughter of a lama from Chalsa; she is the great-granddaughter of the lama who reincarnated in his uncle, the Kusho Tulku, in the first place. See the Chart, p. 318, to untangle some of these relationships.

11. The latter was still seen as powerful: in Kathmandu, after leaving Chiwong, he predicted the 1933 earthquake, telling people to leave their houses and go out into the fields at a certain time. After the quake, a woman asked him to divine the state of her house and family back in Solu. He told her that her family was not injured, and that only one side of her house had been broken, and all of this turned out to be correct. The man who beat up the Kusho Tulku is said to have died young as a result.

12. Von Fürer-Haimendorf 1964, 158–59.

13. The Lhasa reincarnation of the Zatul Rimpoche fled to Switzerland at the time of the Chinese invasion. (The Sherpas refer to him as the Swiss Tulku.) He is said to have broken his vows and married there. He recently migrated to Sydney, Australia, where he is president of the Tibetan Community Association of New South Wales. Thanks to Peter Hansen for this item from Australia.

14. Von Fürer-Haimendorf 1964, 156–58. In other words, the biological grandson replaced the spiritual reincarnation of the same individual as the head of Chiwong monastery. An important lesson from this whole affair is the degree to which the spiritual power of certain married-lama lineages remained relevant to religious politics, even though the status of married lamas had been downgraded.

15. Snellgrove 1957, 217–22.

16. See also von Fürer-Haimendorf 1964, 158. After he died, there were two claimants to the status of *his* tulku. These two boys were about six years old at the time of Robert Paul's and my fieldwork in 1966–68. One was the child of a Tibetan refugee family, and one was the child of a Solu Sherpa family of Ringmo village. People seemed to think that the Tibetan child's claim was stronger, but neither of the children had at that point been taken up by the Chiwong monks as their leader.

17. According to Snellgrove, he had been accused of "political agitation" against the Nepal government, and had fled to Darjeeling (1957, 222).

18. The Mani Rimdu at Chiwong, presided over by the Tushi Rimpoche, was filmed in the mid-eighties. The film is called *The Lord of the Dance* (Kohn 1986).

19. Most of the data on Takshindo is from R. A. Paul 1970 and R. A. Paul's field notes (1967), with thanks.

20. According to some accounts, the tulku who was living at the monastery left and went to California, where he is known as the Thartang Tulku. According to information I picked up in Kathmandu in 1979, the reincarnation of Tolden Tsultim, the son of a Lama clan family in Phaphlu, did become a monk but was living in Kopan gompa in Kathmandu.

21. See Ortner (1989a, 47–48) for the history of the founding of the original Thami temple in the early eighteenth century.

22. Ortner 1989a,188; von Fürer-Haimendorf 1964, 134.

23. Von Fürer-Haimendorf 1964, 211.

24. Ngawang Samden was a grandson of Lama Tundup, the former head lama. If the temple had remained noncelibate, he might have inherited its headship. Instead, the temple converted to celibacy, he took vows at Rumbu to become a celibate monk, and he then ran the monastery in the role of regent while waiting for the tulku to grow up; he also became a virtual father to the tulku.

25. I had known the lama since my first fieldwork, in 1967, when he was about eight years old. While I did not know him well, I saw him every time I came to Nepal, and I spent a fair amount of time with him when we (myself and a Granada Television film crew) were filming *Sherpas* in 1976 (Woodhead 1977). Thami monastery was featured in the film as being in excellent condition, and several long sequences in the film were shot at the monastery.

26. MacDonald 1980.

27. Schwalbe 1979.

28. Sangye Tenzing 1971. I drew substantially on this history in *High Religion* (Ortner 1989a); there is a photograph of Sangye Tenzing on page 10 of the book.

29. In 1976 one of these monks, Ngawang, was running a hotel in Junbesi, called "Chez Ngawang," with the help of another Serlo monk. Although they had not yet fallen, local villagers were predicting they would. As one man said, "They haven't fallen yet, but what kind of work is selling cigarettes and arak [liquor]? Not monk work, but the work of men who marry" (Ortner field notes 1976).

30. I received a letter in 1996 from a monk seeking donations to reopen the monastery. I do not know what happened with this effort.

31. For an extended portrait of the Tushi Rimpoche, see Aziz 1978.

32. Peter Hansen, personal communication.

REFERENCES CITED

Acharya, Mamta. 1993. "A True Heroine." *Himal* (July/August): 5.

Adams, Vincanne. 1996. *Tigers of the Snow (and Other Virtual Sherpas): An Ethnography of Himalayan Encounters.* Princeton: Princeton University Press.

Ahluwalia, Major H.P.S. 1978. *Faces of Everest.* New Delhi et al.: Vikas.

Alger, Horatio. 1962. *Ragged Dick and Mark, The Match Boy: Two Novels by Horatio Alger.* New York: Collier Books.

Allison, Stacy, with Peter Carlin. 1993. *Beyond the Limits: A Woman's Triumph on Everest.* Boston: Little, Brown, and Company.

Althusser, Louis. 1971. "Ideology and Ideological State Apparatuses." In L. Althusser, *Lenin and Philosophy and Other Essays,* trans. Ben Brewster. New York: Monthly Review Press.

Ang Tharkay. 1954. *Memoires d'un Sherpa, recueillis par Basil P. Norton,* trans. (into French) Henri Delgove; trans. (in text) S. B. Ortner. Paris: Amiot Dumont.

Another Ascent to the World's Highest Peak—Qomolangma. 1975. Peking: Foreign Languages Press.

Appadurai, Arjun. 1990. "Topographies of the Self: Praise and Emotion in Hindu India." In *Language and the Politics of Emotion,* ed. C. A. Lutz and L. Abu-Lughod, 93–112. New York: Cambridge University Press.

Aziz, Barbara. 1978. *Tibetan Frontier Families.* Chapel Hill: University of North Carolina Press.

Barcott, Bruce. 1996. "Cliffhangers: The Fatal Descent of the Mountain-Climbing Memoir." *Harper's* (August): 64–69.

Bass, Dick, and Frank Wells, with Rick Ridgeway. 1986. *Seven Summits.* New York: Warner Books.

Bauer, Paul. 1937. *Himalayan Campaign: The German Attack on Kangchenjunga, the Second Highest Mountain in the World,* trans. Sumner Austin. Oxford: Basil Blackwell.

———. 1939. "Nanga Parbat, 1938." *Himalayan Journal* 11:89–106.

———. 1955. *Kangchenjunga Challenge.* London: William Kimber.

Bechtold, Fritz. 1935. "The German Himalayan Expedition to Nanga Parbat, 1934." *Himalayan Journal* 7:27–37.

Beetham, Bentley. 1925. "The Return Journey." In E. F. Norton et al., *The Fight for Everest: 1924,* 155–92. New York: Longmans, Green and Co.

Bellah, Robert N., Richard Madsen, William M. Sullivan, Ann Swidler, and Steven M. Tipton. 1985. *Habits of the Heart: Individualism and Commitment in American Life.* Berkeley: University of California Press.

Besant, Annie Wood. 1983 [1893]. *Annie Besant: An Autobiography.* Madras, India: Theosophical Publishing House.

Birkett, Bill, and Bill Peascod. 1989. *Women Climbing: 200 Years of Achievement.* Seattle: The Mountaineers.

Bishop, Barry. 1962. "Wintering on the Roof of the World." *National Geographic* 122 (4): 503–47.

Bishop, Peter. 1989. *The Myth of Shangri-La: Tibet, Travel Writing and the Western Creation of Sacred Landscape.* London: Athlone Press.

Bjonness, Inger-Marie. 1983. "External Economic Dependency and Changing Human Adjustment to Marginal Environment in the High Himalaya, Nepal." *Mountain Research and Development* 3 (3): 263–72.

Blum, Arlene. 1980. *Annapurna: A Woman's Place.* San Francisco: Sierra Club Books.

Boardman, Peter. 1982. *Sacred Summits: A Climber's Year.* Seattle: The Mountaineers.

Bonington, Chris. 1971. *Annapurna South Face.* London: Cassell.

———. 1973. *Everest: Southwest Face.* London: Hodder and Stoughton.

———. 1976 (American edition of Bonington 1973). *Everest the Hard Way.* New York: Random House.

———. 1987. *The Everest Years: A Climber's Life.* New York: Viking.

Bourdieu, Pierre. 1977. *Outline of a Theory of Practice*, trans. Richard Nice. Cambridge: Cambridge University Press.

Bourdillon, Jennifer. 1956. *Visit to the Sherpas.* London: Collins.

Bowman, W. E. 1983 (1956). *The Ascent of Rum Doodle.* London: Arrow Books.

Bremer-Kamp, Cherie. 1987. *Living on the Edge.* Layton, Utah: Gibbs M. Smith, Inc.

Brook, Elaine. 1985. "Sherpas: The Other Mountaineers." *Mountain* 101:36–39.

———. 1987. *The Windhorse.* New York: Dodd, Mead & Company.

Brower, Barbara. 1991. *Sherpa of Khumbu: People, Livestock, and Landscape.* Delhi: Oxford University Press.

———. n.d. "Geography and History in the Solukhumbu Landscape." Typescript.

Brown, T. Graham. 1936. "Nanda Devi." *Alpine Journal* 48, no. 253 (November): 311–12.

Bruce, (Major) Charles Granville. 1910. *Twenty Years in the Himalayas.* London: Edward Arnold.

Bruce, (Brigadier-General the Honorable) Charles Granville, et al. 1923. *The Assault on Mount Everest 1922.* New York: Longmans, Green and Co.

Bruce, (Captain) J. Geoffrey. 1925. "The Rongbuk Glacier." In E. F. Norton et al., *The Fight for Everest: 1924,* 54–72. New York: Longmans, Green and Co.

Burger, Veit. 1978. "The Economic Impact of Tourism in Nepal: An Input-Output Analysis." Ph.D. diss., Cornell University.

Burgess, Al, and Jim Palmer. 1983. *Everest: The Ultimate Challenge*. New York and Toronto: Beaufort Books.

Cain, Karen. n.d. "Wanda Rutkiewicz," *Rock and Ice* 27:18–24.

Cameron, Ian. 1984. *Mountains of the Gods*. New York and Oxford: Facts on File Publications.

Caplan, Lionel. 1991. " 'Bravest of the Brave': Representation of 'the Gurkha' in British Military Writings." *Modern Asian Studies* 25 (3): 571–97.

———. 1995. *Warrior Gentlemen: "Gurkhas" in the Western Imagination*. Providence, R.I., and Oxford: Berghahn Books.

Carrier, Jim. 1992. "Gatekeepers of the Himalaya." *National Geographic* 182, no. 6 (December): 70–89.

Cheney, Mike. 1978. "Events and Trends 1970–6, Nepal Himalaya." *Alpine Journal* 83, no. 327:218–27.

Chevalley, Gabriel, René Dittert, and Raymond Lambert. 1953. *Avant-Premières à L'Everest*, trans. (in text) S. B. Ortner. France (n.p.): B. Arthaud.

Child, Greg. 1993. *Mixed Emotions: Mountaineering Writings*. Seattle: The Mountaineers.

Clifford, James. 1997. *Routes: Travel and Translation in the Late Twentieth Century*. Cambridge, Mass.: Harvard University Press.

Clifford, James, and George E. Marcus. 1986. *Writing Culture: The Poetics and Politics of Ethnography*. Berkeley: University of California Press.

Collins, Steven. 1982. *Selfless Persons: Imagery and Thought in Theravada Buddhism*. Cambridge: Cambridge University Press.

Conze, Edward. 1975 (1951). *Buddhism: Its Essence and Development*. New York: Harper Torchbooks.

Crossette, Barbara. 1991. "A Changing Everest: Tourists and Toothache." *New York Times*, 11 March, sec. B, p.1.

Curran, Jim. 1987. *K2: Triumph and Tragedy*. Boston: Houghton Mifflin Co.

Dash, A. J. 1947. *Darjeeling. Bengal District Gazetteers*. Alipore: Bengal Government Press.

da Silva, Rachel, ed. 1992. *Leading Out: Women Climbers Reaching for the Top*. Seattle: Seal Press.

David-Neel, Alexandra. 1932. *Magic and Mystery in Tibet*. New York: Claude Kendall Publisher.

Denman, Earl. 1954. *Alone to Everest*. London: Collins.

Des Chene, Mary. 1991. "Relics of Empire: A Cultural History of the Gurkhas, 1815–1987." Ph.D. diss., Department of Anthropology, Stanford University.

Desio, Ardito. 1956. *Victory over K2: Second Highest Peak in the World*. New York: McGraw-Hill.

Dias, John. 1965. *The Everest Adventure: Story of the Second Indian Expedition*. Delhi: Government of India Publications Division.

Dingle, Graeme, and Peter Hillary. 1982. *First Across the Roof of the World: The First-Ever Traverse of the Himalayas—5,000 Kilometres from Sikkim to Pakistan.* Auckland: Hodder and Stoughton.

Dixit, Kanak Mani, and Dipesh Risal. 1992. "Mountaineering's Himalayan Face." *Himal* (November/December): 11–18.

Dowling, Claudia Glenn. 1996. "Death on the Mountain" *Life* (August): 32–46.

Downs, Hugh R. 1980. *Rhythms of a Himalayan Village.* San Francisco: Harper and Row.

Dumont, Louis. 1960. "World Renunciation in Indian Religions." *Contributions to Indian Sociology* IV: 33–62.

Dyhrenfurth, G. O. 1931. "The International Himalayan Expedition, 1930." *Himalayan Journal* 3 (April): 77–91.

———. 1963. "The Mountain Exploration of the Everest Massif." In Toni Hagen, G. O. Dyhrenfurth, C. von Fürer-Haimendorf, and Erwin Schneider, *Mount Everest: Formation, Population, and Exploration of the Everest Region*, trans. E. N. Bowman. 97–123. London: Oxford University Press.

Dyhrenfurth, Hettie. 1931. *Memsahib im Himalaya.* Leipzig: Verlag Deutsche Buchwerkstätten G.M.B.H.

Eiselin, Max. 1961. *The Ascent of Dhaulagiri*, trans. E. Joel Bowman. London and New York: Oxford University Press.

Faux, Ronald. 1982. *High Ambition: A Biography of Reinhold Messner.* London: Victor Gollancz Ltd.

Finch, Captain George. 1923. "The Attempt with Oxygen." In C. G. Bruce et al., *The Assault on Mount Everest 1922*, 273–98. New York: Longmans, Green and Co.

Fisher, James F. 1990. *Sherpas: Reflections on Change in Himalayan Nepal.* Berkeley: University of California Press.

———. 1991. "Has Success Spoiled the Sherpas?" *Natural History* (February): 39–44.

Fleming, Jon, and Ronald Faux. 1977. *Soldiers on Everest: The Joint Army Mountaineering Association–Royal Nepalese Army Mount Everest Expedition 1976.* London: Her Majesty's Stationery Office.

Fleming, Wendy Brewer. 1988. "Another First on Everest: History in the Making." *Nepal Traveller* 5, no. 3 (May): 7–10.

French, Patrick. 1995. *Younghusband: The Last Great Imperial Adventurer.* New York: Harper Collins.

Freshfield, Douglas W. 1979 (1903). *Round Kangchenjunga: A Narrative of Mountain Travel and Exploration.* Kathmandu: Ratna Pustak Bhandar.

Funke, Friedrich W. 1969. *Religioses Leben der Sherpa.* Innsbruck and Munich: Universitätsverlag Wagner.

Gardiner, Steve. 1990. *Why I Climb: Personal Insight of Top Climbers.* Harrisburg, Pa: Stackpole Books.

Geertz, Clifford. 1973. "Thick Description: Toward an Interpretive Theory of Culture." In C. Geertz, *The Interpretation of Cultures*, 1–32. New York: Basic Books.

Gillette, Ned, and Jan Reynolds. 1985. *Everest Grand Circle: A Climbing and Skiing Adventure through Nepal and Tibet*. Seattle: The Mountaineers.

Goldstein, Melvin. 1964. "Study of the *ldap ldop*." *Central Asiatic Journal* 9: 123–41.

Greenblatt, Stephen, ed. 1993. *New World Encounters*. Berkeley: University of California Press.

Guha, Ranajit. 1988. "The Prose of Counter-Insurgency." In R. Guha and G. C. Spivak, eds., *Selected Subaltern Studies*, 45–89.

Guha, Ranajit, and Gayatri Chakravorty Spivak, eds. 1988. *Selected Subaltern Studies*. New York and Oxford: Oxford University Press.

Gurung, Harka. 1985. "Gurkhas and Mountaineering." *Nepal Himal Journal*: 1–2.

———. 1991. "The Pioneer Mountaineers." *Himal* (July/August): 35.

Hagen, Toni, F. T. Wahlen, and W. R. Corti. 1972 (1961). *Nepal, The Kingdom in the Himalayas*, trans. B. M. Charleston. London: R. Hale.

Hagen, Toni, G. O. Dyhrenfurth, C. von Fürer-Haimendorf, and E. Schneider. 1963. *Mount Everest: Formation, Population, and Exploration of the Everest Region*, trans. E. N. Bowman. London: Oxford University Press.

Hansen, Peter H. 1995. "Albert Smith, the Alpine Club, and the Invention of Mountaineering in Mid-Victorian Britain." *Journal of British Studies* 34 (July): 300–24.

———. 1996a. "Vertical Boundaries, National Identites: British Mountaineering on the Frontiers of Europe and the Empire, c. 1868–1914." *Journal of Imperial and Commonwealth History* 24 (1): 48–71.

———. 1996b. "The Dancing Lamas of Everest: Cinema, Orientalism, and Anglo-Tibetan Relations in the 1920s." *American Historical Review* 101(3): 712–47.

———. 1997. "Debate: Tenzing's Two Wrist-Watches: The Conquest of Everest and Late Imperial Culture in Britain, 1921–1953." *Past and Present* 157 (November): 159–77.

———. n.d. a. "Guides and Sherpas in the Alps and Himalayas, 1850s–1950s." Typescript.

———. n.d. b. "Confetti of Empire: The Conquest of Everest in Nepal, India, Britain, and New Zealand in 1953." Typescript.

Hardie, Norman. 1957. *In Highest Nepal, Our Life among the Sherpas*. London: Allen and Unwin.

Harvard, Andrew, and Todd Thompson. 1974. *Mountain of Storms: The American Expeditions to Dhaulagiri, 1969 and 1973*. New York: New York University Press.

Haston, Dougal. 1997 (1972). *In High Places*. Seattle: The Mountaineers.

Herrligkoffer, Karl M. 1954. *Nanga Parbat*, trans. E. Brockett and A. Ehrenzweig. New York: Alfred A. Knopf.

Herzog, Maurice. 1987 (1952). *Annapurna: Conquest of the First 8,000-Metre Peak*, trans. N. Morin and J. A. Smith. London: Triad Paladin Grafton Books.

Hillary, Sir Edmund. 1955. *High Adventure*. New York: E. P. Dutton.

———. 1962. "We build a School for Sherpa Children." *National Geographic* 122, no. 4 (October): 548–51.

———. 1964. *Schoolhouse in the Clouds*. London: Hodder and Stoughton.

———. 1975. *Nothing Venture, Nothing Win*. New York: Coward, McCann, and Geohegan, Inc.

Hillary, Edmund, and Peter Hillary. 1984. *Two Generations*. London: Hodder and Stoughton.

Holmberg, David H. 1989. *Order in Paradox: Myth, Ritual and Exchange among Nepal's Tamang*. Ithaca, N.Y.: Cornell University Press.

Hooker, J. D. 1854 (1969). *Himalayan Journals*. London: J. Murray.

Houston, Charles S., M.D. 1987. *Going Higher: The Story of Man and Altitude*. Boston: Little, Brown, and Co.

Howard-Bury, C. K., et al. 1922. *Mount Everest: The Reconnaissance, 1921*. New York: Longmans, Green and Co.

Hunt, John. 1953. *The Ascent of Everest*. New York: E. P. Dutton.

———. 1978. *Life Is Meeting*. London: Hodder and Stoughton.

———. 1993 (1953). *The Ascent of Everest*. Seattle: The Mountaineers.

Jackson, Monica, and Elizabeth Stark. 1956. *Tents in the Clouds: The First Women's Himalayan Expedition*. London: Collins.

Jerstad, Luther G. 1969. *Mani Rimdu: Sherpa Dance Drama*. Calcutta: Oxford and IBH Publishing Co.

Johnson-Odim, Cheryl. 1991. "Common Themes, Different Contexts: Third World Women and Feminism." In *Third World Women and the Politics of Feminism*, ed. C. T. Mohanty et al., 314–27. Bloomington: Indiana University Press.

Kellas, A. M. 1913. "A Fourth Visit to the Sikkim Himalaya, with Ascent of the Kangchenjhau." *Alpine Journal* 27 (200):25–52.

Knowlton, Elizabeth. 1933. *The Naked Mountain*. New York and London: G. P. Putnam's Sons.

Kohl, Larry. 1988. "Heavy Hands on the Land." *National Geographic* 174, no. 5 (November): 632–51.

Kohli, M. S. 1969. *Nine Atop Everest: Story of the Indian Ascent*. Bombay: Orient Longmans Ltd.

Kohn, Richard. 1986. (Film) *The Lord of the Dance: Destroyer of Illusion*. New York: Mystic Fire Video.

Krakauer, Jon. 1997. *Into Thin Air: A Personal Account of the Mount Everest Disaster*. New York: Villard.

Kunwar, Ramesh Raj. 1989. *Fire of Himal: An Anthropological Study of the Sherpas of Nepal Himalaya Region*. Jaipur and New Delhi: Nirala Publications.

Laird, Thomas. 1981. "Mountains as Gods, Mountains as Goals." *Co-Evolution Quarterly* 31:116–29.

Lambert, Raymond, and Claude Kogan. 1956. *White Fury: Gaurisankar and Cho Oyu*, trans. Showell Styles. London: Hurst & Blackett.

Leamer, Laurence. 1982. *Ascent: The Spiritual and Physical Quest of Willi Unsoeld*. New York: Simon and Schuster.

Leon, Lydia. 1984. "Project Reports: Tengboche Culture Center in Nepal." *Cultural Survival Quarterly* 8, no. 3 (fall): 69–70.

Lieberman, Marcia R. 1991. "A Trek of One's Own in Nepal." *New York Times*, Sunday, 28 July: Travel Section, pp. 14–16.

———. 1993a. "Scott, Amundsen, and Pasang Lhamu." *Himal* (July/August): 7.

———. 1993b. "Marcia Lieberman Responds." *Himal* (September/October): 7.

Ling, Trevor. 1976. *The Buddha: Buddhist Civilization in India and Ceylon*. Harmondsworth, England: Penguin Books.

Lively, Scott Allen. 1988. "Monks and Mountaineers: The Changing Role of Monasteries in Sherpa Society from 1915 to the Present." Honors thesis, Harvard College.

Macdonald, Alexander W. 1973. "The Lama and the General." *Kailash: A Journal of Himalayan Studies* 1(3): 225–34.

———. 1980. "The Writing of Buddhist History in the Sherpa Area of Nepal." In *Studies in History of Buddhism*, ed. A. K. Narain, 121–31. New Delhi: B. R. Publishers.

Mallory, George H. (George H. Leigh-Mallory). 1922. "The Reconnaissance of the Mountain." In C. K. Howard-Bury et al., *Mount Everest: The Reconnaissance, 1921*, 183–280. New York: Longmans, Green and Co.

———. 1923a. "The First Attempt." In C. G. Bruce, et al., *The Assault on Mount Everest 1922*, 121–226. New York: Longmans, Green and Co.

———. 1923b. "The Third Attempt." In C. G. Bruce et al., *The Assault on Mount Everest 1922*, 273–98. New York: Longmans, Green and Co.

March, Kathryn. 1977. "Of People and Naks: The Meaning of High Altitude Herding among Contemporary Solu Sherpas." *Contributions to Nepal Studies* 4 (2): 83–97.

———. 1979. "The Intermediacy of Women: Female Gender Symbolism and the Social Position of Women among Tamangs and Sherpas of Highland Nepal." Ph.D. diss., Department of Anthropology, Cornell University.

Marcus, Steven. 1975. "Mt. Everest and the British National Spirit." In S. Marcus, *Representations: Essays on Literature and Society*, 76–87. New York: Random House.

Mason, Kenneth. 1955. *Abode of Snow: A History of Himalayan Exploration and Mountaineering*. London: Rupert Hart-Davis.

———. [1987. Reissued by the Mountaineers Press, Seattle.]

Messner, Reinhold. 1979. *Everest: Expedition to the Ultimate*, trans. Audrey Salkeld. New York: Oxford University Press.

———. 1981. "At My Limit: I Climbed Everest Alone." *National Geographic* 160, no. 4 (October): 552–66.

Miller, Robert. 1965. "High Altitude Mountaineering, Cash Economy and the Sherpa." *Human Organization* XXIV (3): 224–49.

Mitten, Denise. 1992. "The American Team." In *Leading Out: Women Climbers Reaching for the Top*, ed. Rachel da Silva, 201–17. Seattle: Seal Press.

Miura, Yuichiro, with Eric Perlman. 1978. *The Man Who Skied Down Everest*. San Francisco: Harper and Row.

Moffatt, Gwen. 1961. *Space Below My Feet*. Cambridge, Mass.: Houghton Mifflin.

Mohanty, Chandra T. 1991 "Under Western Eyes: Feminist Scholarship and Colonial Discourses." In *Third World Women and the Politics of Feminism*, ed. C. T. Mohanty et al., 51–80. Bloomington: Indiana University Press.

Morris, James/Jan. 1958. (as James) *Coronation Everest*. London: Faber and Faber.

———. 1974. (As Jan) *Conundrum*. New York: Harcourt Brace Jovanovich.

Morris, John. 1960. *Hired to Kill: Some Chapters of Autobiography*. N.p.: Rupert Hart-Davis in association with the Cresset Press.

Morrow, Patrick. 1986. *Beyond Everest: Quest for the Seven Summits*. Camden East, Ontario: Camden House.

Nebesky-Wojkowitz, René de. 1956. *Oracles and Demons of Tibet: The Cult and Iconography of the Tibetan Protective Deities*. The Hague: Mouton.

Noel, Captain John. 1927. *The Story of Everest*. New York: Little, Brown.

Norton, E. F., et al. 1925. *The Fight for Everest: 1924*. New York: Longmans, Green and Co.

Northey, W. Brook, and C. J. Morris. 1976 (1927). *The Gurkhas: Their Manners, Customs and Country*. New Delhi: Cosmo Publications.

Ortner, Sherry B. 1973. "Sherpa Purity." *American Anthropologist* 75:49–63.

———. 1975. "Gods' Bodies, Gods' Food: A Symbolic Analysis of a Sherpa Ritual." In *The Interpretation of Symbolism*, ed. R. Willis, 133–69. London: Malaby.

———. 1977. *Sherpas* (transcript of all dialogue recorded for the film). Unpublished. (See Woodhead 1977 for film information.)

———. 1978. *Sherpas through Their Rituals*. Cambridge: Cambridge University Press.

———. 1989a. *High Religion: A Cultural and Political History of Sherpa Buddhism*. Princeton: Princeton University Press.

———. 1989b. "Cultural Politics: Religious Activism and Ideological Transformation among 20th Century Sherpas." *Dialectical Anthropology* 14:197–211.

———. 1995a. "The Case of the Disappearing Shamans, or No Individualism, No Relationalism." *Ethos* 23 (3): 355–90.

———. 1995b. "Resistance and the Problem of Ethnographic Refusal." *Comparative Studies in Society and History* 37, no. 1 (January): 173–93.

———. 1996a. *Making Gender: The Politics and Erotics of Culture*. Boston: Beacon Press.

———. 1996b (1983). "The Founding of the First Sherpa Nunnery, and the Problem of 'Women' as an Analytic Category." In S. B. Ortner, *Making Gender: The Politics and Erotics of Culture*, 116–38.

———. 1996c. "Borderland Politics and Erotics: Gender and Sexuality in Himalayan Mountaineering." In S. B. Ortner, *Making Gender: The Politics and Erotics of Culture*, 181–212.

———. 1996d. "Making Gender: Toward a Feminist, Minority, Postcolonial, Subaltern, Etc., Theory of Practice." In S. B. Ortner, *Making Gender: The Politics and Erotics of Culture*, 1–20.

———. 1997. "Thick Resistance: Death and the Cultural Construction of Agency in Himalayan Mountaineering." *Representations* 59 (summer): 135–62.

———. 1998. "Generation X: Anthropology in a Media-Saturated World." *Cultural Anthropology* 13, no. 3 (August): 414–40.

Parker, Anne. 1989. "The Meaning of 'Sherpa': An Evolving Social Category." *Himalayan Research Bulletin* IX (3): 11–14.

Paul, Robert A. 1970. "Sherpas and their Religion." Ph.D. diss., Department of Anthropology, University of Chicago.

———. 1976a. "The Sherpa Temple as a Model of the Psyche." *American Ethnologist* 3:131–46.

———. 1976b. "Some Observations on Sherpa Shamanism." In John T. Hitchcock and Rex L. Jones, ed. *Spirit Possession in the Nepal Himalayas*, 141–52. New Delhi: Vikas.

———. 1977. "The Place of Truth in Sherpa Law and Religion." *Journal of Anthropological Research* 33:167–84.

———. 1979. "Dumje: Paradox and Resolution in Sherpa Ritual Symbolism." *American Ethnologist* 6:274–304.

———. 1982. *The Tibetan Symbolic World: Psychoanalytic Explorations*. Chicago: University of Chicago Press.

———. 1990. "Recruitment to Monasticism among the Sherpas." In *Personality and the Cultural Construction of Society*, ed. D. K. Jordan and M. J. Swartz, 254–74. Tuscaloosa: University of Alabama Press.

Pfeffer, Martin, et al. 1937. "The Disaster on Nanga Parbat, *1937*." *Alpine Journal* 49, no. 255 (November): 210–227.

Regmi, Mahesh Chandra. 1978. *Thatched Huts and Stucco Palaces: Peasants and Landlords in Nineteenth Century Nepal*. New Delhi: Vikas.

Ridgeway, Rick. 1979. *The Boldest Dream: The Story of Twelve Who Climbed Mount Everest*. New York and London: Harcourt Brace Jovanovich.

Risal, Dipesh. 1993. "Pasang Lhamu." *Himal* (May/June): 42–43.

Roberts, David. 1986a. "The Direct Style of John Roskelley." In *Moments of Doubt and Other Mountaineering Writings*, 145–60. Seattle: The Mountaineers.

———. 1986b. "Patey Agonistes: A Look at Climbing Autobiographies." In *Moments of Doubt and Other Mountaineering Writings*, 183–94.

Roberts, (Lieutenant Colonel) James O. M. 1964. "Transport and Sherpas." In J. R. Ullman, *Americans on Everest*, 335–42. Philadelphia and New York: J. B. Lippincott Co.

Roch, André. 1947. *Garwhal Himalaya: Expedition Suisse 1939*. Neuchâtel and Paris: Editions Victor Attinger.

———. 1952. "The Sherpas of Everest." *Himalayan Journal* XVII:157–58.

Roskelley, John. 1987. *Nanda Devi: The Tragic Expedition*. Sparkford, England: Oxford Illustrated Press.

Rubenson, C. W. 1908a. "An Ascent of Kabru." *Alpine Journal* Vol. 24, No. 179 (February): 63–67.

———. 1908b. "Kabru in 1907." *Alpine Journal* Vol. 24, No. 182 (November): 310–21.

Rutkiewicz, Wanda. 1986. "Paper read by Mrs. Wanda Rutkiewicz of Poland [Women's Mountaineering in the Himalayas and Karakorams]." In N. D. Jayal and M. Motwani, eds., *Conservation, Tourism and Mountaineering in the Himalayas*, 134–37. Dehra Dun, India: Natraj Publishers.

Ruttledge, Hugh. 1934. *Everest 1933*. London: Hodder and Stoughton.

———. 1935 (American edition of 1934). *Attack on Everest*. New York: Robert M. McBride and Co.

———. 1952. "In Memoriam: The Late Head Lama of Rongbuk Monastery." *Himalayan Journal* 17:159–60.

Sahlins, Marshall. 1981. *Historical Metaphors and Mythical Realities: Structure in the Early History of the Sandwich Islands Kingdoms*. Ann Arbor: University of Michigan Press.

———. 1995. *How "Natives" Think: About Captain Cook, for Example*. Chicago: University of Chicago Press.

Said, Edward. 1978. *Orientalism*. New York: Pantheon Books.

Samuel, Geoffrey. 1993. *Civilized Shamans: Buddhism in Tibetan Societies*. Washington, D.C., and London: Smithsonian Institution Press.

Sangroula, Yubaraj. 1993. "A National Heroine." *Himal* (September/October): 7.

Sangye Tenzing. 1971. "The Unprecedented Holy Scepter: A Religious History of the Sherpa People." Unpublished translation. Junbesi, Nepal, and Paris/Nanterre, France: No publisher.

Sassoon, D. 1988. "The Tengboche Fire: What Went Up in Flames?" *Himalayan Research Bulletin* 8 (3):8–14.

Scarr, Josephine. 1956. *Four Miles High*. London: Victor Gollancz Ltd.

Schwalbe, Kurt J. 1979. "The Construction and Religious Meaning of the Buddhist Stupa in Solo Khumbu, Nepal." Thesis, Graduate Theological Union, Berkeley, California.

Scott, Doug. 1984. "Himalayan Climbing: Part One of a Personal Review." *Mountain* 100:26–36.

———. 1985. "Himalayan Climbing: Part Two of a Personal Review." *Mountain* 101:26–32.

Scott, James C. 1985. *Weapons of the Weak: Everyday Forms of Peasant Resistance*. New Haven: Yale University Press.

Sewell, Jessica. n.d. "Views of the Sherpas on the Early Himalayan Expeditions." Research paper commissioned as part of this project. S. B. Ortner files.

Shaha, Rishikesh. 1990. *Politics in Nepal 1980–1990.* New Delhi: Manohar Publications.

Sharma, Prayag Raj. 1993. "Don't Belittle Pasang Lhamu." *Himal* (July/August): 5.

Sherpa, Ang Rita, with assistance from Pertemba Sherpa. 1990. "Tengboche Monastery Reconstruction: An Appraisal Report." Typescript.

Sherpa, Donna M. 1994. *Living in the Middle: Sherpas of the Mid-Range Himalayas.* Prospect Heights, Ill.: Waveland Press.

Sherpa, Fran. 1997. "A Comparison of Life and Migration Experiences of Sherpa Spouses Inside and Outside Nepal." Paper given at the meetings of the Association of American Geographers, Forth Worth, Texas. Typescript.

Sherpa-Padgett, Linda M. 1993. "Devastating Words." *Himal* (September/October): 5–6.

Shipton, Eric. 1937. "Survey in the Nanda Devi District." *Alpine Journal* 49, no. 254 (May): 27–40.

———. 1938. "Shaksgam Expedition." *Alpine Journal* 50, no. 256 (May): 34–59.

———. 1952a. "The Everest 'Tigers': The Sherpas and Their Country." *Geographical Magazine* (August): 172–83.

———. 1952b. *The Mount Everest Reconnaissance Expedition 1951.* London: Hodder and Stoughton.

Simmel, Georg. 1959. "The Adventure." In *Georg Simmel, 1858–1918*, ed. Kurt H. Wolff, 243–58. Columbus: Ohio State University Press.

Singh, Gyan. 1961. *Lure of Everest: Story of the first Indian Expedition.* Delhi: Government of India Publications Division.

Smythe, F. S. 1931. *The Kangchenjunga Adventure.* London: Victor Gollancz Ltd.

Snellgrove, David. 1957. *Buddhist Himalaya: Travels and Studies in Quest of the Origins and Nature of Tibetan Religion.* New York: Philosophical Library.

Spivak, Gayatri Chakravorty. 1988. "Can the Subaltern Speak?" In *Marxism and the Interpretation of Cultures*, ed. C. Nelson and L. Grossberg, 271–316. Urbana: University of Illinois Press.

Stevens, Stanley F. 1993. *Claiming the High Ground: Sherpas, Subsistence, and Environmental Change in the Highest Himalaya.* Berkeley: University of California Press.

Stewart, Gordon T. 1995. "Tenzing's Two Wrist-Watches: The Conquest of Everest and Late Imperial Culture in Britain 1921–1953." *Past and Present* 149 (November): 170–97.

Stoler, Ann, and Frederick Cooper. 1997. *Tensions of Empire: Colonial Cultures in a Bourgeois World.* Berkeley: University of California Press.

Streather, H.R.A. 1954. "Third American Karakoram Expedition, 1953." *Himalayan Journal* 18: 67–80.

Survey of India. 1915. *Exploration of Tibet and Neighboring Regions, 1879–1892.* Vol. 8, Pt. 2, 383–99.

Tambiah, Stanley. 1976. *World Conqueror and World Renouncer: A Study of Buddhism and Polity in Thailand Against a Historical Background.* Cambridge and New York: Cambridge University Press.

Taylor, Timothy D. 1997. *Global Pop: World Music, World Markets.* New York: Routledge.

Tenzing Norgay. 1955. (Tenzing of Everest with James. Ramsay Ullman) *Tiger of the Snows.* New York: G. P. Putnam's Sons.

———. 1977. (Tenzing Norgay Sherpa) *After Everest: An Autobiography.* As Told to Malcolm Barnes. London: George Allen & Unwin, Ltd.

Thapa, Deepak. 1995. "Fame Still Eludes Sherpas." *Himal* 8, no. 5 (September/October): 50–51.

Thapa, Vijay Jung. 1997. "Lords of Everest." *India Today International* (7 July): 54–56.

Thompson, Mike. 1979. "Sahibs and Sherpas." *Mountain* 68:45–49.

———. 1980. "Risk." *Mountain* 73:44–46.

Tilman, H. W. 1935. "Nanda Devi and the Sources of the Ganges." *Himalayan Journal* 8:1–26.

———. 1937. "The Ascent of Nanda Devi." *Alpine Journal* 49, no. 254 (May): 13–26.

———. 1946. *When Men and Mountains Meet.* Cambridge: Cambridge University Press.

———. 1948. *Mount Everest, 1938.* Cambridge: Cambridge University Press.

———. 1952. *Nepal Himalaya.* Cambridge: Cambridge University Press.

———. 1983 (1946). "When Men and Mountains Meet," 269–422. In *The Seven Mountain-Travel Books.* Seattle: The Mountaineers.

———. 1983 (1948). "Everest, 1938," 423–511. In *The Seven Mountain-Travel Books.* Seattle: The Mountaineers.

Tullis, Julie. 1986. *Clouds from Both Sides.* London: Grafton Books.

Ullman, James Ramsay. 1947. *Kingdom of Adventure Everest.* New York: William Sloane Associates.

———. 1955. "The Gentleman from Chomolungma." Introduction to Tenzing Norgay, *Tiger of the Snows*, xi–xvi.

———. 1964. *Americans on Everest.* Philadelphia and New York: J. B. Lippincott Co.

Unsworth, Walt. 1981. *Everest: A Mountaineering History.* Boston: Houghton Mifflin.

Venables, Stephen. 1989. *Everest Kangshung Face.* London: Hodder and Stoughton.

Von Fürer-Haimendorf, Christoph. 1964. *The Sherpas of Nepal: Buddhist Highlanders.* London: J. Murray.

———. 1976. "A Nunnery in Nepal." *Kailash* 4:121–54.

———. 1984. *The Sherpas Transformed: Social Change in a Buddhist Society of Nepal.* New Delhi: Sterling Publishers.

———. 1990. *The Renaissance of Tibetan Civilization.* Oracle, Ariz.: Synergetic Press.

Waddell, L. A. 1888 (1959). *The Buddhism of Tibet or Lamaism*. Cambridge: W. Heffer and Sons.

Weir, Tom. 1955. *East of Kathmandu*. Edinburgh and London: Oliver and Boyd.

White, J. Claude. 1909. *Sikkim and Bhutan: Twenty-One Years on the Northeast Frontier 1887–1908*. New York: Longmans, Green and Co.

Woodhead, Leslie. 1977. (film) "Sherpas." In the series *Disappearing Worlds*. Anthropological consultant: S. B. Ortner. Manchester, England: Granada Television.

Younghusband, Sir Francis. 1925. "Introduction." In E. F. Norton et al., *The Fight for Everest: 1924*, 13–30.

———. 1926. *The Epic of Mt. Everest*. London: E. Arnold and Co.

———. 1941. *Everest: The Challenge*. London: Thomas Nepon and Sons.

Zivetz, Laurie. 1992. *Private Enterprise and the State in Modern Nepal*. Madras, India: Oxford University Press.

INDEX

NOTE: Most Sherpas use no last name, or use ""Sherpa" as a last name. Sherpa names are therefore alphabetized by first name.